PROPERTY OF _____

TITLE _____

COMPANY _____

THE
EXECUTIVE
DESKBOOK

Third Edition

Auren Uris

VNR VAN NOSTRAND REINHOLD COMPANY
New York

Printed in the United States of America

Van Nostrand Reinhold Company Inc.
115 Fifth Avenue
New York, New York 10003

Van Nostrand Reinhold Company Limited
Molly Millars Lane
Wokingham, Berkshire RG11 2PY, England

Van Nostrand Reinhold
480 La Trobe Street
Melbourne, Victoria 3000, Australia

Macmillan of Canada
Division of Canada Publishing Corporation
164 Commander Boulevard
Agincourt, Ontario M1S 3C7, Canada

16 15 14 13 12 11 10 9 8 7 6 5 4 3 2 1

Library of Congress Cataloging-in-Publication Data

Uris, Auren.
  The executive deskbook.

  Includes index.
  1. Management.   I. Title.
HD31.U66   1988   658.4   87-10597
ISBN 0-442-28790-9

PREFACE

There are at least two reasons why a publisher asks an author to do another edition of a book:

- The book continues in demand.
- The subject matter has been changing, and updating is necessary to maintain the work's usefulness.

Both of these apply to *The Executive Deskbook,* but the second point is especially cogent. Since 1976, the year of the Second Edition, events have created new problems and opportunities for managers. For example:

Executive obsolescence. Rapidly developing technologies, the proliferation of acquisitions and mergers, and increased competition have pressured companies to streamline staffs and eliminate individuals of outdated capabilities. The result: obsolescence, previously a fate reserved for machines and manual workers, now affects the executive echelons. One career consequence: shorter workspans with a given employer, increasing rates of unemployment, but also, advancement for the prepared.

Women in management. Women continue to enter and advance in executive staffs. But unexpectedly, gender-related obstacles that interfere with performance persist. And executive women suffer the grinding conflict between family and professional agendas.

Management performance. Standards of skills and achievement are more demanding, as the art and science of management grow more sophisticated. Competition has become internationalized, increasing the need for higher levels of performance.

Management style. The nation has gained a new awareness of the process of management. Deficiencies in governmental operations were attributed to poor management practices. The new sense of executive alternatives makes the tools offered in the *Deskbook* of even greater utility.

To help managers meet the new challenges as we head toward the next century, the Third Edition offers:

■ Updating of the entire text, including replacement of the old "he" and "him" usage by recognition of both sexes. New material in substantial amounts extend the coverage in many sections.

■ A thoroughly revised "Women in Management" section, strengthened by input of several experts in the field.

■ Additions to the popular "Key Management Concepts" section, to broaden its value still further.

■ Revision, under the guidance of a nationally recognized authority, of "Fair Employment Practices," an essential and continually evolving area of executive interest.

Despite the many improvements, one aspect remains unchanged. This is the format and typographical style that has been a major factor in the *Deskbook's* appeal and effectiveness.

Tens of thousands of managers worldwide—through foreign-language translations, from Arabic to Swedish—have benefited from previous editions. The Third Edition has been planned both to enhance and to extend the insights and information offered in this practical, easy-to-find and quick-reading executive tool.

Auren Uris

ACKNOWLEDGMENTS

The updates, insights and new information enriching the Third Edition have been gleaned from many whose names are mentioned with their contributions. In addition:

Doris Reichbart Uris, whose criticism and suggestions were helpful throughout. As an executive in the film and television field, her first-hand experience was sought in recasting the "Women in Management" pages. Being my wife shortened the communication lines.

Women's fashion consultant Barbara Pittfield, who added her authortative views on the new directions and their significance in executive dress styles, and what the well-dressed career woman should, and shouldn't, wear.

William Keenan, of the Research Institute of America, whose expertness in the field shaped the total rewrite of the Fair Employment Practices section, not only updating it but also pointing out pitfalls, and offering guidance for action.

Evelyn Mertens and Betty Russo, and especially Margaret Arthur, a good friend and Dutchess County neighbor, for help at various stages of manuscript preparation.

Mary Summers, head of the Research Instute of America library; also, the information-services staffs of the New York and Brooklyn Public Library, for finding and verifying a broad range of data.

Finally, I want to express a special gratitude to friends and colleagues who read parts of the work-in-progress and raised questions and supplied answers that appreciably improved the final product.

CONTENTS

4   MANAGEMENT TOOL KIT   379

THE
EXECUTIVE
DESKBOOK

1

AREAS OF MANAGEMENT ACTION

The executive's job can be sliced up in a variety of ways. For example, the field of general management has traditionally been divided into planning, organizing, implementing, and controlling.

For purposes of *The Executive Deskbook,* fourteen functional areas have been developed which more clearly relate to the executive activity as the executive practitioner tends to see it in the course of day-to-day operations. Here are the fourteen areas:

Time Saving and Self-Scheduling
Effective Communication
Meetings
Decision-Making
Problem Solving
Planning
Delegation and Assignment
Building Group Effectiveness
Leadership and Motivation
Dealing with Problem People
Dealing with Interpersonal Problems
Improving Your Own Effectiveness
Women in Management
Fair Employment Practices

Under each of these headings you will find specific, practical suggestions for handling the most common difficulties. While many of the solu-

1

tions are based on the insights of behavioral science, the recommendations themselves are spelled out in clear operational terms.

*   *   *   *   *

1. Time Saving and Self-Scheduling

Most executives would agree to the following propositions:
- There's never enough time.
- Interruptions and other unforeseen developments threaten or destroy executive schedules.

It is precisely because executive time is of such supreme importance—after all, whatever the executive accomplishes, he or she does *in and with time*—that it deserves your special attention. The catalog of ideas in the pages ahead have worked time saving and effort saving wonders, and they can serve you. Consider the suggestions on a purely pragmatic basis: if they suit you, they're "good," if not, pass them by. Remember that the successful adaptation and application of just one idea can save hours of precious time and be worth thousands of dollars to you and to your company.

FIVE BASIC STEPS OF EXECUTIVE TIME SAVING

1. Develop an overview of your responsibilities.   Your job requires that you perform a particular set of activities. For example, if you're a line executive, you are responsible for overseeing the output of your department, division, and so on. But also, you must maintain contact with other company departments such as personnel, the treasurer's office, production control, and on a long range basis, seek to improve the production capabilities of your unit. As you consider all these obligations, and the activities they suggest, you sharpen the picture of your job, see it in helpful perspective, and get a line on your time requirements.

2. Set priorities—pattern your work schedule according to overall organizational needs.   Obviously, all elements of your job have some importance. But in developing an effective work schedule, it is essential that either on paper or in your mind you set the various elements in a hierarchy according to importance. By setting priorities:

a. you know how much relative time to assign to an activity;
b. you can reschedule; in case an item of higher priority "heats up," an immediate low-priority task can be set aside.

But what is the mental process involved in setting tasks in sequence? Consciously or unconsciously you set your priorities according to a group of factors that affect a task's importance:

- Personal and personnel safety
- Company commitment and reputation
- Profit and loss (the aim being to maximize the former, minimize the latter)
- Urgency (as in a customer's appeal for special treatment)
- Loyalty to company and colleagues
- Personal convenience and personal preference.

The list is flexible, of course. Your own personal scale of values and factors not mentioned—friendship, favoring your own department over others—may be influential.

3. Schedule your routines.   Most executives follow both a daily and a weekly schedule. Typically, correspondence is handled first thing in the morning, ongoing tasks checked, progress reports read, communications with other executives made for a variety of operating reasons, and so on, through the day. Weekly items, regular weekly conferences, for example, are fitted in on appropriate days, as required. In developing your schedule:

a. *Be guided by priority needs,* and see that your subordinates follow your lead in this respect.
b. *Schedule according to your personal energy peaks and low points* (see page 5 for chart and details).
c. *Watch out for spoilers,* those recurring factors that interfere, a colleague or customer who asks for preferential treatment, whether justified or not.
d. *Expect the unexpected.* Try not to be fazed by minor accidents, intrusions, or upsets. Be prepared to borrow personnel, get assistance from colleagues, consult your boss.
e. *Consolidate like tasks, order sequences efficiently.*

4. Delegate.   Assigning specific tasks for which you are directly responsible is a major factor in executive time saving and job accomplishment. (Because delegation is a crucial factor in executive job performance, you'll find it covered at length, starting on page 124)

5. Review periodically.   Few executive jobs remain the same, year in, year out. That's why, every six or twelve months, it is desirable to assess your job responsibility and activity. When changes or trends toward change are spotted, you can make appropriate adjustments in your work schedules.

For those executives who want to really dig into the whole problem of self-scheduling in depth, the item on page 15 offers help in conducting such a study.

➲ **THE IMPORTANCE OF PACE AS A TIME SAVER**

> *"She's a woman on the move."*
> *"He's got a lot of drive."*

Labels like these are thought to identify the outstanding executive; and this may or may not be true. The inexperienced manager who says with pride, "It's drive, drive all day," may feel he deserves high marks for performance. But effective managers are those who pace themselves, who may be going like a jet for a while, work at a leisurely pace a bit later, and completely relax (yes, during working hours) after that.

Athletes understand the need for pacing. The miler doesn't try to burn up the track during the first quarter. Similarly, the real champion has a sense of pace that is partly attuned to the competition, partly to the need for outstanding performance for its own sake.

In your own case:

- Only go all out for the tasks that demand it.
- Take breaks—coffee, a walk down the corridor or to another building, a feet-on-the-desk interlude—before you reach the exhaustion point.
- Add a relaxation period, when you feel either physical or mental fatigue beginning to appear. *How* and *how much* you relax, whether for ten minutes or two hours, depends on your preference. The rest may take the form of a low-pressure lunch, conversations with colleagues or on-the-job friends. One executive, enmeshed in a month-long grueling project, found a stimulating movie a perfect workbreak and mind refresher.

The above points tie into the matter of your daily energy cycle . . .

➲ **ADJUSTING YOUR SCHEDULE TO YOUR PERSONAL DAILY ENERGY CYCLE**

Undoubtedly, you've observed it in yourself: your energies have fairly regular peaks and valleys. There are times during the working day that you feel up to anything, at other periods you would just as soon coast along.

The industrial psychologist, Norman R. F. Maier, studied the working efficiency of a group of executives, and charted his findings, as illustrated below.

Remember that the curve represents the rise and fall in efficiency of the "average." Your own personal energies may closely resemble those charted, or deviate somewhat. In any event, the same factors apply:

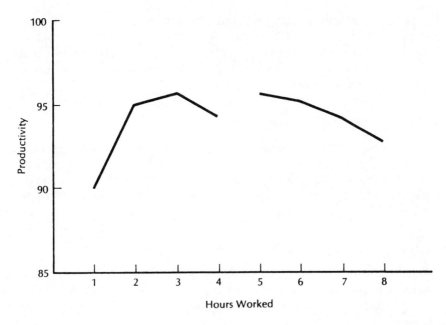

Personal Efficiency Chart.

Warm-up period.   Note the rise from the morning start. Physiologists explain the warm-up on a partially physical basis. Muscles must be limbered; changes in blood pressure and circulation take place.

Fatigue drop.   Fatigue is the usual explanation given for the lowering of efficiency in the course of the working period. In some cases, this tends to be cumulative.

End spurt.   Although not shown on the chart, there is a tendency for efficiency to increase as the end of the work period is approached. In some cases, a similar increase may occur before breaks in general—lunch periods, completion of a task, and so on.

Your own peaks and valleys.   To chart your own ups and downs of daily efficiency, keep a brief record, noting:

- the hours you feel the peppiest
- the times fatigue catches up with you
- the periods you feel most at ease mentally
- the times you find it difficult to work

Tabulate the results over several days to poinpoint your strong and weak periods. Then, take the final payoff step:

Tailor your daily working schedule to your personal chart. For instance, save tough, demanding jobs for high-energy periods. Fit routine tasks into low-energy periods. Fill in mental doldrums with the tasks that almost "do themselves." Tackle new projects, or mentally taxing ones, when your energy peaks are highest.

➲ ONE EXECUTIVE'S TIME TEASER

"It may sound like kidding yourself," says James R. Kray, president of a Los Angeles department store, "but when I have a rush project for my office staff, I set the wall clock an hour ahead. Then, if the job has to be done by four o'clock, say, we've got an hour's cushion. Very psychological, but it works."

➲ HOW TO MAKE ROOM FOR A RUSH PROJECT

Every once in a while, an executive is asked by his superior to "drop everything and push through the X Project." The executive has an immediate problem of responding to the request. Here are the three possible responses:

Okay. This admittedly is boss pleasing, but if it's done off the top of the head, the executive may not be able to deliver.

A flat no. If you have the status and the judgment to tell your superior you are not in the position to perform as requested, this may let you off the hook. However, it may also suggest that you don't understand certain business considerations or that you haven't recognized the exceptional case calling for special effort.

Maybe. That's the third possibility. It's safer all around, but it can be too cautious in some instances and too promising in others. Any one of the three reactions may be correct, but the executive must choose the best one. There are no hard and fast rules, but the following checklists suggest guides.

Consider *okay* if:

- ☐ The boss is willing to accept delays in other work.
- ☐ All facts and information are readily available.
- ☐ Key employees are on the job or can be called in.
- ☐ All necessary supplies and materials are on hand.
- ☐ All necessary equipment is available and in good working order.
- ☐ You can depend on the group to "give a little extra."
- ☐ Your boss will go along with your decisions on overtime, additional expenses, etc.
- ☐ You have checked service departments—everything from engineering to safety—to make sure you'll get any service you need.

☐ You have checked other units that may be involved in helping process the work, to make sure they'll work with you on the emergency schedule.

☐ The company (and you) have a lot to gain by an affirmative answer—and delivering on your promise.

Consider *no* if:

You're sure that the priority of the rush job is less than work currently in the department.

You know it isn't humanly possible to do the job in the allotted time. (This usually means the person making the request doesn't understand as well as you do what's involved.)

There's a modified no answer that really amounts to *no, but.* . . . Here, if someone up the line can help eliminate an obstacle or qualify the request, you may be able to deliver some effective *no, but* answers that can make everybody happy, and you look good:

"No, I can't finish all of it by five tomorrow, but I could give you X at that time, and Y by noon, next day."

"If you will take the report as a rough draft and finish it. . . ." Or, "If they'd be willing to take them packed in bulk instead of individually. . . ." Or, "If they could use the order done with regular materials instead of the special formula on the specifications. . . ."

"No, we can't do it unless you can get Fred Bishop and his crew to assist me. . . ."

Consider *maybe* if:

In this situation, it's wise to use *maybe* only if you're pretty sure you can deliver as requested. The executive who says "maybe," and then comes through on schedule, rates a gold star. The one who falls down, hasn't added to his or her reputation for dependability or capability.

The fact is, almost every job can be done *if*—if your boss or the front office is willing to go along with the extra costs, delays, or other inconveniences of making unexpected shifts in work schedules. The other part of the problem rests with the manager and the degree to which flexibility has been built into the department. Essentially, this means making the entire work force understand that emergency jobs or rush orders aren't a headache, but a challenging part of the unit's responsibility that must be tackled when the heat's on.

➡ DEVELOP A SENSE OF TIME

We're notoriously subjective in our time estimates. To the man sitting on a hot stove, a second is an eternity. The amorous swain out with his girl will tell you an evening passes in a moment. Yet, it's important for us to be more objective about time, because the way we view it will affect what we do with it. These guides can help develop a realistic and useful view:

Be a clock watcher.   Check for the correct time in the course of your daily routines. The more you do so, the better you will become at estimating the passage of time and time expenditures. Remember that people tend to *underestimate* the time involved in what they *like* to do; *overestimate,* what they don't.

Watch out when time drags.   This may be a signal of time waste and may call for your tackling another task that puts you under the pressure of immediate activity.

Come up for a breather.   Absorption in a task *may* be fine. But when you're "lost in work," take time to ascertain that it's a job that deserves the time and concentration it's getting.

Avoid being "rushed to death."   Being caught up in a sequence of tasks may mean you're very much with it, and swinging along at peak efficiency. But it may also mean that you're being pushed along by a series of "demand" tasks that have low priority—in which case, you may be wasting time.

Keep the end of the day in view.   Knowing that you have "just one more hour to go" may suggest a rearrangement of tasks, so the essential ones that can't wait for tomorrow get taken care of.

➔ **THE IMPORTANCE OF FLEXIBILITY IN EXECUTIVE TIME SCHEDULING**

Whether you use a systematic method of scheduling your workday, such as a self-time study, or develop a schedule on a practical, "demand" basis, there are overall considerations about executive time that suggest the need for *flexibility*. That is, you must be prepared to set aside one task for a more important one, or to drop everything for an emergency situation. Three reminders help keep your time more manageable.

1. The executive job is essentially nonroutine.   While every executive knows he or she has recurring tasks (the in-box must be coped with every day, for example) the crucial elements of the job generally do not fit into neat time compartments. A discussion with a group of key subordinates to plan a new project, a consultation with one's superior, may cut deeply into planned time expenditures.

2. Trouble shooting and fire fighting is a standard part of your job. Any difficulty that develops in the echelons below you tends to be kicked upstairs. It may be a personnel problem, or what to do about a plan gone awry. But you, as the court of last resort, are expected to take over if those below you are unable to cope.

3. Single time expenditures tend to be short. A time study of executive activity showed that few executives can spend more than twenty minutes on a single task. This fact probably accounts for executive "homework," at least as much as executive overload. The items tucked into executive briefcases for home attention are usually those that need hours of undivided attention.

The proper response to such considerations is to build time latitude into your time allotments. Be prepared to do a half-hour task in two fifteen minute tasks. Be prepared to do a Monday task on Tuesday, if an emergency conference completely shreds your Monday plans.

➲ HABITS CAN SAVE TIME

Some of your daily habits waste time, others save it. Psychologists make the point that habits are of two kinds:

Adaptive. These are useful. For example, you develop the habit of checking the mail first thing in the morning, because it often contains orders or requests that influence the day's sequence of business.

Nonadaptive. These are illogical and waste time. For example, an executive has developed the habit of going through his mail each morning. But since the correspondence only bears on routine matters that have to be taken up later in the day, he will have to reread it all.

Nonadaptive habits are usually adaptive habits that no longer have a useful purpose. For example, an executive reaches for a pencil in his vest pocket, only to recall he no longer wears a vest.

Getting habits to save instead of waste time means eliminating non-adaptive habits and developing adaptive ones. It isn't easy, but it's possible. Here are two ways to proceed:

Will power and won't power. Take yourself in hand; be tough with yourself. Let's say, for instance, there's a tendency to bog down, become enmeshed in the unimportant. Force, persuade, teach yourself to pull out, get back onto a more productive track. The executive mentioned above, who needlessly goes through his mail, can force himself to give up the practice, with the realization that he'll be doing it later at a more propitious time. Or, he can ask his secretary not to bring in the mail until after lunch.

The systematic approach. Look at the problem in the way a time-study person approaches a work procedure: (1) size up what's to be done; (2) work out a series of movements that do the job; (3) whittle away at the procedure until it's efficient.

Here's how you can substitute a time saving for a time wasting habit:

- Spot the habits that have outlived their usefulness.
- Work out a new habit to replace the old.
- Check the time and other efficiency factors involved; make sure it's really economical.
- Follow the sequence through.
- Repeat.
- Keep on repeating, till the new habit is established, the old one eliminated.

Finally, in getting rid of nonadaptive habits, remember that it's easier to substitute for an action than to simply try to avoid it. For example, the executive who needlessly reads his mail will stop this time waste more effectively by filling the time by a desirable activity—contacts with subordinates, for example.

➔ SUITING TIME TO TASK

It's easy enough to say, "Give each task the time it deserves, no more, no less." But how to do it? These guides help:

1. Take time to take stock. Stop once or twice during the day to see how you're doing. Are you on schedule? Has anything come up to throw you off the track? What can you do to get back on track if you're off (delegate a task, reshuffle your task sequence, get help from colleagues, your superior)?

2. Watch out for time "hogs." A pet project, an intriguing but low-priority problem, the persuasiveness of a subordinate, may get you involved in disproportionate time allotments. Avoid such diversions.

3. Leave time for long-range elements of your job. Thomas Watson's admonition to his IBM managers, "Think," is not misplaced. It's amazing how seldom *thinking* appears in a listing of executive activity. Yet planning, problem solving, and applying creativity to achieving objectives are often the most important, indeed, the payoff elements in your job. If these key items are missing from your workday, do what is necessary to include them, through such means as delegation.

4. Stay out front. In the race with time, you must lead, or you're in trouble. The executive who chases the clock, trying to catch up, is at a disadvantage. Again, if you find you're falling behind in meeting daily or weekly obligations, get out from under routines you can assign to others.

5. Review a sizable work period for overall stocktaking. Be practical, and adopt the Casey Stengel view that, "You win a few, lose a few." Everyone has bad days, when the end of the work period finds one's schedule in a shambles. Assess your performance over a week or a month. If from a longer-range perspective you're satisfied, forget the occasional "black rock" days. But if you're dissatisfied on looking back, tackle the problem of self-scheduling from scratch, as recommended on page 15.

USE DEADLINES AND SUBGOALS

You can store up time just as electricity is stored in a battery. You do it by getting ahead.

Unfortunately, many executives do the opposite. They dig into their supply of time by transferring items from today's calendar to tomorrow's—when a phone call or a short memo could eliminate the items from both. Two devices help:

Deadlines.   A deadline puts you in a direct race against the clock. In many cases you find deadlines built into a task: "Let me know by three o'clock tomorrow whether we'll be able to handle the Johnson matter," your superior asks. When there is no deadline, you gain an advantage by creating your own. For example, you tell your secretary, "We want to get that report out by the last mail of the day."

Subgoals.   It's easier to keep track of progress with several subgoals, rather than one long-term goal. And you have the added psychological spur of dealing with handleable, bite-size segments of time. For example, executive Jane Smith and her staff are starting a project that requires a week for completion. At the end of each day the group meets to evaluate progress, adjust methods of operation, solve problems that have appeared. The alternative, to work with only the final, distant goal in sight, fails to provide the incentive for daily accomplishment. Lacking also is the critique that helps keep the group on top of the operation.

TIME SALVAGING

"The moving finger writes; and, having writ, Moves on. . . ." said Omar Khayyam.

We tend to agree. We can't turn the clock back. *But time is salvageable.* Consider the fact that when you use other people's ideas, you're using *their* time—the time they spent in developing the ideas. By checking other people's experiences you also save time. You avoid the necessity for repeating the time-consuming moves they had to make before they found the right answers.

At the top of the prospect list for time salvaging is your own past activity. Make it a practice to review your own experience. For example, you spend time investigating the possibilities of a new office procedure, but end up in a blind alley. That time is not necessarily lost. At a later date you may get the additional information you need to round out the investigation satisfactorily.

To recap:

- Check back on your own past efforts, procedures, and ideas. Ask yourself whether changed circumstances make it possible to apply them successfully *now*.
- Look for the products of time spent by others that you can adapt and apply.

⟲ DO TWO THINGS AT ONCE

"You can't do two things at once," is an old saying that originated before carbon paper and the coaxial cable. The fact is you *can* do two things at once and save considerable time in the process. Just to convince youself, take a pencil and do a simple problem in arithmetic, say multiplying 9,345 by 2. At the same time, recite a poem you know by heart.

A familiar illustration of multiple activity is the executive who (1) sits in his bathtub; (2) under a sunlamp; (3) reading a fistful of reports.

Here are some suggestions to help you get a double payoff from your time:

- Design dual-purpose activities. An executive, screening resumes for a typist/word processor at the same time watches for the highly qualified applicant who might be able to start as an executive secretary.
- Link activities that can be done simultaneously. Supervising a subordinate who is preparing a highly detailed report, an executive catches up on his or her mail and discusses plans for the week with an assistant.
- Lump together tasks that can be handled in the *same* place. An executive, flying across the continent, takes care of several contacts for the company. Bunching telephone calls is another application of the same principle.
- Start simultaneously different tasks that can proceed alongside one another. If the jobs are to finish at the same time, start the longer operation earlier.

⟲ PUT TRAVEL TIME TO USE

The jet plane is a great time saver, and a great time consumer. More and more, executives are taking to the airways to conduct business in person, because it's now practical to get from New York to Boston, Washington, Los Angeles, London, Sydney, or Tokyo in a reasonably short time.

But whether a business trip takes an hour or a day, on train, plane, or boat, even an hour spent commuting can be a waste if it's spent staring at an unseen landscape, or doing a crossword puzzle (unless you're a puzzle fan, and you put crossword puzzling under the heading of Relaxation).

Fortunately, travel time can be put to productive use. Here are time-saving travel tips:

1. Avoid "jetophilia." Some executives seem to get caught up in a travel, do-it-in-person routine. The result: a certain percentage of their traveling is unnecessary. Before committing yourself to a personal appearance ask, "Is the trip necessary?" Don't travel if a letter or phone call will do. The personal touch *may be* just the factor needed to clinch a big deal. But if something less is involved, can you send a subordinate?

2. Schedule trips at low-pressure times. In arranging for a personal appearance in another city, try to fit the trip into a day or week when you have the most time latitude.

3. Use a tape recorder. Many executives report productive use of hours spent on train and plane by dictating reports, memos, and letters. The newest recorders are small and lightweight. Mailing the tape back to your office means the material can be typed and ready on your return. Double payoff: when a report is to be made on the outcome of the trip itself, executives say that dictating the report on the return trip gets it into permanent form while impressions are still fresh, and puts less burden on note taking and memory.

4. Do brain work. Armed with pencil and paper you can tackle problems, do planning, and develop projects without the threat of the usual office interruptions.

5. Do your "must" reading. The normal reading load of managers has been rising steeply over the years. And some of it just can't be shunted off on subordinates, or neglected. Trade and industry information, new management methods, business developments, books on subjects relevant and helpful to your professional activities—all these require your attention to fill in knowledge gaps. Travel time is often made to order for this type of professional updating.

6. Transact your business at travel terminals. A New York executive recruiter travels from city to city to interview prospects for placement. He saves himself hours of bucking downtown traffic by meeting the job applicants at air or train terminals. Sometimes lunch in a terminal restaurant gives him the "office" he needs. If more than one prospect is to be interviewed, he takes a room at an airport hotel or motel.

7. Bone up for a meeting. Regardless of where the meeting is held, or for what purpose, going over relevant materials during your trip keeps the details fresh in your mind. Not only can you commit facts to memory, but you can plan your approach or strategy with the advantage of the imminence of the meeting as an aid to your mental operations.

8. Schedule visiting time as carefully as office time.   A frequent problem of efficient use of travel time is travel delay. Many an executive has experienced the frustration and time-waste of train schedule slippage, of being fogbound at an airport, or of being stacked up in an air traffic jam. But barring such efficiency destroyers, you can trim trips by some traditional means:

- Travel the most efficient way. If there is a cost differential, consider whether the fastest way may not be worth more to you in dollars and cents.
- Have your secretary or travel department check schedules, and put you on the most convenient runs or flights, both coming and going.
- Try to schedule the actual business contact so as to permit the best travel arrangements. If squeezing a meeting into two hours instead of three will save you several hours of waiting for transportation, let the others in on the meeting know of your time situation, and streamline the meeting.

9. Assess the percentage of your time spent traveling.   Executives occasionally find that, without their being aware of it, more and more of their time is spent "on the road." It may, of course, be necessary, and time well spent. But it also may mean that an undesirable "travel habit" has been developed, where "I'll hop down tomorrow," gets to be the standard response for every minor crisis. Or an increasing travel schedule may mean that your responsibilities have been changing, and too much travel becomes a symptom of job content which has gotten out of hand. It's worth your time to conduct an overall review, if you are seeing too little of your office.

➥ TIME: QUANTITY VS QUALITY

Says a self-satisfied executive: I get to my office any time I like before nine, and leave when I please after six." He feels he's doing right by his job. He's probably wrong.

The *quantity* of time executives spend on the job is less important than its *quality;* that is, *how* it's spent. Hours devoted to routines better done by subordinates may be profitless. One inspired thought developed in a few minutes may make your company rich.

The quality-of-time concept comes into sharp focus in relation to important long-range projects, such as cost and safety improvements, that may remain undone "because there's no time to do them" because of "get-the-work-out" pressure. You make time for these vital long-range goals by scheduling meetings and follow-up sessions. If the threat of bumping arises, use delegation and time trade-offs with colleagues to make time for them.

➔ **HOW TO MAKE A PERSONAL TIME STUDY**

When a well-intentioned novice writes an article on executive time saving, it usually starts by directing the readers to "Make a self-time study. Keep a complete, accurate record of your time expenditures over a one or two month period. . . ."

There's a monumental task, tossed off in a sentence. If you attempted it, chances are you'd have to stop doing the very things you were trying to record, because you wouldn't have the time.

Nevertheless, it is possible to do a brief self-study that will yield helpful information. Three steps give you the data on which to base a weekly work schedule. If possible, get your secretary to work with you, both in keeping track of your time expenditures, and writing down the observations.

1. Keep a record.   Select a normal work week. If unexpected developments disarrange a day, restudy this day during the following week.

Note the starting and stopping time of each activity. For example:

"9:00 to 9:20—Reading incoming correspondence."

"9:21 to 9:40—Conferring with Smith about the new display project."

Keep your record sheets close at hand. Make your notations as soon as possible after a task is finished. Don't overlook small items. A number of five-minute jobs can account for a major chunk of working time.

After you've kept the record for a week or thereabouts, and you feel it's fairly representative of your schedule:

2. Analyze the data.   The next step requires sorting out your time expenditures. Here is a suggested set of headings. Add to it as your own data may indicate.

Contacts With Subordinates	Administrative Matters	Intracompany Contacts	Outside Contacts
Training and instruction Work assignment and discussion General personnel matters "Social" contacts Other	Correspondence Departmental progress review Planning Other	Reports Interviews and conferences Contacting other departments Other	Customers Suppliers Service firms Other

ANALYSIS SHEET

After you have distributed the items from your time record under the appropriate general headings, and indicated the time allotments, you're in a position to evaluate the results.

The first question to ask as you look at the figures is whether the time is desirably balanced. Are your major time allocations going for top priority activities?

Additional questions:

- Am I devoting adequate time for communications with my staff, immediate superior, or other executives?
- Is sufficient time being allowed for planning, both short and long range?
- Am I devoting sufficient time to the development of my staff, both as individuals and as a team?

Your analysis can help you remove some standard obstacles to executive efficiency. For example, wasted time may result from your duplicating the work of an assistant. Or, you may find that unscheduled items (i.e., interruptions) consume sizable quantities of time. This may suggest possibilities for delegation or other means of shedding duties that consume disproportionate amounts of your time.

3. Restructure your time outlays.   What you've learned in your analysis can be used to revise your schedule. But no radical change may be necessary. Rearranging a few key activities can make a great difference in your efficiency. Here are some possible steps:

Group similar items.   You save time if you perform the same types of work in sequence. For example, handle all dictation at one time. Or, consider your contacts with a colleague: you avoid the need to walk back and forth between the same offices, and reduce starting and stopping by transacting all your business at one meeting. If routine matters of mutual interest arise, let them accumulate until you're ready for another session.

Change timing of key items.   You may find it advantageous to reschedule some activities from morning to afternoon, or vice versa. A daily progress check with your assistant, for example, might best take place at the end of the day, and should be rescheduled if it has been relegated to another less logical time.

Marshal miscellaneous items.   Examine the items that don't fall neatly under any of the headings of your analysis sheet. For example, take a time expenditure like casual conversations with colleagues. If possible, shift these around so that they don't break up items that would be better uninterrupted. Your purpose is to enlarge as much as possible the time spans you devote to a given task. And don't overlook the possibility of shifting low-priority interruptions and so-called emergencies that you can relegate to the low-pressure hours of your workday.

2. Effective Communication

> *"Nobody ever tells me these things."*
> *"Why didn't you let me know sooner."*
> *"I should have sent you a copy of my memo."*

The list of obstacles to good communication is almost endless. And each failure can mean serious losses in the form of errors, delays, bottlenecks, or misunderstandings. Accordingly, executives who maintain good communications are making a strong move toward increased effectiveness. In the pages ahead you will find keys toward this goal.

➲ THE FOUR MAJOR CHANNELS

To begin with, consider adopting a broader approach than the one that preaches two-way communication as the height of the art. It can be said that executive communications is *four-way*. The chart below gives the picture:

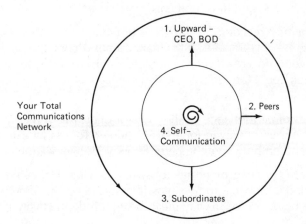

This is the network that managers must master to stay in touch with the entire range of contacts in their organization. Failure at any one of the four links constricts control and sources of information. Here's what's involved for each channel:

1. Upward—your boss, other executives, board of directors.   Every boss has a boss. Even presidents report to CEO's, and the latter reports to a board chairman. Your communication upward is essential for reporting accomplishments, devising or clarifying policies, discussing plans, and getting answers and information from the source.

Goals and direction setting.   Your work objectives and overall strategies emerge from discussions with the higher echelons and a two-way flow of memos, reports, directives.

Performance.   You want others to know *what* and *how* you are doing. Upper-echelon assessment is the most meaningful measure of your achievement, where you are in terms of career progress, and how fast you're moving along.

Consultations.   Key points of company policy and operations are shaped at top levels as a result of your upward contacts.

Information and recommendations.   What the policy group knows about operations is largely based on reportage by the executive staff. Your opinions and recommendations may be instrumental in devising operational strategies.

2. Peers.   What you tell your comanagers, and what they tell you are crucial checkpoints for keeping in touch with your level of operations, personnel, trends, and developments.

Opinions and reactions.   You measure your own responses to some extent by those of your peers. If the manager next door tells you that a new policy is going to create many problems and you feel the opposite, a conversation could turn up some insights and conclusions you didn't foresee.

Standards of performance.   Are you a hotshot? Are you "oustandingly creative?" Are you, heaven forfend, mediocre? To a large extent the answers depend on how you compare. Know your competition.

What's up?   Management has its own grapevine. Happenings, which way the wind is blowing, rumors, gossip, may not be top communications fare but to be out of touch may mean being self-destructively ignorant.

3. Subordinates.   These are your immediate staff, assistants, subordinate managers, and supervisors. Your main business:

Leadership.   This is the channel through which your guidance of the group determines everything from getting the work out to building a team spirit that can power group achievement.

Assigning, giving orders, and directions. Your people are an extension of your own efforts. You must send and receive information continually to keep the group on the work track.

Delegation. This procedure is essential for keeping your own schedule flexible, also to train and prepare certain individuals for greater responsibility.

Ideas and proposals. Eliciting and motivating the creativity of your group can get you ideas and proposals and sharpen your own thinking.

Listening post. Feedback from your subordinates can bring you reactions and opinions to company policies and actions. And the grass-roots grapevine can deliver news relevant to company life, if you want to tap into it. The spoken word, usually informal chats, is the medium of choice for this contact.

4. Self-communication. This channel is most overlooked and least systematized. Yet it can be a crucial, bearing as it does on your own activity and accomplishment. What is involved is the input and output of messages that go on within your own mind. There are three major areas in which you communicate with yourself:

Things to do. You write out a list of tasks in order of priority on your daily calendar. Most executives pepper their desk calendars with future tasks: "Start people on inventory right after lunch" on the day it's to take place.

Reminders. "Meeting on Wednesday should discuss security of sales data." "Check dentist on morning of 12th to make sure he can get me out fast." The string around the finger was a primitive memory nudger.

Idea production. Based on one executive's practices, some suggestions: "Use employees' idle time for reviewing files for discard." "Problem to solve: how can we clean up the mess in the stockroom?" "How about increasing our neckwear sales with a line of ties imprinted with common first names?"

Self-communication is a process of your own mind assisted by various pieces of equipment: calendars, deskpads, tickler files, notebooks, pocket dictation machines. Subordinates can also help. Secretaries and assistants traditionally are good backups for your own memory.

➲ REMOTE CONTROL

Most communication rides along on standard media: meetings, memos, face-to-face talks, and so on. But in some cases you must improvise a system tailored to a particular need. A case in point is keeping in touch when you are away from your desk. One executive's ideas illustrate the basic elements, written, verbal, and liaison aspects:

A stand-in.   It is desirable to have one person represent you: your secretary, assistant, or another manager. In order to eliminate any question of what's expected, or the amount of authority you've delegated, notify those he or she will be contacting.

Instructions.   Written or verbal, to key staff members about their tasks. In order to avoid questions of the "Says who?" type, usually, this should not be left to your surrogate.

Activities list.   Specify the matters that may require your stand-in's attention, to be started, monitored, or stopped.

Possible problems.   "Here's what to do if. . . ." There are likely to be anxiety points for your assistant. You ease the tension if you can anticipate and prescribe for them: "If Mr. Miller of Green Bay calls about his order, explain that there was a delay in getting the pattern, but we'll only be one day late."

Whom to consult.   Tell your stand-in, "If you have any trouble with the transcriptions, check with Molly. If you are short-handed on the monthly mailing, check with Greg."

Where you can be reached.   A written reminder for your assistant, possibly one for your boss, and only to be used in emergencies.

➲ THE HIRING INTERVIEW: SIX EFFECTIVE APPROACHES

Of all your verbal communications, interviews with job candidates may be among the most crucial. They may be a major step in upgrading staff and shaping it for future needs. Most managers are experienced in this one-on-one meeting. See whether incorporating any of the points below can improve your present approach:

1. Sticking to essentials.   Don't be carried away by the conversation and lose sight of the experience and qualities the candidate must have to do the job you're filling. Remember, you don't want to be blinded by the halo effect (see page 357) and let oustanding assets in other areas disguise important lacks.

2. Knockout factor.   Some executive interviewers avoid unnecessary talk by zeroing in on *knockout factors;* that is, those elements of experience or skill the applicant must have: "Mr. Lane, I see your résumé states you spent two years selling in the field. Tell me about it." If field operations and customer contact is crucial and what emerges suggests that the candidate isn't equipped for a key part of the job, you curtail the interview and save both your own and the other person's time.

3. Organizational fit.   Yes or no? Some companies have an image of their ideal employee, and constantly seek to hire those that conform. For example, at one time there was said to be an "IBM type," or a "banking type," or an "advertising agency type." Some organizations may adopt an opposite tack. They conduct a hiring interview like a theatrical audition, seek superior performance by doing what in the theater is called, "casting against type." An actor who looks like a fashion plate is made a villain instead of the hero, a middle-aged character actress is made a private eye. The idea is that the unusual matchup may provide above-average, even sensational performance.

4. Two heads?   This doesn't refer to the candidate, but to the practice of having more than one interviewer assess him or her. For key jobs, this can be a wise move, with conversation between the two or more interviewers rounding out the evaluation. In this procedure, for uniformity's sake, it helps to equip each interviewer with a sheet of qualifications and key questions.

5. "What is your strongest asset for this job?"   The question has several virtues. First, it gives you some idea as to whether the applicant is on track about the job you're offering. Second, you find out how he or she sees himself. Third, you can explore an area of experience or skill and evaluate it. Also possible, in some cases, particularly where you have good rapport, is, "What do you think is a weak area of your qualifications?"

6. Hire for the future?   Where you have a sense of human resources needs in the months or years ahead, you may want to go beyond the immediate job, and assess job seekers on the basis of other qualifications.

In the context of hiring, legal aspects may be relevant. If so, see page 287, Fair Employment Practices.

➲ GETTING YOUR SECRETARY TO SCREEN CALLS

It's up to you to tell your secretary how you want incoming phone calls handled. Calls can be broken down into general categories:

- Business calls—urgent
- Business calls—routine
- Calls of solicitation (salespeople, for example)
- Calls of inquiry

- Calls from business friends that may be either business or personal
- Personal calls

No general rules tell you how to handle calls in each of the above categories. But using the list as a basis for a discussion with your secretary you can tell him or her:

- which calls come through immediately
- which calls require taking a message for a call-back
- which calls require a turndown: "I'm sorry but I am quite sure Mr. Smith is not interested."

It's important to realize that your secretary is a public relations operative in his or her position as call-screener. A secretary may make it all too clear that he or she's on the line to keep people away from the boss. The result can be cold, impersonal, and destructive of your executive image. The effective secretary is one who shows that the job involves not only serving the boss but also rendering a service to the caller.

➲ HANDLING THE PAPER FLOOD

The correspondence load tends to be a highly individualized problem. No two executives face the same situation. Here are some basic methods that you can use to individualize your handling of paperwork:

- *The physical factor.*   It's not unusual to find a lopsided pile of mail in an undersized in-box. Of course, a barrel-sized receptacle would *increase* rather than minimize the problem. But just check to make sure that you have *adequate* containers for incoming and outgoing material.

- *Presort delivery.*   One method of presorting can be especially effective if you can get cooperation from your mail handlers. Here are two versions of such a plan:

Company I. *A color system.*   Rush interoffice memos are sent in red envelopes. Being easy to spot, they can be fished out of a pile of less pressing matters. Certain reports and other key material are distinguished in a similar manner.

Mailroom cooperation.   Mailroom people may be asked to do a rough sorting job, putting correspondence from the outside in one pile, company correspondence in another.

And here is a variation of some of the same elements:

Company II. *Method of delivery.*   "I ask the mail deliverer to hand me really important communications in person," reports one executive. That's possible when you can tell him or her, "If it's from Mr. Smith, it's urgent."

In some cases, of course, you may want to arrange a special delivery for high priority items.

Size.   An executive had routine but *important* communication forms made up on eight-by-eleven cards. This card can be spotted in a stack of mail quickly.

Color.   Rush items from the front office are sent on colored stock— pink, yellow, buff, etc. Each color is keyed to a particular company function: pink for sales, yellow for purchasing, buff for personnel, and so on.

Once the difference among the items is made visual and obvious, presorting can be carried out easily. The only prerequisites are that the system you use be *simple,* so that it doesn't overburden the intelligence of those using it, and it must be *consistent,* so that the chance of your color code getting mixed up is practically zero.

Receiving line.   To be effective, your plan for handling correspondence must include some kind of priority procedure.

What comes first? The executive who doesn't know the answer is liable to waste time on the unimportant, while the really critical matters go begging.

The priority problem is part of administrative detail that usually cannot be delegated. *Your* knowledge of your operation, *your* evaluation of what's important must underlie any priority system.

Priority "machine."   One executive uses what can be called the "three-box method" of assigning priority. In one box she puts the correspondence that requires immediate attention. The second compartment gets the letters, memos, etc., which have to be disposed of in a *week.* The third gets correspondence with *no special deadline.* This last accumulation is either discarded or acted upon periodically.

A variation of the same principle: the executive keeps his correspondence in a pile in the order in which it is to be handled. As new correspondence arrives, he sorts it into the proper place in the pile according to its priority.

The one on top is always the most current piece of business. And, of course, he works from the top down.

➲ ONE EXECUTIVE'S MAIL-HANDLING TECHNIQUE

The top executive of a London cosmetics firm, handles his morning paperwork as follows:

1. Read all mail.
2. Dictate replies to all letters requiring personal attention.

3. Instruct secretary on how to reply to routine letters.
4. Forward mail to be handled by others to the appropriate associate, with comments or instructions, as necessary.
5. File mail to be acted on at a future date in pending files, and instruct secretary to present them when they are due.
6. Sort out reading matter and periodicals, put those to be read in a briefcase for home or commuting perusal.

Even where secretaries are competent to reply to routine letters, the executive signs them. He says, "You should know the contents of any letter that goes out over your name. You owe the recipient the courtesy of a *bona fide* signature."

You may agree with the last statement. On the other hand, some executives use the time saver of having their names signed by an assistant with a notation such as, "Per R.C." the initials of the assistant.

➲ SIX OBSTACLES TO COMMUNICATIONS WITH YOUR BOSS

Even the best of bosses may have qualities that create communications problems. Here are the six major complaints executives make about their contacts up the lines and what can be done about them:

1. When the boss won't listen.   Many top executives say they don't listen to communications from subordinates because information is presented in poorly organized form, or because opinions are presented in a half-baked fashion. Perhaps your boss *ought* to listen; but since he or she is human, you may have to encourage attention. Whenever you communicate-

- Be brief.
- Be clear on the purpose of your communication.
- Define a problem as precisely as possible.
- Organize the relevant facts so that they can be quickly grasped.
- Map out possible alternatives, and give your recommendations—clearly labeling what is opinion and what is fact.
- Appeal to your boss's special interests: do things his or her way, as far as possible.
- Sell the advantages of your plan.
- Present any recommendations you have in terms of their benefits for each party concerned.

2. When the boss won't talk.   "Cancel all overtime starting today!" Nothing more—no further word of explanation to you.

You know your people have been counting on the extra pay. With no explanation to give them, you expect trouble. It's the boss's mistake, but it's your problem.

Often a boss's failure to tell the whole story is simply due to the fact that in the press of business, the matter has been overlooked. Here are arguments that can make your case:

- Lack of information can foul up your handling of a situation for which he is ultimately responsible.
- Incomplete information may send you off in the wrong direction—causing delays in meeting deadlines and similar waste.
- You may know of a better alternative than one that is suggested.

But, be specific. Talk about real cases and actual or potential consequences.

The most alarming aspect of this problem, though, occurs when the boss just hasn't given you any clue at all that something is in the wind.

You have to be on the alert, develop a nose for news, an eye for clues. If your boss has failed to schedule a regular period for getting together with you, make it a practice to keep in touch on an informal basis, at a time when you know the pressure is off both of you.

3. When the boss won't see you. The boss behind the Mahogany Curtain is certainly a most difficult problem for every executive. You may have to prove that time spent with you is beneficial to him or her.

However, the steps recommended above for the boss who won't listen apply to the boss who won't see you. Add one additional requirement: you may have to pave the way with a telephone call, a brief preliminary one-sentence personal comment, or a message relayed through a secretary. In any of those cases, your short message must be well thought out to:

- arouse interest
- suggest benefits that can be derived
- indicate that you will not burden him

4. When the boss is indecisive. Some bosses delay giving needed information. But later, when things turn out badly, they say: "You sure screwed up the works. . . ."

On the other hand, the error into which many people tend to fall is the belief that the top executive will be able to answer any question off the cuff, whether it has to do with a purchase of a box of paper clips or the relocation of an entire factory.

If your superior is indecisive, first make sure that you're not expecting decision making that would be as inadvisable as it would be impossible.

Let's assume, however, that the boss is, in fact, a Hamlet in executive clothing. Here are the moves to make in order to get a decision:

- First, find out what decisions you are expected to make. That in itself is a decision, of course, but it's one that would relieve the boss of a heavy burden.

- Second, when you do have a question for an indecisive boss, marshal all the facts needed for a decision before you put the question to him or her.
- Third, spell out why a decision is needed and when.
- Fourth, if there is any chance of a kickback on the decision you ask for, spell it out. It's amazing how often we delay decisions because consciously or unconsciously we are trying to anticipate any trouble they may cause. If you spell out what such trouble may be, you save your boss the time it would take to think these matters through.

5. If the boss is a bypasser.   A boss may step right in and give orders to your subordinates. It's safe to assume that there are reasons for the bypassing: the boss is in a hurry; the idea is to help you; it's an effort to get quicker or better results. In any case, steps like these can help:

- Don't show personal resentment. The important thing is not the damage done to your pride, but to the work and morale of the department. Keep it matter-of-fact; avoid accusations.
- Be specific about the harm done. Stay on a factual level. Don't suppose or guess. Show what actually happened in the past. (If nothing has happened, there may be no point in raising the question.)
- Watch for long-range effects. In some cases, bypassing may have no immediate consequences. But over a period of time, you may find your position with your people is weakened. They may look elsewhere for information and instructions, for example. Discipline itself may become a problem. In this case, your best bet is to sit down with your boss and present the whole picture as you see it.

Your biggest problem will be to keep the issue from becoming *personal*. Don't let feelings and emotions complicate the situation.

6. If the boss is on your neck.   There are many possible reasons for the boss hanging around all the time. It may be worry about the way things are going and he or she wants to pitch in. In that case, perhaps you should accept the help.   Or maybe there is uncertainty about how well the job is being done. The remedy is to give more information. Ask yourself:

- Is your system of informal feedback inadequate? In that case—
- Are your reports too infrequent? Watch when the boss shows the greatest interest—if it's a couple of days before the regular report is due, volunteer the information earlier.
- Do your reports contain the type of information needed? Pay particular attention to the kinds of questions he or she asks on visits to your department. Make that information available on a regular basis.
- Are your reports too detailed—or lacking in detail? Either may be wrong.

In any event, remember that your first communications duty to the boss is to give all the information wanted.

And, of course, to your subordinates, *you're* the boss. Can you help *their* contacts with *you?*

➔ IMPROVING YOUR PUBLIC SPEAKING EFFECTIVENESS

"The executive who talks impressively in public may not be better than his tongue-tied opposite number, but he sure makes a better impression." That's a common opinion in top executive circles. The average executive has many opportunities for public speaking. Everything from the informal company meeting to an invitation to address an industry-wide convention may come your way. If you are less effective as a public speaker than you would like to be, consider first the three common obstacles:

Attitude. "I can't give a speech," is a common excuse. In his book *People in Quandaries,* Wendell Johnson calls this defeatist attitude IFD disease—Idealization, Frustration, Demoralization. Many people set too high standards for themselves, are frustrated when they prove unreachable, and then consider themselves failures. If you have to coax yourself to accept speaking opportunities, remember that there are very few *great* speakers. Just set yourself a goal of a talk that is *adequate for the purpose.* (Obviously you will improve with practice.)

Stage fright. Everyone experiences it, from the high school valedictorian to the seasoned professional actor.

The fear of being "on stage" can be minimized. You may grope for a word; your voice may develop a quiver; your knees may feel shaky or— even actually quake. *So what.* If you are realistic about your speaking abilities, expect to make mistakes and resolve to speak regardless of your fears, *generally you will do fine.* One speaker, complimented for her impressive performance, responded by saying, "I was scared to death." She may have been, but chances are she was the only one who knew it.

Opportunity. Some executives don't consider speaking to groups important. "Why should I bother. It's a lot of trouble. . . ." Why should you bother? Because you want to be a leader, a motivator, and to grab a piece of the action.

In addition to minimizing the mental blocks just described, there are three approaches that help you score: *Planning, Practice, Performance.*

1. Planning: the preliminaries. In journalism school, aspiring reporters are taught to start out on each assignment with five questions in mind: why, who, what, where, and when? Only when they come up with the answers to all five will they be able to write the whole story.

The same technique can be used by aspiring speakers. When you are to give a talk begin your preparations by asking yourself:

Why are you giving the talk? To tell other executives about a pet project? To alert your people to new plans? To ask for help on a special project? The answer will put your purpose in clear perspective, help you get it across easily.

Who will you be talking to? Rank-and-file employees? Managers? Students? Business people? Will they be knowledgeable, sympathetic, resistant? The more you know about the audience, the less likely you will be to fail with the words you use, the ideas you express, and the way you present them. Knowing the audience and its areas of interest helps you decide what aspects of a subject to cover.

What do you want to say? What is the *one* major idea you want to put across? What points can you include to support it; what can you leave out? The subject must suit the capacity and interests of the audience and be slanted accordingly.

Closely related to *what,* is the consideration of length; *how long* to make the talk. The answer to *how long* depends on the scope of your subject, as well as the actual amount of time allotted to you.

Where will you be speaking? If it's in a conference room, will there be blackboards, tables, and comfortable chairs available? Is it to be in a TV studio? Is it to be in a work area where you may have to contend with noise, interruptions, and distractions? Your talk will have to be planned around the place and its assets or liabilities.

When will you be speaking? Early morning or late evening? Is this to be a one-person show or will there be other speakers on the bill? Will you be the first speaker, or the last? Clearly, your position in the sequence of speakers will influence your approach; for example, you would want to put extra punch into a talk to rouse an audience wearied by a succession of previous speakers.

Once you have the five W's answered to your satisfaction, you can proceed to . . .

Planning: the nitty-gritty.   Planning is an important factor in any successful speech so that you know beforehand what you're going to say. This doesn't mean writing out a talk sentence by sentence. People seldom write the same as they talk, and what reads well on paper usually sounds stilted and dull when spoken. What you're after is a clear outline of your main ideas, plus brief notes, and key phrases to serve as an assist to your memory.

Organize the main part of the talk first.   Jot down the major theme of the talk and then decide on several key points to support it, shuffling and reshuffling until they're arranged in logical order, one leading naturally into the next. Add subordinate points, case histories, and examples to back up each idea, but only those that actually help clarify the idea. Don't try to include too much, it will only confuse your listeners. Better to say less, effectively, and have it remembered. (This principle explains the longevity of Lincoln's address at Gettysburg.)

If you're going to want notes with you when you speak (and most people do), print each key idea at the top of a 3" × 5" or 4" × 6" card. Then under each heading list the necessary subordinate points, brief notes, or phrases that will serve as reminders.

Plan a "socko" opening.   Start with something that will gain the immediate attention of your audience. It may be in the form of a question, a human interest story, a striking quotation, a statement of disturbing fact, but whatever your choice, it should be relevant to your topic. Keep it short and informal. And, unless you're an experienced raconteur, avoid humor—when it doesn't work it's embarrassing, to you and your audience. (Good idea: write out the actual opening sentences on a card and memorize them.)

Plan a forceful, thoughtful closing.   The close of a speech is a strategic element, since what is said last is likely to be remembered longest. Plan your ending carefully, know almost word for word what you are going to say. One of the best ways to end is to briefly summarize your main points. Telling your audience what you said *after* you've already said it, really makes it stick. Or you may want to wind up with an appeal for action, or a sincere compliment for the audience. Your closing sentences should round out your talk, leaving no loose ends.

Keep your talk audience centered.   People are much *less interested* in what's going on in Timbuktu than in what's happening in their own backyards. Talk in terms of the problems facing the people who will be listening to you, and use illustrations and examples that they will recognize. Everything you say, and any visual aids you use, should relate to what they do, want, and worry about.

Plan for participation.   How will you know whether your audience has understood what you've been talking about? One way to find out is to get members of the audience to tell it back to you. If appropriate, plan questions *now* that will promote discussions *then*. Don't leave this to chance. Add the questions to your notation cards, and at the proper time use them to get the group started talking back.

2. Practice.   Once you know what you want to say, prepare for the big day. One realistic way is to get up on your feet and practice *out loud*. You may feel a bit silly at first, but keep at it. Make the first run throughs in private, then move up to appearances before a mirror (where you can see yourself as the audience will see you) or before a sympathetic spouse or friend (who may helpfully point out your goofs and strong points.)

If you have a tape recorder available, one or more run throughs played back help polish rough spots, and give you an idea as to the overall effectiveness of your talk, as well as its length.

3. Performance.   You've done the planning, the practice, now you're on stage, ready to put yourself and your talk across.

Dress neatly and to suit the occasion.   This may mean anything from khakis for a construction site to business clothes for the conference room.

Act confident—even if you're not.   A little nervousness is a good sign; it will give you the extra push you need to put yourself across. But don't let it show. Stand tall, steady down with a couple of deep breaths, glance around at the audience, and smile. You may be judged even before you speak, so make sure your attitude is a friendly one.

Talk naturally—and loud enough.   Today people don't dig the soapbox oration, four-syllable words, or "readings" from a manuscript. They want you—your words, your ideas, your feelings. And, if you have any doubts about "projecting" to people in the last row, ask if they can hear you, *before* you get into your talk.

Vary the tone and pitch of your voice, your rate of speaking, and the stress you put on words. You do this in everyday conversation, why not when talking to an audience? A monotonous, singsong approach doesn't win listeners. Prove the point now by noting the difference between the following:

1. We have the lowest accident rate in the industry. (Read in a monotone.)

2. We have the *lowest* accident rate in the *industry*. (Read with emphasis on the underlined words.)

If you find yourself running dull, running scared, or running down:

- Look at the blankest countenance in the room and direct your words to him or her. In trying to get him to respond, you'll perk up your way of speaking.
- One expert speaker suggests, "Think of the audience as a group of people who owe you money." You could tell them what's what, couldn't you?
- Introduce a new point in the form of a question—then proceed to answer it. This approach makes it easier for you, more interesting for your listeners.
- Pause before and after important points. This adds emphasis to them, gives you a chance to take another deep breath.

Avoid mannerisms.   Pounding fist in palm, pulling off and putting on glasses, clearing the throat, pointing. Any of these, *done once,* may be an effective attention-getter. Repeated, it takes away from your talk—the audience will be so busy wondering if you're going to do it again (and being irritated when you do) that they'll miss most of what you're saying.

End with a smile. And that's all. No thank you's, no apologies for what you've said, why and how you said it. If you've done the best you could, your audience will know it and appreciate it.

A final thought. Don't worry about applause. There wasn't *any* after the Gettysburg Address.

⤷ **SELECTING THE BEST MEDIA**

Executives have five general methods for communicating both up and down the line. None of these is inherently better or worse than others. Each has advantages and disadvantages. You may have to compare two or more to select the most effective. Here are the media available to you and their respective pros and cons:

ADVANTAGES	DISADVANTAGES
MEETINGS	
You can develop a two-way flow; also permits use of visuals—charts, films, etc.—you can show and explain.	Time consuming, possibly inconvenient, and sometimes difficult to keep a meeting on track.
Permits discussion and better meeting of the minds. And you reach several minds at once.	Can be a field day for the long-winded individual or the floor grabber.
PHONE	
Speed, immediacy. Permits questions and answers. May include colleagues on an extension or a conference setup. Can be done from your desk.	Be prepared for the "not available" response (ask to be called back or when the person can be reached) and "I'll put you on hold" (you can say you'll call back later). Also, generally there is no record of the conversation.
FACE TO FACE	
Personal contact.You can set a mood by a show of friendliness and relaxation. You can show, discuss visual material. Conversation is two-way. Rapport may come quickly.	One or the other individual may be subject to pressure by a powerful personality or the other person's high status. May not be easy to terminate.

NOTE OR MEMO

Brief. A tangible record can be filed. You can prethink your message. This can delay responses until you're satisfied with what you've written.

One way. No control over its reception at the other end. A rigid form, limited by permanent words on paper.

FORMAL REPORT

Can be comprehensive. Material may be organized at your leisure. Can be disseminated widely by means of copying. Indexing and other summary devices help reader grasp scope of piece, locate specific subsections.

May require considerable time in reading. Problem of actual writing may be discouraging to a time-hungry executive. When poorly written, they are deadly dull to read.

The five methods above are not mutually exclusive. For special purposes, executives may use two or more methods to get a reinforcement effect.

◗ EVALUATING YOUR OUTGOING COMMUNICATIONS

The contents of an executive's out-box represents an investment of thought, time, and energy, an investment that requires periodic evaluation. One way of evaluating your adequacy as a communicator is to test your own key memos, reports, and letters by questions such as these:

- Does this communication have a purpose?
- Is the purpose well-served?
- Is the communication needed and used by the person receiving it?
- If the communication is a request for information:
  Is it going to the right person?
  Does it ask the right questions?
  Have you clearly indicated what you are asking for?
  Have you set a time limitation; that is, a time by when you need what you are asking for?
- Are you communicating too frequently about the same things? (If the answer is yes, face-to-face meetings may be indicated.)
- Could a form, for example, a checklist form, simplify a message or report?
- Would you understand the communication if you received it? Put yourself in the place of the respondent. How do you feel about your communication now?

➜ EVALUATING YOUR INCOMING COMMUNICATIONS

The in-box is the terminal of a lifeline essential to keeping executives functioning effectively in their organizations. An occasional review of the communications dropped into your in-box can both improve your contacts and save you time. Questions like these should be raised about your mail:

- If you receive a considerable amount of unnecessary mail, should your secretary or assistant be screening your in-box?
- With reference to material received periodically, do you really need it?
- Do items with "perishable" material get to you on time?
- Do regular communications contain all the information you need?
- If a periodic report contains more material than you need, can you have the sender streamline it?
- Should you pass a particular report on to others?

Generally your information needs tend to change. Responsibilities and job content will vary even when job title or status do not. Accordingly, it is a good idea to make a periodic assessment of your in-box in order to maintain a maximum level of effectiveness.

➜ SHOULD YOU TELL IT LIKE IT IS?

Executives sometimes have a basic communications question to answer: is it always best to level with your subordinates, to tell it like it is, regardless of consequences? The problem arises in situations like these:

- The truth is unpleasant and telling it isn't going to be easy. For example, there may be traumatic consequences. Some people are going to be fired, a restrictive policy is going to be instituted, and so on.
- The truth, good or bad, is something management is not ready to reveal.

It's difficult to set down exact guidelines in this explosive communications area. But here are some preliminary considerations that can shape what you eventually say:

Your own sense of integrity. Do you believe that you must always tell the truth, even when it hurts? Or do you think that conditions sometimes justify the "little white lie," modifying the truth? (Would you tell your Aunt Tillie that her new living room rug makes you seasick, or, that you'd never seen such an unusual pattern? If you'd spare Aunt Tillie's feelings, why not those of a subordinate?)

Your reputation. If you hide or stretch the truth often, and without good reason, your employees will learn that they can't rely on you as a source of information.

Where your loyalties lie.   There is to be a personnel cutback but man-agement is keeping quiet: it doesn't want to cause wholesale upsets, and to have people quitting before they're ready to lose them. Do you say some-thing or don't you? You have been entrusted with a certain amount of responsibility and are expected to handle that responsibility wisely. What do you do?

To the question, "Should you tell it like it is?" there are three possible answers: "Yes," "No," or "Partially." And here's how executives arrive at each of these decisions:

Yes.   You *should* tell it like it is if you have nothing to gain by conceal-ing the facts, or by evading the question, or by putting off the answer. For example:

A subordinate asks if she's going to get the promotion she's been work-ing for. You know she isn't. If you tell her you won't know for a while, and someone else tells her No that very afternoon, you haven't really spared Amy's feelings. But you have lowered her opinion of you.

It would have been better to tell Amy straight: "Sorry, Phil's getting the promotion. I know you've been breaking your back for this one, but Phil's experience is more in line with what's needed. However, there's going to be another spot opening up. If you keep going the way you have been, you'll have the jump on all the others."

No.   You *shouldn't* tell it like it is if the truth will be destructive, and there is some way to avoid it; *or* if you have been specifically asked to say nothing. Never violate confidentiality.

Partially.   There are times when you *do* gain something by concealing some facts, giving an evasive answer, putting off the answer, or cushioning impact.

A subordinate wants to know if there's any truth to a rumor he's heard around the office, and you tell him, "A decision has been made on that, but we won't know the decision until Monday." The subordinate assumes that you know something he doesn't—as well you should, in your posi-tion—but you're respecting management's request that you say nothing.

But when an employee comes to you asking your opinion of his work and you know there's room for improvement, the "little white lie" won't help him and putting off the answer won't help you. This could actually be a good opportunity to give some criticism, since he came to you. Tell him you've noticed how much effort he's putting in and you're really pleased. Then, suggest areas where he might work harder so that he'll keep on moving forward.

⊃ BYPASSING

Bypassing is a communications malpractice in which a manager is, in effect, dropped out of a communications chain. There are two ways in which it can happen.

■ **Someone contacts your subordinate without going through you.** Example: Your boss may take up some business matter directly with one of your subordinates, without your knowledge or permission. In other words, someone from up the line, or at your level, goes "behind your back" on some business matter with one of your people.

■ **Contacting your boss without your knowledge or permission.** Here, one of your subordinates undertakes direct communication up the line, or with your superior, without your knowledge or consent.

Bypassing represents an undesirable shortcutting of channels because it has destructive consequences: it weakens bypassed managers' authority; it deprives them of information that sometimes they should have; if procedures or operations are started as a result of the bypassing, managers may remain in ignorance of operations which they should be controlling.

Why people bypass.   To handle the problem you should know some of its possible causes. Here they are:

■ The authority of the manager is either being questioned or flouted.
■ Subordinates feel that they can get a better response, which favors them, by going "directly to the top."
■ When those up the line bypass you to get to your subordinate, it may be because they are under time pressure, or you're not around at the moment and a situation requires fast action.

If you're a victim of bypassing, don't show resentment, particularly if it's a first. Constructive action is more possible if it begins on a factual rather than emotional basis.

The manager who is bypassed must consider some tough questions. First, if it's a subordinate who goes over your head:

1. Are you too slow? In some cases, a failure to respond quickly to an employee's request prompts a shortcut up the line. If you can't act fast, tell the person why and how soon you think you can move. If your communications links are at fault, see if there isn't some way you can improve them.

2. Are you using the "back of your hand"? A manager with so many other items to demand his or her attention, may not give as much weight to a request as the employee does. The manager may show this by the way the problem is dealt with. You have to take pains to show that you share your subordinate's concern with the question.

3. Are you failing to listen? The subject you take up the ladder may mask the one the employee really wants discussed.

4. The employee feels you're out of sympathy with the subject. For example, Olga is after you to get her course in writing paid for by the company. You feel this stretches the policy on furthering job-related studies. Olga knows this and hopes to get approval on her own.

5. Do you use your influence with the boss? This may be the toughest aspect of all. But when a manager doesn't swing his weight with a superior, the employee may feel he can get more consideration directly from the boss.

Don't dismiss the possibility that an employee may expect more of you than is justified. Within the limits of a normal relationship with your superior, you may be going at full power. If that's the case, explain the facts to your subordinate.

But where there's definitely something lacking, you'll have to look for an opportunity to discuss it with your boss. You should have specific information to pass along to him rather than a vague feeling that you need "more authority." Go into the facts of the matter, cite examples to make your case.

If the bypassing is by a superior who goes to one of your subordinates without your knowledge:

1. Is it just a one-time emergency occurrence? For example, your boss needs some information which your subordinate has and you're not around. In this situation the only requirement is that either your boss or the subordinate lets you know what has happened after the fact.

2. Have there been instances where you've failed to respond to a superior's request for information? For the forgetful manager, or the one who procrastinates, the answer to this question must be, "Yes, I've been guilty in the past, but it won't happen again."

3. Is the boss at fault? It may be an unpleasant fact to face up to, but in some cases, bypassing from the top down signifies a disinclination by the superior to recognize the authority of the manager. In this case, what's called for is a tactful discussion with a superior that emphasizes: (a) the manager's willingness to act as a communications link, and get the desired information, or convey it; (b) emphasis by the manager that his or her authority role vis-à-vis the employee, will be undermined if the bypassing continues.

Bypassing situations sometimes are complicated. You might be involved in one for which none of the above points is the sole answer. But you'll be able to uncover the reasons and be guided accordingly if you ask yourself:

- *Why* does the person bypass me?

- Is the reason an indication that I'm not running my job properly?
- What must I do to prevent recurrences?

➜ ART AND CRAFT OF THE MEMO

Everybody in business and organizational life writes and receives memos. From executives down to the lowest echelons there is a more or less continuing flow of messages. Subject matter may range from a simple announcement—"There will be a meeting of the Order Department at 11 o'clock in Mr. Smith's office"—to an alert on an intricate problem. Length may vary from effective one-word statements—"Thanks!", "Yes!", "No!"—to those which run to many pages.

The memo plays a vital function. It's a flexible communications medium that reflects the complexity of organizational life—its conflict, its harmony, its humanity, and even its politics. The ability to write an effective memo is an essential skill. Managers who become adept at handling the memo not only increase their effectiveness, but also improve their chances for recognition and advancement within the organization.

In short, the memo gives you an opportunity to participate directly in the give-and-take of communication. Those who master this medium are vastly strengthened in their quest for status and achievement. The aspects treated below can assist you toward these important goals.

The memo as a personal showcase. When you write a memo, you are doing at least three things:

- You're moving ahead on the subject of the communication itself.
- You're showing your degree of mastery of one of the most important management skills—the ability to put thoughts in writing.
- You're exposing your personality—the kind of person you are.

Since the memo can be highly personal, your output influences how others perceive you. Reputations are not made or lost on the basis of a single communication, as a rule, although *they can be*. But usually, it's over a period of time that the accumulative effect of your memo-writing helps form a part of your image for associates and colleagues.

Two Basic Forms. Many forms and conventions have been developed that aim for convenience, quick comprehension, and fewer errors. Case in point: the physical form of the memo, of which there are many versions. Basically, however, there are two. One is the *organization's* own interoffice form. Here's a sample:

ACME COMPANY
INTEROFFICE MEMO

To _____

From _____

Date _____

Subject _____

The other form is an *individual* one, which some companies provide, or which the manager purchases from a local printer. This form tends to be quite simple and may bear some printed legend, such as "From the Desk of . . ." and the name of the manager, or simply the word "Memo." This is an area where some managers give their imaginations free rein.

Accordingly, you sometimes see memo forms with busy little figures rushing around smoking at the heels, flying Mercurys, sheets of paper being propelled by beating wings, and so on. Each to his own taste.

Another variation is the company name with the suffix *-gram* added; for example, the Ray-o-gram (for the Ray Company). The company's interoffice memo is usually typed by a secretary or typist, whereas the personal memo (From the Desk of . . .) is more often handwritten by the manager or executive.

The "self-mailer."   In some cases the efficiency of the memo exchange is helped by write-in answers tailored into the original form. Note one executive's memo to his staff:

Dear _____ :

Frank Amster, vice-president of Kayline Products, will be paying us a visit on Friday, January 21. He would like to meet the key people in engineering and production. Please indicate below what time period would suit your schedule best:

( ) between 11 A.M. and 12 noon
( ) lunch
( ) between 1:30 P.M. and 2:30 P.M.
( ) between 2:30 and 3:30 P.M.

Other? _____

Soon as possible, please.

Pat Masters

This "self-mailer" technique is particularly useful when:

- You want to obtain fast replies from others within the department or within the company.
- You need 100 percent response. Most people tend to complete a fast check-off form more easily than one that involves the time and thought that goes into an open-ended reply.
- You are asking a number of people the same question. It then becomes easier to tabulate the responses, or plan a schedule, as shown in the example above.
- The answers you're looking for can be *categorized* ("Yes," "No," for example) or put in *numerical form* (0–25, 26–50, 51–75, and so on).

⟳ MEMO LANGUAGE THAT SOOTHES

The experienced memoist tends to write tactfully in touching on certain sensitive situations. One can use tactful language to protect a friend or deal wisely with a foe. The language we are talking about is a euphemistic way of expression, a way of hiding the seamy side of things—if that seems desirable.

A secretary who hasn't been getting along well with her boss is leaving for another job. She writes him a memo that will give him no reason to blame himself for her departure:

Dear Mr. _____

I have just been offered a position which includes special writing assignments, increased responsibility, and a chance to advance to a managerial job.

I hope you will understand my eagerness to accept this challenge. Accordingly, I will expect to be leaving in two weeks. Please be assured I'll do my part during this period to break in your new secretary, to the best of my ability.

Here are some other common usages:

"I have been asked by our President, Mr. Tom Cowley . . ." Tom Cowley has ordered.

"Paul Barba has resigned . . ." Paul Barba has been fired.

"You are invited to attend . . ." It's a command you'd better heed.

"My assistant has requested a two-month leave of absence to give him an opportunity to recoup his health . . ." An employee with a severe alcohol problem is being given a chance to resolve his difficulties.

Ordinarily, openness and honesty are virtues in communication. But in some touchy and even explosive situations, it can be the height of wisdom to use indirectness and euphemistic phrasing.

➔ WHEN NOT TO WRITE A MEMO

Usually there's no problem about when to write a memo. You want some information, you answer a question, and so on. But there are times when memos should *not* be written because of unpleasant consequences: you might lose face because of a memo written in the heat of anger; you might take a stand based on incomplete information; you *needlessly* put yourself on record in a controversial matter.

Here's a rundown of the situations in which managers should sit on their hands until the memo-writing impulse disappears (of course, you can *write* it, just don't *send* it):

When they are setting you up.   "A colleague sent me an inquiry asking for my thinking on our new sales presentation. He knew I had negative views, and wanted me to put them on paper. I wasn't sure how he'd use my memo, but I knew it wouldn't be helping me any. I conveniently 'lost' his request. After a second attempt, which I countered by saying I'd be glad to 'share my thinking when I could get around to it,' he gave up. I never regretted not writing that memo. I know I'd have regretted writing it."

When passions muddy the mind.   "If I'd written my boss about what I *really* thought of his hiring a man for a job that I wanted, I'd have been through in this company," confesses a new company president. "I was burnt up by what I considered an injustice. But soon I found myself working with the new man. We proved to be a terrific two-man team—and I soon sent my boss a memo to that effect. A few years later I was made vice-president, and just recently president, of the firm. And my 'rival' is now my general manager—a great asset."

When one is angry, scared, hurt, in short, suffering from any of the negative emotions, interoffice communications on the upsetting subject should be postponed. It is inevitable that one's thinking is being influenced, and that afterward, when emotional balance stabilizes, the message will be different, and that usually means better.

When you have nothing to say.   Sometimes this is a matter of quantity. It may be okay to write a brief say-nothing memo. But occasionally a gremlin takes over and you may find yourself turning out page after page of nonsense, when a one-sentence rejoinder would do.

"Our president asked the heads of operating departments, of which I am one, to send along ideas for new products," says a production manager. "I dictated a five-page memo summing up a number of third-rate ideas, and even as I was dictating it I knew it was a lot of hooey. Fortunately, I tore up the memo after it was transcribed, and simply sent a note saying I would give the matter some thought. The following week I had a really good idea, and sent that along. It started a whole new profitable line for us."

To paraphrase a great truth related to another medium, "The absence of memos can be golden."

When face-to-face is better.   "My boss asked me to send her my reactions to a lengthy report. Ordinarily, there'd have been no problem. But I hesitated because I wasn't clear on a couple of points, including the basic purpose of the report. So instead of writing, I called and suggested that we discuss the matter over the lunch table. It made all the difference. She was able to clarify some key aspects. I understood what she was driving at, and in the exchange I was able to make some useful suggestions. None of that would have been possible without the advantage of the give-and-take conversation."

In addition to the situations already described, there are others that do not suggest complete suspension of the memo-writing impulse, but *do* suggest either hesitation or some other modification of memo-writing procedures:

When your secretary can do it.   There are many memos that one's assistant can handle. For the executive to get involved with these is a waste of time. For the routine message, the executive's great contribution should simply be signing it.

When the timing is wrong.   There may be nothing wrong with the communication being sent. However, there may be something in the situation that makes for poor timing:

Manager Bill Tompkins comes to work one morning and has a difficult time getting his car placed in the new company parking lot. He rushes into his office and gets off a big blast to the personnel director asserting that the parking rules that have just been put into operation are "useless, stupid, unacceptable, ill-advised," and so on. He shortly gets a response saying, "Dear Bill: Still too early to tell." Sure enough, in a few days, the new arrangement works out well. Understandably, this leaves Bill Tompkins feeling like the rear end of a common domesticated animal.

➲ EDITING YOUR MEMO

For a longer memo you may want to take special pains. This means essentially writing your memo in two phases: First, a rough draft in which you've said everything you want to but without paying too much attention to exact wording and other niceties of writing. Second, you edit the draft, ending up with a finished, ready-to-go version. This is the professional writer's way. It's a process that may almost be called secret, it's so little known to nonprofessionals. As a matter of fact, the nonpro thinks that the skill of writing lies in having such a great command of language that you start with the first sentence and go, chugging flamboyantly along to the end, without a pause, and end up with a finished piece.

The opposite is true. The very best writers, like De Maupassant, Tolstoy, Hemingway, and Faulkner, would do a second, third, and fourth draft before they were satisfied. "I'm not a writer, I'm a rewriter," says one author with many books to his credit.

To start your rewrite, you change your viewpoint. Now you assume the role of reader instead of author. You are about to pass judgment on *what you have actually written.*

First, read for the overall effect. If you run into a point that is unclear or badly worded, make the correction. If you prefer, don't stop to change it, just put a mark in the margin. Similarly, if there is something omitted, note it briefly on the side, and then go right on reading your draft.

As you read, you'll find a word that doesn't sound right; too strong, too weak, not clear enough, not really what you had in mind, or not sufficiently arresting. Change these. Eliminate unnecessary verbiage (called "cutting" by the writing pros). Eliminate a statement you feel is inadequate. Correct the grammar.

Also, look for repetitions. Don't assume the repetition must *automatically* be eliminated. Sometimes there is a good reason for repeating yourself. But if you are doing so, be sure you know why:

For emphasis. To make an important point stand out, you may be perfectly justified in repeating. Only, be sure it is really important.

For clarity. You may want to repeat an old point in a new context in order to make sure your reader will understand. You can't risk the possibility that he or she has forgotten the point, or failed to make the connection. So it may be wise to do your reader the courtesy of saying, "As I pointed out before. . . ." But if you find too many "as I mentioned earlier's," it may signal the need for reorganization.

One word is usually better than two. Extra words are excess baggage. In business especially, it's best to "travel light." When you read over your first draft, concentrate on eliminating heavy phrases. Here are some of the worst offenders:

Heavy	Light
accompanied by	with
afford an opportunity	allow
at all times	always
at this point in time	now
due to the fact that	because
experience has indicated that	we learned
in the near future	soon

in regard to	about
meets with our approval	we approve
prior to	before
subsequent to	after

Here's how one manager was able to edit a paragraph in a memo. First version:

> Please afford my secretary an opportunity to check the Jones file. Since you at all times have cooperated with such requests, I hope you will acquiesce once more. Due to the fact that this information must be forthcoming in the near future, I trust you will be able to grant permission at your earliest convenience.

Here's a streamlined version:

> Do you mind letting my secretary check the Jones file? We need some information urgently and your help would be greatly appreciated.

If you think the first version of the paragraph is exaggerated, of course, you're right. But the sad fact is that it is representative of much business writing, even today.

Your final step: start at the beginning, rewrite as needed. Then reread, tying up all loose ends.

➔ SIX KEY MEMOS—AND HOW TO WRITE THEM

The need to write some types of memos recurs frequently. Their subject or theme is such that you are often called on to put words on paper to express these particular sentiments. Here are a group of sample memos under six headings that can guide your thinking and writing:

1. Admonition.   A subordinate is undertaking a risky course of action; a colleague invades an area that is not his responsibility. You want to voice concern, to warn, advise, caution, suggest alternatives. Another purpose of the admonitory memo: to put your views on record in case later developments raise questions of your judgment, attitude, or alertness.

---

a. *This sample is from a division manager to the company's purchasing chief. A few facts and for-instances would have helped make a stronger, more persuasive message.*

To H.B.:
I understand you're considering placing my order for desks with the XYZ Furniture Company. I have it on good authority that they're an unreliable source. You may not want to take my word for it, but I hope you'll at least check this out before going ahead.

b. *This message was posted on company bulletin boards. The message wisely avoids the angry reprimand for wrong-doing, yet makes a strong and reasoned case.*

To All Employees:

It's been noticed that some employees have been parking in the executive area. This misuse of our available space is causing problems with our overall parking plan.

The new area just completed provides convenient parking for everybody. To the few who are failing to comply: please don't create needless difficulties. Anyone parked improperly from now on will be asked to repark during the lunch hour.

c. *From one production manager to the head of a neighboring department. Somewhat sharp, but to the point.*

To A.R.:

Pete Jones tells me you've given him an assignment to do "on the side." Since Pete is in my department, taking such a step without consulting me is most objectionable. I've told him to disregard your request. And, in the future, if you want to take up work matters with my subordinates, please check with me first.

2. Condolences.   A misfortune, failure, or bereavement may call for an expression of sympathy. What you say and how you say it is a function of your actual feelings, your relationship to the individual, and so on. This is one area of communication where the error of omission is most undesirable. Even a brief message shows thoughtfulness. Silence is likely to be interpreted as indifference.

a. *Message to a colleague before an operation. Maybe hospitals aren't fun, but the writer does a good job of projecting a cheerful front.*

Dear _____:

I hear you're about to join that small and select group known as the No Gallbladder Club. As a member myself, I can tell you that you're going to a hospital that has the prettiest nurses and the best meals in the world. And your convalescence will at last give you a good excuse to do what we all yearn to do, but can't because of guilt—be lazy!

Good luck. It'll all be here when you get back!

b. *A colleague writes to one of his group whose wife has died after a long illness.*

Dear _____:

We all share your grief. Mae was a good friend to many of us and admired by all. Please take comfort in the thought that her pain is over, something that she herself wanted. And certainly, her last months of life were brightened by your endless hours of care and attention at her bedside. She couldn't have had a more loving or devoted husband.

---

c. *A manager writes to the wife of a deceased colleague.*

Dear Mrs. _____:

It is with a feeling of shock and deep loss that we hear of George's demise. He was a most popular and well-liked friend and colleague. In the eight years of our close association, I got to know and enjoy George's wit, his good humor, and unfailing friendliness. His accomplishments were many, and his quick creative mind was a major company asset. Things won't be the same around here without him. We miss him, and I can appreciate your own great sense of loss. Please know that you are not alone in your mourning.

3. Gratitude.   Appreciation falls as the gentle rain from heaven on the parched place beneath. Recognition is one of the holy grails of corporate life, more sought after than found. Any time you have the chance to express thanks to someone, you can be sure, whether the message is aimed at your boss or a subordinate, it will be taken as an indication of your thoughtfulness and sound character.

---

a. *A subordinate voices gratitude for off-the-job consideration from a boss.*

Dear Ben:

Now that I'm back at work, after three weeks of hospital incarceration, I want to tell you how grateful I am for your visits. They certainly brightened the days. And the plant you sent is adorning my desk this very moment, a permanent reminder of your thoughtfulness. I would say the fringe benefits in this company are tremendous!

---

b. *Thanks for an assist in winning advancement.*

Dear Mr. Henley:

We both know that promotions in this company are earned. And I'd have to agree that when the news came through today, my satisfaction included a certain amount of feeling that justice was being done. But I'd have to be both stupid and ungrateful if I failed to recognize the full extent of your contribution. Starting from that day three years ago, when you sat me down and gave me a picture of what the possibilities were for me, and the countless times since that you helped with sound advice and encouragement, your efforts on my behalf made all the difference.

I'll never forget your kindness, your friendship, and your wisdom.

---

c. *Appreciation to a boss for praise in an especially important circumstance.*

Dear Mr. Miller:

That was certainly a great buildup you gave me in the board meeting this morning. I want you to know that my hat still fits—for two reasons:

Only a great boss can have great subordinates.

We both know that it has been your help and encouragement that moved me along every step of the way.

As the song goes, you made me what I am today, I hope you're satisfied. I am— and very grateful as well.

4. "I told you so."   Every once in a while executives get lucky: Something has happened that they predicted, or an action was taken that was warned against and, happy day, they were right!

It's always nice to have one's views reinforced. But the "I-told-you-so" memo is usually written by that not altogether admirable person, the poor winner. However, in certain situations the "I-told-you-so" memo can avoid the crowing and the implied rebuke it suggests. Here are some samples that almost make the message palatable:

---

a. *A superior to a subordinate; the moderate tone and constructive conclusion take the curse off the fault-finding.*

Dear Pete:

Just got the production figures for last month, and although they're better than the previous period, they fall substantially short of target.

Now I'm sure there was no lack of effort. More than ever, I'm convinced that what's needed is an overhaul of the entire operation—everything from more careful work planning to better utilization of your people.

I realize it's a big job, but when the old ways don't work, new methods must be developed. I'll be glad to sit down with you and map out an approach that could brighten up the production picture for the future.

---

b. *When this type of message goes from a subordinate to his boss, the writing problem becomes more ticklish. Here a head-on but humorous approach may just do it.*

Dear Boss:

Hear that Steve Avery quit last week. I hate to say, "I told you so," but I did, didn't I? You'll never get me to admit that I'm smarter than you are, but I did have a chance to see Avery operate at a closer vantage point. If you promise not to hold it against me, I'll try to continue to be right in the future, particularly when you ask for my opinion.

---

c. *Here the writer and recipient are at the same organizational level. "Y-ness" refers to industrial psychologist Douglas McGregor's idea that most people are willing to accept responsibility and work on their own initiative when given the chance.*

Dear Hank:

Never mind the ten bucks you owe me. If your conscience hurts, you can buy me lunch some day. Bet aside, the important thing is that my faith in the Smith-Calvison team paid off. Actually, I was betting on the ability of those two people to respond to a clear-cut challenge, on their own. Everything I believe about the "Y-ness" of human beings was at stake. I'm hoping that aside from a temporary partisanship, you're as pleased as I am at the successful outcome.

5. Orders and Instructions.   "Do this," "Do that," "Come here," "Go there," "See X," "See Y"—on the work scene there is almost no end to instructions. To a large extent orders are verbal. But there are often good reasons for orders and instructions to take the written form to avoid misunderstanding, for the record, etc. Here are some examples:

---

a. *The request form of order written to a subordinate.*

Dear Jane:

Don't you think it would be a good idea for you to stay close to the new expediter, especially for the first two weeks, until he gets the hang of things? Remember, his experience isn't too heavy, and he seems to have enough on the ball to warrant the investment of time.

---

b. *Velvet glove, iron hand.*

Gerry:

I'd like to see the corridor in your department cleaned up by next Friday and kept free of litter and mess thereafter. We'll all feel better for it.

---

c. *Flat order.*

To all supervisors:

I expect all departmental production reports on my desk each morning before noon. Thank you.

---

d. *This memo makes the point that when one speaks with authority, an order can be low pressure indeed. This top executive is saying, "Be there!" The quiet tone doesn't belie the need to obey.*

Dear Harry:

Will you and your staff meet with me briefly in the conference room at 9 A.M. on Wednesday to discuss our compliance with the antidiscrimination laws?

6. Praise.   Someone has done something, achieved something, been honored. You want to state your pleasure, possibly adding your own congratulations. A complimentary memo is a good way of cementing an old relationship or strengthening a new one. It's your chance to make someone feel good and show that you appreciate an effort. It's the business equivalent of the naval "Well done."

---

a. *An executive writes to a member of his staff on the occasion of his twenty-fifth anniversary with the company.*

Dear Jack:
Twenty-five years—twenty-five great years of creative accomplishment! I've had the benefit of working with you for the last ten years of that period and I want you to know that our association has always been one of the big pluses in my job. So, here's wishing you many more years with a company that has every reason to appreciate your contribution.

---

b. *From a top executive to another who does considerable public speaking and has just addressed a national business conference.*

Dear David:
"Another superb achievement" is the comment one always would like to make of an admired colleague. You created an instance where it applies perfectly. I enjoyed being a witness.

---

c. *An executive writes to the editor of the company's house organ.*

Wendy:
I particularly liked the last issue of the company monthly newspaper. The lead article, on customer use of our service, was lively and made me feel awfully good about us. And the tribute to George Planter on his retirement said the right things in the right way—real feeling without getting sloppy.
Keep up the good work!

---

d. *Note written on a report which a boss returns to his subordinate.*

To: Avery Grant:
Sharp and analytical, bright and imaginative. Damn fine job!

3. Meetings—How to Master Them

Meetings are part of business communication. The subject is treated separately here for two reasons:
Despite roars and whimpers about meetings being a "waste of time," they are essential to every organization.
The difference in benefits between a well-run and poorly run meeting is

4. If you tend to accept and apply them, how successful are the out-comes? ☐ Poor; ☐ Not too bad; ☐ Good; ☐ Excellent.

5. Strengthen your mind's intuitive activity. If impulses don't appear readily, seek them out. Try to get in touch with your mind at the level that produces spontaneous judgments. Ask yourself, at appropriate times such as when you face a decision, "What is my gut feeling about the situation?"

6. Do you hestitate to act on intuitive feelings? If so, note that Dr. Weston H. Agor, author of *Intuitive Management,* analyzed the experience of 2,000 managers and found that those who trusted their intuitions tended to be among the most successful.

Some management experts condone the use of intuition. One says, "Managers worth their salt play hunches, and their mistakes are minor compared to their successes."

Finally, remember that your cognitions and intuitions come out of the same brain. You can cross-check. No reason not to weigh an intuitive decision by cognitive probing, or vice versa.

⮕ PSYCHOLOGICAL HURDLES TO DECISION MAKING

More than almost any other executive process, decision making is ringed about with mental blocks. Here are four basic ones:

- *Hamlet's disease.* Committing themselves to a course of action goes against the grain of some people's personalities. They are people of thought rather than action, and taking decisive action is difficult for them.
- *Compulsion.* Some individuals suffer from the opposite of the Hamlet syndrome. They feel compelled to make decisions, to take action, often premature and just as often, ill-considered.
- *Consequence anxiety.* For some, decision making is fraught with mental discomfort. They have an excessive fear of "guessing wrong," and tend to distort the consequences of a less-than-perfect decision.
- *Do-nothingism.* This shows up as a disinclination to act, a tendency to procrastinate. But unlike *consequence anxiety,* the individual who suffers from this difficulty doesn't seem excessively anxiety ridden. And unlike *Hamlet's disease,* the deterrent to action seems to be lack of awareness, rather than a personal antipathy to action.

As opposed to these ailments, "mentally healthy" executives find a certain amount of excitement in decision making, and approach the process with zest and the feeling that their decisions are likely to be as good as anyone else's or better.

⊃ **MINIMIZING UNCERTAINTY**

In many decision-making approaches, an early directive is to get the facts. Unfortunately, there are very few situations requiring a decision in which the executive can have all the facts needed. For example, you have to make a decision about marketing a new product. It would be extremely helpful if you knew a competitor's plans for marketing a similar item. Yet you may have to make your decision without this vital piece of information.

Effective decision makers learn to operate in the face of information gaps. They do their best with available facts; or allow a given period of time for fact gathering: a day, a week, a month, and then set about making the decision on the basis of available data.

However, it's possible to give your decisions the equivalent of "body English." The executive has two recourses after the decision has been made.

■ *Test run.* In some cases you can try out the decision short of full implementation. For example, an executive has decided to adopt a particular kind of package for a product. It is tested in a limited market. If results are satisfactory he goes all out, if not, he can rethink his decision.

■ *Branching.* It is possible to develop a decision with "branching" steps. For example, an executive says, "Let's use training method A with a group of ten people, and training method B with another ten. Then we can compare results, and adopt the method that works best for all our trainees."

⊃ **WHEN TWO HEADS ARE BETTER**

Two heads, or three or four are not necessarily better than one, but there can be safety in numbers. A common method in decision making involving more than one person, involves just *two* people, usually a manager and his or her boss. That is the example used here, although the same format applies to a larger group, of say, up to six.

1. Be aware of the hazards. A single individual may be in mental conflict over a decision, so it's not surprising that two or more people discussing a decision can run head-on into controversy and confusion. Watching for initial simmerings can help you cut off complications before they develop into real problems.

2. Seek compatability. The decision-making meeting can develop an edgy tone because of emotional or partisan hidden agendas. Accordingly, team up with someone with whom you can work in harmony. This should not bar pairing with a colleague who may not always agree but is capable of compromise.

3. Establish congruity.   Start your collaboration by a discussion that sets forth the background, relevant information, and requirements of the decision. Any disagreement about facts or any other element must be clarified and eliminated.

4. Third parties?   If you cannot agree, consider calling in those who can help resolve the contested points. This may be a colleague with relevant experience or simply one in a position to mediate. The executive to whom you both report might be appropriate, as well as a colleague with expertise in solving the problem, or even an outside expert.

5. Clarify the scope and limitations of the decision.   You and your partner must have a common understanding of what the decision is all about; the necessity for it, and any restrictions (as to cost, for example, or timing, degree of change from the status quo, etc.)

6. Will you lead the discussion?   It's generally desirable for one person to be the conference "leader," run the discussion like a minimeeting, keep it going on track. Leaderless, the conversation may sag and lose direction. Consider switching leadership so that neither person is always in the subordinate role.

7. Wrap-up.   More than one get-together may be necessary. But at the end of your sessions, the decision agreed on should be stated clearly and concisely: "At the start of the new year, a system of progress reports will be clarified, amplified, and be carried out by all department heads. A form for this report will be developed by three managers. Mr. Smith has agreed to appoint this committee by the end of the month." The agreement, in written or oral form, should reach all those involved.

IMPLEMENTATION: KEY TO DECISION-MAKING SUCCESS

"Not what you do, but the way that you do it," holds the secret of a successful outcome in decision making. This is the opinion of a veteran executive decision maker who has seen both in her own experience and that of colleagues the crucial role played by implementation in determining results.

You must devise a master plan to bridge the gap between making a decision and carrying it out. Here are the considerations for your implementation planning:

Commitment.   Once a course of action has been decided, others involved must be willing to put aside all hesitations, partial commitments to other courses of action, and so on. You have made a decision. You must move ahead on the decided course with a minimum of hestitations or doubts.

Announcement.   In some cases this element is minor. But in others the way in which a decision is revealed to a staff or an entire company roster can make a difference in its acceptance, and its viability. When a decision is stated with resolution, confidence, and optimism, its chances of success are considerably increased, as compared to a reaction of doubt, hesitation, gloom, and pessimism.

Personnel.   Who gets to do what in putting a decision to work is often a crucial factor. Some alternatives can simply not be adopted because the people to develop it are not available. Consider the historical incident of the "Message to Garcia" in the War with Spain. It was only when the officers of the United States Military Intelligence were able to find a man sufficiently qualified for the task, Lieutenant Andrew Somers Rowan, that the decision to contact General Clixto Garcia could be implemented.

In considering the personnel aspect of implementing a decision, think of it not only in terms of quantity, but quality. You may have enough people to do a job but ascertain that they have the skills, experience, initiative, and so on to achieve assigned objectives.

And more and more, executives are learning to use small groups rather than individuals in personnel assignment in some situations. Ask yourself, "Would a two- or three-person team be better for a given assignment than a single individual?"

Facilities.   Everything from raw materials to production equipment may have to figure in your implementation. Like the personnel factor, every one of the facilities require hardheaded detailed thinking:

Do we have enough machines for the job?
Are they in satisfactory condition?
Must we rent or buy?
Can we subcontract?
Are present maintenance arrangements satisfactory or will they have to
    be changed for this particular job?

In the same way, you may have to go through considerations of space, transportation, materials-handling equipment, and so on.

Time.   Exactly when to start a plan, what deadlines to set, what pace to adopt, must be clearly spelled out. An undertaking started prematurely may suffer just as much as one started too late. On the question of pace, you must consider whether a particular project should get "crash" treatment or may be spaced over time. Considerations may involve the state of mind of a work group. For example, you may want to announce an exciting new program in the fall when people are psychologically "ready to buckle down," rather than during the summer doldrums.

Responsibility.   You may want to stand at the helm to make sure that the implementation of the decision remains on course. Or you may want to delegate this responsibility. If you make the latter move, the individual you select and the manner in which you hand out the assignment may be crucial.

There's a big difference in the motivating effect of "Jim, there's a little project I'd like you to take over for a few weeks," and "Jim, there's an important responsibility I've decided to turn over to you, and the outcome of it so important that it can make a considerable difference in the futures of both of us."

Credit.   There are post facto benefits to gain from a successful decision. Pass the praise, and not only to subordinates. Word to the boss: "It was your decision to give the order top priority at the warehouse that made it possible to meet the deadline."

◑ MOTIVATING THE IMPLEMENTERS

After the decision is reached, you may have to do a recasting job. Those involved in discussing and developing the decision may have to be replaced by a different individual or group to *apply* the decision. This step may be slighted because the sponsor of the decision, fully involved, may incorrectly assume "everybody knows" what the decision is all about. You increase the odds in your favor by a full briefing of implementers, not only to convey facts, but increase motivation. Here are some guidelines:

1. Supply the background.   Convey the full picture in broad strokes, and also in sufficient detail for understanding of the requirements of the job, though certainly not at boring length.

2. Stress importance.   Two aspects of the situation will impress the need for concentration: (a) the difficulties that made the decision necessary; (b) benefits sought. It's at this point that the challenge of the assignment, should be stressed: "This is a tough job, Grace, but if you perform as I believe you can, it will mark a new high for you."

3. Eliminate the negatives.   You want to heighten enthusiasm for the assignment. Three factors may detract, and require discussion with your subordinate:

a. *Disagreement.*   It's possible that implementers may not fall in with the wisdom, effectiveness, or consequences of the decision. If so, you must change doubt to acceptance, or, in some cases, seek other executors of the decision plan.

b. *Threat of change.*   Some decisions may by their nature require alterations in policies or procedures. You may have to neutralize the fears of your implementers as well as others who may be affected.

c. *Overload?*   Make sure that there is no resistance to the assignment because of the feeling that it is an undesirable add-on to the employees' "regular" job. Any such feeling can mar performance, and should be dealt with by providing assistants, cutting down on regular routines, and so on.

4. Use your usual assignment procedure.   In handing over the task, cover the customary points, describing what's to be done: standards required, objectives, resources available, possible difficulties, reports expected, sources of help in emergencies, including your own participation if desirable.

5. Restate benefits of the action.   Two areas are important here: the benefits to the organization and to the individual or group. In one case an executive was able to tell her assistant, "If you do this as well as I think you can, it can have a favorable effect on that promotion we've talked about."

⮑ SIX TRAPS IN YOUR PATH

The process of making decisions can be tough and challenging. But in addition to the routine ardours, mistakes and misdirections can trip the unwary. Here are six to avoid:

Prematurity.   Don't commit yourself before it's necessary. For example, in a developing situation such as sales of a new product, make sure results are significant before deciding to modify the marketing approach.

Impracticality.   The new head of Personnel decides to start a program of after-hour training for low-performance employees. It's not a bad idea but the president overrules it: "Even assuming we could find the facilities, and beef up night-time security, we don't have people who can conduct the courses."

Miscasting.   Who should make the decision? There may be a question of jurisdiction. For example: Supervisors holding a work improvement meeting decide that tool breakage is a factor. The conference leader says, "I'll tell Purchasing to cancel all orders with our present supplier and find another source." A colleague points out that the decision is up to Engineering to make.

The other side of the coin: Some managers flinch at responsibility, kick a decision down to a subordinate. Handing over a hot potato to an assistant is poor management. Some decisions, like disciplining your employees, can't be delegated.

Too many cooks.   Some managers, under the guise of research or "getting background," run around collecting more opinions than are useful. The Research Institute of America has noted:

> The traditional decisiveness of executives has been eroded. Perhaps misunderstanding human relations concepts, they insist on participation of others in areas where they alone hold responsibility. These managers are under the misapprehension that with the group involved in the decision, the chances of error, and consequently blame, are reduced.

"Irrevocability."   There are no perfect decisions in this imperfect world. Even a decision that was sound at its inception may need reworking as circumstances change. Says one executive:

"I make my quota of mistakes, like everyone else. But I never hesitate to reverse myself when I see a decision isn't working out. I don't think of it as correcting an error, but as making a new decision. It's nice to have a second chance. I've taught my people that a 'bad' decision won't be held against them, failure to change it when the facts come in will be."

Out-of-sequence.   Some situations require several decisions, and these may have to be made in a natural order. A young executive decides to budget thousands of dollars to complete the development and full-scale marketing of a product based on his idea.

His boss expostulates: "Bill, we're not even sure we can make that product in quantity, much less whether it's feasible from a marketing standpoint. Maybe we will have to subcontract, or redesign because of customer preferences. Only after we have all those answers can we make the decision you're pushing for."

➲ WHEN DECISIONS GO SOUR

Executives—using one method or another—somehow manage to make decisions. But only a small percentage of decision makers, know how to proceed when a decision goes wrong. And remember, even the most carefully considered, well-planned decision can turn sour. Five positive moves may save the day:

Recognizing.   This move is a "must" prelude to all the others. Clear-headed, honest recognition of the fact that, on this particular decision, you have come up with a clinker. It may not be your fault at all. Other people, other forces, other events may be wholly or partially responsible. But whatever the cause, there is nothing to be gained by clinging to a losing situation. Executives who don't or won't recognize the inevitable, who are determined to make a decision work, to stick it out come what may, are only compounding the wrong. *Your* lead: accept the losses, analyze the causes, try to recoup what you can.

Reversing.   Many a decision is the result of a multistep process. From Step A to Step B to Step C and on and on until the final stage is reached. Somewhere along the line you may have tripped. Can you, after thinking things out, retrace your steps to the point where the misstep occurred? Backtrack from E to B, for instance? Then revising B, begin a subsequent series of steps, this time in the right direction? If so, you're halfway home.

Replacing.   There will be times when you have a decision that looks great—on paper. You've followed all the proper procedures, made all the right moves, said all the right things. Then, in execution, up pops a weak link. And trouble. Does this mean that your idea is not workable? Not at all.

Take the case of the executive who decides to set up a permanent team to handle the selling of a new product, Tom, Seth, and Gene, his three best producers. But it turns out that their sales go down, not up. Why? Analysis of the situation shows that Seth is the culprit, missing orders that he should land. Does the executive scrap the team idea? Indeed not. His original decision is still a good one; only the weak link needs replacing. Seth goes back to his old selling assignment, Jack replaces him.

The weak link replaced, the decision can look good again—on paper and in execution.

Revising.   In some instances, of course, a decision turned bad can't be remedied by simply replacing or retracing. Accordingly, major surgery is called for, a complete revision of the original plan. Now's the time to ask yourself, "Do I have an alternative? Is there a workable Plan B that I can substitute for unworkable Plan A?" Undoubtedly, in arriving at Plan A you had considered other ways, other means of achieving your objective. Can one, or a combination of these, with additions, subtractions, amendments, successfully serve your purpose?

This stage, incidentally, may call for consultations up, down, and along the line.

Reviewing.   Results are the proof of the decision-making pudding. When they go wrong, analyzing when, why, how can teach you a great deal about your own decision-making ability, about techniques that need sharpening, about pitfalls to be avoided, about planning, performance, people. Failure often triggers more knowledge than success.

➲ A DECISIONLESS DECISION

Is it possible to "make a decision" without making one? In a sense, yes. Company president William Mott is fed up with his assistant. The young man seems to have lost the interest he originally had in his job. His performance is sloppy, even careless.

Repeatedly, Mott has tried to face up to the situation and make the decision to fire his subordinate; but somehow, although he has marched up to the hurdle repeatedly, he can't bring himself to take the jump.

Then one day his subordinate comes in late; he fails to do an important job that Mott has assigned, and takes a coffee break that stretches to a full hour. When the young man reappears, Mott, carefully restraining his irritation, calls the young man and suggests that he find a job better suited to his abilities and interests. After it is all over, Mott feels greatly relieved. Actually, the young man takes the firing so agreeably, the company president realizes the assistant also was in favor of the move.

"Why didn't I make that decision months ago?" Mott asks himself. Under the pressures of the moment, he had *acted* without the considered thinking we call decision-making.

The Mott case indicates an interesting aspect of decision making. Essentially, a decision is a resolve to take action, and from time to time situations may arise where the executive takes decisive action without necessarily thinking of the move as a decision. However, such actions obviously are decisions, or rather are prompted by a decision made unconsciously and spontaneously.

So it seems that in some situations you can "decide" without consciously making a decision. Just beware of the pitfall to such executive action: sometimes the spontaneous decision can kick back. For example, executives have fired subordinates in a moment of anger and then regretted it.

➲ RATING YOURSELF AS DECISION MAKER

This rating considers two aspects, how you go about making a decision, and your procedure afterwards.

Precheck.   First, assess yourself on a single point:

1. How do you rate yourself as a decision maker, on a scale from one to ten, ten being tops: 1 2 3 4 5 6 7 8 9 10. You will be asked the same question later, in a different context.

2. Do you feel you've "made peace" with the emotional stress of decision making? □ Yes □ No □ Not sure.

3. Do you have a procedure for handling decisions (other than the small ones you do automatically) in which you move step-by-step, that satisfies you? □ Yes □ No □ Not sure.

4. Are you satisfied with your grasp of the preliminaries of decision making—gathering the facts, assessing the general nature of the decision to be made, developing alternatives, and so on? □ Yes □ No.

5. In the "deciding" phase, when you select an alternative on the basis of matching resources and needs, do you generally find you proceed smoothly, make sound judgments about the specifics: Which alternative will cost least? For which are you best able to assign people? Which has the best ratio of risk to payoff, and so on. □ Yes □ No □ Not sure.

6. Do you give the implementation step all the attention it needs to optimize results? □ Yes □ No □ Not sure.

7. Do you stay with the decision-in-action long enough to ensure that justice has been done to the original planning? (This usually calls for first-hand checks of procedures, implementers' findings, as well as results.) □ Yes □ No □ Not sure.

Postcheck.   After the dust has settled, you are in a position to get a more objective view of what was considered, what was planned, and what was accomplished.

1. How would you rate yourself in retrospect as to your decision-making performance: 1 2 3 4 5 6 7 8 9 10. Is it different from your previous answer (to Question 1 under Precheck)? □ Better □ Worse □ Same.

2. Make a list, mentally or in writing, of the strong points in your decision making and planning. Here note everything from cost estimates to the aptness of your selection of implementers. Is it satisfactory? □ Yes □ No □ Not sure.

3. Now make a list of weakpoints. Are the items surprising? Spotting them, can you eliminate them? □ Yes □ No □ Not sure.

4. This is a stress question. (Remember, decision-making is not only supposed to be a most important part of the executive job, but also the source of greatest pressure.) Which parts of the decision process weigh you down most; for example, is it the responsibility you bear for results; committing yourself to a course of action; the difficulties of choosing among alternatives? Choose one or more and note here:

Using your ratings.   The process you've just gone through is illuminating in and of itself. The Yes and No responses should give you fresh insights in your decision making, and should be evaluated in the context of your job experience. The "Not sure" answers may be of most value. Think them through, resolve the uncertainty that they represent, and they can be the points at which you can sharpen your decision making skills.

5. Problem Solving

"Our progress," says the CEO of a flourishing enterprise, "has been built by effective solutions to our problems." Every business, division and department has problems, that come in many sizes and shapes. The best way to deal with them is by knowing not only what they are, but the processes by which they can be vanquished.

➲ THE TWO BASIC TYPES

Management literature on problem solving usually considers problems as a single class. But analyze a group of problems, preferably your own, and you notice that there seems to be a basic difference in their nature:

"What" problems.   These are difficulties that you cannot solve until you analyze the situation and pinpoint the *precise problem*. For example, Al Grant is an experienced manager who has just switched jobs. He's only been in charge for a few weeks when the large number of arguments and complaints from employees suggest that his supervisors seem to have a human-relations blindspot. Or is it that the rank-and-file are an obstreperous lot?

Grant has a problem, all right, but he must decide *what* the problem is to proceed further.

"How" problems.   For example, you are operating a chemical plant and have recently started up a new process. You get a call from the Mayor. The runoff of your chemical waste is getting into the town creek and killing off the marine life. All the planning and engineering techniques were supposed to prevent this. You know what the problem is. Finding a solution depends on investigating the situation and devising preventives for the lethal leakage—in short, *how* do you proceed?

"Identify the problem" is the first step in most formal problem solving procedures. Remember, sometimes the step is implicit in the situation: you know what's wrong. But if you don't, you have to check the causes in order to pinpoint the element that needs remedy.

⮑ FIVE STEPS TO EFFECTIVE SOLUTIONS

The distinction between "What" and "How" problems is built into the guidelines that follow:

Step 1. Categorize   Decide whether you have a "What" or a "How" situation.

Step 2. Gather appropriate facts   For "What" problems, which you must analyze to pinpoint the difficulty, look for facts that relate to *causes*. Seek answers to questions like these: Who can shed light on the causes? What are the symptoms of the problem? Where do they occur? When do they occur? How long have they been noted?

For "How" problems, already identified, the facts should relate to the *resources* you can bring to bear. For instance: Experts or people of experience and ideas; tools or equipment; techniques, methods.

Step 3. Avoid false assumptions   It's so common a failing, it deserves a separate cautionary step. It's in the fact-seeking phase that there is a tendency to make misleading assumptions. For example, in the case of the pollution-ridden stream, the first assumption the executive in charge has to avoid is that the complaint is justified. He must test to make sure that it is waste from his plant and not some other source that is at fault.

Step 4. Solve in principle.   A solution may require selection from a range of possibilities. For example, is a poor quality record to be tackled by a hunt for better equipment or employee training? It helps to decide the general solution in order to move ahead. But don't limit your ideas unnecessarily. Your best solution may consist of simultaneous action on two or more fronts.

Step 5. Pretest solutions.   Tests are not always possible, but when they are they can save a lot of time and money. Again using the polluted-stream example, a bright engineer may come up with a chemical—mechanical system for stopping the flow of lethal waste. A thorough testing of the procedure in the laboratory will not only ensure results, but may lead to improvements in the system. Of course, in this example, testing is almost routine. But in other types of problem-solving methods, such as those involving training programs, or community-relations objectives, devise tests such as sampling that help make effectiveness more certain.

➲ TAKE A PROBLEM INVENTORY

Problems seldom are viewed as a group. The advantage of listing the problems you have (and those you anticipate) is to analyze the department's general health. It's like being a doctor. You talk to the patient to get his or her sense of well-being: "How do you feel in general?" The examination that checks organs and systems comes next.

You may want to undertake such an inventory yourself, based on your firsthand knowledge of operations. But to get the most out of the approach, draw your subordinates into the act. This can serve to make them more aware of their own areas of responsibility.

➲ COUNT YOUR BLESSINGS

Blessings, in our present context, are nonproblems, situations, procedures, policies, that are without complications.

By listing your nonproblems you:

1. Get perspective on the problems you do have, as a group. For example, if things that are okay are considerably fewer than your list of problems, you don't have problems you have a *problem*.
2. See what you are doing right.
3. May find your department is doing an overall fine job, and treat it with even more respect.

➲ POTENT FACTOR: YOUR ATTITUDE

Your personal attitude can help build a strong approach to dealing with problems. Here are the key elements that make for effectiveness:

1. Develop a "can-do" attitude.   There is more to this concept than meets the eye. Psychologists have proved again and again that individuals who are optimistic about their ability to solve problems have a much greater chance of doing so than their pessimistic opposite numbers. In the area of practical problem solving, the manager who goes on the assumption that a problem *can* and *will* be solved, is halfway to his goal.

2. Mobilize the creativity of your people.   It has been proved repeatedly: we all have unplumbed depths of imagination and ingenuity. Develop the practice of posing challenging assignments and problems to your people to stimulate their creativity. They're not likely to let you down.

Most of us respond favorably to the excitement of a challenge. Many of us will work our fingers to the bone to come up with an answer to a difficult problem because we hunger for the feeling of self-esteem and the increased respect of colleagues and co-workers when we score a break-through. Your subordinates' "need to achieve" can supplement your own.

3. Break problems down to bite-size.   Some work situations cannot be coped with because they're too vast or complex. For example, one manager was told by his boss, "In the next year, we're going to be replacing every piece of equipment in your department. Your employees are all going to have to relearn their jobs, develop new skills."

The problem of retraining about forty people in a dozen different skills, and still keep things running on a regular basis is clearly tremendous. But the department head made his first step an effective one. He got down to cases. He spelled out what each employee needed in order to handle new assignments. Once he had done this he was able to set up schedules that permitted each employee to get the training that was needed to make the transition.

4. Make the distinction between "gradual" and "crash" solutions. Some of the problems executives face can be solved over a long period of time. When the problem you face is of this character, a policy of "gradual-ism", that is, piecemeal and consistent planning, gets you off the hook.

However, some management problems are "emergency" or "rush." Here's where you're under deadline pressure and simply can't stretch out your thinking about the problem, or take your time developing solutions.

You strengthen your approach by using "crash" tactics. Whether you use a braintrust or maintain close contacts up the line and with staff experts, give yourself the advantage of *multiple brainpower*. Don't hesitate to draw on the mental resources and experience of other people in your company—subordinates, specialists, colleagues, and so on. (See, "A Permanent Problem-Solving Committee," page 103.)

➔ **THREE HAZARDS**

It has been said that a problem identified is half solved. An incident in an engineering class makes this point:

An engineering instructor tells a group of beginning students, "Here's a problem. Make up a sketch for a bridge to cross a river a mile wide."

The solutions come in describing suspension, cantilever, and viaduct designs.

The instructor gives all the papers but one a failing mark.

"Only one student is on the right track." He reads from the winning paper: "No solution is possible unless we know more about the problem." Some of the missing elements: how wide a channel must be allowed for navigation? How high must the span be above the channel? How much traffic is the bridge to bear?

Each one of these factors is a part of the problem. Each one must play a part in the solution.

In thinking about a problem situation, these steps keep you on track:

1. Don't assume you know the problem.   In some cases, you can't come to grips with a difficulty unless you know:

- The background. How long has it existed? How bad is it? And so on.
- The causes of the problem. What factors have brought it about? Why does it persist? What factors intensify the difficulty? What factors alleviate it? And so on.

2. Avoid the brass-tacks urge.   Many executives like to strike directly at the heart of the matter. In some cases that's commendable. But hasty approaches may lead to "solutions" that solve nothing. Particularly with a difficult problem, make sure you know not only the one-eighth that shows above the surface, but as much as possible of the seven-eighths that may not readily be visible to the eye. The importance of identifying a problem is that you force yourself to consider its different aspects and details.

A comedian once boasted that he discovered a cure for a disease that didn't even exist. It happens in executive suites every day—we solve problems that don't exist, because we haven't properly identified them.

3. Avoid overenthusiasm.   Appropriate enthusiasm over your solution is fine. But an excessive amount has several drawbacks: overselling it may be unconvincing and make people doubt its effectiveness. It may suggest a lack of realistic expectations. Or, worst of all, it may commit you to an action that is inferior to another course that might be better. The time between developing a solution and putting it to work is one for coolness and objectivity. Save the energy for a celebration of success.

➲ A PRELIMINARY CHECKLIST

International Management, a business journal headquartered in London, offers a series of practical points in the problem-solving process that serve as a good preliminary checklist:

☐ **Is there a solution.**   Not all problems can be solved.

☐ **Write it down.**   Lay it out so that you can analyze its complications.

☐ **Define the problem positively.**   The optimistic outlook inspires a positive solution both for yourself and others.

□ **Have you forgotten anything?**   Don't let the omission of important data fog your focus on the problem.

□ **How deep do you dig?**   Research may bring out facts you've over-looked or simply don't know about.

□ **Look for more than one solution.**   Are there alternative solutions? If so, which is best? Can you combine?

□ **Welcome new ideas.**   And give the new idea the chance to prove itself.

□ **Check your solution.**   Evaluate your answers. Since you can't fore-see precisely how a solution will work, changes and corrections may be necessary.

□ **Don't look for a perfect solution.**   Aim for the best you can get under the circumstances.

□ **Rest your ego.**   Insistence on being right all the time only alienates others. If your problem involves other people, give them the chance to be right once in awhile.

➲ **WHEN THERE'S NO SOLUTION**

You sometimes tackle a problem to which you can find no answer. Should you go on plugging away seeking the key? Or, should you give up? When you face this dilemma take the following steps:

1. Assess the importance of the problem.   Stick with it if it's a major obstacle. There's no point, for example, in conducting business as usual if a bottleneck is obviously going to wreck chances of filling a major commit-ment.

On the other hand, don't tie yourself up over a minor matter while regular operations go to pot.

2. Consult.   You can't get away from sound arithmetic: two heads are better than one. And three are better than two. Take up the problem with your boss, the people in your group who are directly concerned, special-ists in your staff departments who might be able to help.

They may or may not be able to provide immediate assistance. But it's not unusual for your own thoughts and ideas to become clarified in the process of discussion. Even if you draw blanks, you have at least multiplied your chances of success.

3. Can you ease up?   If you have a little elbow room in terms of time, let the teaser rest for a while. Give your mind a chance to cool off. Relaxation can renew your mental vigor, may give you a new approach and new understanding.

In some cases, time may work for you. For example, an executive found herself with the standard problem of two subordinates who couldn't get along. They were both key people; shifting either would have meant further complications. After days of futile thinking, she decided there was nothing she could do. Six months later she observed the problem no longer existed. The two individuals had little by little ironed out their own differences.

4. Review.   If the problem is important, you'll probably be forced to reconsider it from time to time. Do so in the light of changes that have taken place since you last considered the matter. A change may suggest a solution.

WHEN IT'S RIGHT TO BE WRONG

Occasionally a problem presents itself in which all the "right" solutions have failed to work. In such a situation, the "wrong" way may prove effective. In a sense, Solomon's method of dealing with the case of the disputing mothers applied a "wrong" solution. When he suggested that the child both women claimed be cut in two, it clearly was not a good solution. But it caused one woman to agree to give up the child; the other perfectly willing to abide the ruling made it easy to decide who the real mother was.

Here are some situations in which you might want to consider doing the "wrong" thing:

1. When the "right" way doesn't work.   Sometimes you just have to throw the rule book out of the window to save the situation.

2. When the "right" way won't do well enough.   In some cases, the quality of the result you want may persuade you that the "right" track isn't getting you where you want to go.

3. When there's doubt as to what the "right" way really is.   This development may turn up in connection with work methods. One experienced executive says:

"Sometimes in order to solve a problem of technique, I have to go as far off the deep end as I can. That helps me find limits within which a sound solution may be developed."

➲ SOLVING UNSOLVABLE PROBLEMS: AN HISTORIC SUCCESS

"Reaching for the moon" is a phrase that denotes trying to achieve the impossible. But now in our lifetime comes the achievement that gives lie to the old meaning. Neil Armstrong, Michael Collins, and Edwin Aldrin, did the undoable by achieving the objectives of Apollo 11 and being the first men on the moon.

The feat made the whole world proud—and thoughtful. Perhaps other "undoable" tasks are within our reach. At the very least, there's a tremendous lesson to be learned from the moon-conquering accomplishment of the first man-on-the-moon rocket.

Analyzing the steps by which we forged our triumph, key points emerge that may be applied to "unsolvable" problems on the job:

1. Commitment.   In 1961, President John F. Kennedy made a rousing, determined statement that committed the nation to landing men on the moon "before this decade is out." When starting any ambitious project we must resolve to put into the task the effort required. This act of will provides us with the drive and the emotional strength to start and sustain the energies needed for success.

2. Deadline.   In President Kennedy's statement, the words, "before the decade is out," created a sense of time pressure. Compare the effect of Kennedy's statement *without* the time deadline. What if he had merely said, "We must go to the moon." It *may* have been as exciting a declaration. But without the deadline, we would not have had the same feeling of urgency, a highly motivating factor.

3. Resources.   Thousands of companies and hundreds of thousands of people became involved in producing the ideas, the planning, the hardware, and the techniques that eventually landed us on our satellite. In the same way, the manager who is undertaking "mission impossible" must have resources available. Part of the solution is the assessment and gathering of resources, manpower, materials, equipment, and so on.

4. Piecemeal victories.   We didn't get to the moon in a single jump. As a matter of fact, a succession of ambitious projects starting with Pioneer I in 1957, and including Ranger, Mariner, Surveyor, Explorer, and Gemini, preceded Apollo 11. Each added to our knowledge and refinement of techniques. Within the framework of each of these major projects were thousands of piecemeal accomplishments—the improvement of a valve, the redesign of an electrical system, the continuing modernization of vital parts and instruments, such as the onboard computer.

In the same way, the executive should strive to break down his long-range goal into subelements and subgoals. These bite-size tasks or goals *are* attainable. And reaching the overall goal, in a sense, is the sum of many small successes.

5. Refinement and improvement.   A large part of the scientific and engineering talent in our space effort was devoted to continuing improvements in design methods and standards of quality. Accordingly, the executive who may be trying to drastically reduce overall production time on a major item may find that he moves toward his objective when, under his direction, a subordinate comes up with an idea for a special bit for a drilling operation, or a more efficient jig for an assembly operation.

6. Consolidate learning.   As advances were made, the benefits were quickly incorporated into the overall activity. Accordingly, each project benefited by what had been learned in previous ones. For example, the know-how for building bigger, better, and more reliable rockets advanced steadily from 1958 on. The same is true of the improvements in design and application of computers used in the space conquest.

7. Communications.   A part of the space effort that seldom made the headlines: the countless hours of meetings, conferences, discussions; the exchange of memos and reports among the various groups and individuals involved in the space project.

It's both stimulating and helpful to let the left hand know what the right hand is doing. Employee A who has solved a problem in his part of the project may be able to help Employee B solve one in his area. Or, Employee C, struggling with difficulties, may receive an idea from Employee D that will ease the bind.

8. Leadership.   An essential ingredient is continuing direction from the top. With a project involving even a few people—and certainly where larger numbers are involved—a single "command center" must supervise the effort, keep it moving along, and keep the parts of the project effectively related to one another. *This is the ultimate contribution of an executive.* And, as some experts see it, Apollo 11 may be said to be a triumph of American management know-how as well as of "technology."

An "unsolvable" problem? Apollo 11 proves that *if* there is such a thing, the number of items in this category are fewer than we think. Apollo 11 is an inspiration to the entire planet, but to American management, it's a stimulating reminder that any goal we set ourselves is possible—if we work toward that goal and believe in our ability to achieve it.

In World War II, management developed the saying: "The difficult we can to at once, the impossible takes a little longer." Our moon triumph suggests that the "impossible" may not take that much longer.

➜ **QUANTIFICATION, AN ASSIST IN PROBLEM-SOLVING**

Roger Bacon said that knowledge wasn't scientific until it used numbers. Sir Francis Galton, who launched the modern theory of statistics suggested, "Whenever you can, count."

For executives, numbers are an important tool of thinking and problem solving. Problems that seem vague and unmanageable come into sharper focus when you *count* and *compare*.

Clearly, when a problem naturally involves quantities, they become a key aspect of the solution. For example, you have a problem of moving 10 pounds of material across the continent. The solution is likely to be quite different from a similar problem involving 1,000 pounds.

But you are faced with many problems in which the quantification isn't built in. In this case there are two possible approaches:

■ **Assignment of values.**   Let's say you have a problem of evaluating the performance of an employee. Her job involves three different elements, each of which is of different importance. You represent this difference by "weighting": element A, the most important, is assigned a value of 50 percent, elements B and C given values of 25 percent each. Now, as you go about evaluating the quality of performance in these three areas, the quantification step gives you a continuing reminder that accomplishments in element A, or her failings, are twice as important as those in B or C.

■ **Rating scale.**   Instead of numbers, it's also possible to make helpful comparisons by use of a graded scale such as Excellent, Good, Fair, Poor, Unsatisfactory. Another common method is the old school grading method: A,B,C,D,E, and F.

In each of the above cases the objective is to make your thinking more specific. In avoiding vagueness, you sharpen the facts and make possible comparisons that are helpful in problem solving.

➜ **PRIORITIZING YOUR PROBLEMS**

"I have a hundred problems," says an overworked executive. "and one of the biggest is, which to tackle first."

Even if you have only two problems to deal with, you may be stuck with a priority situation. Remember, we're not talking about ordinary tasks here—you deal with those by deciding on a schedule. Task priorities become a problem if you are overloaded and have to find some way of suiting load to capacity.

Problem priorities are complicated because time itself is often a factor.

For example, you have an urgent problem: How to make a rush job more attractive, so that you can get a willing volunteer. But your boss comes in and says, "We're expecting a delegation over this afternoon from the X company to inspect our facilities. Will you please plan a grand tour that will make us look good and tell them what they want to know?" Not being sure how long the solutions will take requires insightful guesswork. Should you take the ten minutes, or hour, to think through the motivation problem, before undertaking the tour program?

Problems vs. Tasks.   Problem priorities differ from task priorities in two ways:

Task	Problem
1. You usually can estimate performance time for a task.	1. Time of indeterminate length may be needed for an answer.
2. Procedures for accomplishing a task are usually routine.	2. Solutions may have built-in unknowns. You may have to test out a tentative solution.

Priority-setting factors.   A number of factors influence your priority judgments:

1. Money.   The dollar outcome may suggest holding off an unplanned switch in operations if the changeover will mean excessive additional set-up and start-up costs. Or the cost factor may be indirect, and reflect the need to retain a big customer's good will.

2. Time.   For example, a manager says, "If I can get simple problems taken care of easily, I get them out of the way for two reasons: first, to cut down on the number of items on my To Do list, and second, to be able to concentrate on the more complex ones without feeling that things are piling up."

3. Stops and starts.   As every industrial engineer knows, stops and starts are time and money wasters. Two considerations arise from this fact:
a. Finish up. It may be wise to stick with a lower-priority difficulty and wrap it up than have the inconvenience of premature switching.
b. The human factor. Many people have a natural dislike of being interrupted before completion of an assignment (see the Zeigarnik Effect, page 358). If time and cost considerations are not decisive, it may be best to permit a subordinate to finish a job before a more important one takes precedence.
The next three factors apply equally to task and problem priorities:

4. Facilities. The availability of equipment, space, materials, and other resources may determine sequence. A meeting may be going on in your meeting room, but you may have to move it elsewhere, or postpone it if an emergency session comes along.

5. Goodwill/clout. An important customer, like the 800-hundred-pound gorilla, may have anything it wants. Unforeseen events may exert similar pressure. For example, a boss may deliver a request you can't refuse: "Drop everything else. . . ." Or a colleague may need help to the point where you must drop everything else.

6. Long-range versus short-range consequences. These are not always easy to figure. A priority you set for short-range considerations may turn out to be costly in terms of long-range consequences, a disappointed colleague, an irate boss, and so on. How to weigh long against short term consequences? Your judgment may be your only measure.

➲ OVERCOMING PROBLEM NEGLECT

A manager says ruefully, "I'm up to my ears in solving immediate problems, everything else gets lost." Getting out the work may kill off other matters deserving attention. However a simple technique can insure against problem neglect:

1. Divide your problems into three categories:

Immediate. These could require attention within a 24-hour period.

Middle range. The time latitude of these could be a month.

Long range. The period involved here is more than a month and is sometimes open-ended.

2. Assign worthwhile problems from all these categories to assistants and subordinates. No problem you have listed should be left floating. If it will help, keep a Problems file, but make it a live file, not a dead one.

3. Provide deadlines. Except for the open-ended, no-completion-time puzzlers, every assignment should include a deadline, as well as interim reporting of some kind.

4. Facilitate. Don't expect to receive bricks without providing straw. A problem may only require thought, but often resources are needed, such as authority to requisition or buy materials, use of machine time, consultation with people inside or outside the organization, all or any of which you may have to set up.

Final point: Should you assign an individual, or more than one person? This question deserves fuller attention.

➲   **A PERMANENT PROBLEM-SOLVING COMMITTEE**

Call it a headquarters staff or a brains trust, a standing committee of effective people to whom you can turn without the need of a hasty group-forming procedure, can improve your readiness to deal with problems. Such an arrangement may improve both the efficiency and effectiveness of your group problem solving. To reap the benefits, and prevent complications, two preliminary considerations are important:

How many?   "Not too big, not too small," is exactly correct. You depend on your judgment of the nature of the difficulty, and the people available for the team.

Who?   This question complements the previous one. Some specifics:

■ Who is available?
■ Who is able to take on leadership of the group?
■ Who has the skills the effort will need?

Experts who have studied taskforce operations say that aside from operating skills—everything from accounting skills to scientific ones—there are "group function" abilities to consider. For example, a taskforce of about six people might include: a leader; an analytical thinker; a practical feet-on-the-ground person; an imaginative head-in-the-clouds individual; a detail watcher; a team player ready to tackle anything any time; a resource person. The last is typically a person of experience who can fill knowledge gaps or dig up needed data. He or she may not have to be a regular member of the team, but should be available.

■ Next select the group members on the basis of merit (as well as know-how, of course.) It can have the virtue of giving you a way to recognize superior performance.
■ Make individual membership temporary. Emphasize the fact at the outset. You don't want to form an elitist bunch that may cause disaffection among non-members. By changing the group makeup, you avoid the appearance of favoritism.
■ Praise for the ex's. Because of the need to keep the group to manageable size, you may have to take a member out for each one you add. Make it clear to those you excuse that they are not being "dismissed," unless that's what is actually happening. Your thanks for a job well done, praise that will be heard by the rest of the group, not only softens any negative reaction by the employee, but reminds everyone else of the recognition that comes with taskforce service.

➋ PROBLEM AS OPPORTUNITY

It's a management cliché that "every problem is an opportunity." The sense of the statement is that the manager may find in the problem the chance to improve the situation of which it is a part. However, there are other ways in which a problem can be the doorway to opportunity.

1. More of the same?   The immediate difficulty that confronts you may have parallels. For example, a manager who finds he or she can cut rejects by periodic on-site sampling of a mainline production unit may be able to work out similar schedules for contributory production operations. A procedure that betters one kind of work may suit another.

2. Related areas?   Sometimes the improvement may be spread to other elements, those physically close, for example. A department head, starting to debug the layout of her supply room, finds she can, at the same time, alter shipping facilities that tie in.

3. One solution fits all?   A manager who has been working to develop the ability of an assistant to deal with customers discovers that arranging to have him visit customers' premises and meet key personnel transforms his understanding and rapport. The manager asks himself, "Who else in the department would benefit from that kind of exposure?"

4. Problems as training?   "We all know that helping an employee 'get his or her feet wet' is the beginning of indoctrination," says the head of a computer operation. "But handing over a tough problem that requires digging, talking to people, determining the consequences and causes of a difficulty is the equivalent of tossing employees into the pool bodily and making their learning an exciting discovery."

A like-minded manager makes it a practice to assign long-range stubborn problems to bright young employees, not only for training purposes but also with the hope that a fresh mind not limited by the knowledge that "it can't be done" will do it.

➋ WHEN IT ISN'T A PROBLEM

There's a linguistic difficulty with the word *problem*. The semantics of problem solving may distort meaning and lead to treating nonproblems as though they are the real thing.

Emotional by-product.   "I have a terrible problem," says a division head. "I must fire a subordinate who is a good friend." He thinks the necessity to fire a friend is *his* problem. But he is mistaken. There is no difficulty in firing. That only requires some paperwork and an exit interview. The real problem is the emotional ordeal the action causes him.

The solution to the problem of firing is not to fire. The solution to the problem of personal trauma lies in mitigating the stress for both executive and subordinate. For example, the firer may help find the employee another job. Or, he could mitigate his feeling of guilt by reminding himself that he did all he could to prevent the separation.

Synonym. "Don't give me any problems," a manager tells an employee she has accepted as a transferee. The employee is somewhat unruly, and is being put on notice. The manager is using the word *problem* as a synonym for trouble.

Mistaking the part for the whole. "I love problems," an assistant tells his boss. He doesn't, really. It's the excitement and test of his abilities that intrigues him. A routine problem that can be solved routinely bores him to death. What he really means is that he enjoys challenge. His astute boss finds that he makes the employee happy and gets better results when he stresses this element of a problem assignment.

➲ WHAT QUALITIES MUST A SOLUTION HAVE?

When the Dutch boy thrust his finger in the hole in the dike to keep out the onrushing sea, he solved a problem. But while the act was heroic, the solution has a major drawback: it was temporary.

Solutions must not only eliminate obstacles or difficulties, they must also deal with a number of implicit requirements. In the finger-in-the-dike solution, the authorities knew they had to come up with a more complete solution to prevent catastrophe.

In *The Practice of Management,* Peter Drucker cites a case in which a company had to replace an executive vice president who had died suddenly. There were complications. The man had made the company, but also had been a bully and a tyrant. Moreover the problem had another part: the president, who guarded the vice president's rights and ultimate status, actually left decisions and responsibility to the V.P.

Solutions were suggested: Appoint an informal committee of functional vice presidents to work with the president. Another was to recruit a replacement for the executive vice president who would assume the responsibility and decision making exercised by his predecessor.

These "solutions" were ruled out because of implicit needs: the company needed an effective top management, thwarted by the do-nothing president. The one-man rule of the former vice president had been a handicap not to be repeated.

Drucker states that solutions must reflect the needs of the organization overall. He suggests the objectives that pertained in the case in point:

- balance and harmonize immediate and long-range future plans;
- take into account a. the business as a whole; b. the activities needed to run it;
- focus on business performance and results.

In your own case, identify and consider the qualifiers of your solutions. Some are general: a solution generally should be permanent, not be too costly, or require too long period to implement. It should adhere to company policy and tradition. But there may also be specific factors: "We must respect the feelings of X." "We can't undercut Y's authority," and so on. (See page 54 for the agenda for a problem-solving meeting.)

6. Planning

"What isn't planned today, won't be done tomorrow," says the experienced executive. Thinking and arranging for future activities—everything from routines like a staff meeting to a major project, such as the launching of a new product or the building of a new plant—is one of the challenges for the effective executive.

Planning failures are of two kinds:

Neglect. "Tomorrow will take care of itself," says the self-deluded manager, and counts on improvisation and fast reflexes to make up for planning deficiencies. But time and tide often find him or her high and dry, and failures become legion.

Flubbing. Some executives go through the motions of planning, but inadequate methods don't do the trick and too often consequences are dire.

Suggestions that follow can help you review and improve planning methods.

⊃ **WHEN TO PLAN**

Planning becomes appropriate when an activity must be prepared for, organized, and scheduled, sometimes as dictated by the calendar. Three planning occasions might be:

- The beginning of a new year with its newly set objectives.
- The quarterly intervals that give you the opportunity for appraising achievements and resetting your sights.
- Any new undertaking or project.

In addition, there are the tasks that may confront you at any time; the need, for example, to cut costs, revise operations, improve quality of output, raise the level of performance of personnel.

Replanning. Replanning is an adjustment of original efforts, and is indicated when-

Initial arrangements have become unsatisfactory. Perhaps people are unable to perform as expected, or a procedure develops unexpected faults.

Standards are raised. For example, quality or quantity performance, previously satisfactory, are no longer acceptable. Actions must be planned that will meet new expectations.

New objectives are set. An air-freight company decides, "We want to keep track of each shipment so that we can locate it within an hour of an inquiry." Old procedures have to be superceded to give greater control.

➡ **TYPES OF PLANS**

The list below can help clarify your approach to planning:

One-time plans. Some situations you plan for are one-shot. They will be used once and may never again be repeated. Involved in this kind of planning, executives will often improvise. Cost considerations may suggest planning at a get-by level, the lowest possible acceptable standard.

For example, the D Company wants to mark the opening of a new building with a memorable and newsworthy ceremony including a buffet lunch for all employees and guests, decorations, speeches by key people, including the mayor; TV and newspaper coverage are major elements that have to be orchestrated. The program is a one-time event, but it has to be put together carefully for optimum results.

■ **Standby plans.** Executives sometimes develop a plan for handling a situation that *may* develop. Such planning must be done with as much care and detail as a plan you will be putting to work tomorrow. Too often a standby plan has been developed with the feeling that the contigency, although possible, is not likely. And when the situation does arise, the standby plans are found to be impractical, incomplete, or unrealistic.

Standby planning may require more imagination and ability to visualize than ordinary planning. You may have to depend heavily on your own abilities or those of others to foresee possible situations in order to plan for them realistically.

■ **Short-range plans.** Short-range planning has the value of immediacy, and can depend heavily on informal and direct communication.

When you are going to start a project that can be completed in a few days, the amount of paper work can be minimal. Face-to-face communication can usually get across the exchange of ideas and information required.

■ **Long-range plans.** Unlike short-range planning, projects that extend over months or years must have three built in characteristics:

1. *Continuity.* You must put down on paper and build in controls that will keep the project moving in the desired direction and at the pace originally planned.
2. *Review.* Periodic considerations must be made of progress in order to make sure that original objectives will be achieved.
3. *Goal reconsideration.* Factors which have helped determine the purposes or goals of a plan may change. Sights may have to be raised or lowered. Along with reviews of progress, the executive may also want to assess original objectives to see if they are still valid or whether they must be modified.

The points above are basic for long-range operations, but this type of planning has taken on a whole new dimension in recent years, and under the name of *Strategic Planning* has been enlarged, refined, and standardized to a specific top management procedure. You will find this subject covered in detail at the end of this section. See page 119.

■ **Back-up plan.** No matter how carefully planning is done, introduction of new factors or performance failures in some areas may bring a project to a point of crisis or failure. In this case, it is desirable to have "Plan B," a back-up plan which can be substituted for the original one (see page 116, "Develop Plan B").

Emergency plans. Organizations are prone to emergencies. Your fire protection may be of the best, but an actual blaze will still be a shock against which forces must be mobilized. Some time ago a chemical plant in New Jersey faced an unprecedented crisis that illustrates what can happen:

Case in point: Catastrophe in the balance. A new employee was directed to remove an empty nitrogen cylinder from a feeding line and replace it. He disconnected the nitrogen container and replaced it with one of hydrogen. Nitrogen is inert, hydrogen can be violently explosive.

Fortunately the error was quickly discovered by an experienced worker who rushed to his foreman's desk with the news. "Shut down everything, clear everybody out," the supervisor ordered his assistant, and phoned Engineering.

"My god!" the engineer in charge said. "A single spark could blow up the building. I'll be there in two seconds." The engineer raced to the scene, verified the mistake. The works manager and division manager appeared and the three, along with the supervisor, had a quick conference. The supervisor's suggestion was adopted:

The end of a long two-by-four was set against the shut-off valve. With gentle taps of a hammer at the other end of the lever, the supervisor closed the valve. Then the system was bled of the hydrogen that may have fed in. The four then agreed all was clear. The recall whistle was blown and people in various degrees of recovered equilibrium returned to work.

Here are the elements of the emergency:

Anatomy of Danger
Sudden, unexpected, unprecedented happening
Discovery of the danger and sounding of alarm
Assumption of command by foreman
Minimizing of the consequences—stop machines, exit people
Forming of crisis committee
Developing countermeasures
Applying countermeasures
Restoration of order

While some of the elements resemble other emergencies, the uniqueness of the accident requires a flexibility that takes special problems into account. For example, many accidents would not benefit by the participation of an engineer but might require another type of expert.

⊃ THE EMERGENCY COMMITTEE

An approach stated in general terms can be specified and the group formed when needed:

■ **From the front line.** Make front-line managers—supervisors, department heads, and so on, the first communication point. All employees should be trained to report trouble to the manager in charge of the area, department, or function involved.

The two next links should be forged simultaneously, or as much so as possible:

The expert. An engineer, scientist, professional, must be contacted, as appropriate. If it is a medical emergency, such as heart attack, the organization should have a doctor to call.

A member of top management. Quick decisions of importance may have to be made off the cuff. Someone must be on hand with sufficient authority to commit the company to action.

➲ **GROUP INITIATIVE**

The team must match the emergency:

■ **Action plan.** The people already mentioned—department and division heads, expert, and top manager—plus any other individuals with something to contribute, confer on countermeasures. The top manager may lead the discussion, or pass the authority on to someone who may be more knowing about the situation.

■ **Authorize action.** The emergency plan is implemented, with resources marshaled as needed by a coordinator who is responsible for keeping the effort on track.

■ **Wrap-up.** When all is clear, clean-up, other efforts required for a return to normalcy should be completed, and if possible, work resumed. In cases where major damage has been done, and normal operations cannot be resumed, procedures for an orderly suspension should be started.

■ **Contingency plans.** We live in lively times. Even more than in the past, change is the order of the day. Product marketing life is shorter, style and taste shifts can kill off old favorites and bring new smash hits in everything from breakfast cereal to rainwear, seemingly overnight.

By definition, contingency planning is the adjustment a company must make when *developing events* make a current plan obsolete.

The consequences obviously involve top management. Equally clear is the chain of alterations that rock through an organization, affecting every division and department. This means contingency planning eventually must involve most or all levels, from the top down. And these linked revisions must be controlled and interlocked by a supervising entity.

■ **Standby plans.** The difference between standby and contingency planning is that the latter is targeted on events that aren't likely to happen, but often do, and the former on developments that are expected. For example, "If the advertising pulls and we're overcrowded," the retailer tells his staff, "let's do the same thing we've done previously, set up counters inside the side corridor." Completed arrangements may call for movement of merchandise, setting up a cash register, appointing the salespeople for the temporary location, and so on.

These points apply to standby plans:

Availability. If the action required consists of more than a few simple steps, but the plan on paper, and have it at hand in a file, or in the desk of the manager in charge.

Advance notice.   Inform those people who will be involved in implementing the standby plan of the possibility of their changed assignment. Materials, equipment, transportation that may be required should be as close to the point of action as possible. For example, in the retail operation, the temporary counters or tables should be at the ready near the side corridor.

On hold.   If people outside the organization will have to be called upon, let them know sufficiently in advance to avoid last minute difficulties. This includes those who will supply materials, equipment, and so on.

Person in charge.   It's desirable to have a single individual take charge of implementing the plan. He or she should be in possession of all details in order to smooth the transition.

➲ 3-SCENARIO PLANNING

In facing future possibilities, managements may confront a development that is in the cards, but its exact form and dimension is unknown. For example:

An urban department store has operated profitably and earned a reputation for service to a middle- and upper-class clientele. Changes in the local economy and related housing developments, and growth of suburban retailing begin to make inroads in sales. Slight pecks have been made at confronting the situation. Higher-priced goods have been replaced by lower-cost and lower-quality items. Advertising has become more sale-oriented, trying to make up in volume some of the loss in profit margin.

Eventually the president brings in a consultant who starts a more intensive effort to face up to the shape of things to come. Working with a selected group of managers and specialists, he starts an analysis of the firm's prospects under three headings of possible change:

1. Best.   The most favorable possibility. For example, the shifts in the market and customer pool will stabilize and earlier profit margins can be reestablished.

2. Worst.   Least favorable circumstances. The neighborhood deteriorates and sales volume drops below acceptable levels.

3. Medium level.   At this dimension of change, the presumption is that an adequate program of operational adjustment makes it possible for the company to function reasonably well for at least a five-year period.

In adopting the "three faces of change" approach, it's up to the participating planners and staff to realistically fill in the shape and implications of the three phases, and come up with countering strategies.

➔ **PLANNING FOR PLANNING**

Management authority Peter Drucker has commented that work planning must be planned for just like any other aspect of management. He recommends five steps:

Setting objectives. What are the things my company and my department wish to achieve—and when?

Determining priority of objectives. If all the objectives cannot be achieved at once, which are the most important?

Identifying resources. What will it take to achieve the objectives set forth? What are the resources of the department, and the company, available to help achieve the objectives?

Executing action programs. What will it take to move the plan off paper? Who must issue what instructions and to whom?

Maintaining control. Are follow-up procedures used effectively and thoroughly? Does the manager know what the score is, on an up-to-the-minute basis?

➔ **GIVE YOUR PROJECT A NAME**

Whether it's the Manhattan Project (atom bomb), or Operation Overlord (invasion of Normandy), you'll generally find that every big project is given a name. It's not an affectation, it's an effective idea for projects, large or small, for two reasons:

■ The name acts as a convenient handle. When you discuss the matter with other people you then have a simple means by which to refer to it. You develop a common understanding of what it is you're talking about.
■ Less tangible but possibly even more vital, in your own mind the project becomes more specific, more concrete.

➔ **PINPOINT THE PURPOSES OF YOUR PLANNING**

It is highly desirable to state goals in terms of specific quantities. In some areas there is no problem. When you are setting production goals or sales quotas, it is perfectly natural to state these in specific terms: January quota, 10,000; February, 12,000; and so on.

But even with less clear-cut objectives, it is sometimes possible to reduce your aims to numbers. Take the matter of quality, for example. In the average office the quality of the work cannot, as in the industrial scene, be expressed in terms of tolerances, types of finish, color range, and so on. But let's say you're out to improve the quality of the typing done by members of your staff. This goal might very well be put in terms of the

numbers of typos or erasures that mean a given piece of correspondence must be discarded.

A threat to achieving planning objectives lies in an unexpected direction:

A department head, alarmed by the figures that jump out at her from a cost of operating report, decides she'd better bear down, fast and hard. She plans an impressive program: close check on every expense item, from stationery to overtime; conferences with her subordinates to sell them on the need to keep a tight rein on expenditures; an intensive probing into current work methods to see where they can be made more efficient.

She gets her assistant and the entire work group to cooperate. They go along, and she's pleased as punch the way the plan is clicking. She considers the matter finished, and turns her attention elsewhere. But, unfortunately, she has forgotten her original purpose. *She never bothers to find out whether she's chopped one penny off operating costs.*

Write your purpose down in black and white. Be as specific as possible: "To cut $500 off monthly expenses." "To get dealers to take 10 percent more of our product." And so on. And, check to ascertain to what extent goals have been met.

➜ SELECTING THE PEOPLE

List all the people who should be involved in furthering a plan. Conceivably, this might include everyone on your staff. More generally, there are a few key people through whom you will work directly.

This helps in two ways:

1. You may sometimes discover that you lack one or more other people needed to implement the plan.
2. In listing the people, you may discover that although you have the individuals, they will require further instruction before being able successfully to tackle the task for which they have been selected.

Once you have spotted this need for training, you will find it becomes one of the subgoals which the plan must take into account.

➜ CHECK OUT AVAILABLE FACILITIES

Planning requires a review of available resources. You may need new facilities, or you may have to revamp those on hand in order to be able to implement the plan.

Make your facilities list as complete as possible. Remember the old story of the kingdom that was lost for want of a nail. Facilities lists will vary, depending on the nature of the project involved. For a plan of production, for example, you might list available resources under headings like these:

Raw materials
Fittings and supplies
Production equipment
Auxiliary equipment
Standby equipment
Handling equipment
Packing materials

The problem of human resources, of course, is an essential and related part of your planning, covered above.

Another approach to assessing facilities is shown in the chart below:

Have on Hand	Modifications, Repairs?	Additional Facilities Required	Date	Sources & Remarks

➔ DEVELOP AND CHECK METHODS

Where tried and true methods have been satisfactory, you may merely have to state briefly the means you intend to use to achieve your goals. But in other cases, this may become the key item of the plan.

Let's say, for example, that the purpose of your plan is to cut down on absenteeism. When you come to methods, your first inclination may be merely to jot down the means that have been used in the past: the record keeping by supervisors, the occasional warnings backed up by a severance of the really extreme cases.

But writing down the method gives you an opportunity to reassess its potential effectiveness. In your plans to combat absenteeism, you may be moved to seek additional methods: development of an absentee record form that will go more fully into the reasons for the absence; or follow-up by a personnel officer of the reasons that have been contributory to absenteeism, such as poor transportation facilities, and so on.

➔ ESTIMATE COSTS

The wise executive keeps the cost consideration in mind in every planning move he or she makes.

You may say to yourself: "Sure, I did a good job on that project. But I wonder whether it couldn't have been done at half the cost."

You're always working within a cost limit. Putting it in other words: if money were no object, almost any plan could be brought to a satisfactory conclusion. But the executive who can do it well and do it cheaply, achieves a double success from his or her planning.

➔ SCHEDULE PLANNING ELEMENTS

Draw up the timetable of the planned operation. Set specific dates for the various phases of your plan:

Preparation.   Under this subheading, for example, you may want to indicate training steps required to equip your personnel for the tasks you intend to give them. You may have to go out into the market to secure additional equipment, more space, and so on. Many of the items here will have been turned up in your filling out of the earlier parts of the guide.

Sequence.   Your plan will be advanced by specific people assigned to definite parts of the total effort. Your usual assignment procedure will figure here. You'll select your people according to their suitability for the tasks you want performed. You'll set up deadlines, subgoals, and so on.

Time targets.   Be specific "Noon, May 20," or "End of business, Friday, June 17." Build a tradition in which meeting deadlines becomes a matter of professional pride. Alter time targets only when unavoidable.

➔ BUILD IN CONTROLS

Whether you call it progress review, follow-up, or checking on assignments, set up some means of reviewing the progress of the plan and of readjusting to unexpected developments. If one subordinate is lagging behind, you may have to put an additional person on the job. If another subordinate is getting ahead faster than you anticipated, you may have to stop her and put her on another job if her completion must coincide with the work being done by a second individual.

The controls you use will depend, of course, on the nature of the effort. You may want to set up a system of written reports by which your subordinates keep you informed of how they're making out. Or where cost is critical and must be checked with a sensitive hand, you may want to have all bills for the project collected in a central agency so that you can be kept continually informed of how fast the money is going out.

If you have been successful in quantifying your objectives, it may be helpful to keep track of progress by means of a visual chart or graph. Whether you chart your progress daily, weekly, or monthly depends again on the nature of the project. But you'll find such visual aids particularly effective in the conferences you may want to hold with your subordinates to discuss the rate of progress and the need to alter methods to changing conditions.

⮕ EVALUATE RESULTS

A progress review is, in a sense, a running evaluation of the plan. In many cases, you and your people have much to gain by taking a retrospective view.

Discuss Project X in terms of the *original objectives* as compared with objectives accomplished. You can survey the methods used, starting from the methods you had intended to employ and ending up with any changes and the reasons for changes that may have been necessary.

The other items mentioned in previous pages—purposes; manpower; facilities; methods; costs; timing and scheduling; controls—similarly suggest points of departure and specific areas that can be covered in your evaluation sessions.

⮕ DEVELOP A PLAN B

When large sums of money or other vital consequences are involved, consider having an alternative plan available if the preferred Plan A fails. In preparing Plan B, keep in mind these two questions:

■ **Can Plan B produce what Plan A was meant to achieve?** Many executives tend to be meticulous about Plan A, but give Plan B a passing glance. Plan B deserves just as much consideration as Plan A, for a state of emergency *already* exists when Plan B is brought in.

■ **Is Plan B free from Plan A's weaknesses?**   Plan B will, of course, be inferior to Plan A, or it would have been your first choice. But even though Plan B has more serious faults than Plan A, they should be *different* faults. If the two plans have similar weak spots, they may be no better than one plan. Actually, *Plan B is an added danger* in this case, since its very presence may lend a false sense of security.

The classic case is the driver who never travels without a spare, but whose spare won't hold air.

➲ BUDGETS AS A TOOL

Usually, executives think of budgets as a financial fence. While in a sense, budgetary limits are meant to deter excessive or misdirected expenditure, budgets also have strong additional advantages:

■ **More complete planning.**   A budget may be viewed as a scheme of operations converted into dollars and cents. As such, it forces executive planning and provides a stable financial framework that can help insure performance. A budget can be especially helpful in times of change, as many companies have learned after living through the turbulence of significantly fluctuating economic conditions.

■ **Measure of performance.**   A budget kept up to date gives the executive a continuous view of how well he or she is progressing. Top management, too, is provided with a check on total company performance. Any significant variations from budget allocations signal the need for investigation.

■ **Control over spending.**   A good budget allows managers to maintain close control over expenditures. Sophisticated executives have learned that properly viewed, budgets can encourage spending where it will clearly improve net profit.

■ **Better coordination.**   The financial controls provide the mechanism for improved coordination between various parts of a business, or between departments. Financial controls may help correct such problems as poor communication between production and sales, faulty timing in the introduction of new products, and improper staffing of operations such as order, service, warehousing, and so on, in the light of projected sales volume. Finally, for many executives, a well-drawn budget is a helpful measure of his or her performance. It tells executives who reach their goals and remain within budgetary limits that they have probably done a satisfactory job. For executives who have done violence to budgetary limitations, no matter what their accomplishment, there is the need to backtrack to learn whether performance, no matter how outstanding, has been really profitable.

➲ A CONTINUATION PLAN—KEEPING THINGS ROLLING IN YOUR ABSENCE

Details of a continuation plan will vary from executive to executive, depending on the nature of job responsibilities, the length of time he or she will be away, who will be left in charge, and so on. Any plan for continuation involves two factors: people and paper. Here are tips for making your continuation plan work in both areas:

1. Always keep your superior and subordinates reasonably well informed about what is going on.
2. Train one particular person to take over your job in emergency absences.
3. Make your assistant privy to as many of your current problems and concerns as possible.
4. Use short absences and your vacation as training periods for both plan and personnel.
5. Prepare a continuation folder to include key job descriptions, an outline of your own duties, whom you report to on what, who reports to you, where key items are located, who can answer questions, etc.
6. Have job descriptions written by key personnel, outlining their areas of responsibility and detailing their duties and the names of all subordinates.
7. Make sure your folder includes a plan of action for continuing present projects, for deciding about upcoming matters of major significance, plus a review of proposals for change, an outline of future projects, and any other helpful information.
8. Revise and update these reports as often as advisable, but at least semiannually.
9. Keep your continuation folder constantly up to date by filing recent correspondence, memoranda dealing with current problems, etc. in it. Weed these out from time to time.
10. Go over this folder with the person you have picked to take over in your absence, and let him or her know where it is kept.
11. The typical executive's secretary becomes a key source of information and opinion: "I believe Ms. Jones would handle that situation this way. . . ." Let your secretary know your expectations in this regard.

12. Should you leave word as to where you can be reached in case of emergency? That's a highly personal decision. Just be sure to give the question some thought, and act on the decision, whichever way you decide.

➜ STRATEGIC PLANNING

In the early 1950s the term *long-range planning,* a general and somewhat loose approach by organizations to set their future course, began to develop into a more scientific and effective one. It acquired the label *strategic planning,* incorporating thereby the additional dimension of an action-oriented method.

Larger corporations tested and developed the idea, and for that reason it remained a big-business tool. But eventually, and at present, medium to small businesses find that the benefits of strategic planning are available to them, and their own needs for growth and survival require its application.

➜ CONCEPT AND PROCESS

Strategic planning can be a highly technical and for-the-bigs only operation. But in its basic and uncomplicated form, it lends itself both to the needs and capabilities of every organization that seeks to assure itself of a healthy future.

■ **Concept.**   According to George A. Steiner, whose *Strategic Planning,* is one of the authoritative sourcebooks:

Strategic planning is a backbone support to strategic management. . . . Everyone recognizes that strategic and operational management are tightly linked. Strategic management provides guidance, direction and boundaries for operational management. Just as strategic management is vitally concerned with operational management so is strategic planning concerned with operations. But the focus and emphasis of strategic planning as with strategic management is on strategy more than operations. [1979, p. 4].

Steiner goes on to comment that a company may survive internal inefficiencies if its basic strategy is solid, but isn't likely to offset ineffective strategies with the best operational performance. The ideal situation, he concludes, is to design brilliant strategies and implement them effectively.

■ **Process.**   The procedures of strategic planning are those which amass the creative, analytical, and practical brainpower of an organization to make the assessments, analyses, the diagnoses and prognostications that will determine future tactics and operations. This may mean a single individual, usually at the helm of an organization, or scores of people.

➲ **FOURTEEN ELEMENTS OF STRATEGIC PLANNING**

Marvin Bower, for several decades managing director of the consulting firm, McKinsey and Company, has enumerated fourteen areas that make up the components of a management system for all business. They will be treated in terms of the part they play in SP. Their sequence has been changed, and explanations modified to suit the SP context:

1. Developing a company philosophy. Strategic planning requires raising a question that first arises with an organization's origins. Peter Drucker has phrased it as asking, "What is our business and what should it be?" In answering the question in the search for future operation, the answers necessarily involve such basics as setting objectives, development of strategies and plans, and the making of decisions about tomorrow's actions.

2. Establishing policies. A set of resolutions regarding the importance and practices of SP should be formed by the company policy-setting group. These may range in concreteness from written statements to ideas tacitly agreed to. But their thrust should add up to the commitment to strategic planning, and the involvement of the organization at its various levels and among key managers.

3. Structural support. Implementing SP must be insured by committees and participation by key executives whose responsibility may be permanent or temporary. Specific assignments should be given so as to leave no doubt as to the need to perform.

4. Setting objectives. The aims of the organization's SP efforts are best formed by a council of top people. The exact nature and directions in which survival and growth is to be sought should emerge from wide-ranging discussion. And the same or similar body should reconsider conclusions reached, for updating and readjustment.

5. Planning strategy. The large, overall actions that are to help achieve objectives should be developed by those in the organization best suited for such planning. Everything from product lines to markets, from production methods to research should be considered to maximize strategies.

6. Establishing short-range goals. Targets shorter in time range and narrower in scope than far-reaching goals should be agreed upon, designed as subobjectives for operating plans.

7. Providing personnel. Recruiting, selecting, and developing people at all echelons, especially top management and high-caliber technical people, should be continuous so that human resources are available as needed for strategic plans.

8. Establishing procedures. Important and recurring activities should be determined, prescribed and periodically refined.

9. Providing facilities. Plant, equipment, and other physical facilities for organizational progress must be available and maintained as needed.

10. Acquiring capital. The money and credit required, not only for current but also future business activity must be on hand. Those in charge of finances, obviously, should be among the continuing participants in SP.

11. Setting and maintaining standards. Measures and levels of performance are a major means of enabling an organization to achieve long-term goals.

12. Developing programs and operating plans. These are for day-to-day operations, with an eye to future needs. For example, a records procedure with a foreseeable obsolescence requires thought about eventual replacement.

13. Providing control information. The facts, figures, and conditions to help people perform will change to suit future strategies. Forces inside and outside the organization must be kept cognizant of requirements imminent and for later on.

14. Motivating people. Even the best-intentioned may have trouble in accommodating to the demands of the future in the crush of present. The image of the future, in its many aspects for your organization must be kept alive and meaningful in order to get an acceptable level of cooperation in activities that are future-focused. The backing and activism of management at all levels is required.

➔ OVERCOMING ANTI-SP BIAS

For those sold on strategic planning, the idea of resistance may seem irrational: "How can anyone be against preparing for an ongoing future?"

As George A. Steiner points out in *Strategic Planning*, negative feelings about SP procedures may operate at two levels:

■ **Practical objections.** This is the kind of thing people say:

"All my time goes into regular operations. I have none left over for possible long-range developments."

"Strategic planning is technical and complicated."

"Too much paperwork, most of it unnecessary."

"I'm not one for future planning. Here and now is my thing."
But behind such expressions may lie feelings of uneasiness:

■ **Possibly unreal fears.**   Wariness, even deep concern, may be the real source of trouble. For example:

Doubts about the future.   "I'll be retired in five years, and out of it." Or, "In a few more years the technology of this business will be so changed, I'll be obsolete."

Power struggle.   Less aggressive people may feel at a disadvantage from possible conflicts of interest and personalities.

Fear of failure.   "What if I guess wrong?" says a manager who has been given the responsibility.of projecting his operations five years ahead.

Lack of imagination.   For some, the future is as blank as a fortune-teller's crystal ball. They have difficulty in making the mental leap required by an exercise requiring looking ahead.

➲ SIX STEPS TOWARD WINNING ACCEPTANCE

Organizations embarking on a stratetic planning effort should consider measures that clarify objectives and persuade those who will participate:

1. *Top management commitment.*   Those at the top must fully back the effort to get acceptance by the other echelons.
2. *Emphasizing importance.*   The message must be communicated: if we want a strong future, we must think about it and plan for it.
3. *Stressing benefits.*   "A better future" has a glow but not much substance. Where possible, benefits to the company and to individuals should be spelled out: "We want to plan to increase our market share by 50 percent in five years. Imagine what career opportunities that growth will mean to every manager."
4. *Fine-tuning managerial skills.*   "You will gain considerable insight and increased planning know-how by participating in the committee. . . ."
5. *Making worthwhile contacts.*   Strategic planners will have the opportunity to work with others inside and outside the organization that will increase capabilities and widen horizons.
6. *Staying on top of change—and offsetting personal obsolescence.* "You know how rapidly our business is developing. Those who are active in future planning will be in a position to update their orientation to industry developments and come out way ahead of the game."

➲ R&D: RACE TO SHAPE THE FUTURE

The research and development (R&D) function has mixed status in business. In some companies, because operations are secret and staff "unbusinesslike," dreamers rather than doers, idiosyncratic in dress and manner, it is viewed either with derision or resentment. In others it is considered where the action is, the origin of exciting new products, services that shape operations.

However, when R&D is put in the context of strategic planning, its true function, goals, and importance become clear. For with the preoccupation of strategic planners with the future, the efforts of most development departments clearly become that of anticipating what is ahead rather than waiting for it to happen as a result of outside forces.

The R&D department that can come up with a new drug, a new computer element, devices to improve basic services, from transportation to water supply, is demystifying the future, and giving its organization a leg up on marketing prospects.

➲ WHEN PLANNING IS ABSENT

Some people assume planning, other than that for immediate operations, is an affectation and an unnecessary frippery. Consider two examples of unpreparedness:

Case of the New York restaurateur.   A Turkish restaurant opened in New York City some time ago. After long weeks of erasing the artifacts of a previous bistro, and all the steps of planning, rebuilding the kitchen, and decorating the dining area in bright good taste, the proprietor, who was also the maitre d', announced opening night. In a midtown area with eating places running four to five on a block, competition was fierce. Mr. R. expected a slow growth, possibly accumulating enough customers to see the light at the end of the tunnel after several months.

Catastrophe struck quickly and unexpectedly. A restaurant reviewer came in to assess the place in the second week. He gave it an ecstatic notice: "Best Turkish food in town." The place was jammed, lines waited outside. And waited, and waited. Diners sat at tables for an hour before the few servitors could start them, and longer to finish. The new kitchen staff was unable to cope with the load. After a week the crowds stopped coming. They never returned. The restaurant closed two months later. It simply hadn't planned for success.

Case of a publisher's oversight.   XYZ Publishing had an excellent reputation. Its reports on business developments, its analysis and prognostication of trends were accurate and helpful to its subscribers. Savvy members of the staff grumbled. "Our competitors are enlarging, doing better than we are. How come?"

Eventually the founder and president gathered his cohorts: "We've had several meetings to figure out why we haven't flourished as well as some of our competitors, why we're not bigger in terms of services, subscribers, and profits. We finally solved it: We didn't plan for growth." And then followed the promise: "Just see where we'll be in five years."

Unfortunately, the insight couldn't deal with the basic problem. There was a reason for lack of expansion the president hadn't spotted. The company didn't change because he liked it just the way it was. He didn't want to share his authority, bring in or promote people at the top to do the planning necessary for growth. The company continued to nurture its good reputation, but in business terms, it was a non-growth static operation.

7. Delegation and Assignment

"Executives work through others. . . ."

That principle of executive action is generally accepted, even self-evident.

It is true that executives satisfy their responsibilities by using the manpower at their command, from secretary to staff and other subordinates. It likewise follows that many executives operate on marginal levels because they have not mastered the methods by which their human resources can be utilized to best advantage.

The techniques of delgation and assignment are major keys to effective utilization of subordinates.

⮑ WHY YOU MUST DELEGATE

Delegation has been called "the secret of executive sanity." No matter how good an executive you are, your responsibilities will always be greater than your personal capacity to carry them out. For example, no one expects the company president to personally purchase, package, and sell the product. The diagram below graphically represents the situation.

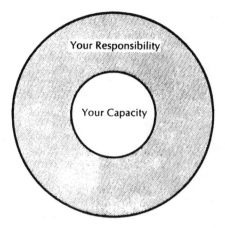

The Area of Delegation.   In the diagram the outer circle represents the limit of your responsibilities. The inner circle marks the boundaries of your human capacity. The shaded ring is the area that you must delegate to others; your secretary, your subordinates, and so on. Note that the tasks you delegate are not parts of their job, they have their own areas of responsibility. What you delegate are tasks that definitely fall within your job responsibility, but which, for one of several reasons which will be described later on, you prefer to pass along to others.

There are two general problems in this area:

Underdelegation.   Executives try to push the inner ring (their capacity) outward in an attempt to make the two circles correspond. Then comes the complaint: "I have to be in three places at once." "I don't dare take a day off." In short, a case of ulcers.

Overdelegation.   Executives who suffer from this misjudgment have so many tasks delegated that they lose control. Their cry: "Why doesn't someone tell me these things!"

The skill of delegation is to know how to concentrate those matters that are most important within the circle of the things you handle yourself. Less important tasks can be passed along to others.

⊃ THE PSYCHOLOGICAL FACTORS

The importance of the mental aspect becomes clear when you ask a key question: "Since delegation offers so many advantages, why is it often underused?"

This query was posed to a group of executives discussing delegation in seminars run by their company. They drew up a list which pinpoints major reasons for hesitation:

Loss of control.   Executives feel uncomfortable when they assign someone else to a task for which they are personally responsible. ''I feel helpless,'' is the way one conferee put it.

Ego.   A delegatee may perform in a way that may cause unfavorable comparison. ''I think Henry did that job better than his boss could have,'' can be a threatening judgment. Executives are reluctant to be judged by the performance of others.

''Subordinates can't handle it.''   True, some employees are unsuited for a specific task. This becomes a test of the manager's ability to match employee to job. But an average work group usually offers a range of capable subordinates for delegation. *Thought:* if no one is able to take on delegatable tasks, a group's resources may be overly thin.

''Subordinates may demand more money.''   The same may be true if they turn in excellent performances in their own areas of responsibility. The rules of pay increases for superior performance are usually matters of company policy and tradition.

Bad experience with delegation.   Understandably, this limits enthusiasm. But successful experiences can rekindle positive feeling. Failure can pose a challenge that leads to success.

➔ OVERCOMING THE DISADVANTAGES

Psychological factors vary considerably from person to person, and most executives have some difficulty. However, these points can help minimize the mental blocks.

1. Be aware.   The mental area is subtle and invisible. Most people must make an effort to bring thoughts about it to the surface. Your awareness of the psychological considerations can be a major help in lessening hesitation about this invaluable tool. Keep them in mind when you undertake delegation. Watch your feelings and monitor those of subordinates, the better to cope with them.

2. Confront specific doubts.   Executives as a group are articulate and sufficiently introspective to pinpoint their feelings. If you sense that you are neglecting delegation, ask yourself *why*. Check the previous list developed by the management conferees as a starting point. If there is a mental block, chip away at it with some objective thinking. If it's a practical reason, such as, "I don't have qualified subordinates," think through the moves that may ameliorate the problem. Training, or partial delegation can give subordinates experience to build capabilities.

3. Anticipate attitudes. The people to whom you delegate may be part of the difficulty. If so, sell the benefits to them in taking on a challenging or unusual task.

➲ **RATE YOUR ATTITUDE TOWARD DELEGATION**

Discover how you really feel about your use of delegation. Answer the questions below, then read the analysis of your score.

SELF-SCORING QUIZ

	Disagree	Doubtful	Agree
1. I like the idea of training people to do parts of my job. I don't mind subordinates knowing what I do.	☐	☐	☐
2. I'm perfectly willing to hand over responsibility and depend on others to perform some of my functions.	☐	☐	☐
3. I think it's reasonable to approve of work accomplished by methods differing from my own.	☐	☐	☐
4. It's okay if subordinates gain a certain amount of self-importance from a delegation assignment.	☐	☐	☐
5. One thing I don't feel: that delegation is a good way to get my work done by others so that I can take things easy.	☐	☐	☐
6. An executive who is personally secure will delegate more freely than an insecure one.	☐	☐	☐
7. I think that the old saying, "If you want something done right, do it yourself," is true in a limited sense and untrue in general.	☐	☐	☐
8. Doubt as to how to manage the finer points of delegation is a frequent reason for not delegating.	☐	☐	☐

Analysis. "Agree" is the preferred answer in each case. To get a numerical score, give yourself ten points for each question answered, "Agree"; each "Doubtful" gets five points; "Disagree" rates a zero.

A high score suggests your attitude is an asset to your delegation practices. A low score does not suggest inability to delegate, but rather inexperience or misunderstanding of the finer points of technique. Now rate your score:

70 to 80.   If you rated in this range, your understanding of the attitudinal aspects of delegation is topnotch. You are unlikely to be stymied by psychological problems with either yourself or your subordinates.

55–65.   A score in this bracket suggests that some areas may be causing trouble. It will be helpful to review the questions in which you gave other than the preferred answer. Think about the statements in the quiz. Try to analyze them in terms of your experience. See whether the results of this analysis may not modify your doubt or disagreement.

Below 55.   A score in this range suggests that you probably have delegation problems. These may result from misunderstanding or inexperience. The recommendations on technique in this section may start you on a constructive course that can improve your ideas and feelings about delegation. Removing some of the obstacles in your thinking could improve your practices.

➲ SIX STEPS TO SUCCESSFUL DELEGATION

A sequence of six moves helps insure the favorable outcome of delegation:

1. Pinpoint the task.   Delineate in your own mind the limits of the responsibility you want to pass along. It may be to do research for a report, or it may be to do the research and the actual writing, or it may be the research, writing, and overseeing of the production of the report. Whatever the dimensions of the assignment, clarify it as your first step.

2. Select the person.   The individual you choose as your delegate may vary considerably:

- If time is short, and you must have acceptable results, select the most capable person.
- If your delegation has as a primary purpose to train or challenge an individual, delegate to the employee requiring this type of attention.
- You may rotate your delegation to broaden the base of trained, flexible people on your staff.

3. Make the assignment.   Let the delegate know what you want done. How much more you tell him or her depends on individual circumstances. For example:

- You may want to put on paper the details of the assignment, wholly or in part.
- You may want to tell the person why he or she was selected.

In any event, you will want to explain why the job is important and the results that are expected.

And finally, you will want to check the individual's understanding to make sure that he or she is perfectly clear on all aspects of the assignment.

4. Supply supports.   Occasionally your delegation can be made on a minimal basis: simply tell subordinates what you want and leave the rest to them. But in other cases, it may be necessary for you to provide additional help:

- Clarify the authority you're handing over.
- Tell others about the assignment so that they will be aware of your backing his or her efforts.
- Tell the subordinate of any danger points in the assignment, or what to do if emergencies develop.
- Make clear your availability in case trouble develops.

5. Check progress.   If the task isn't simple and clear-cut, it may be desirable for you to keep in touch with developments. This gives your continuing control and prevents undesirable complications. Checking on progress may involve anything from a casual, "How are things going," to reports at key points of the project.

6. Evaluate achievement.   If the delegation is something other than routine, you may want to review your subordinate's progress. There are several purposes: you may want to reward achievement or to pin down the learning aspect of the delegation; you might want to go over aspects of the job that have been well done, areas in which performance might have been better. In any event, your subordinate will undoubtedly want the recognition that such a review represents. It can be demotivating for an individual to put effort into an assignment and get no response from a superior for what's been accomplished.

⮩ RETAINING CONTROL

Delegation can be simple. You have a task in your area of activity that you pass along to a subordinate. He or she does it well, you're pleased, the delegatee is happy.

Key element.   But considering delegation in all aspects, including the hazards of an inept subordinate, a poor matching of task and talent, unexpected developments, one element in the process can be crucial. This is control; namely, the procedures and methods you use to stay in touch and monitor progress.

Since responsibility for a delegated task remains yours, you must keep control in your hands—minimal in some cases, considerable in others. Some experts believe that you either delegate or you don't. You either put subordinates completely on their own, or you don't make the delegation at all. Fortunately, there is a wiser, more moderate choice. Degrees of control are possible.

Your best move *may be* to allow complete independence. You simply ask for results. In other cases, you ask for progress reports and to be told of trouble. In the final case, you retain close control, helping the subordinate develop self-confidence by permitting more responsibility as ability is demonstrated.

➲ WHEN A DELEGATEE FALTERS

Despite all your efforts, the delegation may seem headed for failure. A faulty estimate, a miscalculation, his or her inability to cope with mounting difficulties, may threaten operations.

To the subordinate it may seem like a catastrophe, but it shouldn't. Your hand on the reins should prevent such an outcome. And it's up to you to make even a failure have learning value. Usually, you must work with the falterer, take on the more difficult elements of the job. Your two aims will be to:

- Salvage the project.
- Maintain the subordinate's self-confidence. You make it clear you don't think he or she is a failure, and the project a total failure.

➲ HELP THAT DOESN'T UNDERMINE

There are moves that prevent having the delegatee limp away defeated, while you redelegate to someone else or take over the task yourself:

1. Offer suggestions. Don't give complete instructions that must be followed exactly. This may resolve the crisis, but contributes little to improved understanding. Point out a course of action to be tried, so that the delegation can be continued.

2. Be available for consultation. Discuss difficulties. Help the other understand what went wrong, warn of upcoming complications. Let him or her learn by doing. Guide an analysis of the situation. Supply the information that will get the job moving in the right direction.

3. Supply expert assistance. Recommend or enlist the services of an expert or experienced employee capable of helping resolve problems and complete the task. For example, if the difficulty centers on a new procedure, perhaps you can get its developer to step in. Don't have the delega-tee feel replaced. If appropriate, give praise for progress made.

ASSESSING BENEFITS AND CONSEQUENCES

Even if there's trouble, don't launch a premature rescue. Don't intervene because of imminent problems, or even small failures. Learning to deal with crises, taking risks, surviving a rough time, can be invaluable experi-ence.

"We might have lost $10,000 if the man I put in charge of a new project made the wrong decision," says the president of an engineering firm. "But I felt it was worth it to have him understand he was really on his own, and had the resources to do the job."

In your case, the cost of failure might be substantial. But give careful thought as to just how far you let a situation deteriorate before you step in. This may not be at all simple and certainly it calls for your best judgment. A major possible benefit, however, is that your subordinate knows that you have confidence in him or her.

Other costs of error.   In weighing the potential losses, consider the impact on various groups and individuals:

Your department.   Will its reputation fall in the eyes of important peo-ple? If so, what will that mean in terms of status, influence in the organiza-tion? Will group morale be affected? Will confidence in the department's capabilities be shaken?

Other departments.   Will your standing with them suffer? Could there be a lessening of cooperation or an intensification of rivalry?

Customers.   May the quality of your goods or services be hurt by the failure? Might there be damage to customer good will, or even loss of customers?

Your delegatees.   Will they be able to recover from a serious failure? Is it possible that a loss of self-confidence, or damaged prospects to advance-ment aspirations force them to quit?

Yourself.   Will others' confidence in your judgment suffer? Will your aspirations with the company be retarded? And since the failure will be viewed as yours, do you have the resilience to emerge stronger and wiser?

Balance benefits against consequences of unsatisfactory performance. The best lessons may come from a failed task. If your conclusion is that the final result will not be a major loss, stay with your delegation, minimize the damage as much as possible.

➜ AVOIDING DEPENDENCY

Some delegatees may turn up at your office door at the first sign of trouble. They may want specific help, or just the reassurance of contact with you. Unconsciously, they may want to avoid responsibility and force you to retain control.

In most cases your course is clear: Hand the problem right back. It may seem easier to take over, but you must restrain that urge. Rather than giving answers, ask questions that will assist them in resolving the crisis:

- What do you think the problem is?
- What factors do you consider important?
- What are the advantages and disadvantages of each solution?
- What additional information do you need?
- What are some possible solutions?

End your probing when you see that your subordinate's decision making is headed in a promising direction.

➜ YOUR SPAN OF CONTROL

How many delegations can you comfortably make at one time? The point is, how many can you keep track of? The chart below shows how one executive keeps abreast of delegated tasks by means of a matrix chart. You may want to adapt it for your own use. A control tool like the progress chart seems to demand a lot of time. But it needn't be your time. Put your secretary or an assistant in charge of keeping the chart up-to-date.

WEEKLY DELEGATION PROGRESS CHART

Name	Assignment	Progress	Complications	Remarks
Kim Heller	Special inventory	Satisfactory	—	—
Paul Lavin	Attending quality control meetings	Satisfactory	Missed one meeting—ill	—
Cal Hymer	Procedures for better machine productivity	Two weeks behind schedule	Delay in delivery of test materials	Investigate new supplier
Jane Sykes	Report on suggestion system	Slow	Regular work interferes	Consider having Ed work with Jane

⤴ FIVE BASIC DELEGATION SITUATIONS

Here are five basic delegatables:

1. Routine tasks.   Screening your mail, preliminary interviewing of job applicants, discussion of minor maintenance needs, activities like these may be parceled out to subordinates when you're not inclined to do them yourself.

2. Tasks for which you don't have time.   There's another group of activities, not necessarily routine, but of comparatively low priority. When you have time for these, you prefer to do them yourself. But when more urgent matters occupy your attention, these may be passed along to a capable subordinate.

3. Problem solving.   Some executives properly turn over a problem situation to a subordinate. This is usually of a low or medium priority area; and actually there may be one or more of your subordinates with a particular knowledge or skill in the area that qualifies them to take on the task. In addition, they will be motivated to give it special attention, since it will represent a challenge.

4. Changes in your own job emphasis.   For the average executive, job content changes over the years, slowly in some cases, rapidly in others. As executives become aware of these changes in emphasis, they understand that new elements in their activity require more of their time. To "make" the time, the executive must, as a practical matter, delegate "old" aspects of responsibility to subordinates.

5. Capability building.   Last but not least, delegation may be used to increase the capability of individual subordinates and your staff as a group. Properly managed, delegation becomes the means by which you train and develop both the skills and horizons of subordinates. In the item that follows, "Delegation as a Skill Builder," you will find more on this vital point.

⤴ DELEGATION AS A SKILL BUILDER

Greater efficiency isn't the only motive for delegating a part of your job. Enlargement of a subordinate's job or capacity can give three other important results:

Developing a sense of responsibility.   You may wish to make an assignment purely in the interest of increasing ability and self-confidence.

Enlarge general understanding.   For instance, the best way to stress the importance of customer relations for one of your assignments might be to ask a subordinate to take over answering customers' complaints.

Increasing job satisfaction.   Some subordinates thrive on varied assignments; their interest in the job increases along with its responsibility. Delegation of challenging projects helps maintain a subordinate's effectiveness as a team member.

Used in these ways, delegation is another means of getting cooperation, of increasing ability and motivation.

Properly handled, delegation guarantees that your overall job will remain in control, and that the people working under you will keep moving in the right direction. But there are hazards.

You'd be wrong to assume, for example, that delegation is a one-shot affair. Your responsibilities tend to change; new problems come up and make new demands on your time. You must be ready to review past delegations. You may have to make corresponding changes in the tasks that you've assigned to others.

↻ WHEN TO DELEGATE

There are specific occasions in the course of your work when delegation is called for. Here, for example, are three instances:

When you're overburdened.   It's a safe general rule that you simply can't handle *all* your responsibilities and still do a good job on the important ones.

In emergencies.   Your first thought may be to let everything else drop. Yet the temporary suspension of even a routine matter, may leave you with too big a backlog when the crisis is over.

When you have to be absent.   It might be a two-week vacation—or a series of conferences. But someone will have to provide a *minimum* amount of authority while you're gone.

As a starter, check up on the time you spend now in:

- Filling out routine reports, requisitions, etc.
- Making calculations and entries.
- Checking materials and supplies.
- Running your own errands.
- Engaging repeatedly in certain simple, mechanical tasks.

If you can reduce any of these to a matter of a final okay, signature or dispatch of a messenger, consider handing them over to a subordinate. These are the easiest duties to delegate.

➲ WHEN NOT TO DELEGATE

Just as there are situations for which delegation is a solution, there are circumstances which make it inadvisable.

Delegation can cause trouble if the wrong duties are handed over. Some of your responsibilities are yours for keeps:

The power to discipline.   This is the backbone of executive authority.

Responsibility for maintaining morale.   You may call upon others to help carry out assignments that will improve morale. You cannot ask anybody else to maintain it.

Overall control.   No matter how extensive are the delegations, ultimate responsibility for final performance rests on your shoulders.

The hot potato.   Don't ever make the mistake of passing one along, just to take yourself off the spot.

Some jobs must be retained. It's best to hang on to them if:

They are too technical.   Computing a floor load or projecting a cost estimate may be routine for you but completely beyond a subordinate's skill.

The duty involves a trust or confidence.   For instance, handling confidential cost data, dealing with the personal affairs of one of your people, and so on.

To keep things moving at full blast, you may find it necessary at times to delegate duties involving initiative, judgment, and decision. But consider these factors:

- the duty to be delegated
- the ability of the person it will go to
- your ability to keep control; that is, to keep posted on progress

➲ CONTROL AS AN ADMINISTRATIVE TECHNIQUE

When you delegate responsibility, you don't really get rid of it. You must still exercise control.

You *need* control in order to achieve coordination—to see that the assigned task works in with other objectives—and to achieve satisfactory results.

Your instructions must include a standard operating procedure, a list of rules by which the subordinate can handle situations that constantly recur.

Examination of results.   This is the easiest kind of control you can exercise. You simply look at the completed performance. It's sort of "hands-off" policy, used where your assistant is highly capable or where the task is routine.

Control by follow-up.   In many cases, it isn't wise to wait until the performance is complete. Errors may simply be too expensive, too hard to correct. You may want to check progress by inspecting, sampling, or spot-checking. This approach is particularly good where the responsibility is new, large, or difficult to handle.

Progress reports.   For a variety of reasons—time element, location, etc.—you may prefer to have your subordinate report on how he or she is making out. Such a report may be frequent or infrequent, written or oral, by personal contact or telephone. You must decide what is adequate under the circumstances.

⮑ HOW TO PREPARE THE DELEGATE

To get the subordinate off on the right foot, consider these four points:

Give the facts about the job.   Give a clear picture of *what* the delegate is to do, *how* to do it, and the *degree of authority* needed to get it done. "You never told me," is the sorry epitaph on many a well-meant delegation.

Explain the relative importance of the job.   You know to what degree it's important, because you see it in the setting of your overall responsibility. Subordinates will be able to make the necessary adjustments when they run into trouble only if you have given them the background.

Tell with whom they are to deal.   If the assignment will bring contact with new people—for instance, employees in other departments—take care of the introduction yourself. Be sure you let everybody involved know that they're to deal with your subordinate.

Prepare them psychologically.   They may feel an excessive weight of responsibility. Lessen the tension by removing a sense of crisis. Indicate: (1) your confidence in their ability—that's why you picked them; (2) reassurance from time to time; and (3) emphasis on your availability whenever they're in doubt.

⮑ GETTING COOPERATION FOR THE DELEGATE

The responsibility you assign may require a certain amount of authority over others. It may be minor, but, even in the case of a clerk trying to collect figures for a report, you're apt to find people with their backs up, slow to cooperate.

To avoid conflict:

Define scope.   Specify the exact nature of the *responsibilities* that you are delegating. That's essential to keep the delegate on track. He or she may think you're handing over your job, unless you explain what's what.

Tell the others.   Define clearly and publicly the limits of the authority you delegate. And take care of complaints about overstepped boundaries promptly. Make cooperation attractive.

Set harmony as a goal.   Reserve the right to discipline. Don't let your delegate try to enforce cooperation. Impress your delegate with the importance of working harmoniously with the other members of your team. Sell your people on the need for you to delegate the job.

DELEGATION CHECKLIST

The person you delegate won't do the job the way you would do it. Even if you have given instructions, even relatively complete ones, don't be surprised if a delegated assignment ends up in a somewhat unexpected fashion. However, if you are inclined to throw up your hands and renounce delegation as an executive technique—*don't*. Use the list questions below to see if you can strengthen your technique. Ask yourself:

Have I delegated duties I can more efficiently handle myself?   When you have to follow up with constant observation, the game of delegation isn't worth a candle.

Are my delegations boomeranging?   When you pass along a sizable task to a subordinate, you may have to provide him or her with a substitute or understudy. Otherwise, as soon as the employee is absent, you'll have the delegated duty back in your lap.

Are you picking your delegates properly?   Don't mistake a failure in delegation that results from an employee's inability to handle a task with a failure of the delegation technique. Whether it's delegation or just job instruction, unqualified, insufficiently skilled subordinates won't be able to do a job beyond their capabilities.

Have I provided all the help needed?   Generally, in delegation, you want to give your subordinate a free hand. But don't give him or her freedom when what's needed is your assistance or continuing supervision.

Checking on progress from time to time tells you how much autonomy the delegate requires.

Have I set up the right controls?   The ability to make controls work, and work effectively, is a true test of executive leadership. Measure any questionable control by these tests:

■ **Duplication.**   Is this control necessary? Do you get the same information elsewhere?
■ **Reports.**   Are you getting long, rambling reports that consume too much time, or lack necessary information?
■ **Delayed control.**   Are you using "control by result" in a case where too much damage can be done before you can act?
■ **Frequency.**   Are you checking up too often on unimportant matters—facing a pile of progress reports you simply can't read? Or, are you failing to get reports often enough to give you the true picture?

➲ WHEN TO DELEGATE UPWARD

According to the dictionary, delegation is "the act of empowering an individual to act for another." This definition, as well as common practice, suggests that delegation takes place downward, between an executive and his subordinates. But there are situations in which executives might justifiably *ask* or *suggest* that their superior take over an action within the executive's bailiwick:

Praise or reward.   An honor won by a subordinate that, ordinarily, the executive might bestow, can have even greater weight if given or announced by the executive's boss.

Approval or backing.   "I know that selecting the promotion person is entirely my responsibility," an executive tells his superior, "but since he or she will be working with you to some extent, I'd like you to interview the final two candidates, and we'll make the final selection a joint decision."

Supercritical decisions.   "Frankly, J.B., there's so much riding on the outcome, I'd prefer you to make the decision as to the final design of the product." Where the superior is especially capable in the area involving the decision, this approach has much to recommend it.

The full weight of authority.   "I'd rather you announce the new policy," an executive tells the boss, "to make clear its importance."
The obvious hazard of upward delegation is that it suggests dependency or hesitation in making decisions. Make sure that this type of delegation is

undertaken sparingly, and only after one's reasons for the move have been thought through.

In giving assignments to subordinates, executives use a procedure like delegation in some ways, but basically different. It can be helpful at this juncture to emphasize the key dissimilarities between the two.

➲ THE DIFFERENCE BETWEEN DELEGATION AND ASSIGNMENT

There is a tendency to use the words *delegation* and *assignment* interchangeably. Actually they represent two different things:

Delegation.   Here you pass along to a subordinate a task that is essentially within the area of *your* job content.

Assignment.   Here you assign a task within *his* or *her* area of responsibility.

➲ BUILDING INCENTIVES INTO WORK ASSIGNMENTS

In most cases, assignments to subordinates are made matter-of-factly. They are routine, part of the individual's daily job. However, there are some occasions when an appropriate motivating note can make substantial improvements in the level of employee achievement. Here for example, are a number of benefits a particular assignment may win for subordinates:

- Increase in value to the organization and to themselves.
- Gain more responsibility, training, and an increase of skill.
- Practice in connection with any job weakness.
- An opportunity to make suggestions or contribute ideas.
- A chance to make decisions and develop self-leadership.
- An opportunity to demonstrate abilities.
- Psychic reward—the satisfaction of successfully meeting a challenge, accomplishing a difficult task.
- Material reward—special privileges, promotion, or an increase in salary.

➲ WHEN TO USE THE DIRECT ORDER

Assignments can be made in various ways. A direct order lays it on the line for an employee and is an approach to use when:

- There's an emergency.
- You need results fast.
- There's no time for discussion or argument.
- An assignment is simple and its urgency is obvious.

- Earlier instructions have been understood, but not followed.
- The employee doesn't fare well acting on his or her own, but does best under authoritarian leadership.

➔ WHEN TO DETAIL YOUR INSTRUCTIONS

In giving a subordinate an assignment, it's desirable to spell out directions:

- on large-scale, complex assignments
- on tasks that must meet definite standards
- with uneasy employees or those starting important, but unfamiliar projects
- to keep close control

➔ WHEN TO USE THE "REQUEST" APPROACH

Occasionally you hear an executive say, "Bill, do you think you can handle the Jones matter?" It may mean, "Bill, I want you to handle the Jones matter," but worded as a request, the assignment takes on a slightly different character. This approach is effective:

- when you want to know if it's possible to comply
- to build cooperation and rapport
- to encourage volunteers
- when time permits discussion of pros and cons
- when you are dealing with a fully capable old timer who "doesn't like to be told"
- when you are unsure of the means by which a task is to be accomplished
- when you're asking for extraordinary effort or contribution

➔ WHEN TO USE THE "END-RESULT-WANTED" APPROACH

Under some circumstances, you get the best results from your assignments if you simply state the result you want, and leave everything else to your subordinate. This approach is preferred:

- to give an individual the opportunity to show initiative
- when you want individuals to show their own capabilities
- where the uncertainty of the modulus operandi precludes definite instructions
- when you know less about the matter than the person you are directing

➔ ASSIGNING THE UNPLEASANT TASK

From time to time the executive is confronted by the problem of making an assignment that may be tedious, boring, or undesirable for other reasons. A negative reaction from a subordinate in such a situation is understandable:

no one likes to take on a job that may be physically or mentally taxing or distasteful. When you face such a situation:

1. Review your approach.   One Philadelphia executive says, "I was making trouble for myself by giving the desirable assignments as though they were Christmas presents. Naturally, when the lemons came along, the difference in my manner was all too obvious. . . ."

It pays to be matter-of-fact about assignments in general. If you overplay your hand with the popular tasks, by implication, you build up resistance against the less popular ones.

2. Don't call a spade a rose.   If climbing into the bottom of the dye vat is a grimy, nasty chore, say so. No point in telling Harry this is his lucky day if he's tapped for the honor. He knows better; kidding him is likely to have a painful payoff.

3. Be fair, but firm.   You want to be certain that you assign the messy jobs on a fair basis. No one wants to be the fall guy.

Once you make the assignment, expect and insist upon acceptance. If you can point out the basis on which the choice was made, you should have no trouble.

4. Make no apologies.   You can be honest and sympathetic. But your attitude should never be apologetic. Make it clear that work is work—not fun and games. When it's pleasant, then so much the better. When it's unpleasant, the only thing to do is get it over with, and on to the next task.

The odds are that you'll not only eliminate a needless wrangle, but your people will respect you for taking a realistic stand. In this connection, you'll be interested in a jingle by a nameless, but poetic, executive:

> Work is work,
> And can be fun.
> But when it's not,
> Must still be done.

8. Building Group Effectiveness

Most executives have a group of subordinates for whose activities they are responsible. The number and makeup of this group varies broadly. Staff executives may have a secretary and one or two assistants. A production executive—a plant manager, for example—may consider all plant personnel as his "team."

It's clearly in the general interest—the employees', the company's, and the responsible executive's—for the group to function at the highest possible level of effectiveness. In the pages ahead, you'll find a number of specific ideas and methods for improving the capability and performance of your group.

⊃ A WORD ABOUT A WORD

Once *morale* was an important managerial term. It implied great things, specifically, a simple one-track road to improved output. "Build morale and increase productivity," was the belief. But hopes were dashed. Not only did veteran managers warn that high morale didn't necessarily mean increased incentive to perform. Experiments attempting to link high morale to high output and low morale to poor performance failed to prove out. Two practical examples tell the story:

■ **Forced labor.** "Morale in Nazi slave-labor factories," reported one sociologist, "was zero. Output, under the gun, was high."

■ **Saturday night fever.** Men and women from the X Department enter a Saturday night bowling competition. The team wins. Monday morning, morale goes through the roof: "Aren't we wonderful? Isn't our department wonderful?" Euphoria flows freely, but productivity is abysmal. Who wants to work with such a dandy victory to hash over?

The psychological elements of group feeling and unity are discussed in this Section. However, the word *morale* is avoided for semantic reasons. The terms *team spirit, esprit de corps,* are used instead.

⊃ WHAT MAKES A TEAM?

The word *team* resonates with desirable connotations—coherence, unity, effectiveness, shared goals. What elements of the group character make these desirable qualities possible? Here are three major ones:

■ **Spirit.** The French have a phrase for it, "esprit de corps," spirit of the group. It's an intangible element, but it is an arouser of loyalty, pride, and a sense of belonging, all heavy contributors to group achievement.

■ **Interdependence.** A group builds a kind of network of inner struts and ribs, invisible structures that support and strengthen. These derive from the idea dramatized in Dumas's *The Three Musketeers:* "All for one and one for all." It worked for the famous swordsmen, it works for groups.

■ **Self-subordination.** The willingness of the individual to set aside personal convenience, even benefit, for the good of the group, may appear in even the materialistic and self-seeking corporate world. For example, an employee will stay overtime to meet a deadline, finish an important task. A manager will ignore personal preference to favor a choice—in a promotion, for example—that will be best for the group.

⊃ **THREE SIGNS OF GROUP HEALTH**

A group's behavior can signal its unity and will:

■ **Awareness.**   In conversation, do members of your group say, "We?" or name your unit in the context of its being *theirs*? Used in a favorable way, their "esprit" is showing.

■ **Eagerness to get together.**   There are natural times for a group to gather: Christmas and other holiday lunches, anniversaries, the chain of birthdays, farewells, new motherhoods and fatherhoods that traditionally mean "party." Do these flourish within reasonable limits in your department? A "Yes" answer suggests a positive attitude.

■ **Competitiveness.**   "We're the best-run department in the company," an employee may assert. In any contest—safety, "gives best service," "best decorated,"—the group that is out there hot after the honors is constructively group-minded.

⊃ **HOW TO STRENGTHEN GROUP SPIRIT**

You're not likely to be after esprit de corps for its own sake. The spirit of teamwork is worthy in itself, but becomes especially important because of what it produces: greater effectiveness and a higher level of personal gratification for team members. There may be debate as to whether two heads are better than one. But an aggregation that functions as a team is usually more potent than the sum of individual effort.

You reinforce your subordinates' feeling of belonging, and their loyalty to the team by:

■ **Emphasizing your subordinate's contribution to the group goal.** "Thanks to those charts you developed, Linda, the management board okayed the whole project."

■ **Making people aware of their dependency on the group.**   You see it in sports: the star quarterback, named MVP, voices his thanks: "This honor is really shared by every player. . . ." Encourage and applaud this type of thinking.

■ **Compliments to the team.**   You may want to pick out individuals for special honors, but when you recognize team effort, you are reminding your subordinates of their group membership. "The department never performed better. It was shared effort that made our success possible. . . ."

⭢ HOW TO CREATE A CREATIVE CLIMATE

Occasionally, when companies wish to place the accolade of achievement on an executive's brow, they say, "He builds a climate that promotes high achievement among his people. . . ."

When we speak of a "good climate," we're talking about a quality in a company or department that is conducive to some desirable activity. A climate may help good attendance, make people safety-minded, or stimulate employees to offer suggestions and ideas.

Here are some ways to develop a climate that will foster creativity among employees and encourage them to develop and submit their ideas to you:

1. Set a value on ideas.   Start by creating a feeling of excitement and involvement about the whole matter of idea production. You do this by making it clear that ideas have great importance:

"All we need is one good idea," says an executive, "and we'll be able to get this program off to a flying start."

Managers who are able to sell their people on the value of ideas, generally do it by stressing exactly what a good idea can accomplish: Solve a nagging problem, get a crucial project off to a good start, cut costs, and so on.

2. Spotlight the areas of challenge.   Almost any idea has *some* value. However, ideas of particular value are those which eliminate *key* difficulties or increase capability in vital areas.

Whether you talk to your people individually or as a group, let them know the kinds of ideas you're most anxious to get. Do this by focusing on the problem or the activity involved. Avoid the abstract. Show them what you're talking about. Demonstrate the operation, let them observe the condition for which you need ideas.

3. Show your willingness to help develop their ideas.   Seldom do ideas spring full blown from an individual's mind. More frequently, a glimmer, a wispy thought emerges. If properly coddled and developed, it can take on sufficient substance to be considered as an idea with potential application.

Let your people know that you're interested in their ideas at whatever stage they may have reached. If you're presented with an idea that is merely a "gleam-in-the-eye," discuss it with the same interest as you would a fully ripened one.

The experienced manager, the one with an outstanding record for getting ideas from his or her people, is the one who wins the confidence of subordinates in one major respect—he or she *never* reacts negatively to an idea however simple, stale, or inappropriate it may seem.

4. Don't freeze anybody out. "Gilda is our best idea person," a manager confides to a colleague. Perhaps Gilda is the major contributor of ideas. But it may very well be that the reason other employees fail to submit ideas is that they've already been ruled out.

Accordingly, they "let Gilda do it." She has the name, she might as well have the game.

"Ideas don't care who gets them," says one veteran manager. Favoring the bright employee will probably increase that person's motivation, but you are liable to lose out with everyone else. The greater your efforts to enlist all your people in the production of ideas, the more ideas you will get.

5. Reward the successful ones, but encourage the others, too. It's an axiom of the game that those who have come up with good ideas be rewarded for their contributions, whether the reward be patting a back, or fattening a paycheck.

But while giving credit to those who have been successful, make clear your gratitude to the "almosts." Employees who have worked hard to develop an idea that never quite panned out may have labored above and beyond the call of duty. Let the others in the department know how much you appreciate what has been done even though results are lacking.

6. Emphasize the benefits. When an idea has been implemented, generally there is a payoff. The company has gained, the department has gained, and in most instances the contributor of the idea has been rewarded either by tangible or intangible means.

You provide a highly motivational goal to your people when you point out the advantages of an applied idea:

"With the new setup Hank designed, we've been able to cut the cost of these units by ten percent. As a result, Sales has just been able to bring in one of the biggest orders we've ever had. . . ."

Make your idea-building climate a permanent part of the department's life rather than an occasional one-shot subject. When you talk about the department's work to individuals or the entire group, fit in the suggestions described above. The thing about ideas is that almost anyone can have them—when you create the appropriate climate.

→ STIMULATING CREATIVITY IN YOUR PEOPLE

"It's ideas that make the world go round—the management world, that is," says one business expert. Executives, well aware of the need for more and better ideas, realize that their subordinates are a key source. Steps like these can encourage your people to contribute solutions to problems, ideas for improvement, in short, mobilize their brainpower:

1. Pinpoint the problems. Make the problems specific. *General* difficulties are not enough to get your people moving in original lines of thought. "Things around here are in a mess," doesn't give your people anything tangible to wrestle with.

Use your detailed knowledge of the department's functioning to break down a problem and point out the crucial difficulties, the particular bottlenecks.

Here are typical examples:

- how to cut down on telephone interruptions
- how to increase working space without cutting down on equipment
- how to centralize mail pickup and delivery without tying up rush material
- how to assign the work so as to avoid individual dissatisfactions

2. Personalize the problems. Describe the difficulty in practical and immediate terms. Get it out of the realm of abstract. Don't just present it as a "problem," suspended in midair. Instead, talk of it as the problem of (a) the organization; or (b) specific people in the organization. "We're all being slowed up by. . . ." It is emphasis on this aspect that builds team responsibility, and helps people understand that their jobs are part of the organization's total effort. A problem solved helps the entire department.

Refer to the individual involved: the bottleneck that "makes Joe and Steve rush like the devil every afternoon" or "makes Helen stay overtime at least twice a week."

And let everybody know about it—not just the people who are directly affected. People who are too close to a situation may lack the perspective to think of doing things in a new way.

On important problems get the whole group in on the act.

3. Suggest a line of attack. Help your people get started on the problem. That means two things: (a) Make sure they understand the present procedure. They're not likely to improve it unless they're thoroughly familiar with it: (b) Put your finger on the exact troublespots in the procedure

"This is the point where we're apparently going wrong." Or: "If we only could figure out some way of rearranging allocation of sales areas."

Where possible, discuss with your people promising points of departure: "An article I read last week had some good ideas about job enlargement."

4. Keep in touch.   Possibly the most constructive move the manager can make to keep the creativity ball rolling, is to maintain contact. Asking for progress reports, checking back from time to time to see how your subordinates are doing, is concrete evidence of your continuing interest. During these contacts you have the chance to help with any obstacles that may arise. Also, you can watch for the discouragement that traditionally haunts the creative effort. When things aren't working out or a promising development falls flat, encouraging and helpful words can make all the difference.

5. Time to succeed.   Executives who do best in stimulating their people to creative effort find there is a big variation in the *time element.* Some individuals work quickly, seem to be action oriented. These people develop numerous possibilities, test them out one by one, until they hit.

Others tend to be thought oriented. These individuals will spend more time assessing alternatives, and will try to come up with a single one that promises success.

Both approaches work, and it is important that the manager avoid trying to rush the thoughtful subordinate into premature action, or to become impatient with the activist's trial-and-error testing.

➔ **GETTING THE MOST OUT OF EMPLOYEE IDEAS**

Even in the absence of suggestion systems, subordinates will make suggestions or offer ideas that they think bring about desirable improvements on the work scene. When an employee offers an idea, how do you push for a payoff? Consider these moves:

1. Develop and refine.   Often when an employee brings you an idea, it's half-baked. You have to help him develop the idea to where it is usable. You and he—and others who can contribute—put your heads together, eliminate the undesirable aspects, and add the elements that make the idea usable.

2. Prepare.   Few ideas can be put to work immediately. Some ideas may have to lie fallow for weeks or months until the proper opportunity for a trial presents itself. In this preliminary period, you may have to figure such things as costs, people, equipment and facilities, and the situation to which it applies. This is the time to acquire whatever missing elements you may need—anything from a special machine to an employee of particular skill—to test the idea.

3. Arrange for a trial. Some ideas promise advantages that may or may not result. Make sure that a test of an idea is fair and appropriate. For example, you may prove nothing if you take an idea that has been suggested for improving an assembly operation and have the test performed by an inexperienced employee in your group.

Also, for some trials, you may want to have more than one observer. "The results were great," says an employee, following a test of a jig he suggested. "A waste of time," is the opinion of another employee. Of course, your own presence is advisable to evaluate both the trial and the other opinions you get.

4. Don't shortcut on final evaluations. Time and time again it happens that a new method or system passes a preliminary, limited test with flying colors. Then the idea is adopted generally—and the trouble starts. Unexpected developments that didn't turn up in the trial may develop in widespread applications. For example, a new system that was tested successfully by one of your skilled workers gives other employees trouble in full-scale use.

In short, it's wise to stick with the implementation of an idea until it is really proved out in a "production run" or full-scale application.

5. Reward the Idea Man. One way to assure a continuing flow of ideas is to reward those you get. The rewards may range from a simple statement of appreciation to cash payments, bonuses, promotions, and so on.

Assuming that the reward, whether of the psychic variety, that is, a statement of appreciation, or a more material kind—such as a salary increase—is being made appropriately, there is one more move to make. It is desirable both from the point of view of the individual who has been rewarded, and your own interest in getting additional ideas, that the group learn of the return your subordinates get for their efforts.

⤷ CAN YOU UNBRAINWASH YOUR SUBORDINATES?

"I try to get as many original ideas as possible out of a new employee before he or she gets brainwashed—that is, settles down into a rut like most old-timers do."

The implication of the above statement is that a "company way of doing things" eventually erodes originality. After employees have been on the job for a while they get "brainwashed" in the sense that they adopt the views, values, and behavior of those around them.

Where creative thinking is necessary for performance, the executive may consider steps like these to stimulate a subordinate:

1. Explain that the wraps are off.   In giving the assignment or instructions, make it clear that you want your subordinate to strike out in new directions. You may have to say it in so many words: "I'm giving you a completely free hand on this assignment. . . ."

2. Applaud originality; downgrade mediocrity.   As the subordinate goes about the assignment, show your approval by any novel turn taken: "Frank," says one executive, "I'm pleased to see you get away from that old form. I've always suspected it was a major cause of our paperwork problem." Not all original ideas are good—but your reactions can make it clear that you favor the effort towards freshness.

3. Make the "new way" a continuing goal.   It's not enough to limit your approval of originality to special assignments. Make it clear to your group in the course of work discussions, conferences on departmental problems, and so on, that you're always on the lookout for breakthroughs, innovations, new and better ways of doing things.

Of course, managers aren't exempt from the inhibiting influence of company brainwashing. On the contrary, top executives point out that often supervisors or department heads not only puts restrictions on employees' thinking, but also keep their own thinking in a rut.

According to the president of a chemical company, "Ideally, we must walk two paths at once: try to capitalize on the good aspects of conformity: acceptance of company standards, general behavior, and so on. At the same time, we must strive for the benefits of untrammeled thinking, keep vision free, and reward originality whenever it appears constructively on the work scene."

↪ HANDLING EMPLOYEE COMPLAINTS

Justifiably or otherwise, your people may complain. It may be about anything from the air conditioning to dissatisfaction with career prospects.

Your handling of complaints is an important key to the spirit of your group. Consider these guidelines, when you get complaints from employees:

1. Check actual condtions.   Some complaints may be founded in fact; others may represent disguised gripes about anything else. Avoid leaping to conclusions about the justness of the matter. Make checks and comparisons: take a thermometer reading, use the flow of cigarette smoke to check complaints about a draft, for example.

2. Check consequences.   After you've looked into the objective facts, examine the results. Consider taking a "poll" of group opinion on the complaint. This information not only helps you verify the objective situation, but also may represent a measure of the gripe—whether it's appropriate or an overreaction—and how widespread it may be.

3. Suit relief to the problem.   If the complaint is justified, move as quickly as you can to remedy the situation. This may mean changing the directions of vanes in a heating system, or having Maintenance put weather stripping on a loose window. For some situations, you might ask the complainer for suggestions.

On the other hand, if you find the complaint unjustified, present the facts to those involved. Be matter-of-fact. Your people will be much more likely to accept your findings if you avoid the "you're-all-wrong" approach.

As veteran executives know, unfounded complaints may be an individual's bid for attention, or a way of saying, "Show me that you're interested in my welfare." This is a possibility when the gripe is baseless. Then your move must be to review your relations with the employee, to see how you can give the reassurance that he or she is a recognized and needed part of the team.

4. Follow up.   Don't assume that the action you have taken will solve the matter, although it may. But avoid complications by checking back on the condition, as well as the attitude of the person who made the original complaint. When both show improvement, you've got the problem licked.

WHEN ASSIGNMENTS TAKE SUBORDINATES OFF THE PREMISES

From time to time you may have to send one or more employees on assignment out of your immediate personal jurisdiction. It may be an assistant, who must do some research for you in the library, or a team to dig into an operating problem in another office.

When people are new to this type of assignment, working outside the range of your personal supervision may pose problems. You don't want to lose control.

Here are seven steps that can help them perform more effectively:

1. Encourage employees to accept responsibility.   Impress your people with the opportunity to show their self-reliance and reliability. "You're going to be on your own. . . ."

2. Equal status.   Here's where you have to judge the caliber of your people. If you have employees who you know will work together, it may be best to give them equal status. But sometimes, even with just two on the job, you'll have discord. Giving primary responsibility to one may be the most desirable solution.

3. Spell out your instructions. It's even more important than usual to be clear and concise as to what you want done. Be sure you cover two points: (a) the overall objective, (b) the immediate goal.

If necessary, provide written instructions. Where the job can be broken down, write out the steps.

4. Have a send-off inspection. "We forgot to take along the inventory cards.": Forestall loss of time and effort by making sure all necessary materials go out with the employees.

If there's a question of appearance or condition of equipment they're taking with them, set up a regular inspection that will catch oversights.

5. Make sure of what they'll find. "Mr. Smith," telephones an employee from a distant suburb, "I got to the address you gave me, but the supply company moved away three months ago." Obviously a phone call would have prevented a wild-goose chase.

To repeat: check out the situation before sending your people into it.

6. Arrange for a check-back during the job. Tell the individuals or leader how to communicate with you if any trouble develops. It may be clear *to you* that the obvious thing is to send a message if anything unforeseen arises. But sometimes the on-the-spot leader's solution is to call a halt and wait for you to show up. Be sure to spell out how and where they can contact you. If the job's a long one, you may want regular progress reports.

If you have the time, it may be best to visit the scene and check the operation personally. In that case, deal with the appointed leader first, and get his or her version of how things are going.

7. Ask for a report at the end of the job. You may want to make this report written or oral. Use it not only as a check on the satisfactory conclusion of the work, but as a cue for the next job.

➔ THE NEW LOYALTY

Company loyalty inspired by the old paternalism has almost faded from the business scene. To put it another way, paternalism as an effective management technique is dead. Loyalty, if it is to exist at all, must stem from new sources.

There's a relationship between an employer and employee that can be constructive. Call it loyalty or mutual respect, the result of the relationship is clear: it makes the company seem like a good place to work and it makes a superior seem like a good person to work with. It makes employees enjoy their jobs more. Here's what's involved:

1. Imbue employees with a feeling of loyalty to the group. When work problems are presented as cooperative ventures, a manager can build the feeling that the department is functioning as a unit, with each member's presence and best efforts essential to group success. Accordingly, those who feel themselves valued numbers of the group develop ties of loyalty to fellow workers.

2. Foster loyalty to a profession or skill. Whether an employee is an accountant, a production supervisor or a drill press operator, he or she is committed to a particular profession or skill, is a member of a select group, and subject to the standards of that group. These people *may* entertain the idea of working for another company, but aren't likely to *change profession or job category*.

Managers who show employees that they can exercise their professional abilities most effectively and most rewardingly in their *present jobs* can build professional loyalty and derive the benefit from that personal commitment.

3. Create and encourage personal involvement in the work. When managers allow subordinates to share the responsibilities of planning and executing their own work, they provide a chance for self-fulfillment and the consequent emotional reward.

The manager who puts a subordinate on a challenging task, with clearly defined and exciting objectives, is creating the conditions for job satisfaction.

A basic point should be clear: while the old loyalty was based on paternalism and the doling out of *material* benefits, the new loyalty is the result of acknowledging the integrity of employees and creating an atmosphere in which they can satisfy their *psychic* needs, the desire for accomplishment and work satisfaction.

⊃ HOW TO BALANCE A TEAM

Wider rise of the task force or project-team approach means the executive must devote some thought to the makeup of taskforces so that they may function effectively.

Small groups lack some elements that apply to larger ones. First, smaller units, of two or three members for example, cannot be "organized" in the same sense as a large group. And the question of leadership worsens. Consider the problem as it sometimes appears in the two-person relationship, marriage, and you get the picture—unclear division of authority, disagreement as to whose standards are to be accepted, and so on.

When you form a group of two or three people you are not simply adding their skills together. Dause L. Bibby of Remington-Rand put the relationship this way: "With the team approach there is a factor created, a new capability that goes above and beyond the mathematical addition of personalities." To line up an effective team, determine:

- what needs to be done
- the kind of skills required
- which people work best together
- what general guidelines to provide that will help them function together

Here are the considerations for each point above:

What needs to be done.   Different tasks impose different requirements. A team with an informational job must be able to gather data, to probe and analyze, and to come up with conclusions based on the findings. An organizational job would require the ability to plan, direct, instruct, motivate, and deal with unexpected developments. Once you have clarified the general nature of the job you are ready for the next step.

Mixing and matching qualities.   In putting together your team, remember two principles:

The rule of "likes."   Sociologists use the term *homogamy* to describe the fact that some husband-wife teams are formed on the basis of similar backgrounds, economic, educational, and so on. Generally, staffing your group with people who are similar in age and sense of values provides a good basis for mutual understanding and assures a minimum of friction.

The rule of "opposites."   Sociologists used the term *heterogamy* to cover husband-wife pairs who have selected one another on the basis of complementary traits. Teaming according to the principle of opposites works well when the individuals involved respect the differences and specialties of their teammates. While this approach may result in more friction, it often makes for a higher-powered team.

How large should a group be? There are two guidelines:

Use the *smallest* number of people possible to eliminate communication lags and other human frictions that set in as a group grows.

Use the number that will give you the highest total of skill, and that will insure a capability to cover the scope of the job and the speed with which it is to be done.

Appoint leaders.   It is usually advisable to give one of the individuals in even the smallest team, leadership responsibility. The leader not only sets the level of performance expected, but also decides on the means by which goals are to be achieved when there are differences of opinion. One way or another, the leader sets the tone and work pace.

➔ HOW PEOPLE REALLY FEEL ABOUT CHANGE

People are supposed to resist change. And often they do. But the statement "people resist change" is a generalization that muddies the issue. You need clarification because group growth is based on change, and you don't want fear of the future to weaken initiative and group unity.

Allen B. Thomas, V.P. Personnel of the St. Paul Manufacturing Co. says, "I point out to people that change is an everyday norm. Often people want, like, and must have change. Those who resist it are usually insecure. They want to stay put while the rest of the world moves along." Thomas goes on to say that people resist certain actions which have been carelessly categorized as "change." For example:

■ **People resist surprise.**   Few of us like to be caught off balance. A sudden announcement or development tends to throw individuals off balance and, understandably, they resist. On the other hand, knowledge in advance can give individuals the opportunity to digest the change and work it into their expectations for the future.

■ **People resist usurpation.**   No one likes to have someone else come along and make changes in areas which they have thought of as "theirs." This is true in even the most innocent seeming situation. For example, a group of typists have been complaining about their chairs—they jiggle, they cannot be adjusted properly, and so on. A well-meaning executive decides to eliminate the irritation and orders new chairs. The chairs arrive and the girls are indignant. A dozen complaints are lodged against the new furniture: wrong size, shape, color, and so on. Needless to say, they would have been perfectly delighted with the very same chairs if they had picked them out themselves.

The solution, then, is to let people make the changes for themselves in their own areas of competence and responsibility.

➔ PREPARING YOUR PEOPLE FOR CHANGE

Change has been in the cards ever since our ancestors came out of their caves. On the work scene, change has been a tangible and accelerating factor. And ever since World War II, change on the business scene has been developing with jet speed. Result? Employees—and sometimes even executives—view the shifts and alterations of the business environment with uneasiness, sometimes tinged by panic.

A study by the Research Institute of America of a company facing drastic equipment replacement, turned up the basic fears and questions in the minds of employees. Understanding these questions can help you minimize the impact of change in your company or division.

Here are the kinds of questions employees ask, and some suggestions as to how to handle them:

Will I lose my job?   This is the big one, reflecting the greatest fear. And it may come from anyone—old-timers who long for permanent security, newcomers with plans and ambitions, even chronic gripers whose usual plaint is how much they *don't* like what they're doing!

Your answers will usually fall into one of three categories:

No.   Simple, direct, reassuring. The contemplated change will not affect employees' job to any great extent, and they can function pretty much as before. This is the easiest answer to give and the one most people want to hear.

No, but . . .   A company has issued a blanket promise: no one is to lose his or her job, *but* there will be some shifting. Retraining will be necessary. Certain job categories will be eliminated, and people transferred to other departments. New procedures will be adopted, organizational changes made. There will be a place for all employees but they may have to adapt.

Accordingly, you'll be talking to two groups: those who jobs won't change, and those who face a somewhat uncertain future. Here again, you can reassure the people who will be unaffected. For the others, you'll have to walk a straight line between giving them as much information as you can, and not feeding their apprehension. For example, "No matter what happens, there'll be absolutely no changes until the first of the year. And the best brains in the company are making plans to minimize any possible difficulties. . . ."

Yes.   Unfortunately, some changes mean some people will be let go. A company may be cutting back, merging, automating, diversifying. Fewer workers may be required, or more highly skilled, or more experienced, or less. Just who will be kept on may depend on age, seniority (those with ten years or more will be retained, for example), job skills, even your opinion of an employee's growth potential.

It may be difficult to tell a person that he or she is no longer needed. The promise of liberal severance pay can soften the blow somewhat. But equally important may be an offer to help in locating another job—finding out who's hiring, who needs what; helping with job applications; adding a personal recommendation. Considering outplacement firms as a source of help.

How will I find out about new methods, equipment, etc?   Employees look ahead to the immediate effects of job change—and wonder and worry.

There are many ways of imparting knowledge—it's only a matter of deciding on the best method, or methods, for your purpose. Your answer may include one or more of the following:

Talks.   Talks by management, staff specialists, outside experts, yourself. These work well for "thoughtful" changes: company policies, the whys of reorganization, and the like. Care must be taken that they convey full, clear explanations, in the language of the listeners. Where possible, use visual material—charts, graphs, photos—to show the shape of things to come.

Group discussions.   Such discussions offer explanation plus a chance to comment, question, participate. There should be no pressuring of employees who speak up. Leaders must be ready to field all questions (even the most antagonistic), and communicate a spirit of optimism and positive thinking.

On-the-job training.   This should be carried out by the best qualified person, be it you, your assistant, a technician, systems analyst, whoever. Such training should begin as early as possible, be comprehensive, allow for practice, raising of questions, test runs, and thorough review to make sure that all aspects are understood.

Off-the-job-study.   This may encompass anything from reading at home to in-plant classes and out-of-plant seminars. You may have little to do with actual instruction—but you must follow it up. It's up to you to praise what a subordinate has learned, how well it's been learned, and how soon it can be used.

How will the change affect day-to-day routines?   A change in the way of doing things is not a happy prospect for some people. It's unsettling, threatening, suggests inconvenience, even material loss. Employees fight it in a number of ways. They may become sullen or quarrelsome, produce less, ask for transfers, come up with a thousand-and-one pseudological reasons why the change won't work. And when the change becomes fact, they may cheer over each little things that goes wrong, and may even try to help the difficulties along a little.

The most constructive approach is *preventive.* In explaining, be very definite as to *what* is going to be done, *how* it is going to be done, *who* will be doing it, *where* it will be done, *when* it will go into effect. People often resist the new simply because they don't understand what is going on or what is expected of them.

And, while you stress the "good" of the project, admit that there may be some "bad." In anything new, errors and "bugs" are bound to crop up; how can they be avoided?

You want their ideas. Let them know that you can't foresee all the problems; that you respect their knowledge and experience; that you need their suggestions and help. And that you want it to be a continuing thing—the new way may have to be revised, little kinks ironed out. Can they come up with solutions?

Will new people be brought into the department?   Many of today's changes herald the arrival of departmental newcomers. Sometimes they will be better educated, more highly skilled, younger than those already on the work scene. In other instances they may be lacking both knowledge and training. They may look different, talk different, act different. And on all counts, they may be regarded as outsiders, threats to previously comfortable togetherness.

To minimize the feeling of threat, clarify the kind of personnel that will appear, and the company's reason for hiring them. Don't hedge or equivocate—be factual:

"Two technicians start Monday. They're going to iron out the 'bugs' on Operation X. That means we can stop worrying about the headache and get our own work done."

Offer opportunities for advancement?   One step that will minimize the newcomer's threat is the knowledge that old-timers will be given the chance to better themselves. Where the opportunity exists, tell your people how they can learn advanced skills and procedures—and have a chance to bid for future job openings.

Equalize pay scales?   It's hard for a loyal, long-time worker to accept the fact that Joe Newcomer is making as much or more than he is. Yet this can be the case. Today, business hires at higher rates, pays more for education and training, and doesn't always put the same monetary value on loyalty and in-company experience. The hard reality of this situation should be tactfully explained to old-timers.

Will I have to move?   Even if an employee won't be going to a different building or department, major changes in the physical aspects of his or her work station may be upsetting.

When employees are told that they must move—be it across the street, down the hall, to a new machine, a strange department, a different shift—they may object strongly. They may feel they are being asked to leave the familiar and venture into unknown territory, where, in many respects, they will have to start anew. They worry, "Why me? Can I handle a different setup? How will I fit in with the new gang?"

It's up to management to minimize the threat. A three-step process may help:

Explain the reasons for the contemplated move.   Production bottle-necks, poor layout, constant equipment breakdowns, safety hazards, space and storage problems, employee retirements or dismissals. What-ever the reason(s), get involved in the discussion.

Point out the advantages of the move.   More space, brand new lathes, air-conditioning, more efficient layout, chance to keep regular hours, earn more money, learn another skill. Whatever the advantage(s), emphasize the benefits to them as individuals. There's plenty of time later to talk about the good of the department, the value to the company, and so on.

Can they participate?   Are there any improvements they would like to see in the new work station layout? Any suggestions on eliminating safety hazards? Ideas on what to do with old equipment? Suggestions on improv-ing the comfort of the new operation?

Whatever the answer(s), listen attentively and when they're good, usa-ble, tell them so. If some of their ideas are being incorporated in the new "home," they will be happier about moving in.

How will the change affect my status? Chances for salary increase? Promotion?   We all have fundamental needs, and one of the most basic is security. On the workscene, this takes the form of money and the chance to make more, a job and the opportunity to better it.

Some changes do not affect either earnings or chances for advancement. For example, moving a person's work station from the right side of the aisle to the left, doesn't influence take-home pay. But switching the employee to another department, or expecting him or her to learn another skill, *may.*

In such cases, put it on the line with employees. Make it clear that those who make good in new assignments will make gains. On the other hand, refusal to learn and grow could affect chances for promotion and raises adversely.

Faced with change, people respond in individual ways. One person will worry about the opinion of her peers. Another will be concerned chiefly with his status in the department. A third will fight zealously to guard any small prerogative, even something as simple as the desk nearest the win-dow or the "chore" of collecting the time cards every week.

A person sees change from his or her particular viewpoint. Take an overworked machine operator who is assigned an assistant. This may be regarded as criticism of the way he or she has handling the job. Yet another employee in the same circumstance will see it as proof that she has "ar-rived"—with an assistant, she feels status is that much higher.

Knowing your people and their individual needs can help sell them on change. Is Jenny too gregarious for the silent confines of the supply room? Will Sol be more amenable to moving if his machine is placed first in line? Can Will be "turned on" by titling him "Squad Leader?"

Once you can see employee-plus-need, you'll have a better chance of melding employee-and-change.

Things were going along okay before. Why rock the boat?   Some companies, particularly those in high technology fields , move in an aura of change. Their employees learn to expect the unexpected, and thus have far fewer problems in adapting.

But in more static companies, it can be difficult for employees to understand why "something different" is being considered for an operation that, at least on the surface, has been proceeding smoothly. Especially since the path of change, in the beginning, may not run smoothly.

The reasons will vary as much as the changes themselves. For example, the need to lower costs, increase output, improve quality, change a product, may spark major shifts. And the pressures favoring alterations may originate with the company, a department, or you. It will generally be up to you to explain them to your people. And in so doing it is important to relate the purposes and goals of the change to those of the individual. For example:

- The company is modernizing and expanding to meet today's competition.
- This means *your* department is going to have more work, and will be able to produce more.
- That can mean a bigger paycheck for *you*, Joe.

Don't gloss over the fact that any new system will have its delays and errors. And that it may take time to work them out. If people have been given a completely rose-colored view of change—and then things start going wrong—they are apt to react with an immediate "I told you so," and a subsequent loss of faith in your leadership and in management's sagacity.

In other words, don't oversell. And leave the group with two thoughts:

- Problems are likely to arise in the course of changeover. Expect them. Be ready to deal with them.
- The ability of the group will help solve or minimize almost any complications that come up.

Will it mean more work for me? Harder work? Less desirable work? People have different attitudes toward their job tasks. Some want the challenge of the difficult or demanding assignment. Others balk at any hint that they may have to work harder, longer, and so on.

Typist Sue Sloan, resists the idea of acting as part-time receptionist—
"You expect me to greet callers and type too!"

To employees in this situation, three points can be made:

- In an organizational reshuffle, the fact that she didn't do the job before is no reason for it not to be added to her new assignment.
- With the new task added, her workload is still not top-heavy. (You don't ask anyone to do nine hours work in eight hours.)
- The best way to see how a new assignment will work out is to give it a trial—a fair trial.

Right from the start, any shift in workloads should be spelled out in detail, with duties and responsibilities well defined. The idea is to have everyone in the department know who is doing what, how much, and why. To make double sure of perfect understanding you might have employees make out charts of what they think their new duties and responsibilities are. When their version doesn't jibe with yours, you can work together to bring the two versions into line.

What if I can't handle the new job?   In our highly competitive world, the idea that what people know isn't enough, or that what they do is no longer in demand, can be frightening and confidence-destroying. So it's only natural that employees will voice doubts aoubt their abilities to learn new skills and methods. In some cases, *they may be right.*

One way to manage this aspect of change is to set up a probationary period. This may be thirty days, sixty days, or longer, based on the intricacies of the new job and an estimate of how long it should take the average worker to master it. And the time span should be made clear. While there may be difficulties, basically the employee should absorb the new ways and be able to utilize them in that period.

What if, despite all the breaks you can give, the worker still fails to make the grade? Perhaps there can be a return to the old post. But realistically, such moves are not always possible: the position may no longer exist, or it may be filled by someone else. Then a transfer to another department may have to be arranged. Or, the employee may have to be let go, if fairly new in the company.

The problem of retraining is largely psychological. Most doubts arise from fear of the unknown, the untried—or a lack of self-confidence. You can do much to dispel them if you show that *you* have faith in a subordinate's ability to handle the new job. Encouragement can work wonders.

EIGHT WAYS TO START A COST-IMPROVEMENT PROGRAM

For some executives, the always-important problem of controlling costs is one of motivation. However, respect the Rome Factor, as in, "Rome wasn't built in a day." Winning acceptance and cooperation is often a gradual process. Don't try to rush a three-minute egg.

"How can I get my staff to develop their cost-consciousness?" is the way some executives see the problem. Perhaps your people are not suffering from disinterest in costs. But a brief catalog of "starts" may be useful to help cost-cutting efforts. The items below are specific. They aim to win the interest and cooperation of your people. Finally, they tend to lessen the frequently damaging consequences of the "cut-10 percent-across-the-board" approach:

1. The "consultation" start.   One executive describes this use of the idea: "It's almost like a ritual. I find my key people and we begin to talk about the need to tighten up on the cost line. What often happens is that this key group comes up with an idea, a point of departure, an approach that puts cost control in proper perspective."

2 The "performance review" start.   Some executives get their bearings in the cost area by appraising the performance of departmental operations for a given period: annually, semiannually, quarterly.

Analysis of operating records is an effective starting point: production records, recheck records, sales volume, customer complaints, service records, downtime—almost every aspect of departmental operations helps clarify the cost picture.

Out of this review and analysis of past performance can come new resolves and new goals. Says one executive: "Maintenance costs are dragging down our overall performance. We have got to zero in on that area."

3. The employee meeting.   Some executives find that a full-dress meeting of the entire employee roster is an effective cost-improvement starter. Most successful examples of this approach involve getting employee participation and involvement. Here are a set of notes used by an executive for the agenda of a cost-control meeting:

   a. Introduction. Tell the group why our costs must be cut: competition, need to maintain profitability of selling price, and so on.
   b. Relationship of the division to the company. Describe the importance of our unit to overall company performance: the lower our costs, the better the department's and company's performance record.
   c. Individual employees. Tell of the importance of each employee's activity to departmental performance.
   d. Rewards. Describe what increased profitability will do for the company ("We will be able to grow," etc.) and for the individual employee (perhaps higher salaries, greater career opportunity, and so on).

   e. Improving procedures. Ask: What can we do; what are your ideas for getting us moving?

The important thing, says the executive who uses the above approach is to listen to the solutions and ideas suggested, and put them to work as far as is possible.

4. The "dramatic device start.   Flamboyant executives can profit from the example of an Oklahoma City plant manager. He got a large photostatic blowup of a stage money bill and used it to spark a "save-the-buck" campaign.

There are numerous ways to dramatize a cost-saving effort:

- Mount scoreboards in each department or area showing recent sales or production figures, or possibly for expenses such as the cost of materials, or maintenance.
- Another executive staged an "idea day." After several weeks of prepublicity, employees were asked to turn in their cost-cutting ideas. Since employees were not limited to "one to a person," it was found that the average was 3.6 ideas per employee. Out of this vast number of suggestions, the company was able to adopt 76 that paid off.

5. The key operation start.   Some managers prefer to select the element of their unit's operations that is critical, where improvement will have the broadest effects. They then get the best brains among their staffs working on the key areas.

6. The "grain-of-sand" start.   Instead of seeking a single large area, some executives prefer a comprehensive tightening up of all areas of operation. One executive had his supervisors work out with their respective groups the many small ways that lead to operating losses. For example, a supervisor in charge of a polishing room spotted these "loss leaders": machines left running when not in use; breakage due to careless handling of stock; sandpaper being "borrowed" for personal use; pumice wasted; polishing wheels discarded before full use had been obtained.

This pinpointed approach may sound like paperclip saving, but for the executive who can get participation down at the grassroots level, the small savings add up to an important percentage of operating costs.

7. The red tape start.   Companies often become entangled in forms and formalities. When communication channels become clogged, when procedures get slowed down, when people who need attention or material or equipment cannot get it because of "procedures," your red tape is going to turn into red ink.

The effective manager looks for procedural bottlenecks or red tape and improves efficiency and profitability by eliminating them.

8. The interdepartment team.   Many companies find a major source of wasted effort and delay exists between departments. Each department may work well on its own but the department's activities are not well-meshed.

For example, Department A produces work and stacks it in the corridor for Department B to pick up and process, but "B," for various reasons, does not move the work right away, or sometimes the lots are mixed, and so time—and money—is lost.

In a Texas electronics firm, an executive sat down with a colleague also in charge of a major operational area. They proceeded to list a series of questions:

- At what points do our operations touch or overlap?
- What inefficiencies occur in these areas?
- How can we minimize these?
- How can we get better cooperation between the staffs of the two departments?

A list of revealing questions of this kind can help turn up answers to close an operational gap through which wasted dollars have been flowing.

FILLING PERSONNEL GAPS DURING VACATIONS

The vacation period frequently leaves a work roster looking like Swiss cheese. The checklist below can help you cope:

- If regular employees will take on duties of those who are away, will they require some breaking in, such as brushup training?
- In the case of the assignments of vacationers, can you hold off on some crucial aspects till they return?
- Can you use the vacation period as a trial period for some of your people; that is, give them the opportunity for new assignments?
- If you are going to need replacements or temporaries, have you decided how many, and what their qualifications must be?
- Should you take up the question of replacements with Personnel at an early date?
- Do you know of any skilled ex-employees who might be willing to serve as fill-ins on a temporary basis?
- Can you use the "buddy system" to help temporaries break in; that is, have veteran employees act as guides and sources of information for the newcomers?
- Can you modify work methods to meet personnel shortages; for example, have two subordinates share a secretary when their regular assistants are away? (Be sure the secretary knows it's temporary, and ask your subordinates to eliminate low-priority typing.)

➲ WORKLOAD ADJUSTMENTS DURING SUMMER VACATIONS

When the vacation period strikes, you may have to do more than hire temporaries or ask your experienced people to take over someone else's assignment. Adjusting the workload may be essential. Moves such as those below can help:

- Can you move critical jobs up on the schedule, or defer them till the return of vacationers?
- Can special arrangements with other executives ease some of the standard problems?
- Can consultations with your superior lighten workloads or modify work peaks and valleys?
- Can you "trade" work with other departments?
- Can you make mutually helpful transfer of employees with other executives?
- If you plan to hire temporaries, can you have them come in for training beforehand, so that they'll know the ropes when they report for active duty?

➲ MEETING A CRISIS

Avoid undue hesitation, speed up decision making, then move! Talk and act fast.

Get your people into the act—ask for help.

Tell everybody what's going on—especially your superior.

When you give orders, use the autocratic method. At this stage, you only want your decisions implemented.

Borrow people, material, machines from other departments.

Develop backup solutions.

Ride herd on solutions and be ready to modify them in action.

Don't leave crisis procedures in force when the crisis is over.

➲ CHANGE OF PACE

Monotony can put a damper on employee job interest, increase the number of errors employees make, increase the possibility of accidents, and depress their output.

What makes a job monotonous depends largely on the individual. But if you sense a harmful degree of monotony in work situations, consider some relief measures:

■ **Rotate assignments.** Many executives consider this one of the best ways to build job interest. Filing duties might be rotated among a number of employees, for example; so could posting. Note too that this does more than introduce variety into the job. It enlarges each employee's understanding of departmental operations. It gives you greater flexibility in the face of unexpected absences or periods of pressure.

■ **Reduce endlessness.** Psychologists have repeatedly demonstrated that "signposts" are necessary to the feeling of progress. Managers put the principle to work when they break the day-long job into a series of steps. Processing invoices in sets of twenty-five, for example, would be one way of doing it.

■ **Off-the-job missions.** An executive points out that these can be rotated among those employees who seem to show the greatest restlessness. Frequently, trips off the premises are all undertaken by one employee. This may be the more efficient way of handling it. But placing such assignments on something like a roster basis gives more people a chance to "get away."

■ **Emphasize challenge.** "This isn't just a routine assignment," Executive A tells his assistant. "If you can come up with a plan for promoting this new product, it will be the first time it's been done in this division.

➔ READING THEIR MINDS

The Clue	Common Inference	Alternatives
No complaints, gripes, or grievances	Smooth sailing ahead	Explosion brewing, or apathy building up
Eagerness to confer with superior	They like you, respect your knowledge	Sagging initiative, overdependency
No questions being asked	Everybody in agreement	Afraid to show ignorance, or doubt of boss
Arguments among themselves	Friction and internal strife	Healthy exchange of ideas

Executives pride themselves on their ability to take a "reading" of their group. "The mood is up," one executive says. Another reports, "There's a feeling of tension and dissatisfaction."

It's important to be aware of group mood. However, there is a tendency to misinterpret. The chart above gives you an opportunity of checking some common evaluations of group feeling.

But when it comes to reading the mind of your group, here's how to avoid mistakes:

1. Check alternative theories.   Don't latch on to the first explanation that comes to mind. No matter how well it seems to tie the clues together, keep trying new possibilities.

2. Look for additional evidence.   Don't let one clue, or even two establish your theory. A single observation can be very revealing, but at best it requires verification. Getting further proof should not be difficult. If the situation suggested by the clue has any significance at all, it's bound to create additional evidence. Look for it. Sometimes it pays to go after more evidence on your own instead of waiting for things to turn up.

If you're relying primarily on detective work for information about what's happening, you have a strong clue that regular communications are sagging. Spend more time talking to your people. Probe beneath the surface behavior to get real feelings. It will pay off in terms of understanding and your ability to improve group well-being and performance.

➲ WHEN THEY ALLOW TOO BIG A MARGIN OF SAFETY

Every business tries to build a margin of safety, or "fudge factor" into operations. Budgets, inventory controls, production and quality controls, all contain such a cushion. But many people try to build in a little extra protection of their own, if they get the chance.

An employee wants his production quota set low, so that he won't have too much trouble looking good. A well-meaning employee may "hide" some scarce material, so she won't get caught short. The consequences can be immobilizing and expensive.

When you find subordinates building in their own fudge factors, playing *too* safe, consider:

1. Are they revealing overanxiety?   The employee who lives in terror of being caught short clearly is afraid of the snapback—a severe reprimand, loss of status, and so on. If this seems to be the case, the fault may lie with the supervisor. Everyone, from top to bottom of an organization, should have a certain amount of freedom to err. Without this freedom, initiative will diminish.

2. Are they making a power play against a colleague?   "Ted would rather have someone stand around idle than share his backlog of work," asserts a colleague bitterly. The subordinate who hoards, whether it's manpower, equipment, or materials, while a colleague suffers from shortages, obviously hasn't gotten the idea of team play and cooperation.

3. Are they aware of the cost facts of life?   "Why shouldn't I keep these hundred drums in reserve?" a mixing-room supervisor in a paint factory asks her boss. "You wouldn't want us to run out of solvent, would you?" The cost of storage, the cash tied up in the materials, apparently is not appreciated by this well-intentioned employee. Her boss owes her a session on hidden costs.

4. Does use of the fudge factors suggest unsatisfactory controls? These may be at the level at which the fudging is taking place, or at the next higher level up the line. A manager whose worksheets reflect excessive hours of employee idle time *may* have too much standby help. Or, there may have a legitimate complaint: "I never know from one day to the next what kind of orders the Front Office is going to load on me."

Admittedly, there never can be a perfect balance between ability to perform and performance requirements. However, using a fudge factor beyond accepted limits often reflects either anxiety or uncertainty. The conditions that cause these problems must be spotted and dealt with to control fudging.

➲ WORKING WITH TEMPORARIES

Your assistant comes down with a sudden illness and she's out, several days or weeks. Or one or another of your staff is out for reasons of health, vacations, and so on. These days, the use of temporary help has become a pervasive practice on the work scene. And the range of job categories made available by the temporary agencies has been increasing. Stenos, typists, clerks, salespeople, engineers, scientists, the list continues to grow.

Temporary help can be an excellent solution to a roster gap, but temporary workers also represent a tough problem—that of getting them into the act quickly. Here's how to make temporary help more productive sooner, a method that you may want to pass along to your subordinates, if and when they have to hire temporaries:

1. Specify the kind of help needed. According to one agency, success of a temporary depends 90 percent on the quality of the job description. Requesting a "typist" gives you only a slim chance of getting what you *really* need. Copy typist? Manuscript? Statistical? Each requires different skills; you won't get what you need unless you specify.

2. Keep your department in the know. An unexpected face invites speculation. Has the regular job holder been fired? Is the new person really there to see which jobs could be automated? Don't let rumors start. Tell your department a temporary is coming to *help them.* Keep them informed, and they'll be eager to cooperate.

3. Plan work and prepare supplies.   You waste time and money trying to organize assignments and equipment after the temporary arrives. Decide in advance which work will be assigned. A checklist can help you be sure you have all supplies ready. Where possible, have the regular employee help in the preparations.

4. Give complete instructions.   A temporary comes into your department cold, whom you hope will perform like an experienced hand. It's not "the impossible dream"—if you give complete instructions. A job instruction sheet, prepared by you or the regular employee, helps cover all points, and lets the temporary review them. Or, if you give instructions orally, encourage the temp to make notes of key points. Work samples help get it right first try.

5. Explain company procedures.   The temporary will feel like a member of the group, not an outsider, if you explain rules regarding lunch hours, rest periods, smoking, etc. This prevents mistakes which would annoy you and embarrass the newcomer. If possible, use a "buddy" approach: assign a seasoned employee to help with routines.

If you've chosen a reputable agency, the temporary has been tested, trained, and placed according to skills and personality. He or she is a professional and should be treated as one. Expect good work, and you'll get it.

➲ GROUP GROWTH AS A VITALIZER

A group, like an individual, is stimulated by progress. Advancement of your department builds respect for it. Most people prefer to be affiliated with an entity on the move than one that is going nowhere.

Groups within an organization, a department or division, may not always be able to advance. The usual growth signs, increased physical area, expanded function, enlarged facilities, or extended roster, may be limited by the needs of the organization of which it is a part. Yet, even under this constraint, a group can grow internally. You can set increasingly high standards of performance. Through continuing training or new hires, the group may acquire heightened skills and capability, available if and when organization needs are more favorable toward its future.

And while it may seem a contradiction, a group can brighten its image by losing its top people to other parts of the organization by promotion or transfer. The reputation of being good training ground, of offering the value of apprenticeship with an outstanding manager, can create respect.

However, for many groups, advancement comes naturally. An excellent executive is given increased responsibilities, which may mean larger staff, acquisition of new or related areas of operation.

There are invaluable benefits of belonging to a dynamic group:

- It builds the image of the group in the eyes of members, as well as others.
- It increases the self-esteem of group members. "I work for the X Department," as they say it, becomes an acceptable boast.
- Gives individuals a forward tilt in their work. They are challenged to stay abreast of the advancing group, are motivated to greater effort in performance. They have somewhere to go in their personal aspiration.

9. Leadership and Motivation

President Eisenhower defined leadership as "the ability to get people to do what you want because they want to do it."

This statement also includes the concept of motivation: the ways and means of getting people to *want* to do whatever is to be done.

Some management observers feel that the idea of leadership is outdated. The traditional image of the business leader who stands at the head of his or her "troops" and guides them along, doesn't suit the image of the modern executive. Motivation has come to be the preferred concept and to some extent it encompasses the ends of leadership. However, the burial of the leadership concept is premature. The contemporary executive has good reason to want to keep up-to-date on the subject of leadership, as well as motivation. Accordingly, you will find both areas covered in this section.

➲ **WHY LEADERSHIP WORKS**

Everyday experience plus the assurance of industrial psychologists tells us that leadership on the business scene is an important element in effectiveness. And yet, as important as this fact is, very seldom is the question asked, Just why is it that leadership works?

Analyzing the response of the individual and of the group to good leadership yields considerable insight into managerial effectiveness:

1. Leadership and the Individual. Individuals working in constructive relationships with their superior can accomplish tasks that surprise even themselves. Personal productivity and creativity take an upward bounce. Often, individuals can make gainful innovations in their jobs and on the entire work scene. Here's why:

Goal alertness. The president of a New Mexico public service company puts it this way: "I get my people lined up on the target, make them aware of what contributes to our goals and what does not." Leadership that is expertly exercised makes individuals aware of desired goals, steers them away from dead ends.

Talent latency.   A New Jersey electronics manufacturer reports that one of his managers without prior factory experience became one of their most capable men. Explains the executive, "His boss was able to arouse an emormous amount of talent that the employee didn't even know he had." There is latent energy and untapped talent in all individuals—no matter what their position, no matter at what level they are performing. The good leader is able to bring out the wealth of these hidden gold mines.

And a key point: the improvement in performance *doesn't* come about by employees working themselves into a lather. They don't work harder, they work smarter—to use an old axiom.

Self-doubt eradication.   Most people are affected with varying degrees of self-doubt. "I can't do that assignment, I've never done it before." Or an employee will accept an assignment and spend hours worrying whether he or she can fulfill it. Performance is bound to be adversely affected.

A good leader gets a subordinate to improve performance by breaking the chains forged by self-doubt. Superior performance results from this upsurge in self-confidence.

2. Leadership and Groups.   There are times when the manager wants the workforce to tackle an assignment as a team. Good leadership turns individuals into team members. Here's what happens:

Common goals.   "The leader creates a concept of common goal," says a Pennsylvania manager. "I can take programmers who are out for themselves and help them see that it's more important for the unit to win the ball game, so to speak, than for each one to try to hit home runs."

Mutual help.   A South Carolina cotton mill manager recently presided over the installation of semiautomatic equipment in his department. "I realized," he said, "that if employees would help one another learn the new ropes, we'd have fewer mistakes. The faster learners could teach the slower ones, not leave them to fend for themselves." By talking to the workers, he was able to get them to help one another. Soon the entire department had mastered the new equipment. The reason? Good leadership, which created, in this instance, a department-wide atmosphere of good will and mutual helpfulness.

Team effort.   The leader takes an aggregation of people and molds them into a team. You see it done by good sports coaches, on the diamond and gridiron. You see it on the work scene, when masterful managers are at the helm.

Leaders who know their business can put the work of individuals in phase with the work of colleagues. "I can modify subordinates' assignments," said a California aircraft plant manager, "or put them on a different task entirely, until the work is ready. If I do my job right, individuals work smoothly, in step with one another. There is less time wasted, fewer starts and stops."

The result of this "phasing" of the work, and the result, too, of providing common goals and a spirit of mutual helpfulness, has been expressed as: the whole is greater than the sum of its parts. It is the sign of the effective leader.

➲ **A BRIEF REVIEW OF APPROACHES TO LEADERSHIP**

Historically, leadership concepts have been of three types:

The trait approach.   This explains leadership in terms of the personal traits of the leader. Ever since the dawn of the human race, people have been aware that leaders often possess qualities that set them apart. Personal courage, for example, was one of the traits generally ascribed to early tribal leaders.

The trait approach has advocates today. There are some management authorities who say, to be effective, a leader must:

be enthusiastic
know himself or herself
be mentally alert
be self-confident
have a sense of responsibility
develop a sense of humor

The list is far from complete. Dozens of items could be added.

No one can really quarrel with the value of many of these traits. However, the trouble with the trait approach is that it's about as useful as a handbook on traffic rules would be to the motorist who needs a road map. No one would deny that an enthusiastic leader can be a highly inspiring one. But, if would-be leaders are not *naturally* enthusiastic, they could work themselves into a nervous breakdown trying to develop an artificial enthusiasm. And the insincerity of phony enthusiasm can be disastrous.

The same handicap pertains to other leadership traits—they're fine in theory, but not practical when it comes to developing leadership, or applying it.

The situationist approach.   Some experts feel that the situations in which the leader operates hold the key to effectiveness. Accordingly, this concept stresses the characteristics of leadership situations. Norman F. Washburne, in *Nation's Business,* lists a number of actions performed by a good leader that reflect the situationist approach:

A good leader initiates action;
gives orders that will be obeyed;
uses established channels within his group;
knows and obeys the rules and customs of his group;
maintains discipline;
listens to subordinates;
responds to their needs;
helps them.

Although Washburne's ideas go a step further than the trait approach, we need something more. The trouble with the situationist approach, in general, is that, it's *descriptive* rather than *prescriptive*.

For example, we have all verified the fact that a good leader initiates action. However, the statement "a good leader initiates action" raises more questions than it answers. *What* kind of action does the leader initiate? *When* does he initiate it? And, exactly *how* does he do so?

The social activist approach.   Some authorities view the role of the leader as one of putting together the elements, human and material, required for successful performance. This method includes the assignment of individuals or groups to specific tasks, and stresses the nature of the relationship between the leader and followers. It has the same drawback as the situational idea. It tells you *what* needs doing. The *how* remains a mystery.

The method of Selective Leadership, the next item in this section, is an example of practical method.

⮩ SELECTIVE LEADERSHIP: A SYSTEMATIC APPROACH

Should a manager approach an experienced subordinate in the same way as a novice? Should one manage a group of laborers the same way as one might a group of scientists? What difference if any do the personalities of .subordinates make in the boss's approach to them.

In the early 1960s the author developed a systematic approach to leadership. (*Techniques of Leadership,* Auren Uris, McGraw Hill, 1964.) The concepts and practices that make up Selective Leadership derive from key experiments by psychologist Kurt Lewin at the University of Iowa. To explore the nature of leadership, Lewin set up experimental groups of two sorts:

One type was dominated by an *"autocratic"* leader, who determined policy, decided what was to be done and how, assigned tasks, and chose work companions for each member. He or she was personal in praise, criticism, and general comments.

The second type was led by a *"democratic" leader,* who brought up matters of policy for group discussion, encouraged group members to choose their own work companions, and was "objective" in comments about performance.

Then came an unexpected development: observers noticed that one individual playing the role of "democratic" leader created an atmosphere different from that of other "democratic" leaders. He exercised virtually no control over the group; permitted group members to shift for themselves; let them tackle problems unaided, as best they could. The group's response to this technique was so different from the reactions of other democratic groups that Lewin set up a third kind of group under a type of leadership which he termed "laissez-faire."

Significant differences emerged in atmosphere, behavior, feelings, and accomplishments:

Autocratic.   Group members were quarrelsome and aggressive. Some individuals became completely dependent upon the leader. When the leader was absent, activity tended to stop altogether. Work progressed at only a fair rate.

Democratic.   The individuals got along with one another on a friendly basis. Relations with the leader were freer, more spontaneous. The work progressed smoothly, and continued even when the leader was absent.

Laissez-faire.   Work progressed haphazardly, and at a slow rate. Although there was considerable activity, much of it was unproductive. Considerable time was lost in arguments and discussions between group members on a purely personal basis.

Pros and cons.   Actually, each method has built-in strengths and weaknesses; each method has its value. The three methods developed in the University of Iowa investigations provide the framework of the *Selective Leadership* approach, welding the Lewin concepts into a unified and systematic method.

Using the *Selective Leadership* approach, the manager selects whichever one of the three tools is most appropriate:

Autocratic leadership.   The leader mainly seeks obedience from the group, determines policy, and considers decision making a one-person operation.

Democratic leadership.   The leader draws ideas and suggestions from the group by discussion and consultation. Group members are encouraged to take part in the setting of policy. The leader's job is largely that of moderator.

Free-rein leadership.   (Lewin's "laissez-faire" method) The leader functions more or less as an information booth, plays down his or her role in the group's activity, and exercises a minimum of control.

These definitions provide the basis for a systematic approach to leading people. *Autocratic, democratic,* or *free-rein* methods may be considered as three tools of the management leader. Contrary to common belief, the three approaches are not mutually exclusive. No one has to choose among using autocratic, democratic, or free-rein methods. That would be like telling golf players they must choose between using a driver or a putter; in the course of a game both will be used:

Note Manager Frank Z. in action:

He *directs* (autocratic method) his secretary to make a report.

He *consults* (democratic method) with his employees on the best way to push a special project through staff operations.

He *suggests* (free-rein method) to his assistant that it would be a good idea to figure out ways in which special orders may be handled more smoothly in the future.

This type of leadership suggests that mastery lies in knowing *when* to use *which* method. In short, Selective Leadership is a logical adaptation of autocratic, democratic, and free-rein techniques to appropriate situations.

➲ THE PERSONALITY FACTOR

Once the three basic approaches are understood, it remains only for the manager to learn to suit the appropriate approach to a given situation. For example, the personality factor is taken into account in this fashion:

The hostile subordinate.   With individuals of this type, the autocratic method is likely to be most effective. While they resent authority, they respect it at the same time. Accordingly, hostility must be met by a show of authority. The autocratic approach has the effect of channeling aggressions, confining energies to constructive ends.

The group-minded individual.   Subordinates who are team-minded, who enjoy "team play," will probably function best if led by democratic techniques. They need less direction, regard work as a group job, and are willing to accept group goals as personal ones.

The individualist,   the solo player. He or she usually thrives best under the free-rein type of leadership, likes to develop personal methods and ideas the more latitude given, the greater freedom for mobilizing his or her creativity.

In addition to adapting to the personality factors of a situation, selective leadership also takes into account the nature of the response the manager seeks in any given context. For example:

Compliance.   If the subordinate or group is working along routine lines, with well-established goals, the autocratic method is appropriate.

Cooperation.   A rush order may put a group under pressure to perform above standard. Calling the group together, describing the nature of the crisis, asking for help and suggestions, are democratic techniques that will best help meet objectives.

Creativity.   Productivity can be stimulated slightly by autocratic, means, considerably by democratic approaches. But creativity poses different problems. When novel ideas are sought and imagination is needed, the free-rein approach is usually most effective.

(See Section III, "Key Management Concepts," for a further description of Selective Leadership.)

➲ THE CHARISMA COMPONENT

The experienced executive knows that above and beyond the procedural and rational aspects of leadership, there's something else. Intangible though it may be, it can make major differences in results:

- Some executives "do things all wrong" and still run effective departments.
- Some executives "do all the right things" and still get only the most meager payoffs.

What is this X factor? One explanation is *charisma*. "Charisma," says the dictionary, is "that special personal quality in some people that makes others want to follow their lead." King Arthur had it, so did Joan of Arc. And John F. Kennedy had it in outstanding fashion.

Can a leader "develop" a charisma, improve this highly personal aspect of leadership? Unexpectedly the answer is *yes*. Keen observers of outstanding managers in action report that the charismatic leader is usually one whose dedication, involvement, and sincerity regarding work and goals are self-evident, *sufficiently so to rub off on subordinates.*

Charismatic executives inspire their people, spur them on, motivate them, get improved performance, in ways ranging from increased output to more wholehearted participation. In ultimate development, well-led employees view the company's problems as theirs.

➜ YOUR PERSONAL LEADERSHIP STYLE

"In a society overrun by people trying to be carbon copies of one another, anyone with the nerve and verve to be different can lead an exciting life filled with a sense of personal satisfaction."

These words are from, "They Dare To Be Different," by Elmer G. Leterman and Thomas W. Carlin.

There's no doubt that for many, the path of individualism and nonconformity can lead to high achievement. The names and accomplishments of some high achievers make the point—Lee Iacocca, head of the Chrysler Corporation, who led his company out of the slough of near-bankruptcy to profitable operation; Helen Gurley Brown, the Californian whose best seller ripped the veil from the subject of sex and the single girl; Dr. Wendell Phillips, whose unique approach to exploration and development of oil lands made him one of the wealthiest men in the world.

What does "daring to be different" mean for executives? Answer: unconformity represents a style, a *working style,* a way of thinking about and doing things. And as such, it deserves your objective consideration.

There's no doubt that the executive who moves out in new and nontraditional directions may well come up with novel ideas and solutions to problems. For example:

Department head Bill Woods has a production problem. Ordinarily, he would set about solving it either by consulting with Engineering, or by getting his most experienced employees together for probing discussions. But, Bill Woods decides to try a different tack: he arranges to have a working lunch with three or four of his fellow managers, and along with the food, he puts his problem on the table.

The example is not only illustrative, but suggestive, because the executive reading the Bill Woods tactic, will make the logical observation: "Woods's approach *may* work if his fellow managers have some knowledge of the circumstances surrounding the problem."

In other words, "daring to be different," has a good chance of working *if* certain conditions prevail:

■ If "daring to be different" isn't simply being different for its own sake. In short, the differentness must give you an edge.

■ If the new tack, takes you in a direction where there's a possibility of finding pay dirt. (As pointed out, discussing problems with colleagues may yield results *if* the colleagues have know-how in the problem area.)

Tough-minded executives know that a concept is only as good as its payoff. And they need only look about on the work scene to know there must be more than one road to the top. No one concept can claim to be "the way" to success.

Accordingly, executives evaluating the worthwhileness of "being different" may say, "Sure, taking the unorthodox, unprecedented approach to things is one way of accomplishing objectives, if it happens to be your thing. But it's not the *only* way."

Doubtless there are benefits to "being different." However, studying the work patterns of successful executives suggests that there are other keys to success. For example, some outstanding managers owe their achievement to persistence, sticking with a problem till a solution is developed. Others accomplish objectives by making the best possible use of resources on hand. Here are a number of keys to leadership success, philosophies of work, tactics for achievement—call them what you will:

- "being different"
- persistence
- mobilizing available resources
- attention to detail
- follow through
- analyzing a problem accurately
- knowing how to get and use expert help
- other (add your own): _____

In scanning the list, ask yourself, "Which of the items have I used, or do I use, separately or in combination?" Remember, each has the virtue of potential success. To a large extent, the question, "Which is best?" is answered by three other questions:

- Which suits the particular problem best?
- Which can I implement best?
- Which suits my natural propensities or "personality" best?

Perhaps you'll decide that being different is your thing. Or, you may see the advantages of another alternative, or combination of alternatives.

In any event, the increased awareness gained by thinking about the approach to work and work problems can improve one's leadership performance. Executives who know what "their thing" is, have a much better chance of doing it well.

➲ WHAT TO TELL A MANAGER WHO'S JUST STARTING

Occasionally, executives face the task of putting new people in supervisory jobs. Their qualifications naturally have been found adequate. But a personal "message" from you can help them approach their responsibility with more understanding—both of the job and your expectations.

The following suggestions probably won't be made in one sitting, but over a period of time. These management principles have helped many a tyro make the grade:

Be firm, but fair.   You can lead, direct, coach. You can and should speak and act with strength and conviction. But it's also important to realize that circumstances change people; people change situations. What works in one instance, won't in another. What's fair for one person may be all wrong for someone else. A good supervisor knows how to be flexible, in order to be fair.

Take advantage of the experience and abilities of other people.   Few people are geniuses who know everything. Be receptive to the ideas and advice of others: your subordinates, your boss, staff people, other department heads. Being interested in what they have to say can provide a twofold benefit: they'll be stimulated by your interest; their ideas may save you many a headache.

Use authority constructively.   Authority, vested by top corporate management in all managers commensurate with their responsibility, is a support, not a weapon, a backup of the right to give orders, request acceptable behavior, prohibit undesirable practices and give rewards.

For the beginner in management, there may be a tendency to make an overly quick display of authority, use it to impress and intimidate. Some other undesirable actions include:

Don't play favorites.   One of the morale destroyers managers should abjure. It may also be self-destructive and tarnish one's ethical values.

Avoid arbitrary decisions.   "We'll do it my way because I'm the boss," may be technically correct, but it is a shaky foundation on which to base a decision. It is better to say: "Since it's my responsibility, I shall rely on my judgment."

Use persuasion rather than pressure.   An employee who grudgingly goes along with an order isn't likely to perform as well as one who sees the logic or good sense of a directive. When the time is available, persuasion is always more effective than acceptance under duress.

Admit your mistakes.   Even the greatest executive can't always be right. When you goof, don't alibi, don't try to shift the blame to someone else. Just admit that you were wrong and offer a brief explanation, if you think it's pertinent. This applies whether the mistake involves one person or all the people in your group.

Be truthful.   Even when it hurts. Don't be afraid to tell subordinates they are doing a poor job—it's for their own good—but at the same time point out how they can improve. That way, you make them feel that even though they're low now, there's no reason why they can't move up. Remember the reverse side of the coin, as well—give credit where and when it is due. Everyone welcomes a word of praise and appreciation for a job well done.

Be consistent.   People won't willingly follow a leader who goes from mood to mood, who flatters one day and frightens the next, who talks a blue streak in the morning and clams up in the afternoon. They simply end up confused and unsure.

Maintaining an even disposition isn't always easy. Sometimes you have to bit down hard on your tongue so you won't say something you'll regret. Or it may take a colleague's blunt, "What's the matter with you?" to alert you to your attitude. Accept such comments in good faith—and snap back to normal.

Don't be afraid to train assistants.   Recruit the kind that can serve as good right hands, take over when you're not there, move into your spot when you go higher. Executives who "run scared," who hold onto each bit of their jobs and authority lest someone else prove smarter than they are miss the boat. A good assistant can make a good manager look even better.

Be a self-starter.   Don't wait for someone else to set the rules and the pace. Be open to inspiration, learn to translate thought into action, dramatize action with salesmanship. To sell an idea, stress its good points, tell people what it can do for them, the company, and for you as well.

And when you start something, see it through to the finish. Don't be disheartened when something doesn't run smoothly. Give it time, patience, and some enthusiastic follow-through. It may take on a new vitality.

Keep people informed.   Don't try to put things over on your group, to keep them in the dark. If you expect them to work as a team, you have to treat them like a team, one that is in the know about what's going on and why. This builds their confidence in you as a leader and keeps spirits high.

Continue reading and learning.   Moving from supervisor to executive demands new knowledge, new techniques, almost a new way of thinking. You progress with experience, reading and listening. A course in labor relations community relations, the latest in computer or information systems technology, can prove invaluable. The same holds true for books and magazines dealing with various phases of management. One part of management is common sense, but another is knowledge and know-how. Both are available—if you know where to look for them.

➲ WHEN YOU NEED VOLUNTEERS

No executive has ever complained of having too many volunteers. Complaints, if any, are usually: you need help, but no one comes forward. To make sure you can count on helping hands when you need them:

1. Clarify what you want done.   That includes how long the job will take. "I need someone to stick around with me for an hour or so Wednesday night," says the head of the Computer Room. You can cross Johnny's name off the list for all future volunteering, if he gets stuck till midnight.

2. Stand ready to pitch in.   Where a job's being carried through on a voluntary basis, the manager should be prepared to lend a hand himself. "You inventory the first aisle, I'll take the second," is the attitude that gets lasting cooperation.

3. Highlight your appreciation.   That's a time-honored rule, too often disregarded in the rush to get home. Whether you're dealing with one volunteer or twenty, it's always good practice to make a curtain speech: "Thanks a lot for the way you've pitched in to clean up this job."

4. Reward their efforts.   They'll like that best of all, and they'll give you the most in return. Be sure to include their record of cooperation in merit rating and progress reviews. "I'm putting in a pitch for you," is sweet music to anyone's ears.

Follow these rules, and you'll be much surer of seeing the hands go up, rather than the thumbs down when there's a call for volunteers.

➲ WHEN YOUR LEADERSHIP IS CHALLENGED

Occasionally, and for a variety of reasons, executives may find their leadership rejected or evaded by their group. Even the most seasoned executive may run into trouble. The important thing is to recognize the development in its early stages, and eliminate causative factors before the virus spreads. Here are some of the symptoms:

■ **Excessive need for discipline.**   You find increasing instances of people bypassing regulations, becoming negligent, even acts of insubordination.

■ **Grievances galore.**   Complaints of all kinds begin to pile up. The trivial matter that's passed unnoticed for months suddenly becomes a major issue. A grievance you considered settled flares up again.

■ **Cooperation down, goldbricking up.**   Tom, Dick, and Harry, the faithful three you could always count on to stick with a job until it's finished, beg off on staying overtime. You find you've got to do more arguing and explaining to keep your group on their toes.

■ **Performance records skidding.** "Look at the errors made last month!" That may be the soundtrack on your first picture of leadership trouble. Or maybe the mail is accumulating in the correspondence department, and Word Processing is falling behind, with no increase in the workload.

■ **Leadership ignored.** They stop asking questions. They no longer look to you for advice. They make their own decisions on matters that normally require your okay.

Any one of those situations calls for a two-dose treatment:

Keep your head. Start out by dealing with the individual cases. Don't use any single case as a test of strength, to show you can crack down. Resist the temptation to "make an example" of the latest offender. That may be the spark that sets off the explosion.

Look for the underlying cause of the trouble. Check up on the answers to the questions in this self-examination:

- ☐ Have you been failing to make decisions when they were called for?
- ☐ Have you been getting all the facts before making a decision?
- ☐ Have you been selling your decisions by explaining the "why," or have you been relying on your authority?
- ☐ In running your "shop," have you been influenced by personal feelings— friendships, animosities?
- ☐ Have you been getting your staff in on the solution of group problems?
- ☐ Have you been taking positive steps to underline the group nature of the work—group goals, group achievements?

⇨ THREE TYPES OF MOTIVATION

Why do people do things? For example, what makes an employee get out of a comfortable bed to brave the problems and ordeals of a job? What makes an executive apply herself to a task, work overtime to complete a particularly challenging project?

In general, people are moved to act by three types of motives:

1. External motivation. Many people do what they do because they're *told* to do it. A parent tells a child she must get high marks in school. A teenager mows a lawn because his father orders him to do so. Or, a young man goes to college because his parents believe it's essential for his future. On the job, an employee "obeys the boss."

2. Social pressure. Many people are motivated by social or group pressures. For example, 90 out of 100 people work because our society expects them to. Similarly, many people get married when they do because society expects them to. Or, on the job, individuals seek advancement because it's expected by their employers or colleagues.

3. Self-motivation. Occasionally, we find people who take action on their own. They do something because *they* want to do it.

The self-motivated individual in many cases lives where he wants to, in the manner he prefers, and works toward objectives that he has decided are desirable for him. It's important to understand these three basic types of motivation. The executive who is most effective in motivating subordinates is the one most able to get them to act *not* because they are commanded to by a superior, *not* because they are pressured by the expectations of those around them, but because they are aware of the desirability of attaining the objectives of their efforts defined by their superiors.

What self-motivation comes down to, finally, is subordinates' conviction that they desire the fruits of success, want them so badly that they are willing to strive for them with both heart and mind.

➔ TELLING THEM WHAT'S IN IT FOR THEM

You're explaining a new policy to your group, and you want to get its full support. Or you give an individual an assignment, and he very properly seems to hestitate, because he's not clear on his stake in the success of the effort. In cases like these, the key to effective motivation may be in explaining to the individual, or group, the benefits they stand to gain. Perhaps the most crucial specific application of this approach lies in the cost-cutting area. You, as a representative of management, know the importance of holding the cost line. Some of your people may be reluctant to "knock themselves out" to save the company "a few bucks."

A considerable amount of insight into this problem is gained when you hear the answers given to a probing question: "If your company announced a cost-cutting drive, what would it take to get you to cooperate?" The answers given here provide the key to effective motivation, not only in cost cutting, but in any other job project where employees may be unclear as to what they stand to gain:

■ **Personal payoff.** "I'd want to feel," said a New York City insurance office clerk, "that my boss would notice me if I did a good job. And I'd expect him to remember my cooperation when it came time for a promotion or a raise."

■ **Dollars and cents.**   A Connecticut bakery employee said she'd want to know the dollars and cents of the matter. "Let my boss show me figures. If I saw figures showing, say, that $1,200 went down the drain every month on unnecessary electricity, I'd sure turn off lights. But if my boss just talks about 'waste' or 'high costs,' that's too abstract for me."

■ **Necessity.**   Says a California aircraft worker: "I'd want the company to tell me they're in financial trouble. Or if they told me my job depended on it, yes sir, I'd try to cut costs. and I'd want to be kept informed of the progress made: how we improve each week after the drive goes into effect."

■ **We're all in the same boat.**   Said a Chattanooga insurance-company employee: "Why me? That's what I'd ask my boss. I've got a sense of responsibility like everyone else, but I'd want it appealed to honestly. If I thought that somebody higher up was just passing the buck down to me, I wouldn't do anything. But if I felt that everyone above me was getting into the act, sure I'd help out."

Should this hardheaded attitude be discouraging? *Not at all.* Notice that the employees indicated that they would be *perfectly willing to participate* in cost-cutting efforts *if*—the reasons behind the activity were made clear, their position were given some consideration and justification, and so on.

If your company and your department plan to do any belt-tightening, try to think what each subordinate in your department would react to, then spur that interest. For some employees it will be involvement—just asking for help, getting them into the act. For others it will be the carrot—or the stick. Chances are, you'll have to use all of the techniques at your disposal. Your flexibility with these techniques—the aptness with which you satisfy each employee's "What's in it for me?"—will determine *how* your staff cooperates.

⊃ **WHY PEOPLE WORK**

Chances are, your subordinates want:

- recognition as a person—treatment as an individual, not as a "cog in the machine"
- fair treatment—a square deal
- job security
- suitable working conditions—reasonable schedule, comfortable facilities, protection against hazards
- a chance to be heard
- pride in their work—the feeling that they are useful

- knowledge—the meaning of the job, clear instructions
- the help of leadership—guidance (as needed)
- challenge—a chance to prove ability
- the sense of belonging—acceptance by others in the department

⮌ EIGHT DEMOTIVATORS

Obviously, not every case of lack of motivation among your subordinates is your fault. But, without being aware of it, the executive can contribute to a subordinate's apathy. Watch these areas:

- *Freezing them out.* Employees who don't have sufficient contact with you will begin to feel that nobody cares about them.

- *Chewing them out.* Make sure criticism is reasonable and accompanied by constructive suggestions for improvement.

- *Letting them flounder.* Don't let employees struggle aimlessly, with what you expect of them. When you don't communicate clear standards, they may decide "anything goes."

- *Ruling by whim.* When you don't enforce rules consistently, you are depriving workers of the leadership they need.

- *Aiming too high.* When goals are set too high, people give up, say, "Why should I knock myself out?"

- *Aiming too low.* If employees are not challenged, do not have a chance to use their full potential, they become bored.

- *Skimping on equipment.* Inferior tools or materials will "turn off" the employee who is trying to do a good job.

- *Insufficient recognition.* Failure of a boss or leader to register awareness of an individual, either on a day-to-day basis or in appreciation for notable performance, may lead to demoralization. The ritual "Good morning," and "Good night," may have little value in today's working relationships, but they're better than no recognition at all. And subordinates who feel their accomplishments go unnoticed, regardless of strong inner incentive will lose steam.

These demotivating factors suggest a key principle: high levels of performance from subordinates are forthcoming not only as a result of positive motivation, but also in the absence of actions that demotivate.

⮌ HOW TO CRITICIZE

You want the improvements resulting from criticism without demotivating side effects. Accordingly:

Focus on the act, not the person.   Don't suggest to the individual that he or she is unworthy. Get the facts, concentrate on them. Tell the employee that:

- An error has been committed.
- Good people have made the same mistake in the past.
- They corrected their errors and "you can too."
- The way to correct the error is thus-and-so.

Be specific about the error.   Avoid generalities, exaggeration.

Be specific about the remedy.   Spell out just what can be done to improve.

Watch reactions—go slow enough so that you are sure you are being completely understood.

Choose the right time and place.   Make it private. Avoid criticism just before lunch or closing time. If possible, allow for a second, constructive talk the same day.

Use only friendly humor.   If you can't keep it friendly, avoid it. Misplaced humor often makes enemies.

Follow up on criticism.   Don't repeat your criticisms or instructions. Follow up to:

- Reassure subordinates that you're in their corner.
- Give them a chance to ask questions.

HELP FOR THE GOAL-MINDED SUBORDINATE

Not everybody wants to be president—either of the U.S.A. or Acme Universal Manufacturing Co. On the other hand, for many of your subordinates a feeling of career movement is necessary to maintain performance.

In considering the attitudes of your people to their work, you'll find that they tend to fall into three groups:

- Those who are happy in their routine. These are the small minority.
- Those who are happy just knowing there is a chance to move up—even if they do nothing about it.
- Those who want to go places. The better your staff, the more such people you have.

Yet, not everybody is qualified to move ahead. Or the nature of the work may be such that there is no opportunity for advancement. If your people get the feeling of being dead-end kids, you're going to have disciplinary problems, absenteeism, high turnover, frequent gripes and grievances, as well as inferior performance.

How can you prevent the dead-ender from getting the "I'm-in-a-rut" feeling? Keeping in mind the special condition in each case, see which of these recommendations apply.

1. Are there chances for promotion or transfer?   Give this point a pretty thorough going-over before throwing up your hands. And don't let a person's present performance, by itself, guide your thinking. We all have undeveloped potentialities.

Search the work record. The present job may have disturbed an old aspiration. Perhaps past work experience can be reapplied.

Talk to them about their interests. They may reveal additional possibilities.

2. Can you expand the job?   You may be able, without any loss of efficiency, to incorporate other operations into the job. They may be steps that either immediately precede or follow the employee's regular task. Or they may be entirely unrelated, but still make use of special abilities.

3. Can you improve job methods?   Without changing the oldtimer's job, you may still be able to increase its efficiency, raise quality standards, or both. That provides a sense of progress in the job promotion without involving promotion to a new job.

4. Can you put employees on their own without losing control over the various activities?   An old-timer may tend to set herself up as a "separate department." This may be a good solution. A feeling of independence usually carries with it a sense of responsibility.

But you don't want to create a problem situation. If you give Hank the feeling that he can run things his own way, you'll have trouble if that way doesn't agree with yours. In other words, you want to give him independence of action that makes it possible for him to get results, without removing him from the group and your leadership.

You can accomplish this by subjecting Hank to a lesser degree of direction. "Just put through that report. With your experience, I don't have to look it over."

In addition, this attitude on your part gives him the feeling of superior status.

5. "You're doing an important job."   Employees who feel they are in a rut will be more content if they know they are accomplishing something worthwhile. These more than any other type of worker, need a constant reminder that their work is necessary. Offer:

- an understanding of their relation to the company, how their job fits in.
- an understanding of how the company serves the community, our national interest, and so on.

(Some of management's greatest scientific minds have contributed revealing concepts of motivation on the work scene (see the Motivation heading in the Index for the ideas of Herzberg, McGregor, Skinner, and others).

10. Dealing with Interpersonal Problems

"Among the touchiest, most explosive problems an executive must face," says Lee J. Smith, president of Tri-Tex Advertising, of Dallas, "are those dealing with attitudes, values, or habits of subordinates."

What's referred to are situations that arise on the workscene that cannot be dealt with on a simple matter-of-fact basis. For example:

A valued employee tells you he's leaving for another job.

You must fire a subordinate.

An employee complains to you about the offensive body odor of a neighboring worker.

Difficulties of this type can tax executives' understanding of people and their resourcefulness in developing satisfactory solutions. In the pages ahead, you'll find some of the most challenging interpersonal situations that turn up on the work scene, and suggestions for dealing with them. Success, of course, brings the possibility of converting a problem into an asset.

⊃ WHEN AN EMPLOYEE SAYS, "I QUIT!"

A valued employee who unexpectedly tells you he or she plans to resign, precipitates a need for careful reaction. Consider these points:

1. Decide what the employee really wants. Harold Ickes, Secretary of the Interior under President Roosevelt, used to "quit"—again and again. "Mr. President," he'd say, "I've got to leave." To which the President would reply: "Now Harold, what is the matter?" Roosevelt sensed that Ickes didn't really want to leave. What he wanted was a sympathetic ear.

Good executives follow Roosevelt's example. They listen to the words the employees says, and look for their meaning.

Of course, there are some employees who talk about quitting when they really want a raise. Here are some of the other gambits that are used:

"I have another job and I'm giving you notice."

"I'm thinking about leaving."

"I'm just not happy. Perhaps I ought to leave."

Each of these speeches means something different. The first is final, the last is tentative. It's obvious the employee can be made to stay—if you want it that way.

2. Decide if you want to keep the employee.   There's a natural response you must make when someone says, "I want to walk out." The executive tends to object—and perhaps shouldn't.

If you believe the employee is serious about leaving, mentally review the record, decide if this is a valuable employee. If not, clearly you shouldn't try to keep him or her. A certain amount of turnover is healthy, brings in new blood. A quit in some cases can be a desirable development.

3. Get the employee's story.   When Walt S. walks in and says he's through, ask yourself, "Is there something causing a problem in Walt's work situation?" Maybe it's going to affect other people under your supervision. Maybe it already has.

How do you find out? By encouraging Walt to talk freely. You want him to tell his story. That story may suggest what's gone wrong. It certainly will suggest lines of questioning.

Needless to say, you have to be careful that nothing the employee says elicits argument or criticism. You must be a fact finder in this situation, not a judge.

4. Get the "picture."   Let's say Walt tells you his story. But your mind's been racing: thinking of what another employee let slip last week, what one of your fellow managers said, and so on. What you're doing is seeking the real reason for the employee's desire to leave. A quit may be a complicated thing. Experienced executives find that employees who say they're quitting for one reason may have different, more basic reasons.

You can find the deeper reasons by tactful questioning. And, perhaps, the employee's statement suggests questions to be asked of the employee's co-workers, one's own colleagues, Personnel, if need be.

5. Decide how far to go.   Based on what you learn, you decide whether the employee is serious about leaving or just wants some hand-holding—or a raise.

You may want to offer inducements. *But watch out.* Don't make unrealistic promises that only kick back. Regardless of how good employees may be, it's wiser to let them go than to make efforts to keep them that you'll regret later on.

In general, your moves are likely to take you in three directions.

■ *Eliminate or alleviate a source of dissatisfaction.*   "I just can't start at nine," a typist may say. You may want to permit her to make a change—start at nine thirty—keeping in mind that your reasons must be good enough to explain to others why you did so in one case, and are not bound to do so in another.

■ *Offer reassurance.*   In some cases, employees may actually have better prospects in their present job—chance for a better position, higher wage bracket—than they are aware of. Make sure, then, that if employees are dissatisfied because they see no chance to improve their situation, that they are set straight—if it's in the cards.

■ *Offer tangible improvement.*   It may be anything from special privileges to a raise (if deserved). But, again, there must be justice and logic in the move, to protect you from a parade of "quits," aimed at winning some advantage.

Finally, if you think an employee is too good to lose, you may want to pass the question upstairs, let your superior in on the problem. There may be steps that your boss knows about that are worth taking for a key employee.

➜ HOW TO FIRE

Of all the situations that confront the executive, the one that represents the greatest personal ordeal, is that of firing a subordinate.

And, strangely, this fact may be true even when the dismissal is fully justified or when the prospects for the reemployment of the individual are excellent.

When you must fire an individual, these steps insure that you are being fair, and minimize possible adverse effects:

1. Use existing procedures.   Your company probably has a specified method for dismissal. While the details of such procedure may differ from one company to another, generally the steps follow a pattern. For example, unacceptable conduct calls for:

■ A verbal warning informing the subordinate of what is wrong and possible consequences.
■ A written warning informing the employee that the offense is continuing and that his or her job is hanging in the balance.
■ A final warning to the employee to the effect that if by a specified time the infraction has not stopped, dismissal is possible.

2. Back-up for your decision.   If you are on the point of firing an employee, it's desirable that:

■ You have some kind of written record in which the history of the employee has been kept.

- If the employee is supervised by a manager on your staff, remind your subordinate that a dossier should be kept in case the decision is in question. The record should contain dates and descriptions of the infractions and corroborating evidence or statements, if available.

3. Try to make the dismissal interview constructive.   Occasionally, an executive fires a subordinate under the spur of anger or frustration. Generally, such off-the-cuff dismissals are undesirable. As a matter of fact, if the executive is in a highly emotional state, it is wise to postpone action until a later time, when the employee can be interviewed in a quiet and relaxed atmosphere.

To make the final discussion as helpful as possible, it is wise to avoid recriminations, accusations, or derogatory descriptions of the employee's performance. Any such opinion should have been communicated to the employee at a much earlier time in the "warning" phase of the dismissal. The actual firing should give the employee a chance to speak fully. But for the executive's part, it must be a firm but friendly parting of the ways. If the situation permits, the executive may insure the constructive aspects of the action:

- Commenting on the favorable or worthwhile aspects of the employee's tenure.
- Making suggestions as to possible future employment.

If the employee raises the question of references for a future employer, you may reveal just what you feel you can say honestly, that will either help get a job or at least not interfere with job finding efforts.

→ HOW TO FIRE AN EXECUTIVE

Very few executives are ever fired. One reason the top echelons are usually fire-safe is that while lower-level employees are still, in a sense, "hired hands," executives are "family." Other reasons: it's bad public relations; it hardly speaks well of the management that did the original hiring, or failed to help toward a successful performance.

However, executives obviously *are* separated from time to time. Here are some of the methods used to bring about a parting of the ways:

- *The Siberia assignment.* An executive is given an undesirable task, a come-down from previous activities. The hint is usually taken.
- *"Find yourself another job."* Usually on full pay, and even without a time limit, the manager is told to seek another affiliation.
- *"We'll help you find something else."* Some companies retain guidance counselors, employment agencies or executive recruiters to help their managers get new situations.

■ *The bypass technique.* This harsh method is sometimes employed when no top executive is willing to face and fire the manager. Instead, his or her name starts being omitted from important memoranda; excluded from lists of conferences, etc. Eventually, the message catches on and the manager starts a job-hunt.

No matter what technique is used to break the news, even when the firing is done directly, the art of face-saving has been highly refined. Devices like these are considered almost mandatory:

■ "He has chosen to resign." For example, "Our vice-presdent is leaving because he's always wanted to go into consulting."

■ "It's a matter of health." For example, "J.D.s wife needs a change of climate, and so, reluctantly, we must accept his decision to leave. . . ."

■ "She's gotten an attractive offer." For example, "Tess was offered an opportunity she couldn't refuse. . . ."

One of the reasons for management squeamishness in this area is the identification, often subconscious, of the executive who has decided to fire, with the firee. "There but for the grace . . . etc." However, much of the sensitivity about firing relates to a tradition of dire consequences. These days, executives tend to be professionally more mobile, and with the aid of career counselors and executive recruiters, the executive job market is a fairly lively place.

➲ WHEN BEAUTY BECOMES AN UGLY PROBLEM

The executive, told that a beautiful female employee may represent a work problem, is likely to say, "It's a problem I'd like to have."

He probably is underestimating the magnitude of the complications that may arise. It's said that beauty is skin deep. But that's deep enough to cause trouble. Executives may face these difficulties:

■ *Favoritism.*   Justly or otherwise, they are accused of treating the Keen Kates better than the Plain Janes. And, sometimes, attempting to lean over backwards to avoid the digs, executives have been blamed by the super-beauties of unfair treatment.

■ *Social whirlpool.*   The beautiful employee becomes the center of a situation that may involve one or more ardent admirers, or one or more envious females. And it's even been known to happen that the presence of a latter-day Helen has caused upset even in the executive echelons, when a higher-placed official may be drawn into the emotional maelstrom.

At any rate, if you decide in favor of beauty on the job to the point of recruiting and hiring one or more, it is helpful to know what to do and what not to do to prevent the beauty queen from turning the executive suite into an overheated trouble spot:

1. Avoid the ridiculous.   Don't try to keep admiring colleagues in line by arbitrary rules of the "boys can't talk to girls" variety.

2. Build an invisible barrier.   The executive who knows how to play it cool injects a sense of propriety into the working atmosphere. For example, horseplay or teasing on a man–woman basis is kept within reasonable bounds. Or, if a woman must work overtime or come in on Saturday, she shares the work with another woman.

3. Apply the rule of reason.   Appeal to the common sense of the woman who is too popular for her own good. Make it clear that the office is a public place. Conduct that might be perfectly proper at a summer resort or the beach is not necessarily acceptable at a desk.

■ *Try to prevent explosions.*   Of course, any relationships after hours and off the premises are outside your province. But when a situation is causing difficulties on the job, discreet action is called for.

■ *Talk to the latter-day Helen, and keep the conversation business-like.*   Make it clear that your concern is for the smooth progress of the work and the state of mind of others who may be affected. To emphasize the friendliness in your approach, you may want to use the "people are beginning to notice" line.

4. Final step—transfer or dismissal?   If your low-pressure, friendly efforts fail, if the consequences are becoming increasingly serious, you may want to warn the males in the case that if they cannot cope with the situation, someone may have to be transferred, even discharged.

Remember, under no circumstances, should the executive in such a situation, become either a censor or wet blanket. A cardinal rule must be: Make no move unless there is actual interference in the work of the department.

⊃ HANDLING EMPLOYEE FEUDS

When two of your employees are in conflict, the consequences can involve your entire staff. The case may even resound in the highest echelons of the company.

On the other hand, it's easy to distort differences between two individuals. A mild disagreement, even a quarrel, may represent a temporary state of affairs. People, being human, don't always like or respect one another. They can still work together.

However, when you become aware of friction between employees, there are steps to take to avoid a widespread conflagration:

1. Should you act?   Even a violent quarrel may not signal a call to action on your part. It's not unusual for people under tension to let fly at one another with angry words. When the tension relaxes, the hard feelings may go with it and often the feuding pair will repair the situation themselves and be thankful that no one has interfered, formalizing the trouble and making it more difficult to smooth over.

2. Think your way through.   Once you decide to take the initiative, give some thought to what you are going to do:

■ It's important that you understand the reason for the disagreement, even though you will probably *not* want to judge the merits of the case, and exonerate one individual and find another "guilty as charged." (Of course, the assumption is that this is not a situation where one individual is bullying or victimizing another. In this situation, your intervention may be desirable at an early date, with the full weight of your authority thrown into the approach, if necessary.)

■ Keep in mind that your objective is to terminate the conflict, making it as easy as possible for the individuals to get back to normal without any scars.

3. The procedure you use.   With the preliminary steps taken care of, you want to talk to the feuders either individually or together. Which of these approaches you use depends on the nature of the quarrel and the character of the individuals involved. Then consider:

■ *Timing.*   Delay may incubate the trouble, but overeagerness may be as bad. Again, the nature of the disagreement and the characters of the principals tell you whether they will be easier to handle the day after a flare-up or on the spot.

■ *Breaking the ice.*   This may be the toughest part of the procedure. You may want to take up the problem head on. "We have got a situation here that we'd better deal with before it gets completely out of hand." Or else, directly, "You both must realize how important it is for us to have a friendly atmosphere in the office."

■ *Third party?*   In some cases, the presence of another employee not directly involved in the feud may help. This is especially true when the other person has some information that will help clear the air.

■ *Place for the discussion.*   Your choice of a meeting place may make things easier. An invitation to go out for lunch or a cup of coffee may smooth the way.

4. The agenda.   Once your discussion is under way, there are three points to be covered, preferably in this order:

■ *Areas of agreement.*   If the quarrel hinges on differences of opinion, you may be able to point out that there are points on which the arguers agree.

■ *Areas of difference.*   In many cases, if you clarify the nature of the differences, a basic misunderstanding may be found at the bottom of the hard feelings. In any event, spotlighting the differences will put the situation in better perspective.

■ *Means of ending the disagreement.*   If possible, leave it up to the principals themselves to resolve the situation. If the argument is about some action or decision that must be made, a flip of the coin, a compromise, admission by one of the individuals of wrongdoing, or that the issue was petty, may end the crisis.

5. Strengthening the bonds.   A well-set break in a bone often turns out to be the strongest section. In the same way, a rift between two people, after healing, may find them on better terms than ever before.

Frequently, such improved relationships happen as a natural result of the efforts you have made. But there may be additional ways you can help. Any moves that show your goodwill toward both individuals to assure both that bygones are bygones, and that you have not taken sides or placed blame, will help mend the situation.

➲ HANDLING A COMPLAINT BY ONE EMPLOYEE AGAINST ANOTHER

A subordinate comes to you saying that a fellow employee borrowed a fairly large sum of money and now refuses to pay it back within the agreed time. Would you:

1. Tell him it's not your affair and refer him to a lawyer.
2. Call in the other employee and try to work out an agreement.
3. Hunt up the second worker privately and bawl him out.
4. Try a fourth alternative?

This apparently simple complaint raises several questions you would have to answer to make *any* move:

Are the circumstances described by the employee correct; that is, was a loan actually made?

Was there an understanding about the time within which the debt was to be repaid?

Why does the second employee refuse to return the money?

Once the facts raised by these questions have been verified, it's possible to act. What can be helpful is a *gradualistic* approach. It is not unreasonable for the employee to look to you for help, but it is unreasonable for you to move in with the full weight of your authority. Accordingly, alternative (2) originally suggested, is a wise opening gambit.

And since your authority really doesn't cover collecting debts for your employees, the ultimate move might be the suggestion to the lender to take legal recourse.

⮑ WHEN A KEY EMPLOYEE STARTS THROWING HIS WEIGHT AROUND

Jerry Z. is a highly skilled man, who knows he can get another job for the asking and would be hard to replace. He has been taking advantage of the situation—coming in late, giving you arguments instead of cooperation, and even, you suspect, talking slightingly of you to other employees. Should you:

1. Recommend his discharge?
2. Close your eyes and hope for the best?
3. Appeal to his team spirit?
4. Warn him to get on the ball or he will have to go?
5. Try to find out what's bothering him?
6. Try another alternative?

Two of the alternatives above should be used in sequence. Start with (5); try to find out whether Jerry is being annoyed, frustrated, or troubled by something in the job situation.

Eventually you might have to apply (4) if your efforts to win Jerry's cooperation fail. Not only is his recalcitrance lessening his value to you as an employee, but such undisciplined behavior is likely to affect the morale of your entire work group.

It goes without saying that early in the game it would be advisable to make plans for getting a replacement should this become suddenly necessary.

⮑ HANDLING OFFICE PILFERAGE

Supplies begin disappearing from your storage cabinet. Should you:

1. Change the locks and let it go at that?
2. Call your group together and issue a mild warning?

3. Keep a weather-eye open, snoop around, and try to catch the thief?
4. Try to figure out who the prime suspects are and give them individual, clear warning?
5. Try a fifth alternative?

Definitely avoid (4). Problems of petty pilferage are difficult to handle because in one respect, they're sometimes acceptable. There probably isn't an executive who hasn't taken a handful of clips or a few sheets of graph paper home for the kids. But once you get out of this relatively small and unimportant pilferage area, it's important to act because the problem may mushroom. In this case, start with alternative (2) above. Let your people know that there is a problem. Try to get their cooperation to stop it.

Certainly go in for new locks and any other move that will eliminate temptation. Finally, if caught, it's probably wise to turn the thief and his fate over to Personnel, since pilferage tends to be a company-wide problem and undoubtedly your Personnel Department has a policy on how to handle it. Needless to say, you must have a foolproof case before pointing an accusing finger.

➋ WHEN YOU GET A COMPLAINT ABOUT A NOISY EMPLOYEE

It may be a youngster who whistles—gratingly. Or it may be a would-be drummer who practices on a file cabinet. A variety of noisy habits may draw protests from other employees who feel put-upon. It's a thorny problem because you have to speak to the nuisance without hurting feelings over something that is essentially trivial. These steps can bring both quiet and peace with honor:

1. Don't be trigger-happy.   Be sure that the noisemaker is a nuisance before you act. If the whistling or other habit does not upset anybody, there's no reason to clamp down. You've got a problem only if the habit upsets others.

But if the complaints begin coming in—

2. Blow the whistle.   You can break it to the whistler gently: "Tom, would you mind killing the canary? Not that there's anything wrong with your whistling, but it is out of place here."

The light approach is best because the situation is not serious; but make it clear that you mean business.

3. Try to head off a feud.   It's natural enough for the miscreant to resent the complaint. Usually there is no point in revealing who complained, unless you are sure there will be no ill-feeling. Best bet: make it seem like your own idea.

4. Make it stick.   Once you've served notice on the troublemaker, your job is usually finished. But sometimes it takes repeated warning, even the promise of disciplinary action. This, of course, should be in proportion to the misdemeanor—usually mild.

5. "Gag up" the penalties.   One executive solved this problem by levying a nickel fine at each infraction after the warning. You may adopt this approach or devise some other kind of penalty that puts the situation in proper perspective.

⮕ THE B.O. COMPLAINT CAN BE TNT

"Mr. Jones, I hate to bring up this matter, but that new woman works right next to me, and she has such a bad case of body odor I can hardly stand it."

From time to time, executives get a complaint about the appearance, behavior, or other aspect of an employee from a co-worker. The culprit may be accused of smoking a smelly pipe, or using too much perfume. Whatever lies at the heart of the complaint, you're faced by a delicate problem.

Consider the "bad breath" problem. Contrary to the message of a TV commercial for a well-known mouthwash, the problem can't be handled by leaving the anti-bad-breath product on the offender's desk. Even less realistic is the expectation that the offender will welcome the attempted assist. You're in a highly booby-trapped situation. One wrong move and the whole works will blow up in your face.

The problem is usually intensified by the urgency of the complaint. As in the case mentioned above, the employee says, "I just can't stand it any more." And the fact is, the complainer may come to you under the pressure of strong upset, further complicating your situation. Don't minimize the difficulties of handling this type of situation. Consider these suggestions to help you think through the difficulties:

1. Check the charges.   There's always the chance that the complaining employee is distorting the facts. This may come about either because of hostility toward the other employee, or an exaggerated reaction. For example, Gloria Z- may come to you and say, "I just can't stand the outrageous dress the new woman is wearing. It's okay for a nudist camp but it's out of place in an office like ours—and it bugs me terribly."

On checking, you may find that while the new woman is wearing an unorthodox costume, it's within acceptable limits. Then the problem is to calm down the complainant and gently persuade her that her feelings *are* somewhat exaggerated. For example, you may point out that she's the only one registering the adverse reaction.

2. Figure out the course of least trauma.   Once you verify the situation and feel action must be taken, your immediate objective is to act in a way that will stir up minimum fuss.

Don't underestimate the sensibilities of the individual involved. Even the best-natured person will resent being told of a personal deficiency. It's not easy for anyone to accept the fact that he or she is guilty of unknowingly offending others.

Consider then that you may not be the best person to broach the subject.

3. Let someone speak for you.   Executives in the past have discovered that their most effective approach is through a mature individual from the group. For example, in handling the body odor problem, an executive went to one of the motherly and discreet people in the department and explained the problem to her. She agreed to talk to the offender in an informal heart-to-heart chat.

Another possibility: a good friend of the offender may also be an effective intermediary. In any case, the person who conveys the message must do it without any suspicion that *you* have initiated the action.

4. Avoid going through channels.   One executive *thought* he was taking the easy way out. He got the head of the Personnel Department to agree to talk to an engineer who was the source of trouble, in this case an overly free use of obscene language. The interview seemed to go fine. The technician listened while the Personnel manager delivered a well-reasoned lecture on the undesirability of obscene language in the hearing of the people who couldn't take it.

The executive complimented himself on his perspicacity. But the employee failed to show up the next day, or any other day thereafter. Once Personnel had gotten into the act, he felt a "big thing" had been made of it, and his resentment registered in the form of a quit.

5. When the problem can't be eliminated.   All that has been said up to this point suggests that your subordinate *can* eliminate the complained-of problem. For example, if it's something like body odor, bad breath, and so on it has been assumed that intelligent use of soap, deodorants, mouthwashes, and so on, will successfully erase the fault.

But some difficulties of this category aren't easily dealt with. Where the difficulty can't be eliminated, you may have to think of making changes. One manager, for example, gave an employee of excessively sloppy personal habits a workstation next to an employee with whom he spent a lot of time outside. Or, a person whose appearance upset one employee was given an assignment in which she worked next to an individual with much less sensitivity to this particular attribute.

One aspect of the complainant problem may mean that it will be coming your way more often. We live in changing times with values and attitudes undergoing revolution. For example, language that might only be whispered in privacy is now trumpeted to mixed audiences from stage and screen. Accordingly, you may be getting complaints from traditional-minded older employees who find some aspects of the "new behavior" difficult to take. In a sense, what you'll be asked to do then is to help bridge the generation gap. You may have to work on both the "accused" and the "accuser" to get them to compromise a little.

➲ WHEN A TRUSTED SUBORDINATE IS CAUGHT STEALING

There is a traditional problem that hits hard and deep because it triggers a conflict between heart and mind, loyalties and responsibilities. How do you handle instances of dishonesty among subordinates, perhaps friends or long-time colleagues?

The case of the tempting cashbox.   Office manager Claire Simmons leaves the building one evening, and out in the street, realizes she has forgotten to lock the petty cash drawer. Annoyed with herself, and feeling it would certainly be safe overnight, she nevertheless goes back to the office. Standing over her desk is her assistant Frank Coe, cashbox in hand.

He hears her, turns around, suddenly pale. "I was just getting some change for a five-dollar bill," he stammers. For a moment time is frozen, as Claire Simmons stares at the handful of bills he clutches. "I mean, I was going to borrow carfare to get home. I'll repay it." They both know he is lying. He concludes miserably. "I saw the drawer was unlocked. I'll never do it again, I promise." Simmons looks at the other, torn by emotion. She has already made one decision: "Put it all back. I'll talk to you in the morning." She's at least given herself time to think.

Whatever her preliminary thoughts, she has five choices:

- **Restitution, and letting Frank off with a warning.**

- **Turning him over to the police.**   (Although a possibility, in this case it's the least likely. If it were to be made a police matter, it usually must be decided on the spot. This kind of action, taken in the heat of the moment, is understandable. But even the police would wonder why there had been a delay.)

- **Informing higher management.**   This move has the advantage of sharing the responsibility. Simmons might still want to make a strong argument in favor of forgiving Frank because he has, up to this moment, been an honest well-performing employee. But if a higher echelon feels there is a policy reason for punishing Coe for his depradation, she may have to go along.

■ **Discipline on the spot.**   In most cases, the judgment would be for firing. Ordinary disciplinary measures—enforced time off, for example— doesn't make sense in Coe's case.

■ **Addressing the cause?**   Two other factors occur to Claire Simmons. Why has Frank done this, she wonders? And here she feels partly guilty. By failing to lock the cash drawer, she has put temptation in his way. And then, she has heard a vague rumor, unsubstantiated, that Frank had started a drug habit, "but only in a small way," her informant had said. That suggests the petty theft is only the tip of the iceberg of Frank's troubles.

In this case, Simmons, because of her sympathy for Frank, questions him and he confesses to the stealing because of being hooked on drugs. She says she will forget about the attempted theft if he will next day start efforts to deal with his habit. He agrees.

What would you do in Clair Simmons' circumstances? It would depend on all the factors mentioned, specific to you, the subordinate, and so on, and your evaluation of the choices available.

➲ DOUBLECHECK YOUR JUDGMENTS?

Interpersonal problems are one area in which your attitudes, conscious and unconscious are strongly tested. Decisions made in interpersonal matters require special attention for the following reasons:

1. You yourself may be a principal.   As a possible participant in a situation (e.g., an employee accuses you of unfairness) your professional standing, your ego, and self-interest may come under fire.

2. Your sympathies or biases may be involved.   Among your co-workers will be friends, possible enemies, people you like or dislike. More than usual care may be required to avoid errors when you must judge, discipline, exonerate, or blame.

Three steps can keep you in the clear:

a. Go as far as you can in collecting evidence.   Get more than one opinion on a matter, check statements, verify facts.

b. Watch your biases.   We all have them, and they can be well disguised. Review your thinking and feelings. Watch for judgments that may be suspect. For example, if you are arbitrating an argument between a friend and a subordinate you dislike, put your mind into a "I've-got-to-be-impartial" gear. Such self-monitoring thanks to the complexity of our brain, is within our power.

c. *Be even-handed.* In your dealings with the participants, try for equal and fair treatment, and avoid prejudging. Premature decisions about rights and wrongs will probably lean toward those you favor. Make an effort to stay uncommitted until the situation and it's supporting facts are fully in your grasp.

11. Dealing with Problem People

One of the most exasperating and demanding parts of the executive's job involves dealing with individuals who represent difficulties in working relationships—a recalcitrant employee, a careless one, an apparently well-intentioned, but destructive individual who may wreck harmony in a group.

Dealing with problem people is best viewed as a special kind of human relations area. The individuals are usually unique problems, and handling them requires policies and practices specific to this area. Accordingly, you will find two elements in the section that follows:

- A discussion of what makes an employee a "problem," since one of the difficulties may be the failure to understand *when* an employee is or isn't a problem.
- Specific suggestions on dealing with "problem people."

➡ WHEN IS A "PROBLEM EMPLOYEE" A PROBLEM?

Problem employee is a traditional term in management literature. Early in the development of human relations awareness in business, executives were alerted to "different," or "nonconforming" individuals, who sometimes represented a work difficulty. But fully as many destructive beliefs began to flourish around "problem employees" as did helpful practices for dealing with them. Some typical myths:

- An individual who doesn't conform to group standards—in behavior, attitude, dress—is a problem, and must be dealt with summarily.
- A nonconforming individual automatically threatens group unity and teamwork.

Both of these ideas are usually false. Individuals who are "different," no matter how much the deviation from group norms, is not a problem *unless:*

- They actually interfere with the progress of the work.
- They interfere with fellow employees in their work activities.
- They damage the image, reputation, or services of the company.

If none of these consequences apply, the individual is *not* a problem employee, regardless of appearance, or what his or her values or behavior.

And a final point: as far as the nonconformer threatening group unity is concerned, most groups are surprisingly accepting of nonconforming individuals. Workers have a live-and-let-live tradition. They know people are there to earn a living, which is seen as a right.

Usually, the executive is a key to acceptance. Groups generally follow their leaders. If they treat the nonconformist the same as other contributing members, the group will do likewise.

But dealing with problem employees can be subtle and complicated. The pages ahead offer suggestions.

➲ INCOMPATABILITY—OR A PROBLEM MANAGER?

It's the opinion of some experts that a problem employee may hide a problem boss. The implication that a manager may have a personality trait that causes an employee to become a problem is possible, but relatively rare.

More common—and a factor that managers should consider in this psychological and behavioral area—is that boss and employee, like other paired humans, may have personalities that clash. For example, a strongly authoritarian boss may make a problem employee of one who is a libertarian and fares best under a less strict hand. A free-rein boss may make life difficult for a dependent, wants-to-be-told subordinate. In either case, unacceptable behavior may result.

In analyzing the case of a possible problem subordinate, add "incompatability"—either with you, or some condition of employment—as a possible diagnosis.

➲ MAJOR PITFALL TO AVOID

Don't play psychiatrist. That tendency occasionally trips up an executive and the consequences can be catastrophic. There are several reasons to avoid donning the therapist's mantle:

- You haven't got the time.
- You almost certainly lack the skill—unless you've been trained.
- You can get trapped by your own emotional entanglements in the problem. This can make you the most regretful person standing in line at the psychiatrist's door.
- You don't have to play psychiatrist to provide effective help to your people, and solve the company's problem at the same time. Approaches detailed in the pages ahead, show you how.

⮕ SHOULD YOU PLAY PARENT?

It's natural that your subordinates should see you as a person of power, possibly a parent image. As a result, some of your people, particularly those who are dependent, may look to you for assistance with their personal problems. Some requests will be unjustified and embarrassing. On the other hand, you often *can* help. The answer seems to lie in *how* the help is given. These pointers can give you the benefits, avoid snap-backs:

1. Don't mistake your role.   Before you offer help, think through your relations to your employee. If you see yourself as the benign, "I'll-take-care-of-everything" parent, you are doing harm before your help has even begun. Being overprotective does violence to the other person's dignity. He or she is not a child, no matter what the trouble. The employee is an adult in need of adult advice.

Putting yourself in the parental role is wrong, because it exaggerates the nature of what you are planning to do. You're going to offer help because of your unique position. You're not involved in the situation, and can see things about it that your employee may not be able to see. Being on the outside you can be objective, bring your experience to bear.

2. Don't carry the burden.   Once you decide to help, act in such a way that the problem remains the employee's. Unlike a doctor or a lawyer, you will not be giving the kind of help that requires employees to put themselves in your hands. On the contrary, the advice you give will be strictly limited, requiring that the employee continue to *think through the problem.*

3. Don't recommend only one expert.   In some cases, you may suggest that the employee get professional help—it may be as simple as saying, "Go to an eye doctor." The employee asks, "Whom do you recommend?" It is important that you recommend a *number of sources.* Or that you suggest a call to your company doctor for a list of names. Or you may suggest contact with an organization—such as a local chapter of the American Medical Association—that can provide a list.

The point is that you want the *employee* to make the choice of whom to consult. If you give only one name, in effect you have chosen the consultant, and your prestige, rightly or wrongly, is linked to the professional's success or failure. It's a chance that you don't have to take—and shouldn't.

4. Describe alternatives.   Maybe you've pointed out that a move to another location will solve a commuting problem.

Being objective, having a clear view of the situation, you can suggest alternatives that were overlooked. The subordinate makes the decision, although you help with the process.

Shown the alternatives, employees start ruling out alternatives until left with the best one. You broaden their horizons when you suggest options, help the other reach a solution based on combining the best features of several alternatives.

5. Watch out for escalation.   For example, with your help, a bank has been selected as a possible solution to a man's financial troubles. He takes your advice and discusses with a bank officer how to get a loan to consolidate his debts. It works. Then he comes to you one day and says. "You were so helpful on that loan problem, could I ask you another question?"

You say, "What?"

He says, "Well, my brother has a problem. . . ."

He is reflecting a tendency that people have, which is to become more and more dependent. And without knowing it, you may experience an equal pull in the direction of giving additional help. *Don't.* Impose reasonable limitations on the help you offer.

5. Don't judge moral issues.   Sometimes the problems dumped into your lap involve the shady side of human conduct: gambling, drink, immorality, even infractions of the law. But you're not going to help by being horrified.

Accept such information as matter-of-factly as possible. Above all, make sure you are sympathetic and friendly—so that the individual does not feel his or her personal position is even more difficult because you know. Then suggest professional help—a lawyer, psychologist, minister.

6. Don't betray a confidence.   Only the most unusual circumstances could ever justify repeating the information the employee has imparted.

The employee has come to you in good faith, seeking you out as a friend and as a leader capable of providing help. It would be a breach of faith for you to reveal to a third party anything that you've learned. And the loss of prestige you would suffer from such an error could be immediate and devastating.

◑ WHEN YOU HATE THEIR GUTS

An executive faces a difficult situation. His subordinate is quite capable, but for one reason or another the executive dislikes him. The hazards of the situation, both in terms of the individual's performance and even in staff morale, are obvious.

However, once the problem is identified, resolve and self-candor makes several steps possible:

1. Spot the bug.   Try to understand what it is about the employee that's bugging you. You may find that you've judged a person unfairly. One manager, for example, discovered, "One of the women in my group wore a constant smirk and I always felt there was some sly or sneaky feeling she had against me. Thinking about her, it became clear that what I had construed as a sly expression was really a grimace that simply revealed nervousness and tension."

Executives have discovered their hostility or dislike directed at an innocent victim because the person reminded them, of someone else. Self-understanding can relieve this type of illogical feeling.

2. Do not broadcast your attitudes.   Try to cover up negative feelings toward a subordinate. While getting a load off your chest may bring relief, it may cause your people to wonder what you say about *them*. In addition, an employee may become marked and lose standing in the group, if the boss's low opinion is known.

3. Lean over backwards to be fair.   Managers have to make a special effort to administer equal treatment. They should establish uniform standards, either publicly or in their own minds, that apply to discipline, assignments, raises, and so on.

Once these standards are established, you have double protection. You can be more certain that everybody's getting a fair shake. And, if your judgments are questioned, you can spell out the thinking behind a decision.

4. Agree to disagree?   Is the source of the trouble a conflict of viewpoints? People with widely differing ideas about life—very liberal and very conservative, say, or very gregarious and very quiet—can get along with one another by "agreeing to disagree."

In essence, they decide not to challenge each other's differences, to concentrate, instead, on cooperating in areas where they agree. This may work when feelings between you and your subordinate are mutually known, and accepted.

5. When you can't make peace, make distance.   What about a transfer for a disaffected subordinate? This may be a good solution, if it is in the interest of the company, and those involved. A special project or job where you and the other person do not naturally come into contact may ease matters. And in some cases, time may improve the situation.

➜ **THE PESSIMIST**

Individuals who are excessively pessimistic have it tough. Give them an assignment that is a little different, set up a goal for them to shoot for—and they are sure they'll miss the mark. Of course, pessimism is a problem because it undercuts self-confidence and performance. Sometimes, pessimists even succeed in wet-blanketing others on your staff.

Dealing with them is a matter of probing with questions like these:

1. Is the condition curable?   Experience with overly-tough assignments may be a handicap. Lack of your personal interest can be discouraging. Where factors like these add up to a pessimist, you can do a lot to ease the mental load.

For example, you often praise for a mighty effort, or you make it a point to recognize progress. But you may find an employee who hangs on to his pessimism regardless of what you do. In such cases:

2. Can you keep it from spreading?   If you're introducing important changes, don't assign the pessimist to lead off. *Pessimism is infectious,* and might dampen the entire proceedings.

3. Can you improve the self-image?   One executive suggests this shot-in-the-arm: "I know you're doubtful about how this is going to work out, Tom, but then don't you always do about twice as well as you expect?" Encouragement has been known to work wonders.

Happily, optimism is infectious, too.

➲ THE OVEROPTIMISTIC SUBORDINATE

Optimism is usually a virtue—except when it is so excessive it blinds the individual to the facts or reality of a situation. For some people, optimism is an escape hatch from failure. Errors are shurgged off, not mended. "Things could be worse," the optimist points out.

Behind overoptimism may be a considerable degree of irresponsibility and immaturity. In attempting to modify this viewpoint, plan a continuing campaign:

1. Start by putting solid ground underfoot. Stress the importance of each assignment at the outset—plus the necessity for success.
2. Tighten up on the reins. Ask for reports on progress. And introduce intermediate deadlines.
3. Bring other members of your group into the act. When the other's overly-rosy expectations interferes with their work, stand back; let colleagues set him or her straight.
4. Show that you, too, can be optimistic: "Okay, let's look at the bright side—by making sure there is a bright side, next time." And then go on to suggestions that will assure success.

➲ DEALING WITH THE ALSO-RANS

For every promotion you make, there may be one or two people who have been left standing by the roadside. For every person who merits praise for outstanding performance, there are those who may have tried and failed. These people who never quite make it, these failures in the competitive race that marks the typical work scene, deserve attention because they can be helped to succeed.

Of course, some people may lack the innate ability or skill to perform at outstanding levels. But before you conclude that personal deficiencies explain their failure, look into these factors:

1. Did you motivate the employee sufficiently?   Almost everybody would like to be promoted—but not everybody is willing to work for it.

Many people don't know what possibilities of self-betterment exist in the company. If your people are to improve, they have to see what specific goals are within their reach. Don't assume that the average employee knows the line of promotion. Tell him or her.

2. Did you define clearly the standards you use in deciding on promotion?   In addition to knowing what the next higher job is, the employee must understand what qualifications are needed.

This factor is important, both in preparing people for possible promotion, and in explaining to the also-rans why they didn't get the job. If you've never explained the standards, disappointment at not making the grade can turn into anger at you, for insufficient guidance.

3. Have you suggested study possibilities that would qualify employees for advancement?   A highly skilled subordinate may move into line for promotion simply by spending a few evenings a week at a vocational school. Your people may look to you as the one with the experience and judgment to make such recommendations.

4. Have you taken steps to give your people additional training on the job?   A Grade B mechanic might need just a half-hour's instruction a week from an old-timer, over a period of several months, to qualify for promotion to Grade A mechanic.

➲ HANDLING THE "JOHN ALDEN SYNDROME"

You may have an employee like the historical John Alden, who hesitates to speak up on his own behalf.

Instead he'll tell you, "Bill Jones thinks thus and so, . . . or Tom Blakely says we ought to . . . ." His failure to advance his own views or interests can cost you information, ideas, and a valuable point of view. In addition, it creates a communications barrier between him and others.

To get the "John Aldens" of either sex to speak for themselves:

1. Explain your need for opinions.   "It's important for me to get everyone's views, John. That's the only way I can get a complete picture."

2. Call for action.   Frequently, a "John Alden" holds back because he or she is not self-confident. A good antidote is to start by asking questions to which the person is likely to know the answer. Note relative strengths and weaknesses in these areas:

- *Facts*. Giving information about the individual's work usually finds him or her on firmest ground.
- *Opinions*. Making comments about other people's ideas for work situations is next easiest.
- *Ideas*. Here's where this type of person needs most encouragement. Demonstrate that you like people who voice their views—gripes or otherwise; that you applaud suggestions, even if they don't pan out.

➔ THE LONE WOLF

The loner may be a productive employee. Or might be one you are just about ready to fire.

Either way, remedial steps might save a potentially good employee, or improve present performance. Many different factors can turn an employee into a lone wolf. To start the de-isolating process, answer these questions:

1. Is the loner tendency creating a problem?   The answer may be *no*. If so, no action is called for. Or it may be *yes*: there is insufficient cooperating with co-workers, or lack of communication with you. If this latter is the case, you must probe further.

2. What's the personal history?   Just check your memory; perhaps a comparatively recent development, such as difficulties at home, problems in personal life, cause a craving for solitude. In some instances, a special competence may mean being left alone because there was no doubt about the job getting done. However, instead of building self-reliance, this move may have further built up the need for a protective shell.

At any rate, further your understanding of the situation by trying to pin down the reason for the behavior.

3. Can assignments minimize the tendency?   If in your opinion, the lone wolf, because of personality makeup, really prefers isolation, your most effective move may be to give assignments which call for operating independently. For example, it can be an advantage to you if a subordinate with this preference took on assignments at remote places, after hours, and so on. But don't permit complete separation from the group.

4. Can a low-pressure program of interpersonal contacts improve the situation?   You may decide that your problem child is a shy sheep in lone wolf's clothing. Accordingly, despite a desire to mix with the others, it is difficult to do. You can help by establishing a bridge to others on your staff; or in arranging at first, minimum contacts with some of your friendly nonaggressive people, then building the contacts when you see you are getting good results.

5. Should you consider a transfer?   It's seldom that even the most extreme representative of this type is fired. But where the loner's tendencies are a definite handicap to job achievement and all your efforts are in vain, you may be able to do both yourself and another executive a good turn by arranging a transfer to department, where the behavior will not represent a handicap.

➲ THE SNOOPER

This individual goes to ridiculous lengths to get into the act. Anytime something is going on, the snooper must try to enter into it—whether advisable or not. There may be a neurotic need for recognition, and perhaps is more sinned against than sinning.

Consider:

1. What is the incentive?   *Ambition?* Does the employee barge in to show how much he or she knows? Here your problem is to learn why this particular tack is taken. Has there been a denial of opportunities open to the rest of the group? A denial to join in group decision making as much as the rest? *Exclusion?* Location of the workplace may be at fault. Or it may be the nature of the work. An assignment may have to be finished later than the rest. Does this put the employee out in the cold? Relocating may be the answer.

If ostracism is a "personal" matter, you have a tougher nut to crack. But whatever the cause, you'll want to make certain that the group isn't withholding information or work that prevents the problem child from doing a satisfactory job.

2. Does he or she crave recognition?   In many cases this person needs a feeling of importance—at least of being as important as other people around. The more you can do to build self-esteem, the more you make this person feel a respected member of the work group, the more you can ease the compulsion to barge in. Accordingly, recognize performance; approve of accomplishments. Praise outstanding achievements.

➔ THE IRRESPONSIBLE EMPLOYEE

Consider the case of Charlie T. He's a youngster, new to the world of work. (But he might be an older, immature person.) Because of his attitude, a situation that seems obvious to you may be obscure to him. He may become involved in delicate matters, without realizing the consequences.

The typical job, with requirements for promptness, conformity with working rules and policies, obedience to instructions, may seem unnecessarily confining and "an establishment approach" that demands to be flouted. If the problem of his irresponsibility is not too extreme:

1. Give Charlie the big picture.   As clearly as possible, preferably in the early days of induction, acquaint him with the history, traditions, objectives of the company, the department, his job.

The older, mature worker understands the general pattern of his job life. But the youngster often has no experience on which to draw. Perhaps curiosity may bridge the gap. At any rate, encourage questions about company operation, product, marketing, and so on.

2. Go out of your way to give the reason why.   That goes for whatever comes up: work, instructions, pay rates, inspection procedures, schedules, and so on. Keep your explanations clear and non-technical. Don't hesitate to repeat them at a later date, if you are not sure he has grasped the point. Assign an experienced dependable worker as an official or unofficial "buddy." A friendly relationship with a fellow employee can help eliminate a certain amount of the immature employee's recalcitrance, and a well-informed sidekick can answer the many small questions that may arise. The individual can pick up a good deal from such a buddy in terms of facts and attitude.

Use care in selecting the partner. He should have understanding and tolerance.

3. Treat him as an adult.   Particularly in the presence of others, don't talk down, show any impatience you may feel. They may take their cue from you and begin making life unbearable for the individual. Even when you deal with him in private, don't let your interest in his life appear patronizing.

4. Assign responsibilities and hold him to them.   Do this gradually. Don't overburden him with responsibility. He may seem to be eager to take on big assignments; but in part the explanation may be his intention not to take them too seriously.

Test him out step by step. Check up regularly on the assignments that you give him. See that he follows instructions closely.

5. Keep his achievements and goals constantly before him.   This individual is likely to be easily discouraged by failures. Emphasize what he has accomplished, and show him how he can turn his abilities to further self-improvement or advancement.

6. Utilize his energy.   Suiting the challenge to his capacities is an important aspect of developing this individual. It can be particularly effective to use his energy capabilities for the benefit of the group as a whole. Success here can make him both a hero and a permanent member of the group. Keep him occupied. Help him to continue to learn. Use his curiosity and maintain his interest by a variety of assignments. This will also help him develop a broader understanding of job responsibilities as a whole.

Maturity may be a bit slow coming to Charlie T. and you may be able to help him grow up.

➜ THE SUBORDINATE WHO IS NEVER WRONG

Carol S. says it, often: "Of course I admit when I'm wrong—but I'm never wrong."

Even if she doesn't say it, that's her feeling. Generally her braggadocio is a cover-up because she has a hard time holding on to her self-confidence. She may have been overcriticized or overpraised in childhood.

Consider these steps in your general dealings with Carol:

1. Let her know it's no crime to make mistakes.
2. Avoid unnecessary criticism.
3. When criticism is in order, don't criticize *her* but the *method* she used.
4. Build self-respect by appropriate praise when she does an oustanding job; then she will have less need for a phony defensive shield.

➜ THE OVERLY DEPENDENT INDIVIDUAL

The strange fact about George B. is that he is a capable individual, and clings not because he needs help, but because he needs reassurance.

It takes time to get an unsure or overly cautious employee like George to stand on his own feet. But if you want him off yours:

1. Go light on the criticism.   It isn't so much that you have to pull your punches. It's just that a small amount will have a strong impact. Usually he overreacts, magnifies a correction into a major dressing down.

2. Watch for signs of trouble.   If he does get into a tight spot that he can't handle, be ready to assist as soon as possible. This doesn't necessarily mean that you take over. When he gets into deep water, the best help you may give him is to help him figure his own way out.

3. Keep feeding the ball back.   When he comes to you for help prematurely, without trying to cope on his own, help him see that he does have the answer: "How do you think we should handle it?"

4. Can you consult George?   To reinforce his own self-confidence, let him participate, where appropriate, in discussions of problems and so on, and from time to time consult *him* on decisions *you* have to make when you can use his help.

➲ WHEN SHE'S TOO POPULAR

Standouts are great in the living room, but hell on the work scene. Occasionally, the executive is confronted by the problem of dealing with an overly popular subordinate like Melanie E. What with phone calls, visits by friends from other departments, she's at the center of a constant social merry-go-round. The usual result is that performance goes down as her disturbance rating goes up. To exercise some reasonable control:

1. Check your own performance first.   If you are extending special privileges—such as long or excessive number of personal calls, you may have to change the signals and make Melanie live up to the same rules as others do.

2. Avoid a frontal attack.   Bawling her out for misplaced social activity might leave you open to the charge that you are "butting into my personal affairs."

3. Focus on her job performance.   It is appropriate for you to call the turn if her activities affect the work. These points apply:

- Disturbance with the work of others. Even if they don't complain, your observation is enough to bring action—and warning.
- Slapdash work, to make up for lost time. This gives you an opening to discuss the quality her work and the need to perform up to standard.
- Low-quantity level. Be specific in discussing her below-standard performance. Refer to a recent job in which she ran short of expected goals.

➲ **THE CARELESS EMPLOYEE**

"The employee was careless."

The statement is often used to explain an error or accident on the work scene. But seasoned executives know the "carelessness" designation is a coverup, rather than a diagnosis.

The trouble with attributing mistakes or mishaps to carelessness is that it automatically puts the problem out of bounds.

It is practically impossible to cope with carelessness—as such.

Experts of the Institute of Scrap Iron & Steel have analyzed "carelessness." They found it to be a catchall term, covering many forms of failures. Through their analysis, they revealed that many of the specific faults that hide behind the carelessness designation *can be* dealt with. Here is the list of possible employee faults disguised by the term "carelessness":

( ) Didn't follow instructions.
( ) Didn't follow rules and regulations.
( ) Didn't use safe work methods.
( ) Didn't follow standard procedures.
( ) Didn't pay attention to what he was doing.
( ) Didn't foresee an action or movement.
( ) Didn't wear personal protection equipment.
( ) Didn't think ahead and plan his actions.
( ) Didn't consider the consequences of his own actions or the action of a machine or equipment.
( ) Didn't know his own physical capabilities or limitations.
( ) Didn't have the physical fitness necessary for the work.
( ) Didn't have the skills necessary for the work.
( ) Didn't know the limits of strength of materials.
( ) Didn't know the properties or actions of chemicals.
( ) Didn't use tools or equipment properly.
( ) Didn't anticipate safety or health requirements.
( ) Didn't use good sense.
( ) Didn't look.
( ) Didn't think.
( ) Didn't have a good safety attitude.
( ) Didn't care about the consequences.
( ) Other: _____

The value of the list is that, unlike "carelessness," most of the items suggest remedies. For example, the man who "doesn't follow instructions" can be asked *why* he didn't. Weren't they clear? Any development interfere with following the original orders? Could he have prevented the failure by informing you of unexpected changes? And so on.

↪ THE ALCOHOLIC

Of all the problem employees you may be called on to deal with, an alcoholic will be most difficult. According to Dr. J. J. Walsh, Medical Director of Union Carbide, "Some of our best employees are alcoholics." And it's heartbreaking for the executive to see individuals of outstanding ability victimized by an addiction that destroys them both as functioning employees and as human beings.

One of the reasons that makes alcoholism so difficult to deal with is that two things tend to hide the problem:

- Alcoholics tend to become extremely ingenious in covering up.
- Social drinking is an accepted aspect of our society, and it isn't easy to make a clear separation between the social drinker and the one who is a victim of the bottle.

When you are faced by a suspected case of alcoholism, it is the height of wisdom to think through your actions, if any. To clarify some of the aspects of the problem, consider the following information and insights developed by medical and psychological experts.

A booklet, *The Alcoholic Employee,* put out by Alcoholics Anonymous, states that there is general agreement on these basic facts:

- There is a distinction between the heavy drinker and the alcoholic. While the former may overindulge on occasion, he or she does not let alcohol disturb the pattern of his living or obscure his objectives.

- Once a person crosses the invisible border line between social drinking and compulsive drinking, he or she is never going to be able to drink normally again. A single drink may be enough to start the alcoholic on the merry-go-round. Alcoholism may be arrested, but it can never be cured.

- The only way for an alcoholic to cope successfully with this unique problem is to abstain completely from even the smallest quantity of alcohol in any form.

Alcoholism, a pamphlet issued by the U. S. Department of Health, Education, and Welfare, suggests indications of alcoholism:

One of the more obvious early signs of a predisposition to alcoholism is that the individual drinks more than is customary among his associates and makes excuses to drink more often. This is an indication that he is developing an insistent need—or a psychological dependence—on alcohol to help him escape from unpleasant worries or tensions.

As the condition progresses, he begins to experience 'blackouts.' He does not 'pass out' or become unconscious, but the morning after a drinking bout he cannot remember what happened after a certain point. If this happens repeatedly or after taking only a moderate amount of alcohol, it is a strong indication of developing alcoholism.

As his desire for alcohol becomes stronger, the alcoholic gulps, rather than drinks, his beverage. He senses that his drinking is getting out of hand and he starts drinking surreptitiously so that others will not know how much he is consuming.

Finally, he loses control of his drinking. After one drink, he feels a physical demand so strong that he cannot stop short of intoxication. Suffering from remorse, but not wanting to show it, he strikes out unreasonably at others. As he realizes that he is losing the respect of his associates and hurting his loved ones, he tries to stop or drink moderately, but he can't. He becomes filled with discouragement and self-pity and tries to 'drown his troubles' in more liquor. But his drinking has passed beyond the point where he can use it as a way of coping with his problems, and he is faced with the disease of alcoholism.

To act constructively when dealing with an alcoholic employee consider these guidelines:

1. Don't act until there is work interference.   While this point applies to problem employees in general, it has particular cogency in relation to a heavy drinker.

2. Develop a realistic view if an off-the-job drinking problem exists. Occasionally, an executive is contacted by a spouse or other member of an employee's family with the information that drinking is a problem at home. As much as you might like to help, it is unwise to do so in your professional capacity. Any moves you make could justifiably bring the accusation from the employee that you are meddling in personal matters. This point must be made clear to the relative, even while you are conveying your interest and sympathy.

3. Avoid moral judgments.   The least effective and most damaging action a superior may take is to criticize an employee's drinking. The perfectly common-sense statement, "You have just got to stop drinking. You're ruining your health and your career," will be completely useless. This point is clarified when you:

4. Understand the psychology of the alcoholic.   There's no point in telling alcoholics they are ruining themselves, for two reasons. One is that they won't believe you, no matter what the circumstances are. The other, deeper reason, is that often the drinking is for precisely that reason. It's *because* drinking is in some cases a form of slow suicide that the individual is an alcoholic. He or she seeks self-obliteration in a limited way, just as the suicide seeks the ultimate permanent form.

Some authorities feel that alcoholism is physiological, that is in its later stages the body develops a need for alcohol that must be satisfied in the same way a starving man must have food. This concept explains why the strongest arguments may become meaningless to the alcoholic. There isn't enough will-power to stop by wanting to.

5. Make your approach nonthreatening.   The most effective thing you can do when you approach the subject with the individual is to do so on a nonaccusatory basis. You may not be able to end the drinking. You *may* be able to call for some action that may help. If you can, make a specific suggestion. You may want to suggest a conference with the company doctor or psychiatrist, or other agency that you know about.

The Alcoholics Anonymous groups have a good record of rehabilitation. But perhaps the employee will refuse to accept your recommendation to seek help from any source that is so easily identified, since he or she may not accept the "alcoholic label." For this reason, the visit to a doctor or psychologist may be a more practical suggestion from you.

Nevertheless, it's helpful to know that most large communities have alcoholism information centers operated by volunteers affiliated with the National Council on Alcoholism. These centers provide information about the problem, have resources for limited support or counseling, and can make referrals to doctors, psychologists, clergyman, family agencies, and hospitals in the community.

Most large companies have sufficient experience with the problem of alcoholism to have both a policy and a tested procedure for dealing with the problem. It would be wise for you to check with your superior or appropriate person in Personnel to get their recommendations in dealing with this type of problem individual.

⮑ EMOTIONAL FIRST AID

It can be an upsetting experience: one of your subordinates displays emotional disturbance. It may either be a fit of crying, a prolonged or intense display of anger, a mood verging on depression.

The following approach is based on suggestions made by the professional staff of BFS Psychologist Associates of New York City.

Of course, you don't want to play amateur psychologist. If behavior displayed is extreme, what's called for is immediate medical assistance. However, if the emotional storm is within normal limits—such as reasonably justifiable anger or tears, there are steps that you can take to help matters. What you do will vary, depending on the nature of the problem.

1. In case of crying or other similar behavior:

a. Show your serious concern to the individual. Make clear your desire to help.
b. Take him or her to a private place, your office for example, as unobtrusively as possible.
c. Give the employee a moment or two to compose themselves. Avoid exerting pressure, to make it clear that you're not annoyed by the situation.
d. Ask, "What's wrong?" If the employee doesn't wish to respond, however, don't press the point.
e. Ask, "How can I help?"
f. When the tears have subsided, give the employee the choice of returning to work or leaving early, if it's in the afternoon.
g. If the employee explains what's wrong, listen; offer sympathy. If it's a complicated or highly personal matter, don't prescribe. You may want to suggest that he or she seek professional guidance.

2. For an outburst of anger:

a. Face the individual firmly and assert your authority.
b. Show a strong mien. Be firm without showing anger. Make clear your intention to have things cool down before any action is taken.
c. Isolate the individual by taking him or her off to a corner or separate room.
d. If you don't know, ask the reason for the upset.
e. Listen to the person's complaint. Generally this will help calm him or her down.
f. Be prepared to deal with shame or sheepishness. Usually, there's a revulsion of feeling in which the individual is sorry for the display of temper. Alleviate this feeling by assuring him or her that it's "just one of those things."
g. If the individual needs counseling or guidance, suggest that he or she see a professional person. Preferably, don't use the phrase, "See a psychiatrist," or anything similar. This suggests that you've made a diagnosis of abnormal behavior, which may be resented.

3. In case of despondency:

a. Approach the individual and show your concern.
b. Isolate the individual.
c. Ask for the reason for his feelings. If this confidence is refused, don't press the point.
d. Show your friendliness and desire to help.

e. If the individual begins to cry, don't interfere. Weeping in this case might be a desirable alleviant.

f. If the upset suggest serious causes, recommend that the individual seek professional help or guidance. If your company has a medical department, leave it up to the nurse or doctor to refer the employee to proper channels.

In all cases where there may be some kind of reaction from other people, talk to them to make sure that they keep their curiosity under wraps. As far as others are concerned, try to smooth over the situation as quickly as possible to help bring things back to normal.

◑ TYPICAL CASES

One thing about problem employees: You can usually deal with them, because if an individual is too badly off, he or she wouldn't be your responsibility. Workers who become seriously depressed, for example, or develops a bad drinking habit, probably can't "hold a job," without professional attention.

Notice that the recommendations made for dealing with the previous cases take two directions:

■ **Symptom treatment.**   In the average case, it is desirable to understand what drives your subordinate's problem behavior. However, this may be too elusive to identify, and so, you concentrate on minimizing the symptoms. For example, you tell a busybody who spends considerable time on his or her preoccupation, "Pat, please stop playing detective on what's going on between Jim and Helen. That's their personal concern, and you're making them both uncomfortable."

■ **Addressing the cause.**   In some cases you can figure out the reasons for a person's aberrant behavior. Even when the roots are deep in the psyche, you may be able to make offsetting moves without playing professional. For example, if your subordinate is a constant self-belittler, because of insecurity and lack of self-confidence, you can try to increase self-esteem by praising satisfactory performance. This may not transform the individual, but it can ease some of the inner tension and brighten outlook.

Keep these two alternatives in mind when planning your moves. Your choice is a major factor in effectiveness. Note: usually you try to treat symptoms, turn to causes as a final effort.

◑ DEALING WITH A PROBLEM BOSS

In dealing with problem employees, you have two advantages. First there are a broad range of initiatives you may take, in your authoritative managerial role. Second, your authority usually will cover the remedies you want to apply.

But when your boss—because of personality, attitude, or incompatible ways of managing—is the problem employee, what you can do and what you can't, take you into another area of methods and choices.

◑ WHAT'S THE PROBLEM?

There are as many varieties of problem bosses as there are rank-and-file employees. One executive, vice president of Personnel for a pharmaceutical company says, "Problem bosses? I'd say the number exactly matches the number of bosses."

You may not be as cynical. Many executives find their boss relations rewarding, even inspirational. One's superior is most valuable when he or she is a resource and career expediter. The working life becomes immeasurably more satisfying when you establish good relations upward. Since the relationship is one-to-one, your situation is specific, and largely depends on the kind of boss you have. The five problem bosses discussed below may increase your insights and ability to cope with a superior who may be somewhat less than perfect.

◑ THE PROBLEM BOSS: FIVE CASES

The examples selected suggest the range of difficulties that confront the manager for whom a difficult boss threatens the working relationship. The recommendations for action illustrate the limits of possible action.

The intimidater.   "I've only been in my job for three months," Anne Varney says, "and I'm on my boss's hit list. She once chewed me out for putting an oversized clip on a sheaf of papers. And I'm a manager, not a volunteer clerk."

Understanding the reason for a boss's punishing behavior may not make things easier for the victim. However, there are helpful questions people in Anne Varney's position may examine:

What's the beef?   "What did I do wrong?" may be a misdirected question. You may be a scapegoat, not a cause. You can be pretty sure the paperclip wasn't the reason for the explosion. Try anything from indigestion to serious home matters for size. Or, there may be a work difficulty, but it's probably removed in time and place.

Can others explain?   Varney is a relative newcomer. Her colleagues undoubtedly are familiar with their manager's outbursts. Talk to other subordinates of your boss, get their experience and opinions of the boss as work associate.

May you be at fault?   If other explanations are lacking, check your own role. In Varney's situation, the boss may feel she is not making the grade, is not satisfying expectations. This kind of reason may be easy to verify. Reviewing recent work crises may turn up a reason for the boss's discontent. If not, initiating a talk in which the boss gives feedback on progress should confirm or rule out the possibility.

Out from under?   If the boss can be made to level, the truth will out. Does the boss hold out hope, and reassurance? Then perhaps you have been overly impatient. But if the prospects are presented in a pessimistic way, perhaps a transfer to another department is possible. Or, if you feel you are not getting fair treatment, consider taking the matter to a higher-level executive.

The boss with feet of clay.   No one likes feet of clay—that is, ineptness, ineffectiveness—in a person of authority. Most hope for superior qualities—vision, perceptiveness, wisdom, the ability to get things done.
   If you think you're losing out because of a superior's inability:

Check it out.   Pin down your reasons. Are they convincing? Can you cross-check with others in the department?

Fantasy at work?   Perhaps you are overidentifying with your boss. Your expectations may be unrealistic. The "perfect parent" syndrome sometimes persists into adulthood. We fantasize about an authority figure who is a combination of Jove and Solomon, all powerful and all wise. Real life provides few from such a mold.

Do the boss's feet test over 50 percent clay?   So what? As a subordinate you have several choices, only one realistic:

- Try to straighten the boss out? Forget it. His or her spouse, friends, colleagues, and psychiatrist probably have been trying for years.
- Blow the whistle? Take up the boss's failings with a higher-echelon executive? They probably know the shortcomings as well as you do. But they also may find virtues and abilities that you may not see. A doubtful move.
- Figure out where your best interest lies? Yes. Two directions to look. Ask, "How can I optimize my relations with the boss?" (You will find some help on this, page 244, under the heading, "How to Handle Your Boss.") Then, "How can I advance my status so as to move ahead to a more advantageous situation?"

The boss plays favorites—and you're not one.   Favoritism, as managers and the good Lord knows, cuts two ways. If it's on your side, try to use it constructively to further your goals. But if you are not among the anointed your job satisfaction and future may be dimmed. In some situations the unfavored are locked in, and at best they must play a waiting game. But if you want to act, here are some suggestions:

Investigate. Assess the pattern of favoritism. Is just one person the beneficiary? Perhaps this represents the boss's mentorship, focused on a particularly able or promising employee. This relationship is less a threat since it usually represents an effort to build a departmental asset.

But if the partiality is based on a bias, of whatever nature, from the old school tie to attractive members of opposite sex, then you may want to probe further by asking the following questions:

What losses? If you can't come up with any, you may want to let well enough alone.

Is there unfairness? For example, do you get the lemon assignments, or lose out on raises freely given to the "in" group?

Should you bring up the matter of unequal treatment? Avoid the murky, treacherous area of the boss's bias. Make it a discussion of a work problem. Stick to the specific instance. If indeed wrong has been done, marshal the facts and figures. Be matter-of-fact, avoid injecting anger, reproach, or other emotional element in your talk that makes satisfaction less likely.

Can you get the boss on your side? In some instances, a boss's favor goes to those in the department who want to get ahead and have a potential for advancement. If you feel you have both these attributes, perhaps letting the boss in on your aspirations, asking for help in advancing them, will bring a favorable response.

The nonrelating boss. Some executives seem to avoid any but the routine exchanges necessary for the work to keep moving. Any initiatives to improve the relationship are left up to you. And, in some cases, any attempts made in that direction meet with a polite but firm rebuff.

There is nothing "wrong" in such behavior. True, it creates a state of contactlessness that makes the job more mechanical. And it may deprive you of a resource for growth of outlook and skills that would improve your professional potential. But, in theory, a boss has as much right to be a "loner" as any of his or her subordinates. However, if the situation bothers you, consider the following:

What do you think explains the unusual behavior? An aloof boss is basically an anomaly, like a football player who can't stand body contact. Is shyness a possible explanation? Or, how about total preoccupation with his or her own job, into which the need to supervise others is an intrusion? (Some executives in the sciences tend to fit into this category.)

Does the reason suggest an opportunity for an initiative? If you feel the boss is susceptible to action:

- Can you enlarge your work-oriented contacts? Some technical aspects of your assignment may benefit from discussion, and could be the magic trigger that eases the aloofness.
- Increase social contacts? That great socializer, the lunch table, may be a possibility. A suggestion for lunch at which to discuss some work situation might do it.
- Is there a misunderstanding in your past? For one manager, the explanation of a distant boss lay in a mixup in a procedure that aroused mutual resentment never dissolved. If this may be your case, consider overtures that may excise the scar.

The boss who drinks too much. Earlier in this section, the problem of the alcoholic worker was discussed at length. The executive suite is unfortunately not off limits for the uncontrolled drinker. As you will see, the situation, though similar in cause, is different in effect and what you can do about it when the alcoholic is a boss.

You might think there is no such category. How can an executive with ongoing responsibilities possibly function for any length of time despite the inroads of inebriation?

The seeming contradiction, unfortunately, does exist. For one thing, there is the matter of degree. Some drinkers just go over the edge. Their behavior and judgments are marred only marginally. They are a problem, if only to a slight extent. Then there are those who impose a major burden on their secretary, assistants, and the entire staff.

Says one assistant manager in a retail store, "My heart sinks when I hear his voice from down the hall. That means he has had a liquid lunch, and I know the damage he can do in that state."

Another manager in the same department says, "I try to take up all questions with him in the morning. He's out of it too many afternoons. Pity. He's such a good boss."

His secretary says, "I keep covering up for him—with the head of the company, other executives, even his wife. I don't know how much longer I can continue like this."

The emotional involvements of this situation can be strong and upsetting. Some points to consider:

It's the boss's problem. And there may be little you can do to help. Some subordinates carry compassion too far, and like the secretary above, hurt themselves. While you may want to help as much as you can, you may have to draw the line.

Understand the limitations of intervention. To people who can control their drinking, the compulsions of the alcoholic seem like an arbitrary self-indulgence. They take the victim aside and say, "You've got a problem, Phil, and it's showing. You really must put on the brakes." If it were that easy, there would be no such problem as alcoholism. One case tells the story. Ms. X. whose fantastic skills as a copy chief were able to forestall retribution for a long period, was finally persuaded by her boss to see a psychiatrist. End of the problem, right? Unhappily, no. It took long months of therapy before she was able to finally admit that she even had a problem, and many more months before the habit could be, not cured, but halted. Ms. X. tells her friends, "For me there is no such thing as drinking a little. One step back, and I'm in the pit." The awareness keeps her healthy.

Should you continue to cover up for the victim?   Perhaps, minimally. But at some point say, "I'm sorry. I'm hurting you, not helping you by lying about your absences, and mistakes. Please don't depend on me to do that any longer."

Get help?   Yes, but tentatively. With the major problem up front, of the alcoholic resisting even the idea that help is needed, a blunt, "See a therapist," or, "Go to Alcoholics Anonymous," or other treatment center, will go unheeded. One approach that has worked is to use an incident or accident—a fall that injures an arm or leg—to seek medical first aid. A word to the doctor may lead to a referral.

If you are on good terms with the victim's superior—but only if you are absolutely certain as to the need and the superior's trustworthiness in such a matter—describe the situation: "I wouldn't bring this to you, but I'm afraid failing to take some action will mean serious damage next time."

A happy concluding thought: The "problem boss" category, though a serious threat, is not large. Modern management, with its standards and competitiveness, seldom tolerates for long the handicaps of a manager whose problems show up on the job. But there is a final thought for you: As a manager, you know bossing is a skill to be fine-tuned, like any other. You may want to give some thought to the ways and means of improving your contacts with all members of your staff, for the mutual benefits that it can bring.

12. Improving Your Own Effectiveness

Your fate and job are linked. What you become professionally is not only a measure of capability, but a playing out of a significant part of your life. And since your responsibility is part of a larger entity, your company, your achievement impacts on that entity's fortunes. The better you may do for yourself, the better you can do for your organization.

Executive performance is a crucial factor on the work scene. The result-getting manager multiplies his or her personal effectiveness through the activities of subordinates. Another way of conveying the same fact: a 10 percent improvement in the effectiveness of an executive can boost the performance of a department, division, or company significantly.

Improvement depends not only on doing things "better." Also involved is your long-range development. To this end, continuing self-improvement is the order of the day, week, and year. The ideas in this section can make you more effective in your job, and can speed career progress.

There are two aspects to updating capabilities: Keeping Up With a Runaway Technology: Mastery of Day-to-Day Schedules.

Keeping Up With a Runaway Technology

View your effectiveness from a time perspective and into focus comes a phenomenon that promises to be overriding: Employer requirements are being altered by an exploding technology and changes in corporate growth resulting from acquisitions and mergers. Updating managerial qualifications can no longer be a leisurely activity. As Lewis Carroll's queen reminds us, sometimes we must run desperately just to stay in the same place.

➲ OBSOLESCENCE: THREAT FROM THE FUTURE

Contemporary managers face a threat to their effectiveness. Ignore it, and they risk alienation by time and technology, and thwarted career aspirations. However, on the bright side: meet the threat and the odds for your success become much more favorable.

That hazard, obsolescence, is advanced not only by automation, computers, robots, and the information explosion, but the many lesser developments that affect job content, performance, and employment itself. Undertaking the battle against obsolescence gives you two immediate advantages:

- The moves that help you offset obsolescence also put you on top of your job.
- In initiating the activities that keep you relevant, you gain an edge over your professional competitors.

➲ WINNING THE FIGHT AGAINST OBSOLESCENCE

A pebble rolling down a mountain is unimportant. But if huge boulders and tons of earth come roaring down, that's an avalanche and can mean catastrophe. In obsolescence, managers may face an avalanche created by a number of factors that, taken together, threaten job and professional stability.

Marguerite Zentara of *Computerworld,* writes, "How can working computer scientists and electrical engineers possibly keep up with increasingly complex and rapid technological change? The Institute of Electrical and Electronics Engineers alone published 200,000 journal pages" in a recent year. And that's only the tip of the iceberg.

The information explosion is just one of several factors that make previously qualified people no longer adequate. To help you neutralize possible inroads of career-upsetting developments, two things: first, identification of the factors that may destabilize your career situation; and second, seven moves that can help you stay in command.

➔ **EIGHT CAREER-SHORTENERS**

Here are a list of major threats to job stability:

1. Advances in technology.   Almost every industry in our time is seeing development of its hardware, software, or both. Equipment or procedures can in the course of their development, leave behind workers and managers whose skills are no longer viable. In the film/video business, for example, the appearance of computerized tape-editing equipment for video not only replaced many film applications, but thinned from the ranks editors who could not handle the new methods.

2. "Youthifying"   of a company or industry. Another reason for job loss: the influx of young people, newly trained to the latest procedures, and often better able to perform the new operations than the incumbents, and at less pay. When a technological advance is of a sufficient magnitude, a generation gap is created that puts the older person at a disadvantage.

3. Alienation.   A psychological factor can be a major handicap. It doesn't create obsolescence, but it intensifies the victim's feeling of being pushed out the door, professionally speaking.

4. Changes in the marketplace.   Where are the buggy-whip braiders of yesteryear? Or the hotshot executives who ran things during the early computer years, now left behind by a whirlwind of innovation? Entire crafts can be outmoded because of cultural or economic changes. The advent of new products, the passing from favor of old ones, leave a swath of obsolescent workers, and their managers, in their wake.

5. Individual inflexibility.   Happily, not all managers snap in the winds of change. Some have the resilience of skills and outlook that can adapt. Those who can't, or refuse to react to the invasion of tomorrow, face rough going.

6. Inflexibility of the employer's facilities.   An advance made by competitors sometimes cannot be matched. And a department, division, or an entire company becomes noncompetitive, and must curtail operations or go under with all hands.

7. The inside and outside of obsolescence.   For the individual, losing relevance has an inside and outside. The outside may be easy to figure. You can anticipate the facts of technological change. It often comes on big elephant feet, and whole communities shake.

The inside aspect is what goes on inside the brain of the individual victim. His or her perceptions may react strangely to imminent change, and to the individual's feelings of self.

The person you least expect may face the threat with self-confidence. Those you thought would adapt easily get the shakes and feel incapable of meeting new conditions. The pressures of innovation may put strains on unexpectedly fragile emotional resources. Low self-esteem may surface in a person unexpectedly. A rejection of retraining may take place. Bitterness and resentment may appear and become problems in themselves.

8. Shortened workspan.   This is an indirect consequence of our rapidly-changing technology, and is only slowly being recognized as a major career obstacle. In the olden days it was common for a person out of school to start a first job and at his or her retirement dinner some thirty or forty years later, say it was supposed to be temporary. Tenure of several decades are not unusual in a stable, slowly developing economy. But when the tempo picks up, things change. For instance:

Vince White becomes a technologically displaced person when his employability in the electronics toy firm he's been with for six years is terminated. His job has been robotized. He gets a job in another toy company, but his department is discontinued when the mechanized games it produces fall out of favor. Well, he had three pretty good years. Next he accepts his brother's offer to join him in a small home-repair enterprise. Things go well, so well, in fact that after four years, Vince's brother gets an offer he can't refuse, and sells out to a real-estate developer. The brother stays on, there's no room for Vince in the new setup.

The contemporary interest in acquisitions and mergers proliferates foreshortened workspans. Both in terms of profession and industry, rapid changes tends to shorten careers. Roy B. Helfgott, Professor of Economics, New Jersey Institute of Technology was quoted in the *New York Times;* as saying: "Today we are once more on the threshold of new and dramatic technological innovation, and I am sure that early retirement will again be a means of easing its impact."

Professor Helfgott's observation touches on a major trend affecting the working life of almost everyone.

CAUGHT IN THE MIDDLE: A HAZARD OF OUR TIME

There is an ironic confrontation of opposed forces created by two different lines of development:

■ **Increased life span.**   Due to better health concepts and care, improved diet, people live longer and retain energies longer.

■ **Obsolescence-shortened career span.**   An advancing technology may shorten the years of employability. Just recognizing this situation, or even better, anticipating it, makes possible the planning of a career that can satisfy both your personal ambitions and economic needs.

NEUTRALIZING OBSOLESCENCE

Somewhere along the road to the future the manager's job ceased being the secure affiliation with a single employer that traditionally it had been. Shortened workspan and technological change are by now deeply imbedded in our system. But career aspirants can take steps to minimize the the conflict in their own situations:

1. Continuing appraisal.   Understand what's coming. Although the changes are business wide, and you should be aware of general trends, focus on the situation in your profession and company.

2. Be aware of new career patterns.   There will be some protected enclaves of employment immune to firings and layoffs. For example, some branches of government and education will provide unbroken tenure. But for many, career patterns will be affected in ways like these:

■ The number of job changes in a typical career history will increase, from an average of five or six to twice that.
■ Length of employment by any one organization will be shorter. "Old-timers" will be those with the company for just a few years.
■ Periods of unemployment will increase. In the past, job hunters needed a minimum of three months to find another job. These gaps will lengthen as job finding becomes tougher.
■ Careers will often show a succession of new employment directions. Career chains will acquire more links as enterprising individuals seek or create opportunities.

3. Career designing.   This will virtually become a new cottage industry. People in effect will be on a continuing alert for new employment or income-earning situations. The response to jobs of doubtful tenture will be a willingness to move with little hesitation to one of more promise.

Your pension situation is one of the factors to consider. There has been talk of "portable pensions," which would be transferred in a job change. Until this becomes a reality, your pension status must be a part of your pro-and-con calculations in a possible change.

4. "What do I want to do?"   That traditional self-question of the career developer will now bring more flexible answers. A self-imposed job category—"I'm an accountant," "I'm a systems analyst," and so on, will become a restraint to be shed.

5. Decide on a policy.   One executive says, "I used to think of myself as a production engineer. My past affiliations were good, but three mergers put me out on the street. I eventually decided I would look for, or try to develop independently, any use of my background, experience and know-how I could. Accordingly, I am a part-time consultant. I give courses in a technical school, I write articles for an engineering monthly, and I have a job as a production coordinator in a local food factory." Avoid locking yourself in, but also, be aware of the range of activities open to your earning potential.

6. Check your organization's obsolescence-creating pattern.   No company seeks to make its employees obsolete. But the nature of a firm's operation makes it more or less susceptible to the inroads of technolocal displacement. Analyze three factors:

Your department's technology.   A warehousing manager for a book publisher has seen the old hand-picked order methods replaced by automatic picking, stacking, and wrapping. He knows present equipment is not the end of the line. Explore and probe the future of procedures in your area of responsibility.

The techniques of your profession.   Whether you're a scientist in Research and Development or a producer of television commercials, you can be sure the technology in use today is not frozen. What's coming up, and how will it affect you? You may not have the answers, but there are industry sources from which some insights may be gotten.

Your industry's situation.   Some industries innovate slowly. Others change on an active ongoing basis. And usually, most companies have several technologies or areas of potential change. For example, an executive in a furniture-manufacturing firm drew up this list:

- Interior design and decorating trends
- New art styles
- New construction materials
- New methods of construction
- New tools and machines
- New materials for finishing—paints, varnishes, etc.
- New finishing processes
- New methods of packing and crating
- New ways to broaden markets

Your checking need not be limited to your own industry. Activity in related business areas—such as home construction for the furniture executive above—might be auguries.

In most industries a handful of organizations or individuals are at the forefront of innovation. Try to keep a line on these.

7. Programming your self-development. Implicit in the previous pages is the recommendation that staying current has become an ongoing preoccupation. In many cases, letting down means getting out. In addition to the tracking of the direction and speed of obsolescence that may be heading your way is the advisability of activity aimed at updating your preparedness:

Don't leave school. It has been pointed out repeatedly: Continuing eductation may be essential. Consider the fact that a professional education, whether in medicine or civil engineering, that could once carry you well into the future—say five or ten years—now may be only sufficient to get you started and keep you going for a year or two. Even real estate salespeople take continuing courses to stay abreast of the changing "rules" that affect them.

Several strings to your bow. If you can prevent it, don't depend on a single line of activity to stay relevant. Reading professional magazines is certainly a major source of new information. But courses, books, seminars, joining colleagues to form a small study group of new developments in your field, teaching your specialty—and getting the benefit of your students' questing minds—are among the possible paths you can pursue in the quest for updatedness.

(See "Personal Obsolescence," in the "Key Management Concepts" section, page 375.)

➡ HOW WELL ARE YOU KEEPING UP?

The questions below help you rate yourself on the degree to which you are keeping abreast of change. The score you get is not too important. But what may be crucial is the revelation of your success in staying abreast of developments that month to month, year to year are changing the requirements of your job, and what is needed to advance your career.

The questions in this self-test give you the opportunity to rate your preparedness efforts, and equally worthwhile, remind you of the resources available to maintain a program of self-development, which, as top personnel executives repeatedly state, is the most meaningful type of development there is.

In answering the questions, combine both management activity and that in your specialty, for example, engineering or MIS/dp, or personnel work, etc.

SOURCES AND RESOURCES—HOW ARE YOU DOING?
A SELF-QUIZ

	Often	Some-times	Never
In the past year or so—			
1. Did you attend seminars on job-related subjects?	____	____	____
2. Did you attend professional meetings or conferences?	____	____	____
3. Did you participate in any training or development sessions sponsored by your employing organization?	____	____	____
4. Any training or development sessions sponsored by a trade or professional organization?	____	____	____
5. Read books in your field or on general management, either as refreshers on new developments?	____	____	____
6. Read trade or professional journals, or newspapers either in your specialty or in the management field?	____	____	____
7. Initiated any research or experimental programs (for example, one manager set up a test to see how shortening or lengthening rest periods affected productivity; a chemist did some reading of the literature to see if procedures other than those used by her company might suggest improved methods).	____	____	____

8. Do you initiate or participate in informal discussions with colleagues about management or technical subjects?   _____   _____   _____

9. Aside from day-to-day matters, do you discuss problems or situations about the work with your boss—take advantage of his or her experience or educational background?   _____   _____   _____

10. Do you think about your work when you are off the job (not talking here about concerns with current problems, but ways to improve your skills and status, your job future).   _____   _____   _____

Scoring.   Your score is at best a rough estimate, and not critical. But as a straw in the wind, rate your answers by giving yourself a 10 for each *Often,* 5 for each *Sometimes,* and 0 for each *Never.*

80–100.   If your total is in this bracket, you're doing fine. Just keep it up.

55–75.   You are doing a reasonably good job. But stand back for a moment and consider the speed with which your particular profession is changing. Is your pace, satisfactory for some professional areas, good enough for yours? If the answer is no, consider the sources for keeping up that are available to you and see what you can do to get on track with the ones that can help you most.

Below 55.   Unless you are near retirement, it is possible that the whole subject of updating your skills and qualifications requires some serious rethinking.

The quiz questions have raised some questions in your mind as to weaknesses in one or another area. Consider them separately, now, and think through the possibility of a one-sided update that means you are doing well in one part of your career preparation, but slighting others.

The questions themselves suggest ways in which you can build a qualifications-advancement program. And if you spot any areas that you feel need some attention, perhaps a consultation with one or more experts—this may include your boss or other staff people—might optimize your planning. (Adapted from Auren Uris, *Real world Deskbook,* Van Nostrand Reinhold, 1984).

Mastering Day-to-Day Challenges

Fine-tuning present skills and acquiring new ones helps you zero in on the current demands of your job. Involvement in these activities, procedures, problems, and challenges can set you in a mode that permits you to raise your sights for present performance and accomplishment.

➲ BECOMING A COMPANY STAR

"How to be outstanding in your company?" a CEO repeats an interviewer's query. "Why, be the top performer on the executive staff."

The way to satisfy this savvy manager's suggestion is to master forward-looking aspects of your job. The pages ahead offer guidelines for improving your handling of them.

➲ FOUR BASICS

What are the foundations of superior executive functioning? An analysis of case histories of successful managers suggest these attributes:

1. Mental fitness. The capable executive has a broad-ranging, mature outlook on the work scene. Values, standards, expectations of behavior and performance of others and of self are realistic—which doesn't interfere with setting high goals. An emotional tone is set well below hysteria and decidedly above passivity. "The job" is considered the second most-important thing, the first, of course, the individual's own well-being and life goals.

2. Physical fitness. Good physical health is characteristic of those who are productive, although as has been demonstrated over and over, so-called handicapped people can be top performers. Generally, the health area is one in which we can help ourselves considerably. Advances in medical knowledge have increased our understanding of the role of diet, exercise, sleep, and so on. Also important is the raised level of awareness of physical fitness needs and possibilities. Regular checkups and proper medical guidance can extend life spans, and equally important, the persistence of youthfulness into what used to be called "middle age."

3. Personal efficiency. The ability to map out his or her areas of responsibility, and the work to satisfy it, is a conspicuous achievement of the good executive. "Well organized" are among the most-sought after words of praise.

4. Self-image as booster.   One more major element helps foster effective self-organization. Successful executives develop a mind-picture, a favorable self-portrait that operates as a benign taskmaster.

It's a fact established by many studies, from schoolroom to workstation: Expectations of one's self can be a major motivator. The principle is simple: A person who expects to do well, does so, while one who expects to do poorly, is less likely to do well.

The implications of these facts are directly relevant to your personal effectiveness. Ambition may then be seen in the light of a self-fulfilling wish. Those who believe they *will* achieve, considerably increase their chances.

⮕ FITTING YOUR PERSONAL STYLE TO YOUR ORGANIZATION'S STYLE

Your organization influences your approach to your work. Consciously and unconsciously, executives develop work patterns that reflect the organization of which they are a part. One observer of organizational realities sums up the idea in a sentence: "Managers must learn to suit their work style to the character of the company.'

Most experts agree that organizations have a style of their own. Managerial candidates may be hired or not on the basis of how well they fit the company stereotype. The "organization person" in a computer firm may be a neatly dressed individual with a positive demeanor, well-informed on professional matters. No heat wave has yet proved hot enough to cause the removal of his or her jacket. For one large advertising agency, the typical manager is flamboyant, offbeat, creative, pushy, and loves and lives the job.

Old-time managers usually have adapted to their company, its pace, priorities, values, turn-ons, and turn-offs. A new manager meets the challenge of advancement by learning these things, working hard, and developing a work style in tune with the standards and work habits of his or her peers. As one W.R. Grace executive has put it, "If your workstyle matches the company's, it becomes easier to get things done. If your methods are at odds with those about you, you are hampered in a dozen ways."

Should you ever break the pattern? Of course you should, because you may get more accomplished by a tactic directly opposed to the organization style in special circumstances, such as an emergency when standard approaches aren't working. For example, one manager in a sedate, slow-paced outfit broke the pattern by advocating a marketing policy he felt was essential for the company's survival. The vehemence of his arguments won the day because it was at variance with customary bland company tone.

A change of style can be effective when used judiciously. Choose your situation and analyze it carefully. If a fresh approach seems appropriate, forge ahead. It will at least set you apart from those who never make changes or take chances.

➲ HOW TO DICTATE

Most executives can and do dictate letters. But considerable time can be saved by dictating other material—reports, long memos, articles for business journals, and so on.

Anyone who can speak can dictate. Practically everyone can develop a reasonable dictating skill sufficient to cut writing time by 50 percent or even more. There's no mystery in how to go about mastering the dictating skill. These points can help you:

1. What to dictate   While almost anything to be written can be dictated, there are some types of writing that effect greater time savings by dictation than others. Reports, for example, are particularly worthwhile for dictation since they tend to be lengthy. Undictated, they represent large investments of time.

Unsuitable for dictation are long lists of names or other proper nouns, numerical tabulations, and highly mathematical copy (i.e., where more than half of the copy is comprised of equations).

2. Human or Machine?   The dictater may have a choice between a stenographer and dictating machine. Recent years have seen dictating equipment refined. Machines are lighter and operate more easily. Some companies have dictation systems where one dictates into a telephone. A recording tape or other medium in a centralized location records the dictation, subsequently transcribed by a typing pool.

Regardless of the particular mechanism, machine dictation and dictation to a stenographer have advantages and disadvantages. A comparison of the two is on page 236.

3. Getting Started   Gather your information, background material, and so on, in advance. Don't start your dictation and be forced to interrupt yourself because you are missing a piece of reference matter. Have available all the backup sources you will need—if possible, in the order in which you will use it.

Make a rough outline.   An outline has the virtue of giving a track to run on, a framework on which to build your final product. And, except for lengthy or complex projects, you needn't get involved in the kind of elaborate outlining that is sometimes taught in school. At a minimum, a number of words or phrases that give you a logical sequence of ideas will do the trick. For example, here is the outline used in dictating this section:

Introduction: Benefits
Everyone can do it to some degree—
a. What to dictate
b. Girl or machine
c. Getting started (after the preparation steps)
d. Common hang-ups and how to overcome them
e. Improving your copy
f. Reviewing your weak and strong points and improving your technique
Conclusion: By-product benefits.

4. Common hang-ups and how to overcome them   Discussions with individuals who dictate material other than letters or memos reveal some common problems:

"Writer's block." Some people say that when faced by the need to start dictating, they freeze. This is similar to the paralysis that occasionally stops even the professional writer in his tracks. To counter this problem, check back and make sure that all your preparations have been made. In some cases, the feeling of not being ready to dictate may be the obstacle. Then, start! Throw hesitation to the winds. Don't worry about finding the "right" word, phrase or sentence. Plunge in!

"I can't get down to brass tacks. I ramble and digress." The solution here lies both in having and *following* an outline. If you find you're straying from it, go over it to make sure it covers your subject adequately. Then stick to it, forcing yourself to stop when you seem to be digressing.

"It's disconcerting to have a stenographer waiting for me to grope for an idea." Try using a machine, or change stenographers; or make some disarming or humorous comment, letting your stenographer know that you don't expect to talk smoothly and incessantly. If you have not been doing much dictating, it is no disgrace to admit it, and to imply that your stenographer will have plenty of time to catch his or her breath while you gather your thoughts or grope for the phrase you want.

"I never liked gadgets."   Talking to a lifeless machine can be disconcerting. Try a stenographer. Or, the particular make or model of your dictating machine may be a poor choice for you. In today's market, one can find a wide variety of dictating equipment. If you are having trouble with a machine that you have tried, a trip to an office supply company will make it possible to test other types of equipment.

"I lose too much time searching for a word or phrase or even an idea." This is a common and major hang-up. To overcome it, bull it through—put down any word or phrase that will get you over the hurdle, knowing that you will be able to improve the word or phrase or idea later on.

The important thing is to aim for a *rough draft*, because once you have your copy in black and white, you have something to work with. The professional writer will often push on to complete his or her draft, regardless of how many word gaps or idea gaps there may be.

5. Improving your copy.   The greatest misconception about dictation is that you say it once and that finishes the job. *Neither* the dictated nor written copy is "right" the first time. Every writer will tell you that the *rewriting* is an essential part of the operation.

So consider the typed pages you get either from your stenographer or from the typist who has worked from your machine-recorded material as merely a draft, a preliminary version. What you should strive for is to turn your first rewrite into "final copy." In some cases, you may have to do two rewrites; that is, revise your copy twice before you have a final draft. It's in the editing or rewriting that you can eliminate oral habits that are objectionable.

6. Improving your technique.   After you have tried dictating once or twice, review your technique. Use the above discussion of hangups as a kind of checklist to spot your weak points. Then try to improve your technique via practice. Even someone very much used to dictating letters cannot expect to undertake longer communications without some preliminary difficulties.

If first attempts are discouraging, try again, dictating material on which you have a good grasp. Don't give up too quickly, because the rewards of success can be substantial. Repeated attempts can help you score a breakthrough. Then, not only do you save time, but you're more likely to undertake a long but important report with good will, even zest. The quality of your writing will benefit from your new attitude.

➲ STENOGRAPHER VS DICTATING MACHINES: HOW THEY STACK UP

Stenographer

Advantages

Useful rapport can exist between steno and dictater.

Can make corrections and insertions on the spot, and supply quick readbacks.

Can be helpful in giving instant feedback to dictater (in terms of reaction to wording, ideas, etc.) Can ask questions immediately if something is not clear.

Disadvantages

Usually works eight-hour day or less, and may resist overtime.

May tire after an hour or so.

If steno is absent from work and has not completed transcription of her notes, chances are no substitutes can read her shorthand. This means a delay until steno returns to work.

Dictating Machine

Advantages

Doesn't complain, has no personal habits or traits that can irritate you. For example, doesn't chew gum, or make long calls for social or romantic purposes.

Available twenty-four hours a day, and is tireless.

Some people are less self-conscious when they dictate to a machine. There is no need to apologize for pauses or interruptions.

Conserves secretarial time, and can be taken along on a business trip without precipitating office gossip.

Disadvantages

Can lend themselves to corrections, but some people find machines difficult in this respect.

Cannot supply a missing word or phrase.

If transcriber has difficulty in discerning some words or phrases dictated, the dictater may not always be available to be asked.

Transcriber might feel it's a waste of time to listen to the entire recording before typing it, preferring to take it down in shorthand to facilitate transcription of corrections, changes, and punctuation.

➔ ON BECOMING A BETTER LISTENER

The average manager spends up to 70 percent of working time listening. But psychologists know that the average listener forgets about three-fourths of what is heard in a few hours.

What can be done? How can you listen more effectively at conferences, discussions, seminars, interviews? Dr. Ralph Nichols of the University of Minnesota has these suggestions to improve retention of what you hear?

1. Know what makes a poor listener. Mainly, it's the difference in time that it takes to say words and to think them. Even the fastest speaker can think words several times faster than he can talk. So listeners tend to race ahead of the speaker, anticipating what is said and then "tuning out."

Frequently, the listener's mind wanders until continuity is broken completely and key points lost.

Dr. Nichols advises listeners to use constructively the time difference between thinking and hearing. Evaluate what is being said. Is it supported with facts? Can you find a weakness in the presentation? Or use the extra thinking time to go back and review what has already been said?

2. Avoid distractions. Another common listener's fault is allowing oneself to be distracted. However, concentration is no easy trick. In addition to tight discipline, it takes *involvement.* You have to find a reason to *want* to listen—and stay with it. But look out for this common trap: you can work so hard at trying to listen and appearing to listen that you don't hear a word.

3. Don't "argue." You'll need to analyze your own emotional reactions, especially the "red flag" variety. This can be a major barrier to effective listening. Certain statements—those with which you violently disagree—can arouse you to the point where you feel you *must* interrupt to make an opposing point. And if for some reason you can't interrupt (you don't want to offend, or it's a formal speech), you likely will do so mentally and miss the words and thoughts that follow.

4. Listen selectively. The really good listener doesn't listen indiscriminately. He or she selects, searches for what can be used, professionally or in private life. Whenever possible decide in advance what you will listen to and eliminate topics that, for you, are of little or no interest or value.

5. Make notes. Few of us listen for listening's sake. The purpose of listening is to retain the important aspects of what's being said. In "formal" listening situations, such as a lecture, or seminar, listening acuity can be improved by note-taking, in two ways. First, the notes you make help put the ideas and information you're hearing into permanent form. And second, the process of notetaking itself, forces you to analyze what's being said, so that you zero in on the significant points and ideas.

Finally, it's been said often enough to require only passing mention here: we hear what we want to hear. The statement has pertinence because it pinpoints the motivational factor. If we are eager to get the opinions and views of a speaker, we tend to adopt all the proper listening methods automatically.

➜ FRIENDSHIP WITHOUT TEARS

The problem of friendships on the work scene have troubled many an executive. You can avoid the hazards and maximize the rewards of friendship by a better understanding of exactly what is involved:

First, realize the difference between two ideas:

Friendliness implies a warm and sympathetic attitude.

Friendship involves intimacy and special consideration.

If you develop friendships on the job it's advisable to:

- compensate for it by even greater efforts at friendliness with others;
- make it clear to your friends that they, like yourself, must be prepared to pay a price for the friendship. You have no choice but to lean over backward, since you cannot allow friendship to interfere with your judgment on the job.

Then, to protect your friendships, show real friendliness to all your people. These guides can help.

- Show no favoritism for one employee over another.
- Don't accept friendly overtures from cliques. While it may be pleasant to be "in" with one group, it's likely to lead to your being "out" with everybody else. Try to avoid showing recognition, and hence, approval of cliques. A barrier between you and the nonclique people would become unavoidable.
- Show friendliness to newcomers and to those who have less standing in the group. This move boosts their morale and emphasizes that you play no favorites on the job.

Finally, to maintain friendships with colleagues or others on the business scene:

1. Don't be overly selective.   It's not simply a matter of avoiding the accusation of snobbishness. More important is the need to make your friendships across the board for the fullest rewards and enrichments.

2. Act with a sense of the appropriate.   This isn't a matter of a stuffed shirt concern with "what people think." For your own sake, good judgment must temper the contacts you foster.

3. Be aboveboard with the other person.   Your motives, your real feelings toward a superior, a customer, or a subordinate, may be neither simple nor clear. If you have doubts about the motives of your friendly interest or feeling toward an individual, think twice before undertaking any social gambit. Nothing is as cold as a chilled friendship.

➔ ADJUSTING YOUR SIGHTS TO CHANGE

Executives, in addition to helping their people meet the challenge of change, face the same challenges themselves. To help yourself ride on top of the crest of the future:

1. Prepare yourself emotionally.   For some people this may be easier said than done. But those who regard the future with apathy, are likely to be steamrolled by it. The one who makes the effect to adjust will have the best chance of riding the future to new triumphs. Accordingly:

- Don't kid yourself and hang on to the idea that, "It can't happen here." Eventually, it *will* happen. The only question is exactly *how* soon and to *what* degree.
- Reject defeatist thinking and anxiety about age or capability. Attitude, not the calendar, determines 'youthfulness' in this situation. And there is a pleasant surprise in store for many: some will find they're even better *suited to the future* than they were to the past.
- Concentrate on your professional assets—experience, skills, general know-how. These are the tools that can help you assure a place for yourself in a changing situation.

2. Management specialization.   The day of the "generalist" will never be over. Companies will always need people with a broad understanding that cuts across departmental and functional lines. However, paradoxically we'll be entering an age of super specialization. Sign of the future: some years ago, a single executive could take care of all a company's financial problems. Today the financial function is often broken up into a number of specialties, such as taxes, investments, fund raising, and so on.

The increasing technical content of management will see the innovation of new staff functions. Managers in production and departmental operations will be served by specialists in operations analysis, statistics, and so on. Purposes: to bring new knowledge from many disciplines to bear on operating problems, and for strategic planning.

3. Watch for opportunities to change.   Examine each development that comes your way from the point of view of the new chances it gives you. Remember, almost every problem can be turned to advantage when examined constructively.

Finally, to ride the wave of the future will require a positive and active participation. You will have to respond to challenge and do your homework. No matter what the tomorrow will bring, the qualities of flexibility, energy, and creativity are never out of date.

PUTTING THE MOST INTO YOUR WASTEBASKET

Many how-to subjects have titles such as "how to get the most *out of*. . . ." The wastebasket is a major administrative tool and to a large extent, the more you *put into it*, the greater the benefits you reap. One executive says that the wastebasket is the "secret trap door to efficiency." Here are some golden rules of wastebasketry:

1. Take care of the physical details.   Size, shape, and location of your wastebasket should reflect not only functional requirements but also personal procedures. Obviously, the basket you use should be big enough for all you can feed it. And it should be convenient to your hand, rather than occupy a spot determined by the whim of your maintenance people or even your secretary. Some executives with limited capacity requirements find that a small, flat-sided basket works out well, particularly where it can be fastened to a wall bracket or a panel of the desk inside the knee-hole area.

2. Pinpoint the extreme cases.   In your use of the wastebacket, two types of material pose no problem:

- *Natural wastebasketables.* A mail order ad for a product of no conceivable use to you, written announcements of developments with which you are already familiar, fall in this category.
- *Obvious retainables.* Weekly production figures that you keep on file, information you will need at a later date, require processing other than by wastebasket. The chart below can further help you decide on the wastebasketability of materials that lie between these two extremes.

For the Wastebasket	To Be Retained
1. *Use and discard.* A memo announcing a conference, for example, can be tossed out after you've noted the conference date on your desk calendar.	1. *Reports.* Key periodic reports that fit into a series you use for comparison, etc.
2. *Extra copies.* You may be sent several copies of printed material. Where you need only one for the record, the others may be discarded.	2. *Items with a future.* You'll hold correspondence that contains: a. queries that require reply b. information you need for an as yet unmade decision c. ideas on which you'll want to follow up
3. *Unnecessary bulk.* Voluminous material of which you need only a summary or portion can be abstracted.	3. *"Evidence."* Letters sent you "for the record"—terms of an agreement, for example—are file material.
4. *Irrelevant material.* Circulars, form letters of no interest to you should seldom survive at desktop level.	4. *Reference material.* Manuals, instruction booklets, etc., for equipment or procedures in your area.
5. *Recorded elsewhere.* Sales figures that are posted on a centralized permanent record may be noted and disposed of.	5. *Copies of your own memos, letters, etc.* These help clarify the record in case of misunderstanding, or qualify you for "credit," if due.
6, 7, 8, etc. Add your own!	6, 7, 8, etc. Add your own!

A common executive practice requires your examination. It's summed up in the question, "Should you use the other person's wastebasket?" From time to time, you receive material of no importance to you. Routing such matter to a colleague who may be interested can be of real help. However, occasionally this procedure becomes the means by which an executive evades a wastebasketing decision. Before sending along a letter, brochure, or memo to a fellow executive, clear it with your conscience.

➔ PREPARING FOR YOUR OWN VACATION

Your absence need not shut down your operation cold, or handicap the staff you leave behind. To keep things moving when you're away, consider questions like these:

- ☐ Have you scheduled your own time off so that it will handicap operations least?
- ☐ Have your immediate staff, your assistant, and so on, been informed well enough in advance of the time you are going to be away?
- ☐ Have you arranged to tie up loose ends of important pending responsibilities?
- ☐ Have you arranged to notify those outside the company, suppliers, customers, etc., who should be informed of the time you are going to be away?
- ☐ Does your boss know when you are to be away?
- ☐ Will you be able to make satisfactory arrangements for a fill-in or an assistant to take over routine operations?
- ☐ Has your assistant or replacement been fully briefed for the take-over—
- ☐ (a) key jobs described?
- ☐ (b) critical equipment pinpointed?
- ☐ (c) manpower problems discussed?
- ☐ Do you want to leave instructions as to where you can be reached in case of emergencies (for your own peace of mind, as well as your assistant's)?
- ☐ Do you know when *your* boss plans to be away, so that you can settle crucial matters before *he or she* leaves?

➔ HOW TO SAY NO

An abrupt no is usually painful to the person to whom it is addressed. What is worse, it can sever a relationship, sever communications.

As a rule, a no is necessary in three types of situations:

- an offer of service from a subordinate
- a question asked for the purpose of getting information
- a request intended to produce a favor or benefit

If a no is followed by thank you, the offer of service shows the individual your appreciation and will usually conclude the exchange satisfactorily.

A no to the second query is usually a simple matter of fact.

But it's in the third instance, when you have to turn down a request, that trouble appears. For example, an employee asks, "May I have the afternoon off?"

You may have this thrown at you, followed by any one of a number of reasons—a visit to the doctor, special shopping, "personal business," an early weekend start.

Analyze the request and note the three possibilities:

1. The request may show a poor work attitude. You're going to say no, but remember that you're saying no to the basic attitude as well as the request.

Lay your cards on the table. Tell the worker you feel the request isn't justified, and show that the job rates more attention than it's getting. And since an attitude of this kind may be built on a fundamental dissatisfaction, try to find the real cause and discuss it.

2. The request is justified, but because of the work situation, must be refused. Assume that the worker has a good reason for wanting time off, but his absence will mess up your schedule. Or the effect on the rest of your staff will be bad—what you grant to one, you can't very well refuse to others.

You're going to say no, but you want the worker to see it your way. "No, we can't spare you this afternoon," isn't very satisfactory.

Try this:

"No, Mary, much as I'd like to, I can't let you go this afternoon, because. . . ." and from there on be frank.

Unlike your worker who has a poor work attitude, Mary is basically conscientious. When you tell her why you're saying no, she may even go back to her work with a renewed sense of importance—if your explanation plays up her part on the team.

3. The importance of the reason for the request isn't clear. Before saying no, be sure you understand the real reason behind the request.

Here's the same request that calls for two different answers.

a. Frances wants time off to go to the dentist because she has a severe toothache.

b. She wants to go to the dentist to have her teeth cleaned.

In the first instance, of course, you say yes. In the second, you may say no, and after explaining why, suggest that she make an appointment outside work hours. But this is clearly a case where you have to get the facts first.

In general, the simple no, has the sting of a crack across the knuckles. *In all cases, no by itself is no answer.*

➔ **HOW TO BE A "COMER"**

"How am I doing?" It's a question that executives are asked by their subordinates. And for progress-minded executives, it's a question they ask themselves.

Are You With It?

A series of questions about you and your job activities constitute a realistic self-audit that can give you an idea of how solidly you are progressing, and help you locate any soft spots in the road:

- Have you recently sat down to assess your knowledge of company policy and the reasons behind it?
- Can you cite specific instances where policy has changed in the last year?
- When is the last time you had to grapple with an ethical question in carrying out your responsibilities?
- Can you describe the traditions of your business?
- Your company has added new equipment, methods, etc. Have you stopped to think what basic implications these changes have for your job?
- The last time you made a comprehensive report, how well were others able to grasp what you were driving at? If they did poorly, was it because of lack of facts? Assumptions and impressions not identified as such? Incomplete examination of alternatives in light of overall effect?
- Have you broken any new ground in the past year, taken on new tasks? If not, why not?
- Did your company make more money last year than the present one? How much of the gain or loss were you responsible for?
- When was the last time you defended the organization against attack from within or without?
- How many proposals did you come up with in the last year for new products, procedures, materials, handling personnel?
- How many of your basic responsibilities do you handle in the same way you did two or three years ago? What? No improvements?
- How often in the past six months have you asked why something is done one way rather than another?
- When is the last time you were in the minority, defending an unpopular proposal in which you believed?
- Can you recall occasions within the last year when you got upset about your work? If so, was it because something went wrong in an area you deemed important? Was it because somebody else couldn't see the value of what you were doing?

Naturally, this isn't the kind of self-test on which you can give yourself a score. For one thing, some of the questions are more important than others to your job. But wherever you had trouble answering, or your answer troubles you, you have uncovered an opportunity to sharpen your management skills and strengthen your potential.

➲ HOW TO HANDLE YOUR BOSS

Your boss, the person you report to, can be a problem or opportunity. Not only is he or she your immediate superior, with the authority to make demands on your time and energies, but also is the monitor of your performance and professional destinies. Your boss is usually the one who can help you mount the heights of your aspiration, or to hold you back.

You can ask the question, "What are good boss relations?" and come up with as many opinions as there are people to answer. To get insight into the ingredients of a satisfactory relationship, it's helpful to analyze some of the deterrents.

To begin with, relations can be *too* smooth between you and your boss. No matter how excellent a performer you are, a boss can make you muscle-soft by too easy acceptance of your ideas, incessant approval of your accomplishments.

Think back to your school days. Don't you feel most respect and gratitude toward the teacher who put you over the jumps, but in so doing developed your interest and capabilities in the particular subject?

An examination of case histories in which both manager and boss agreed they got on well together showed these elements:

1. mutual respect
2. mutual approval
3. mutual stimulation
4. a more or less tension-free personal relationship

Why strains may exist.   Certainly, the logic of the subordinate-superior relationship itself cannot explain the frictions that frequently arise. Both parties have every reason to want a good relationship. What forces explain the contradiction? Several possibilities suggest themselves:

Difference in standards.   One company vice-president stated recently, "The president and I are at loggerheads. His opinion on a major policy matter was so unethical, it ruined my opinion of him irretrievably."

Unacceptable authority.   "It's extremely difficult for me," said the division manager of a plastics plant, "to take orders from a manager I don't respect."

Feeling of threat.   "My boss thinks I'm trying to take over her job," reports the manager of a bank department. "Accordingly, the better I do my job, the tougher she becomes."

It's silly to suggest that those who have poor relations with the boss are always "doing something wrong." Obviously, it's just as possible that the boss is at fault. Fortunately, poor relationships can be improved, and good ones can be made even better, by the efforts of the subordinate executive. The aim is to probe the relationship itself.

Handling Trouble.   You have several ways to go:

1. Search for the roots.   The first step when relationships are unsatisfactory is to track down some causes. Many symptoms have standard origins:

"My boss is afraid I'm going to take his job." Whether the difficulty stems from an overly aggressive subordinate who actually has been thinking too big or from a supersensitive boss, the remedy is the same. It's up to the subordinate to ease off sufficiently to remove the element of threat. Get time on your side.

"My boss doesn't think much of my abilities." Regardless of the abilities in question, the subordinate has failed to impress.

To reverse the situation, action in two directions is necessary:

a. a review of past incidents that may have led to such an evaluation
b. development of ways to eliminate negative impressions and to build a more favorable evaluation

"I have hostile feelings I can't altogether cover up." It's common enough, and the last thing called for is a feeling of guilt. But analytical thinking can pinpoint and ameliorate causes. A grievance, real or fancied, may explain the hostility. "Once I got to thinking about it," reports one 'cured' executive, "I realized that I had always resented my boss's snobbishness. He came from the right side of the tracks, I didn't. Once I dragged that realization out into the daylight, I could properly ask, So what? I even realized it was my attitude rather than his that made the difference seem important."

In addition to healing specific ailing relations, you have other ways to deal with a tough-boss problem that can help make a poor situation good and an impossible one, bearable and constructive.

2. Ask for the tools.   In some cases, the core of an executive's problem with his or her boss is simply that the superior expects a particular set of results, without being willing to provide the means to achieve the expected performance.

In other words, the superior says, "Here's what you'll do," without completing the plan by adding, "And here's what I'll do."

Specifically, the difficulties may show up in terms like these:

"I'm supposed to keep my people informed. But nobody tells me!"

"The boss needles me on output, but refuses to discuss maintenance schedules or machine replacement schedules."

The more strongly a superior presses for a given result, the more justification there is for a realistic discussion of the ways and means by which the result is to be achieved.

3. Selective contact.   "My boss is unreceptive to new ideas," one executive says. Another complains, "My boss is too demanding." The explanations for poor relationships, as we've already seen, may range all over the lot. But they are based on the unsound assumption that the superior, unlike other people, is a monolithic, one-faceted individual.

Often a quality is singled out as the cause of the friction. But, like any other oversimplification, it may hide certain facts. Every person, viewed objectively, has weak and strong points, attractive and unattractive features.

"My boss," an engineering executive reveals in confidence, "is unimaginative. Half the ideas he turns down are wasted, simply because he lacks the imagination to understand what I'm talking about."

But if the executive is correct in her assessment, she ought to know the answer to her problem. Perhaps her boss is eye-minded rather than ear-minded. Accordingly, she ought to frame her ideas in the boss's own language. For example, rather than presenting ideas with a thumbnail sketch and minutes of enraptured prose, she might get further with detailed drawings, and step-by-step visual illustrations of what she has in mind.

Some people resist the idea of dealing with their boss in their strong areas because it seems to be playing up to him or her. The issue is one of intent. Talking to a superior or any person in understandable language is the way to facilitate the business at hand. It is not like seeking a special privilege or self-ingratiation for personal advantage.

The principle of selective contact applies in other areas. Suppose the boss is obviously annoyed by a subordinate's preoccupation with projects to improve work methods. A wise individual would reduce his or her efforts in that direction and back up the boss's efforts, for example, to work out a better cost-reporting system. By scoring successes in the latter area, better understanding and working relationships may be achieved.

4. Show "the real you."   Naturally you want your boss to know of your virtues or successful performances, etc. How about your weaknesses? Should they be hidden?

There are good reasons for *not* hiding them.

Knowing your weaknesses, your superior is in a better position to help you—to back you up in the areas of critical performance.

If you outgrow your handicaps with the boss's aid, he or she cannot help being favorably inclined toward an improvement in which they have played a part.

The boss who has a real feeling for people (and most of them have, you know) wants to know strengths and weaknesses rather than feel only part of the picture is being presented.

More specifically, if you can avoid rigidity and formalism in your communications, the boss at once gets a clearer idea of what must be done to click with you.

In general, the strongest move is to use one's talents and resources to lighten the boss's load. Work cooperatively, and the boss will be *your* "man" as much as you're *his* or *hers*. Out of this mutuality can come the productive, stimulating, tension-free relationship that takes an enormous part of the executive burden off your shoulders.

(See also, "Dealing with a Problem Boss," page 218 .)

→ **PLANNING A SUPERIOR EXECUTIVE-SECRETARY TEAM**

Every executive's relationship with his or her secretary is unique, because it involves two unique people. Nevertheless, some rules are basic.

1. Hire for compatibility.   When you go about hiring or selecting your own secretary, you face the problem of evaluation. You judge the candidates on a number of key points: job skills, appearance, intelligence, experience, education, knowledge of your particular job activity, and so on.

Not likely to appear on any personnel rating sheet is the factor of *compatibility*—how well you and the candidate hit it off. But the fact is, it's crucial for good teamwork. The average executive may do better to hire a less skillful person but one with whom he'll get along well.

Does this suggest that you favor your biases? Absolutely!

Don't misunderstand. This approach is not recommended for hiring in general. If you're the president of a company looking for a marketing executive, obviously a biased personal preference may play little part in your choice.

A secretary is something special. Normally, the executive spends more time with his or her secretary than with a spouse—and we're talking about the normal working relationship.

In the Loesser–Burrows musical, *How to Succeed in Business Without Really Trying*, the audience is assured at one point that, "a secretary isn't a toy." Indeed. But he or she *is* a crucial status symbol. *You* are judged by your secretary's efficiency, appearance, and manner. An overly slick person outside an executive's door imparts an air of frivolity and pleasure-before-business. On the other hand, an attractive, dignified, efficient secretary signals a person of laudable stature.

In a literal sense, you must live with your secretary in close quarters. "If you want to know people, work with them" goes the old saw. For the secretary that goes double. Few people are heroes to their haircutters. If Tom Z. is the greatest guy in the world to his secretary, it's probably because he or she knows all about him and likes him anyway.

2. Try to understand.   The story is so old, it's got whiskers. But amazingly enough, it continues to happen, and happen, and happen:

The young executive, confident and dynamic, zooms into his office. "Good morning, Miss Train," he says, and sits down to his day's work. As the morning wears on, he vaguely becomes aware that there's something wrong with his secretary. He rings for her to give some last-minute instructions before going out to lunch. No answer. With some annoyance, he steps to the office door, and there at her desk is Miss Train sobbing convulsively.

He rushes to her side. "Miss Train," he says, "what's wrong?"

Through her tears she stutters. "Everybody else sent me a card—or wished me Happy Birthday—and not a *word* from you.. . .''

There's no avoiding it: you must give some thought to the secretary who works for you. You must find out what kind of person he or she is; interests; what kind of life the person leads on the outside; their friends within the company.

And you have to do this simply and tactfully, without seeming to pry, without getting too personal. If necessary, keep a record of his or her birthday (Personnel has this information); hiring date (in some companies, this "anniversary" date is celebrated rather than birthdays); names of family members—spouse, parents, brothers, sisters. Make notes at the beginning of the year when you get your new desk calendar, so that you won't have the sad experience of Miss Train's boss. To what end? A birthday card, a birthday (or anniversary) lunch. It's the gesture itself, not the expense, that's important.

3. Give your secretary "voting stock." In some areas, you must be autocratic in your dealings. You give direct orders; you brook no questions about what you want done or how you want it done. But these areas should be relatively limited. For the most part, get your secretary into the act. Encourage him or her to make suggestions about procedures and arrangements that are within the secretary's areas of operation and competence; for example, design of the filing system for your correspondence, or the record of departmental expenses—if the business office has no uniform method. After all, it's your secretary who uses the material.

But further: in matters that are squarely within your province, but on which you'd like another opinion, try him or her.

Case in point. Henry Jones is head of the collection department of a large Midwest department store. From time to time, he must write to customers who have rolled up large debts. Their letters in response to his requests for payment occasionally are difficult to interpret. He calls in his secretary:

"Anne, read this letter and tell me whether you think Mrs. X. really means she'll pay within the next couple of months, or whether it's just a stall."

Two extremes.   How far should you go in soliciting opinions depends on two factors—you and your secretary. If you can consult without abdicating, if the advice doesn't lead to a distorted idea of self-importance, then the more the better, within reason.

The things to watch for are two:

Overdependency.   Don't weaken your own effectiveness by using your assistant as a crutch. One executive describes his plight:

"My ex-secretary was a bright, capable woman with a need for power. She started making suggestions, then recommendations, and pretty soon, she was preempting me in most routine decisions. Finally, I realized I had gotten myself in the situation where I scarcely made a move without calling Miss Lincoln. It was all my fault, of course, but eventually it became so nerve-wracking, that I simply had to have her transferred."

Inconsistency.   It's generally inadvisable to set up rigid boundaries on job activities or job roles. On the other hand, even worse than rigidity for rattling a secretary is inconsistent behavior.

"A woman was in here just a few moments ago," a personnel manager explains," and she was very confused. Her boss kept changing the signals on her. One week he'd give her almost a free hand, the next week he'd play things close to his vest. He just wouldn't let her know what was going on."

You may not want to put it in writing, but at least get it straight in your own mind—the procedures you put in your secretary's hands, those you retain for yourself, and those in between, where you consult your secretary before taking action.

4. Rule emotions out of bounds.   We're not talking about romance or love or an affair. But any stickiness, a tendency to become overly friendly, to make the relationship a social one, will undercut the secretary's usefulness to you.

Chester Burger, in his book, *Survival in the Executive Jungle,* points out: "By nothing more than the tone of your voice or the look in your eye, you can draw a line between you and your secretary which must not be crossed. . . . Your secretary must always realize that she is your employee, not your social acquaintance, however friendly you may be."

5. A bridge, not a barrier.   Marilyn French, in *American Business,* points out that a secretary may either aid or impede his or her boss's communications with outsiders, as well as those within the company.

Certainly a key part of a secretary's job is to screen calls and callers. Being closer to the work group than you are, he or she often can keep you in touch with developments through the grapevine that otherwise might never reach you.

But in order to maintain your secretary as a constructive communications aid, you must provide instructions; that is, give directions as to who you will see and who you won't, for example; and make sure you don't put your secretary in the role of informer.

There's a thin line between listening to the things your secretary brings you from the underground and pumping the individual for more than he or she's willing to tell.

6. Ego feeding.   You want to praise and encourage your assistant, without overinflating a sense of self-importance.

When your secretary acts for you, you will want to back him or her up. This means, among other things, not passing the buck. Don't shift the blame for your failings onto your assistant. A letter you've neglected to dictate shouldn't be explained by "My secretary forgot to send it out." Even further, when a mistake has been made, be reasonable in your reaction. When you do criticize, make sure to follow the traditional human relations injunction, "Criticize the behavior not the person," and do so as mildly as the situation allows.

➲ REMOVING OBSTACLES TO A GOOD RELATIONSHIP

The behavior that rankles most painfully with the secretary is neglect: a boss's failure to say good morning or good night, failure to observe the small amenities. These oversights can create great job dissatisfaction. Three explanations account for the bulk of such instances of executive misjudgment:

1. Thoughtlessness.   Under the multiple pressures of executive life, amenities are easily forgotten. When the executive is preoccupied with thoughts of the new ad campaign, he literally may think of his secretary as a working machine, expected to deliver service, not to receive it.

2. Callousness.   Embittered or cynical, some managers consciously take the stand that, "These people are paid to do a job. Let 'em do it, and if they don't like it, let 'em quit. They'll get no head-patting or soft soap from me."

It's usually the secretary who has already been hurt by lack of attention and insufficient regard, to whom coldness seems a particular affront.

3. Lack of communication.   "I'm not afraid of hard work," the secretary of a bank official says. "But the thing I can't stand is this feeling of being completely out of touch with my boss."

Some secretaries say they resent lack of contact with their superiors more than they would be disturbed by rudeness or sternness. Contactlessness grows out of the inability or the lack of desire on the part of the executive to communicate. It represents both a procedural and psychological hazard:

"My boss just refuses to keep me informed of his plans," averred one overwrought assistant to an East Coast real estate executive. "It gets to be so bad that I don't even know from one day to the next whether he's going to be in the office. He may be a thousand miles away seeing a customer. What am I supposed to do? No wonder I'm a wreck at the end of the day."

The positive aspect of "removing obstacles" involves all the elements of a good working relationship: a feeling of friendliness, mutual respect, open communications, and the kind of pleasant attention to individual likes—from Christmas cards to birthday lunches—that make clear your appreciation.

→ HOW YOUR SECRETARY CAN HELP

"Happy is the man with a wife to tell him what to do, and a secretary to do it," says the English nobleman-humorist, Lord Mancroft.

You may or may not let yourself be guided in your career or your day-to-day job by the suggestions of a helpful spouse. But there's no doubt that your secretary is a major factor in helping you get things done on the job. And how you train and guide him or her in job performance, can make a major difference in easing the strains and pressures of your responsibility.

Here are some guides to maximize the contribution a secretary can make, based on the experience of a top executive known in his company for the loyalty and efficiency of the secretaries he has had:

1. "Let her in on your worries—and your hopes."   When your secretary is privy to your worries, he or she can help offset some of your anxiety. It's not at all a matter of misery loving company. Rather, the assistant knows the problem, the factors that enter into the situation. You gain a certain amount of reassurance in feeling that you have an informed person with whom you can discuss the problem and bounce ideas or solutions around. But balance this off by sharing pleasant anticipations about the department's work, growth, prospects.

2. "Let your secretary take over tasks you don't like—and that he or she can do."   This does *not* mean buck-passing, or handling over the hot potato. For example, if you have to fire a woman in the department, it's your assignment, not one you can delegate. But there are many nasty little problems that come up in offices that secretaries can often handle more tactfully than the boss. For example, a female employee in your group is going to be married. What should you give her as a wedding gift? Your secretary not only can discreetly discuss the subject with the employee, or one of her close friends, but can also do the shopping for it.

Or, you're miffed at the lack of cooperation you're getting from a super-visor who reports to a fellow-executive. You don't want to lodge a formal complaint. But your secretary, if she's on friendly terms with the offending supervisor, can act as a good-will ambassador to repair relations.

3. "Let your secretary screen nuisances and timewasters."   In the life of every executive, some rain must fall. Good-hearted, but verbose people drop in to pass the time of day—and take an hour to do it. Overdependent subordinates, seeking a shoulder to cry on, adopt the boss as an emotional parent. Often the mantle is shifted to the secretary as surrogate. He or she is then expected to listen to and discuss highly personal matters—every-thing from marital relations to what to do about a hostile mother-in-law.

Then, there are salespeople, fund-raisers, community organization peo-ple, all deserving different degrees of time and attention. Screening the boss's callers is a vital function of a secretary. *But* you must take care that this delicate function is performed both efficiently and with finesse.

Your own public relations, as well as efficiency, is at stake. Never to be forgotten—and certainly to be learned by your secretary—is the need to respect the dignity and worth of every individual at your doorstep.

In almost all cases, it's the executive who supplies the cue. A secretary who is disdainful and arrogant, who gives the red carpet treatment to the people "who matter," and the back of his or her hand to the unimportant ones, almost invariably takes a lead from the boss.

Your attitude, even more than your instructions, will set your secretary's style of screening. If you show by your manner that you consider a sales-person a worthy professional—even when he or she is making a cold call—your secretary too, will be courteous when telling the salesperson that you're not available.

➔ WHAT YOU SHOULD—AND SHOULD NOT—EXPECT OF A SECRETARY

"It was a revolting sight," an executive says. "I walked into this executive's office, and his secretary was massaging his neck and back muscles, pre-sumably to 'relax him'. . . ."

The executive as Oriental potentate doesn't look too good to his peers. Yet, there are personal services that a secretary may do, short of becoming a personal masseuse, depending on the secretary's willingness.

Morning coffee, is usually permissible. When a visitor is included—"Would you like some coffee too, Mr. Smith?"—the atmosphere of pleas-ant relaxed work pace can be most enjoyable. Deskside lunch and dinner also fit in here.

Personal shopping—gifts for a wife, children, a business friend—can bring to bear both better taste and judgment than the executive may have, and also gets him or her out from under a chore. But only with acquaintances and within reasonable limits of expertise.

Additional small personal services depend on the exact nature of the relationship and the kind of individuals involved. In general, it's wise to request no services that the secretary resents giving. For example, one executive almost caused a crisis by asking his female secretary to return a purchase made by his wife. The secretary hated "returning things," and while she didn't mind doing a favor for her boss, she resented his thinking that this personal service was transferable to the distaff side.

➲ FIVE STEPS TO PERSONAL CREATIVITY

Everyone capable of thinking at all can produce ideas. Sometimes, all that's lacking is a systematic approach. Here's one that has stimulated many executives to creative thinking:

1. Problem orientation.   Don't start by looking for ideas. Instead, start by thinking over a problem or difficulty.

The problems should be written down, in detail, so that the mind has something concrete—words on paper—to work on. Any problems can be listed, for any obstacles or bottleneck can benefit from an apt idea or solution. But the number of problems should be restricted to three or four; otherwise, energies may be scattered.

2. Mind loosening.   Some executives limber up their thinking about the problems under investigation. Says a Toronto executive, "When I'm looking for a workable new idea, I tell myself, anything goes. I'll let my mind think about any thought I get, even if it seems unorthodox, contrary to all my experience, or just plain dumb."

3. Fact ingestion.   "It's true you've got to examine a problem to come up with an idea," says an executive. "But it's rare to look at a problem and—presto—solve it. I have to go outside the problem first; research it.

"I had a materials handling problem," he adds, "and I went to a friend of mine, an engineer, for some advice. He told me about similar problems that managers in other companies were having. When I got home, I wrote down what he said, then put it in a folder which I marked SIMILAR PROBLEM—OTHER PEOPLE. By the time I wound up talking to friends, reading articles, I had six different folders. One was marked HISTORY OF MY PROBLEM, another: SOLUTIONS RECOMMENDED TO ME. And so on. The fact I was classifying everything kept me from getting lost in the data I was collecting."

4. Mental rambunctiousness.   When all the preliminaries are done, it is time for your creative thinking to start. This doesn't mean your thinking must proceed in a straight line. On the contrary. In many instances, the creative process finds you shuttling back and forth between the problem and various ideas.

But at some point, you take the problem in front of you and start thinking of solutions, ameliorating ideas, and so on. Questions like these can start you off:

What are the different parts of the problem?
Is any one of them the key to another part?
What can I borrow from another situation that will apply to this one?
What if I carry this to extremes? Could exaggeration help?
What's the opposite of the "normal" way?

5. Triggering the unconscious.   It sometimes happens that ideas come—and then have to be discarded. They're not the "right" idea; or, you're after a better one. Perhaps your unconscious can help.

You contribute little to this step directly. You simply rest from any form of conscious thought about the problem by seeking recreation or sleep (if you've been working on the problem at home), or by thinking about other matters.

If you have concentrated on the problem, and stored up considerable data, the unconscious is most likely to spring into action. That's the way we get "inspiration," the sudden idea that bursts into the mind.

One manager reports her success at stimulating her unconscious. She is so successful, in fact, she carries around a small notebook when idea hunting:

"I'd been having a tough problem meeting a specification. I'd tried everything: defined my problem, researched it, asked myself hard questions about it, even let my mind just roam. I got nowhere.

"I went to bed that night and was about to fall asleep—when the ideas began popping like firecrackers. I got up, went to my bureau, wrote them down on a laundry slip, and went back to bed. Five minutes later, I had to get up and write down another idea: on the back of a check. Within minutes I was up again: two more. I spent half the night looking for scraps of paper to write down ideas."

Many people find that the greatest discovery they make is their own potential creativity. The human mind is a tremendous idea machine—possibly the most underused resource in the world. With a minimum of stimulation and direction, we can all become that much-admired, sought-after individual—a person of ideas.

➲ **MAKE YOUR READING TIME MORE PRODUCTIVE**

Most executives, busy as they are, need to read to learn about new developments in their fields. The main problem is: how can they read with greater speed, comprehension, and enjoyment? According to Norman L. Cahners, chairman of a Boston publishing firm, *good readers aren't primarily readers at all*. They are detectives, explorers, scientists, critics, and editors—all active, seeking roles. Writing in IBM's *THINK* magazine, Cahners points out that the effective reader wants information—*and uses reading as a searching technique to get what is wanted*.

As Cahners sees it, reading is a kind of treasure hunt. The trick is to find one's way to the gold nuggets in the most direct fashion, and in the shortest possible time. Unfortunately, reading habits, as usually taught, aren't too helpful in this approach.

Cahners claims there is no point in telling a time-hungry executive to seek a relaxed posture in reading, or to insist on quiet or freedom from interruption. Most of a manager's reading has to be done under pressure and with constant interruptions. He or she has to read whenever a few minutes can be found.

Here are the author's ideas on how you can get the most out of your scarce reading hours:

■ *Make a habit of casing a book or article before actually reading it.* Who wrote it? When? What are the author's qualifications? What is he or she trying to get at? How is the material organized? Take a few minutes to answer these questions in advance, and you may find it's not worthwhile reading the book or article. Or, you may identify what it is you want to look for, what is is you want to learn.

■ *Be impatient.* Don't wait for the meaning in writing to "come to you" through long meaningless paragraphs. Reading requires your active participation. *Go in and get the meaning.* Make a habit of opening the sandwich and getting at the meat. If you pick a dozen business letters at random, you will find that most of them are constructed like a daycoach sandwich—a thin slice of meat between two slices of spongy and conventional prose.

■ *Organize what you have read.* *The reason for reading is to recall a useful idea later, when you need it.* The secret of retrieving an idea, according to Cahners, lies in spotting the dominant theme. The main theme serves as a magnetic field around which facts cluster in patterns like iron filings. Any method that helps you organize the meaning, will make it easy for you to rebuild the details when you need them later. For example, when you finish a session of reading, ask yourself, "What have I read?" Close your eyes for a minute and try to recall it.

■ *Find time to read.*   Merely by trying harder, most of us can double our customary reading speeds without loss of comprehension. Paradoxically, the swifter your reading, the more effective it becomes. Another source of more reading time is to learn to read in snatches—such as on a commuter train. Cahners mentions that the great Methodist leader John Wesley, read history, poetry, and philosophy, mostly on horseback. If you can't read in snatches, try to set aside a specific part of each day for concentrated reading—ten minutes, an hour—however long you decide. The definite spot on the agenda is a way of saying, "There's a time and a place for everything. This time belongs to reading."

➔ WHICH JOB COMES FIRST?

When you have two or more jobs to be done, which comes first? Essentially, what's involved is the establishment of priorities.

Of course, when the urgency of one project is obvious, there is no problem. But frequently the sequence in which to tackle a series of projects isn't self-evident. In such a situation, consider these four principles:

Principle No. 1: Do the easier job first.   With the easy job out of the way, the executive can concentrate on the tougher one without worrying about the other hanging overhead like the sword of Damocles.

Principle No. 2: Start the longest of equally easy jobs first when they must finish together.   This is the old lamb-chop-and-baked-potato principle used by the kitchen-wise cook who starts the potatoes baking first, puts on the chops later.

When your requirements are such that all items must finish at the same time—as when you must make a shipping deadline—this principle is decisive.

Principle No. 3: When the products of both jobs are equal in value, do the short one first.   The virtues of this course include the following:

■ With the brief assignment out of the way, the decks are cleared for you to go all out for the remaining item on the agenda.
■ In the process of getting the shorter task completed, you may have partially mobilized resources which can then be swung on to the bigger job.

Principle No. 4: Question off-the-cuff judgments and check the accuracy of estimates.   Assigning priorities to a job often means you've got to guess at some pieces in the puzzle. In one case, it's the time it will take to repair a machine. In another, it's the completion time of an unfamiliar job. It's wise to ask questions about estimates, get other opinions. Now you're better able to set job sequence.

You're the one who has to make the decisions. But that doesn't mean you can't use the experience of others to guide you on the preliminaries.

➔ QUALITIES OF A "GREAT" EXECUTIVE

What's the difference between a good executive and a great one? Dr. Mortimer Feinberg, a consultant psychologist to American business for many years, in a personal interview, says:

"The best corporate officers, the men who are recognized as tops, have a lot of energy and drive. They do many different things simultaneously—not all of them well, necessarily—but they are *driven* people. Napoleon could do seven things at once. Look for such traits in your subordinates.

"I have never seen a top executive who was passive, contemplative. Hamlet would never have become a good executive, in my view. There may be some Hamlets around, but they aren't holding the top jobs. Fred Friendly, a former president of CBS News, was known in the industry as 'Frenzied Fred,' because he expected others to tackle projects with his own clock-defying zeal. He was described as always looking as if he had just gotten off a foam-flecked horse.

"There are some other, more subtle characteristics that distinguish the potential presidents from the also-rans on the executive staff:

"*Dedication.* Just plain, sheer devotion. You call in the person and you say, 'Listen Jack, you've got to fly to Chicago and get that order. Get out there tonight.' Occasionally, he may have a good excuse—his wife is sick or his child is in the hospital. But if he goes 99 percent of the time, he is committed to the game of making your company successful.

"*Competitiveness.* First-class executives can't bear to lose. They are only interested in winning. They are constantly evaluating themselves against the competition and striving to do better at each opportunity. They change their frames of reference. One executive, a self-made man, told me when he was on the way up: 'Here I am, sitting at the feet of the elephants, and I'm just a mouse. They might kill me. Just by accident. Because I'm a mouse and they are elephants.' I asked him, 'What are you going to do?' He said, 'I'm going to become an elephant, too.'

"*Honesty.* How honest is he with himself? Does he wear expensive suits and dirty underwear? Is he aware of some of his own limitations? How honest is he with you? How consistently does he produce what he said he would produce? Are his aspirations out of touch with reality? Or, are they close to what he can actually achieve? If he says, 'OK, I didn't do too well that time, but I learned a lesson and I'll do better next time,' then he's honest with himself.

"*Realism.* He has his feet on the ground. He doesn't just dream about how great he's going to be someday. If he's always seeing the big picture and never the details, he's in trouble. The outstanding executive is looking at how he's going to get where he wants to be; he is almost compulsive about the little things, the short cuts.

"*Maturity*. He knows that his own future rests on what happens to other people. He can fire a man who does not contribute to the good of the organization. He respects differences of opinion. He doesn't meddle in office politics and he refuses to manipulate people. He is patient. He doesn't accept the first solution when it presents itself. He bounces back when he's hurt.

"Finally, a potential president is able to handle multiple pressures. A New York boss puts it this way: 'Anyone can do a good job if you give him one problem at a time and all the time he needs to solve it. But when I see a man unwilling to pay attention to anything else until he gets his own little problem solved, I worry. That kind of man never knows there's a fire next door until the whole company burns down.' "

⮕ TIPS ON ETIQUETTE FOR THE EXECUTIVE

The subject of etiquette for the executive is as much a joke as it is an area of concern. Look at some of the books that have been written on the subject, and it's all too clear that good manners on the business scene are a simple extension of etiquette in everyday life.

Then, what are business etiquette books about? The well-intentioned authors, after stressing how important it is to cultivate good manners and good appearance, then go on to such vital matters as how to dress, how introductions are to be made, and so on. But once these areas are exhausted, the writers tend to take one of two paths:

■ They go into the lore of etiquette *in general*—visiting cards, orders of precedence, and forms of address (one English book on business etiquette goes into great detail on how to address mail to the royal family, and dukes and duchesses of royal blood.)

■ The other direction in which the subject-matter-starved writer tends to turn: that of business situations. And these don't involve etiquette as much as they do management procedures. For example, one authority discusses meetings and committees, offering perfectly good suggestions that constitute good management practice rather than considerations of etiquette.

Perhaps it's unfair to take these business writers to task so harshly. There is some justification in considering some management procedures from the viewpoint of courtesy and general appropriateness.

For our purposes, coverage in three areas will suffice: dress; introductions; phone usage.

1. Dress.   The key to acceptable appearance largely depends on the "climate" in your company. For example, the informal, even flashy attire that's considered "good form" in an advertising agency, might be inappropriate in a bank.

Give some thought to the way you *want* to look. It is possible to be conservative without being "square." It's possible to follow current trends without conforming to the last detail. And "political" consideration enters: it may be advisable for the executive on the way up to be somewhat more conservative and leave it to better-established executives to be the style innovators and trend setters. However, dressing for the "level above you" is a tactic sometimes recommended for those who aspire to bigger things. See "Women in Management" for a discussion of women executives' dress.

2. Introductions.   Frequently you're called on to introduce people: your secretary to a visitor; a vistor to another executive. Introductions in the business world tend to be informal. But they *should* be audible. In addition to pronouncing names clearly, a title or descriptive phrase is helpful. For example, if you're bringing a customer in to meet one of your company's officers, you might say, as you enter, "Bill, this is Mr. Green, Chief Purchasing Agent of the Acme chain. Bill Smith, our General Manager."

If you are being introduced, any one of a number of traditional phrases uttered in a pleasant tone is acceptable: "Very glad to meet you"; "Yes, I know of your company and think very highly of it," and so on.

Handshaking is almost always in order among men. Women may or may not shake hands, as they prefer. Yes, still.

Finally, if any of the names involved in the introductions are difficult to pronounce, you may want to make it a point of spelling out: "Mr. LeBeau, capital L-e- capital B-e-a-u."

3. Phone usage.   It's in the area of telephone utilization that business practice does tend to vary with practices of the nonbusiness world. Some of the specifics of business phone use involve the executive, some his secretary. In any case, here are some guidelines:

Prompt response.   People calling you, customers, suppliers, other executives, and so on, get a bad impression when phones ring and go unanswered for any length of time. On the other hand, people appreciate the businesslike and courteous impression made by prompt answering.

Identification.   The "Hello" response of the everyday world isn't satisfactory on the job. Your secretary will avoid guessing games by answering a ring with: "Production Department, Miss Jones."

Screening.   Train your secretary *not* to ask, "Who's calling?" It's more acceptable to say, "May I tell Mr. Smith who's calling?" or, "Mr. Smith is attending a meeting. May I have him call you when he's finished?"

Explain delays.   If you must leave the line, you may want to provide a word of explanation, or at any rate, indicate approximately how long you'll be. Generally, if it's going to require some time to get information, it's wiser to offer to call back.

Taking messages.   Here's where secretaries may need coaching, particularly if they are beginners in the business world. Train your secretary to spell names if there is any question and to verify numbers by reading them back to the caller.

As we've said, good manners on the business scene are a simple extension of etiquette in everyday life. And there is no doubt that good manners are an asset to the executive, while lack of courtesy can lose good will, customers, and destroy morale within the executive's own organization.

13. Women in Management

Sometime in the future a chapter like this one will be irrelevant, the subject matter totally outdated. Until then, the information and insights on women's progress toward workplace equality and the upper echelons, and the situations relating to it can be useful to management, and managers of both sexes.

➜ BREACHING THE MAHOGANY CURTAIN

Three developments changed the all-male ballgame in the executive suite:

- legal pressures, in the form of antidiscrimination laws
- increased social consciousness of men and women caused by the women's movement.
- women's proven managerial capabilities, especially in the decades since the Fair Employment Practices acts.

The increasing upward mobility of women on the work scene has brought with it disruptions and new patterns in interpersonal relationships. While women have been present ever since the Industrial Revolution, their jobs were generally menial. Following the Civil Rights Act of 1964, barriers against women in the executive echelons gradually weakened. New problems then arose, as you would expect from a major social and economic change—and are still with us.

➔ EQUALITY UNDER THE LAW

The Civil Rights Act of 1964 prohibited job discrimination based on race, color, religion, sex, or national origins. The Equal Pay Act prohibited wage discrimination—such as the assertion that women "couldn't do" a given job, or that pay differentials were justified because certain elements (often minor) distinguished a male job from a female job. Organizations were directed to see to it by affirmative action that executive rosters show a reasonable percentage of women in higher echelon jobs.

Key cases pushed by the enforcing agencies levied sizable penalties for noncompliance. Affirmative action programs, that is, plans and projects to recruit, train, and promote women along with other minorities, into higher-echelon jobs won significant gains, particularly in larger companies.

(For further coverage of the legal aspects of women's status see Section 14, "Fair Employment Practices.")

➔ ONE WOMAN'S VIEW OF MALE DOMINANCE

There are many organizations in which the climate is reasonably egalitarian. Women employees balance the roster and are themselves convinced that bias will not impede promotion.

But some proponents of sex equality aver that male dominance still persists widely, not only in practice but in spirit. What, you may say? Decades after the inception of civil rights legislation? An account appearing in the *New York Times* January 1987, by Nancy Bazelon Goldstone provides a partial answer.

The girls in bikinis. At the age of twenty-seven, Nancy Bazelon Goldstone became chief foreign-exchange options trader at a major commercial New York bank. At her desk one day she became aware that her colleagues, all male, had vanished from their customary work stations. A brief search discovered them gathered around a table in an alcove. What could it be? Obviously something of major business importance. She rushed to join the group, hoping it wasn't news of an assassination. There, spread out in bright color on the table appeared the cause of the excitement. The "swimsuit issue" of *Sports Illustrated* had arrived.

Okay, you may say, that's one office. But is it? Less obvious but even more significant. Despite the passage of years, studies still show that the dominance of the male spirit shows up in the statistics: women constitute about 30 percent of executives and the percentage becomes scanty at the top levels. And earnings are substantially below male averages.

➲ REVIEWING THE RECORD

A graph of women's progress toward equality shows upward movement, along with hesitations. Instead of a steady rise, the data suggests lapses and reduced rates of progress. While fairly large numbers have entered lower management levels, a *Fortune* article asserts that as of 1984, only *one* of its 500 largest industrial corporations has a woman chief executive, and she, Katherine Graham of the Washington Post Company, admits family ownership of controlling shares got her the job.

Clearly, legally erasing restraints to women's career mobility fails to solve the equality problem. History will show that heading into the 1990s, women have less than equal status in American business. This result is as ambiguous and puzzling as the realities on which it is based. The score:

Victories	Defeats
General acceptance of antidiscrimination legislation	Persistence of suits against employers for discriminatory labor practices
Affirmative action programs	Figures show inequality in many desirable job categories
Fringe benefits, such as child care and related matters, have been instituted by many companies	Many women find working conditions, such as inflexible hours, in conflict with family demands
The success of some women to "have it all," meaning both a career and family	The conflict between economics and biology is a continuing anguish for many

What emerges from the appraisal is that favoring legislation and good intentions of most employers is not enough. Equality continues to be a grail, more sought after than found. One cynic says, "As long as we have separate washrooms for men and women, equality can never be total." But the struggle goes on, still confused by the irregularity of the lines between the opposing forces. A unique factor: women constitute the only minority that may have close personal and social contact with nonminority members: husbands, fathers, brothers, men friends, and so on. This is often a complication rather than an amelioration.

➲ THREE WAVES: THE PATTERN OF PROGRESS

The adaptive behavior of women in management in the past twenty years has registered in three waves:

1. Catching up. Catapulted into the terra incognita of the executive suite, women were told, and with apparent logic, that their first order of business was to learn what becoming a manager was all about. The publishing and academic world obliged, and a flood of books, magazines, courses, and seminars, offered the information and insights that roadmapped the reefs and opportunities.

From a somewhat raunchy, *Games Mother Never Taught You* by Betty L. Harragan, which aimed to prepare women for the worst, to the somewhat more practical *Ambitious Woman's Guide to a Successful Career,* by management veterans Tom Quick and Maggie Higginson, management beginners and aspirers were introduced to the mysteries. Wives asked their manager husbands to talk shop, even to repeat anecdotes they had heard before, but which now took on personal interest. Women who wanted to be managers initiated talks with their bosses, heads of personnel, people in their companies who could help them learn what they had to know to break through the mahogony curtain.

2. "Ape" Men?   Once over the border and into an entry-level management job, women had to know not only what to do, but how to do it. How do you instruct a subordinate? How friendly could you be? What if you gave an order and got backtalk instead of obedience? What about your boss? Is he now a pal, or must your stance still be pretty much what it was to your supervisor, Mr. Smith, when you were a secretary?

A general assumption was that a woman manager had to resemble as far as possible her male opposite number. An article in the *New York Times* Sunday magazine presented the extreme of this view in describing a star of the investment world. In addition to being smart and hard-working, "she ascended on Wall Street because she is tough, can swear, tell dirty jokes, drink with the boys and not let her family get in the way."

The advice to women managers to get as masculine as they could get had battalions of women taking assertiveness training, getting fitted for tailored suits, and discouraging small courtesies that suggested their femininity. (Who enters the elevator first, what about the tab for lunch with a male colleague, and so on).

3. The wised-up woman.   In the last half of the 1980s, a new type of woman manager began to develop. As the prototype for tomorrow-

- She has learned the lessons of the first wave, of fitting into the executive scene, accepting the ascendency of men, and the effort required to achieve parity with them.
- She also knows about the second wave, but faults it. Aping men, in the end, will not work. First, the masquerade is likely to seem ludicrous in the masculinized uniform affected by man, complete to shirt and bow tie, and in terms of behavior, in attempting to seem a bull-of-the-woods. To succeed in her work and achieve equality, women must perform on their own terms, be themselves as a group, and as individuals. The wised-up woman manager:

- Retains her psychic and female integrity;
- Looks within herself for the strengths on which to build her effectiveness and to achieve professional fulfillment;
- Feels she doesn't have to check her femininity at the office door.

The third wave is growing, strengthened by a sense of its "rightness." Interestingly enough, it is dress that foreshadows the woman executive of tomorrow, in image and role philosophy.

➲ WORKING ATTIRE—AS DRESS AND STATEMENT

It was the semanticist Samuel I. Hayakawa who expressed the dual and ambiguous role of dress for women. Speaking of a woman whose hat style startled her colleagues, he said, "It looked awful on her, but great on her self-image."

Hats were once a key to status identification at work. Up until 1950 it was not unusual for female managers, sometimes at their desks, to wear hats. The reason: To set them apart from secretaries, clerks, and so on.

In *Women in Charge*, Aileen Jacobson has twenty-three separate references to the matter of dress. Here is one that contrasts female and male:

Because of the dictates of our society, most women wear makeup and dress more elaborately than men, and jewelry, multi-colored dresses and high-heeled shoes are features that most people have not been accustomed to associate with people in power until very recently. These days, "dress for success" has become a cliché, but it is applied much more frequently to women than to men. Men do not have to worry much about how they dress, while women often must spend time and energy on it that they could more usefully spend on business matters.

For women the question of dress has always been a career problem as well as a personal one. A major factor has been the part clothing plays not only as attire, but as a projection of the persona. It is this dichotomy that explains the conflict between the styles of the day, and how a woman sees herself.

Observers of the work scene have noted the roller-coaster changes of dress styles among women managers. "Total confusion," say some. Many managerial women are at a loss to know how to dress in their unaccustomed role. In an extreme case, employees of an advertising firm were startled by a new department-head who showed up her first day on the job in a see-through blouse.

More generally, a trend in the early 1980's was the severely tailored suit, usually tweed, and silk blouses occasionally worn with bow tie.

Subsequently, a style appeared that reflected the "wised-up woman" approach. Alcott & Andrews, operating a chain of retail apparel shops catering to career women, scored a quick success by offering clothes that -

- eschewed any hint of the "mädchen-in-uniform" look (which marked the concept of dressing like men);
- were feminine, informal, and individualistic;
- avoided lines reminiscent of military uniforms;
- favored graceful, flattering curves, in collars, necklines, and featured scarves and accessories such as chains and pendants.

The brains behind the Alcott & Andrews look, experienced marketers Michael Jeffries and Coleen Brady, developed a concept that encouraged career women toward more relaxation in dress. "Stylish but not trendy," the fashion press reported, "updated but not forward."

In training their salespeople, and indirectly their customers, Alcott & Andrews taught "how clothes work together, about fabric content and the fit of garments, that certain jackets fit certain body types." To broaden their line, and more fully satisfy the needs of business women, pants, coats, shirts, sweaters, jackets and accessories are stocked. "The working woman," says Michael Jeffries, founder and president of A & A, "wants to look pretty, not like a man, but not outlandish."

One male company president, sympathetic and understanding the female manager's problems with role compatability says, "Women's dress problem is to create a favorable impression without being provocative. A man looking at a woman manager should think, 'She is well dressed,' and stop short of sexual fantasies. It may mean a neckline that is an inch higher, or avoiding a slinky skirt. The separation line is thin, but many women are able to stay on the right side of it."

→ FIVE TIPS FOR THE SHOPPER

Barbara Pittfield, fashion consultant to manufacturers of women's wear, offers these suggestions to women who are rethinking their business attire:

1. Dress for comfort and personal style. All the self-discovered rules about "your" colors, necklines that are flattering, the fashions that suit you and those that do not, should guide your choices.

2. Job status and company style are factors to consider. A top executive can afford—financially and in terms of latitude—a degree of expensiveness that might be off-base for a beginning manager. And organizations have their individual standards, depending on the spirit of its management—conservative or less restrained—or even location. For example, firms on the West coast are notably more informal than their Eastern counterparts.

3. Think in terms of "wardrobe" rather than in single items. A day's schedule that includes a top-level meeting might suggest a jacket, as it would for a male manager. This piece of attire is a formalism that may well be eternal because of its function—it minimizes distraction. A task requiring crawling around in a warehouse to check inventory might call for pants. Your closet should make such choices possible.

4. Accessorizing is one key to an enhanced image.   "Don't be afraid to look interesting," Pittfield counsels. One hedge: "Avoid the fussy look."

Accessories assist in several ways: individualize your attire, signal a personal style, and can eliminate the "bare neck" look that Barbara Pittfield cautions against. "A scarf or necklace, preferably not too delicate," is her prescription.

5. Personalize according to body shape.   Not everyone is tall and slender, or chunky and five feet tall. Being well dressed is often a matter of fit, as much as any other factor. A detail like shoulder pads inside a blouse can replace sloping lines by horizontals that suggest authority, a belt can help or hinder appearance, depending on figure and suitability.

Female-fashion: savvy for the men in the crowd.   The guidelines above are offered not only to assist managerial women in their wardrobing, but also to suggest the direction and spirit of career women's ideas of self-presentation in the future. While the information is directed to women managers, it is hoped that their male counterparts will benefit from a practical insight into an area of their female colleagues' concern.

The quest for identity and equality is ongoing. For the individual woman, the problems and their solutions are shaped by dozens of factors, from the personality or her boss to the level of enlightenment in her company, and especially that part of it in which she works. The pages that follow deal with some of the situations that linger on in a society that has not yet caught up with itself.

⮑ FRIENDSHIPS AND THE WOMAN MANAGER

Even though there are a higher percentage of women in higher-echelon jobs, attitudes may not be ready for them. Two sources of friction:

Male colleagues of managerial women   resist their presumptive equality. Hostile behavior may show up in subtle but unmistakable form. For example, in some milieus, women managers are not included in activities not necessarily all male, such as an afterwork drink, or bowling. In the work setting, antagonism may appear in a meeting, for example, where disagreement takes on an extra edge when between a man and woman. The heat of argument may invite derision, either open or by innuendo: "You women don't seem to understand."

Below-surface bias may be revealed in a quickness to criticize behavior simply because it is different. The dictum of Mrs. Patrick Campbell is a commendable guide. The world-famous actress averred that she didn't much care what people did "as long as they didn't frighten the carriage horses." Women managers, like any other group, are best judged by results.

Women themselves.   Women may be uncertain of their management roles and how to act them out, may become defensive or overly aggressive. Male colleagues, even the well intentioned, may react negatively, and the climate becomes tainted with tension and ill-feeling.

A case history tells of one woman manager's adjustment problem based on an old bias:

Ruth Bertram, well educated, divorced, and in her late thirties, has recently been promoted from assistant to office manager. She is the only female department head in her organization. She does not have much in common with the other women in the office, who are secretaries and assistants and, for the most part, younger than she. She has, however, developed a friendship with another manager, Tony Frye—a man about her age. They frequently have lunch together and chat in each other's office.

Now there is gossip. A friendship that would be taken for granted between two men is being misinterpreted as an affair. Apparently we have not progressed far enough from the era when every adult male-female association outside of marriage was presumed to be illicit. Whether it's a holdover from the bad old days, envy, the result of prurient curiosity or boredom on the job, some people still speculate when a male manager and a female manager pair off for lunch.

What can a man and a woman like Ruth Bertram and Tony Frye, who have a nonsexual relationship, do to stop the talk? Some possibilities:

- *Break off their friendship?* But this is the soap opera answer—making a personal sacrifice to prevent scandal. Men and women can be friends without necessarily having affairs.
- *Meet on the sly?* Very bad, because this really would make it look as if they have something to hide. However, it may be smart to avoid anything that looks more like a date than a business relationship—dinner for two, for example.
- *Restrict the friendship to business hours?* This way Ruth and Tony give no grounds for surmising about what they may do away from the office. There may still be gossip, but sooner or later the grapevine will switch to hotter topics if they do nothing to encourage gossip.

For the woman, it's a temptation to grasp the first friendly male hand that is extended—and cling to it. But this friend may not be the most helpful in the long run. If other managers feel shut out, the female manager is even less likely to gain their acceptance.

One realistic remedy: Ruth and Tony should never be exclusive. Inviting other managers to join them gives everyone a chance to see that the relationship is aboveboard. Bringing others into the group has another advantage for the woman manager. In organizations with few women managers, life can be lonely at the executive level. Adding to the circle can enrich social life as well as reinforce professional contacts that can be useful on the job.

→ HOW THE PAST LINGERS ON

Some women are reluctant to accept promotions. A survey of women in eight large corporations showed that 50 percent of women managers or potential managers have turned down job promotions. A major reason for rejection of the higher job offer: the women believed that the promotions were a "fake," offered to help the organization comply with antidiscrimination pressures, or "were created for women because it looked good," as a kind of tokenism to make the organization seem to be in the forefront of social change.

While promotion-wariness among women is likely to change, it may persist in individual cases. This attitude is worth remembering if a woman is offered a promotion and refuses it. Of course, men also turn down offers of advancement because of unwillingness to accept responsibility, not wanting to get too deeply imbedded in the "establishment," health reasons, and so on. But when a woman turns down an offer of a job of more responsibility, her motivation is likely to be ascribed to the weakness or unpredictability of her sex.

A recommendation to women facing a decision on accepting a promotion: think through the pros and cons. Avoid being persuaded or dissuaded by other people's attitudes or advice that may reflect their own particular biases.

Recommendation to managers who are about to offer a promotion into managerial ranks to a woman: set forth the proposal in the same way you would to a man. However, if the candidate indicates an interest in discussing the special aspects of the position, as they might interfere with family schedules, for example, level with her and give her full opportunity to clarify her doubts and ask her questions.

⊃ FIVE ASSUMPTIONS TO AVOID IN JUDGING WOMEN JOB CANDIDATES

Antidiscrimination laws aside, people who screen and interview job candidates sometimes proceed on the basis of false assumptions. Here are five that can lead you astray:

1. *Don't* expect to find a woman with qualities just like those possessed by men already holding similar jobs. Most jobs can be done equally well in several ways. A woman can have qualities quite different from those possessed by male incumbents and still perform satisfactorily. As in any job-filling procedure, list the job demands and gauge the applicant's qualifications as a measure of capability.
2. *Don't* judge the candidate by stereotyped female roles. For example, don't assume that a "masculine," that is, assertive type of woman is necessarily the one you need to be a manager. Or, if you're hiring a person for customer contacts, don't hang your hopes on finding a woman heavily endowed with female charm, as a mainstay of her job tactics.

   In the former case the expectation is that the masculine manner will nullify "female weaknesses." In a second the assumption is that an excess of femininity will help in "manipulating" others. The only cure for this pitfall is to avoid thinking in stereotypes altogether. Try to see job candidates of either sex as worthy for what they are in themselves. Judge them by what they can do.
3. *Don't* make assumptions about a woman's motivation. For example, it's widely believed that married women coming into the labor force do so for "fur coat money," that is, just to be able to indulge their special acquisitive whims. Another widely held feeling is that married women with young children inevitably become a high risk in terms of attendance. As long as the woman has made realistic plans for the care of her children while she's working, her attendance will be as good as anyone else's. At one time it was a common assumption that a young woman would stop working when she met and married Mr. Right. Nowadays that's even less likely.
4. *Don't* expect women applicants to be less realistic or hard-nosed about the job you're offering—salary prospects, benefits, and so on—than a male counterpart. Why should they be, now that the law guarantees them equal pay, benefits, and so on?
5. *Women aren't "little men."* In the dark ages before the women's movement one expert on that intriguing subject known as the "difference between the sexes" maintained that it was really very easy to

understand women in terms of what they were and were not capable of:

"Just think of women as being little men," he maintained. "This explains not only their physical limitations in terms of stamina, weightlifting, and so on, but it also explains their limited ability to plan, make decisions, wield authority, and so on."

The high performance level of today's women managers is the simplest rebuttal to this view.

➲ IF YOU'RE A MALE WORKING FOR A FEMALE BOSS

"The women's movement has created a new minority, and I'm part of it," asserts a manager. "Who are we? We're males who have female bosses. And like other minorities, we have problems." The "problems" referred to are less common as more women enter management. But for some men psychological adjustment may still be necessary.

Of course, the "working-for-a-woman" problem isn't limited to men. In one case a female secretary literally could not take dictation from a woman. The few times she was asked to, she became sick to her stomach—clearly a symptom of psychological trauma.

The overreacting secretary, though a rare case, does suggest the turmoil that may result from what some people see as a reversal of the natural order of things. Actually, there is a range of reactions possible. Some men take the news they will be reporting to a woman by threatening to quit, others demand a transfer. Sometimes the resentment is more covert.

The fact is that resentment is likely *any* time a new boss takes over. When the person who gets the promotion is a woman, the stereotype of male superiority may increase the sense of being unjustly treated, unappreciated, or, even harder to take, inferior.

Even if a man has no strong negative reaction, he may find that his family and friends do. (In fact, some male subordinates confess that what troubled them most was having to tell their wives they were now reporting to a woman.) Acquaintances declare, "You work for a woman boss? I'd rather starve!" It seems as though the male subordinate lacks machismo if he keeps his cool.

Males, from rank-and-file to executives, who are concerned about their female bosses should consider points like these to ease the pressure:

- *Accept actual feelings.* Unless a man works in an organization where women have traditionally been managers, there's going to be some kind of adverse reaction. And it is far better for a man to be aware of any feelings of hostility than to deny them and have his dealings with the new boss colored by disturbing below-surface emotions.

■ *What will it mean in personal terms?* Even if secure enough to feel no threat to his manhood, a man may nonetheless be concerned about his situation. In companies which have promoted a woman because of legal pressure, there can be legitimate concern that top management won't really support her and that subordinates will suffer along with her as a result of her shaky authority and lack of clout.

In addition, if the only women a man has known well have been his mother, his wife, and his secretary, he may be very uncertain of how to act around a woman superior. But if he is able to face up to his own feelings of discomfort and uncertainty, it will be possible to adjust more easily:

■ *See* the real problem. It is a mistake for the male subordinate to see his problem as one of "adjusting to a female boss." The real problem is, "How can I learn to work productively with this particular individual?" It is when the subordinate stops seeing himself as confronting wide-ranging social change, but rather sees the goal as one of developing a practical working relationship that the solution is at hand. One approach to developing a positive relationship involves three phases:

Phase 1: Opening gambits. It is best to let the boss provide the cues as to what she expects and how she will exercise her leadership.

The subordinate, however, does have some options. He may choose to remain passive and leave it entirely up to his boss to determine the pattern of their relationship. Or he may register a pleasant, accepting attitude. After all, the woman is probably expecting, and dreading, resentment from some of her male subordinates. She'll be looking for cues for her behavior from subordinates, also.

Or, going a step further, a male subordinate can show friendliness. One manager reports he greeted his new boss by saying, "I want to congratulate you on your promotion. I'll give you any help I can." He wisely did *not* offer to help her learn the ropes but decided to let her ask him, if she chose.

Phase 2: Testing. Will the new boss be formal or informal? Will she run a tight ship? How, and how much, will she delegate? How much initiative does she expect from subordinates? Will she be tough, demanding, or will she prefer a consultative approach?

The answers to these and related questions come through day-by-day contacts. The subordinate usually gets the message automatically. But the more awareness he brings to these contacts, the faster and better he'll understand what's expected.

Phase 3: Optimizing. After some time has passed, the subordinate is in a position to size up the situation between him and his boss by thinking through the answers to specific questions: What are the satisfactory areas of our working together? What areas are unsatisfactory (if any)? Why are they unsatisfactory? What can be done to minimize or eliminate the difficulties? Here the question might be reworded: If my boss were male and I had the same problem, how would I tackle it?

With these rocky spots out of the road, the way is prepared for a good working relationship. The three phases of developing it are, in fact, those a subordinate should expect with any boss. One secret of adjusting to a woman boss is to regard her, and treat her, as an executive. Whether the approach succeeds depends ultimately on the individuals involved—not on their sexes.

SPECIAL PERFORMANCE OBSTACLES FOR WOMEN

A major fact to keep in mind in order to avoid misunderstanding, disappointment, or conflict is that equality for women and an end of discrimination will *not* transform them into men. They should never be expected to look like the opposite sex, behave like the opposite sex, or necessarily have work styles that are similar.

In specific cases, some standard management situations may represent obstacles to them. For example, in the lower echelons a common problem in sex equality has to do with a woman's ability to lift or carry heavy burdens that may be a part of the job operation. In the upper echelons there are few physical tests that militate against women. But there are some patterns of activity that may represent difficulties, particularly for married women who have responsibility for home and children.

Traveling in the field may mean serious personal disruption for women. Attendance at management or professional seminars or assignments on certain types of company committees may cause family or home problems. Obviously how large the problem looms is entirely an individual matter. Enlightened organizations and executives should take these practical problems into account just as they might give special consideration to male employees in special personal situations.

A possible and touchy complication: hostility by a male manager to a female colleague because she *is* a female. Suspicious and exaggerated reactions may still further complicate the basic situation. For a higher echelon executive, this conflict, usually below surface, represents a problem in forbearance and tact. The best course is to give the woman manager the chance to resolve the problem herself. Supply guidance, if it's asked for. Only as a last resort, and if the hostility of the male manager is clear, should the executive in authority intervene. Perhaps the best approach to the recalcitrant is to remind him that he's behind the times, causing a work problem and opening the company to a possible discrimination suit.

➲ THE ROCKY ROAD TO EQUALITY

Women have two obstacles that confront them as they seek true equality in the world of work. One, obviously, is the external blockage, the bias, resentment, and resistance of males who feel threatened by both the thought and actuality of women in management echelons. Much has been said and written about the *external* obstacles. Less talked about, but more insidious, and for some women an even greater difficulty, is the *internal* or psychological problem.

Women who have reached their maturity in a world which is still sex-differentiated in many ways find it difficult to free themselves of these pressures. The journey from dependency to independence may be beset with difficulties. Just consider one major point: Many women have had as their role one that is subordinate and dependent on other people—as daughter or wife. In the working world a position most widely held by women is that of secretary—a role usually dependent on a male executive.

From this limiting position, the woman who wants to succeed in management must learn to operate on her own, lead and counsel other people, know and state her own views, and in some cases be assertive enough to persuade others, including her superior, to see things as she sees them. These difficulties, though great, have been successfully surmounted by many women. Individual struggle will become less difficult as many of the old stereotypes weaken and fade into social history. But for some women, equality will continue to be a two-front battle, external and internal, and this should be kept in mind by both the women themselves and male colleagues.

Men and women should be aware of the possibility of overreaction in attempting to compete in what perhaps is less a male world, but is still bound by some of the old traditions. The ambitious woman may try too hard. Knowing that in some cases she may have to prove herself significantly superior to a man to get equal recognition, she may drive herself into modes of behavior that aggravate her situation. Many businessmen have expressed themselves on the matter of the overreacting woman manager: "They are aggressive witches who can do a good job, but no man would want to marry one."

You can be sure that such views are not objective evaluations but represent male chauvinism at its worst. You'll certainly never hear an aggressive *male* manager described or put down in any such terms. Then why apply it to his female opposite number?

♦ THREE ASSISTS FOR THE NEW MANAGER

"Women will never perform as ably as men," say some diehards. "They don't have the mental equipment, the stamina, or the drive."

It's an old bias that may persist even into the distant future. But for the practical executive such rigid views are unacceptable. As would be true of any group being thrust into new situations, there must be a period of adjustment and accommodation. Here are some of the considerations that should be made in instances where women in management represent a recent change:

■ **Avoid lowering performance standards.**   It may seem unfair to expect new women managers to perform at the same level as male old-timers. But it may be wiser to do this than to have it seem that female managers just aren't expected to do as well as their male counterparts. Once this expectation becomes ingrained, it becomes a continuing handicap to the advancement and promotion of other women.

■ **Give them time.**   There is a distinction to be made between women just starting out in a new responsibility and what's expected of them eventually. It's a recognized technique in sports that less skilled participants may be given a handicap or assist. This concept should be applied to women only at the start of a training or development period. The ultimate objective should be equality of expectation in terms of performance—objectives accomplished, results achieved, and so on.

■ **Avoid a premature overload.**   It's an invitation to trouble to give women major responsibilities before they are capable of handling them. The "sink-or-swim" approach to test capability *may* be acceptable under special circumstances such as lack of time or absence of an alternative. Yet, with all the resources used in preparation for management today, there is no reason why women shouldn't be given the benefits of adequate preparation before being placed in demanding jobs.

Finally, it's unwise to keep anyone in a job in which, despite all efforts and help provided, performance expectations aren't being met. The same measurements of adequacy should be applied to women managers as to men. Where failure seems irreversible the policies of transfer or dismissal should be applied the same as they are to unsuccessful male managers.

➲ THE MALE–FEMALE TENSION AXIS

Although enlightenment has flourished and the upward mobility of women has generally increased, a tough residual core of friction, conflict, competitiveness, call it what you will, still persists. A study, Managing Sexual Tension in the Workplace, conducted by Catalyst, a nonprofit research and advisory organization concerned with issues involving women in business, finds that executive women continue to face problems of adjustment and acceptance. The result is discomfort and uncertainty among both men and women in corporate life.

The report identifies areas that constitute a second phase of male–female adjustment, following an earlier one that included hat-tipping, removal of same in elevators, to open or not to open doors for women, men having trouble accepting female assertiveness, and so on.

➲ TYPICAL SECOND-PHASE SITUATIONS

Some typical persistent problems:

- A male executive hesitates to send single women on out-of-town assignments because they might be uncomfortable on the road.
- A female manager can't get her male supervisor to provide the honest feedback she needs to improve her professional skills.
- A male executive shies away from criticizing women subordinates because he fears they will react emotionally, and he's not sure how to handle such an emotional response.
- A male manager is uneasy about traveling to a distant convention with a female colleague, although they have a cordial business relationship.

➲ MISCOMMUNICATION, DISCOMFORT, UNCERTAINTY

The Catalyst study speaks of a desirable but hypothetical "comfort level" between the sexes, and suggests that it is distorted by miscommunication and uncertainty. Felice Schwartz, president of Catalyst, believes that failure to face up to feelings explains the persistence of the problem: "We believe there is a real need to open up communications on these issues," she says.

Central to the difficulties seems to be the persistence of traditional attitudes between the sexes, for example, men's failure to understand, and so accept, women who choose a career at the expense of a home and family. Schwartz, referring to men who wax romantic over female colleagues, says, "It's a two-way street, since some women imagine having a romantic relationship" with a male colleague.

➲ EASING THE TENSION

The Catalyst report views the male–female difficulties as a transition period reflecting the unprecedented numbers of high-level men and women working together. However, the study suggests some remedies:

1. Awareness of the problem and seeing it as an adjustment of one-to-one working relationships offers a solution for individual situations. In this connection, Lisa Hicks, senior associate at Catalyst suggests

that "new roles and working relationships have to be defined" for men and women working together.

2. Some companies, aware of the interpersonal problems, and the drain they can represent on mental and physical energy, have hired consultants who run "gender-awareness" sessions to help people work through some of their misperceptions and hangups. Role-playing and discussions help conferees clarify their feelings and view their situations objectively.

3. Some personnel executives, aware of the special nature of male–female confrontations nevertheless see them as being not too dissimilar from other kinds of interpersonal conflicts and disaffections. Says one, "The objective in considering male–female tensions is the same as for any other workplace friction, the need to restore both parties to their optimum functioning and productivity." While the depth of the feelings on both sides of a male–female difficulty are likely to be stronger, the personnel executive's approach does encourage objectivity and adds the important element of matter-of-factness in the attitudes and reactions of those involved.

Sexual Harassment and the Woman Manager

Despite the authority and status that comes with her job, the woman manager is not immune to the toils of sexual complications. There are four ways in which difficulties may appear:

1. Victimization by a peer or executive of higher rank.
2. Development of romantic ideas about a subordinate which are not altogether controlled.
3. Empathetic pressures, subtle but strong, when a subordinate comes to her to complain about harassment from a third party.
4. Threat from outside: unwelcome personal interest from clients, customers, suppliers or other business contacts expecting sexual favors.

Here are considerations for each of these situations. Note that no moral or ethical judgments are made despite their relevance to the general subject. Within the purview of this book, our concentration is on the personal and career problems vital to managers of both sexes.

1. Victimization by a peer or executive of higher rank. Conceivably, individuals of any rank and either sex may be subjected to unwelcome attention. One might think that higher-echelon women would not be vulnerable to such advances. But court records of harassment cases show the facts are otherwise.

In a way, female executives may face a more formidable situation than women down the line. Consider:

■ It may not be as easy for her to appeal to a superior for help in dealing with the situation. Her ability to handle problems may come into question.

■ She is probably playing for bigger stakes. Her investment in her career is likely to be bigger, in terms of time and aspirations. And even a small controversy would most likely undercut her prospects.

Any weakening of her resolve to turn aside advances is likely to commit her to patterns of behavior that might affect her professional goals and future.

Discussions with executive women who have observed this problem suggest possible responses aimed at mitigating ill feeling. They are listed in order of intensity. Of course, the degree of applicability depends on the specifics of a given case.

"I'm already involved with someone . . ."

"I'm flattered, but we can be better friends without any entanglements . . ."

"It would be unwise for us to start anything that is likely to turn into a business and professional handicap (or disaster) . . ."

"I'm sorry, but a relationship with someone in the company would cause complications that would injure both of us . . ."

"If you persist, I will have to consult X (a superior) about your behavior." (An undesirable action but a strong threat, and worth considering if the boss is trustworthy.)

"If these attempts don't stop, I will resign . . ." (A possible course if the boss is the molester or it becomes the ultimate choice.)

"If X won't intervene, I have a good lawyer who might . . ."

The dialogue may seem stilted out of context. It is assumed that the basic ideas would be adapted and worded appropriately for the speaker and the situation.

2. **Interest in a subordinate.** The woman executive who is attracted to a subordinate and has thoughts of following up is in a precarious position. The ways of the heart are often illogical, but reason often triumphs. What profits even a highly placed woman to gain her amorous objective if she loses, among other things, her peace of mind?

For some the answer may be, "Enough." For these, caution may seem preachy and even hypocritical. But the danger is real. The vaunted single standard is still only a hope. There are three things to be said:

■ This is a good time for the manager to consider romantic alternatives outside the organization. Perhaps *reconsider* is the more suitable word.

■ Unless the attraction is overwhelming, it should be resisted for practical reasons. One female consultant, turning autobiographical, said she had been deterred by the thought of having to work alongside the man on a daily basis.

■ If nothing else, think through the possible consequences, sometimes especially dire for higher-echelon people. At the very least, the presence of an inamorato on the premises is likely to interfere with work, perhaps at the most inopportune times.

3. Handling subordinates' complaints. Some managers will have no trouble dealing with an employee's request for help in an harassment situation. But for others there may be intensifying factors:

■ Identification. The manager's own propensities may be triggered. A description of the aggression may uncover or arouse resentments that could lead to distorted appraisals and judgments.

■ Lack of self-confidence. For some executives the context of the complaint may cause embarrassment or uncertainty. In a person capable in most other areas, one of rampant sexuality may cause uneasiness and self-doubt.

A possible action recommended by one of the consulting group: "In the usual interpersonal problem a manager investigates the facts. In this case, the probing should be done with particular care. For example, it's typical for the subject of the harassment to view it in strongly emotional terms. The harasser often avows his surprise and innocence. Both these attitudes have to be assessed carefully."

One consultant suggests: "If the facts in a first-time-complaint are not serious, it's usually best to conclude by warning the alleged offender to cool it, and assure the woman that you believe there will be no more trouble, but not to hesitate to return with any further complaint. If there is a repetition, the judgment must be uncompromising: 'Stop or else.' "

This is a case in which the "or else" has clout. Most companies have strict rules about harassment, especially with the antidiscrimination laws backing up company policy. The manager may decide to invoke company-policy support by reporting all cases of harassment in her area to the head of personnel or to her boss.

4. Threat from the outside. In organizations that deal directly with the public, women in contact with customers may be open targets. "In some industries," says one executive, "it's a quid pro quo for doing business." For example:

Bea Ford is an account executive in an advertising agency. She is intelligent, good-looking, and good at working with people, three good reasons for her boss to give her the job. But being bright, good-looking and having a pleasant manner also makes her personally attractive to clients. Most of them are satisfied to keep things friendly, but there is one client—and it only takes one—who has more acquisitive ideas. And he lets Bea know it.

Bea Ford realized two things. First, she is not interested in encouraging the man. Second, she knows she is vulnerable, open to this unpleasant complication in her job.

Should she level with the client, tell him she's got a perfectly satisfactory special friend? She tries that. His response: "What does that have to do with anything? I'm a married man myself." (Note the willingness to espouse the single standard.)

Should she tell her boss? That's the last thing she wants to do. She can hear her boss, perhaps not saying, but thinking: "If I had a man in that job, I wouldn't have this problem."

The consulting panel put together this set of suggestions for Bea Ford and others in her bind:

■ Be friendly but police your behavior strictly to avoid any hint of seductiveness, flirting, excessive cameraderie. One of the group added, perhaps unnecessarily, "Be a lady even if it hurts."

■ Be ready, at the first clear sexual overture to quietly but firmly make clear that it's not welcome. If the reaction you get is "Why?" use the most effective response, the one you feel most strongly. No. Modify that. If you find the man personally obnoxious, find some other face-saving excuse—his face, of course.

If matters get out of hand, consider going to your boss and explaining the situation matter-of-factly. It is not unlikely that you both suspected this type of crisis might be in the cards from the day you took the job. Your boss will probably offer one or more suggestions, from bawling out the client (yes, it's been done) to switching accounts with a colleague. Don't be too quick to go along with anything that weakens your professional standing (as might be the case if the boss intercedes with the client on your behalf). Decide in advance what you would like the boss to do and persuade him to do it.

A member of the panel said, "I once had a client problem and told the boss about it. I said, 'I want you to know what's going on. I believe I can handle it, but if the dirt hits the fan, I want to tell Mr. X myself that I plan to hand over his account to another representative."

It is interesting that no one suggested that the boss might be asked to break off with the customer, even though one of the women said she knew of a case in which that was done.

(See also sexual harassment as covered in the Fair Employment Practices section.)

➔ THE MOTHERHOOD DECISION*

A successful young manager says, "I'm one of a small group of women managers in their late twenties and early thirties. I don't know of a topic we discuss more than the question of whether, and when, to have a baby."

The accepted wisdom once was that you'd better have it by the time you're thirty. While the optimum ages are still seen by the medical profession as twenty-five to twenty-nine, the "maternity window" remains open until the late thirties, and sometimes beyond. One of the most stressful situations confronted by women is awareness of the inexorable closing of that window. There is a constellation of crises clustered around the motherhood decision:

■ **"Will it hurt my career?"**   It may not hurt at all, but it certainly is an influential factor. Fortunately, there is a law against penalizing a woman for having a baby. Among other things, she is entitled to maternity leave, and the Supreme Court has ruled that states may require employers to grant special job protection to employees who are physically unable to work because of pregnancy.

But there are subtleties. A purchasing agent for an office-supply company said, "Around the seventh month there wasn't anything more cleverly cut dresses could do. Boy, was I pregnant! I gloried in it. But I could feel people edging away from me in the elevator. I noticed nobody sat next to me at meetings. These guys acted as if I had a disease. Did it hold me back? Listen, I loved every minute of it, and little Penny is the light of my life. But I don't kid myself that it was a career plus. It wasn't, at least not in the short run. And in business, the long run is made up of a lot of short runs."

■ **"What's the matter with me?"**   The balancing of motherhood versus career is a major decision requiring cool assessment. But applying so much objectivity can cause problems. "Am I a monster?" asks a woman in the anguish of the dilemma. "This is a baby I'm thinking about, not a new briefcase!"

■ **"Can I handle it?"**   The *it* usually refers to the heavy load imposed by the simultaneous raising of child and pursuit of a career.

This is the point at which some women begin to think of themselves as inadequate. What they feel inadequate about depends on which side of it they come down on. Some envision career damage: coming unprepared to a big conference because a child's illness has held center stage all week-

---

* Adapted from *Career Stages,* by Auren Uris and John J. Tarrant, Seaview Putnam, 1983.

end; embarrassing phone calls from the sitter, etc. Others foresee their problems in terms of flaws in motherhood: neglect of the spiritual nurturing of a child because of excessive concentration on the job, and so on.

■ **"What do I really want?"**   Myra R. consults everybody, her husband, mother, best friend, a colleague at work, finally her boss. She gets several good opinions, but unfortunately, they conflict. And finally she comes to a realization: it's her decision, hers and her husband's. And he is willing to go along with her wishes. Now it's doubly up to her. Okay. "What do I *really* want?" No matter how she puts the question to herself, it is difficult. The pros and cons are not only strong and numerous. They also depend on developments she can't anticipate, from how much will she have to give up for a child, to how good a mother will she make. And what will it do to her job, now and future?

■ **"How do I decide?"**   Having a baby is serious enough, but it inevitably gets mixed up with other serious subjects. Some women go through considerable anguish because they feel that their decisions about working and mothering will somehow make a profound statement about their lives. Sometimes they suspect that the longing to have a baby is really a cop-out—an excuse to drop out of the career race, or a handy alibi for not going farther and faster. Others find that the decision leads to soul-searching that probes into the dark corners of the self. "What am I trying to prove? Do I have the right to do this? Is it selfishness or mother love?" And so on.

Few career crises are so riddled with unanswerable questions. Waiting until all the questions are satisfied before making a decision is in itself a decision. The answers don't come and the window closes.

One woman, unit manager for a giant communications firm, was, at age thirty-six, deeply involved in the process of sorting out these knotty questions when a surprising thing happened. "I plan everything! How could I have forgotten? Anyway, there I was, pregnant!"

She says people thought her pregnancy was funny. "You have to understand that they had me pegged as the original PB (pushy broad). Maybe they were right. Even the fact that I could be a mother knocked them on their ear."

She found, to her astonishment, that "it really did change me!" She felt being a mother had made her more human. However, the difficulties of being both a good mother and a good business person cannot be ignored. The seriousness of the thought that leads to the decision is justified. The important thing to remember is that women have chosen either the single or double career and made it work successfully.

And some people have found that the most difficult crises may be that associated with making the decision. After the baby is born, things tend to sort themselves out. It's hard, but there are far fewer questions with no decent answers.

➔ PREPARING FOR SUCCESS

Women and men share the career experience: they struggle, resolve, and their adroitness leads to success, the executive bastion is won. In fairy tales the result is living happily after. In case histories of successful women and men, other outcomes are more common. For women possible dissatisfactions can cut deeper because the struggle has been harder, the losses more painful.

But success need not turn rotten, and in individual cases being forewarned can clear the vision and make expectations more realistic. Anticipating some key factors can help keep the fruits of achievement unspoiled:

1. Expect new burdens.   Not every executive office sports a miserable tenant. On the contrary. A high percentage of executives love their jobs and relish their accomplishment. Often this outcome results from realistic expectations of pressure points:

Overtime.   Yes, a sixty-hour workweek is not unusual, and you don't get time-and-a-half. Along with this goes a top-heavy work schedule, obvious interference with home schedules, and physical fatigue. However, remedial procedures, from delegation to better priority setting can mitigate the crunch.

Decision making.   Often described as the crux of the executive job, some choices are hard to make. Says one executive, "If only our typical decision were, 'How big can we make bonuses this year?' But others grind you down: cutbacks, layoffs, consequences of a fatal accident to an employee, operational failures that threaten the survival of the company, the continuing battle against the twists and turns of the marketplace." And executives down the line must wrestle with their pieces of the action.

Men often suffer along with women from procedures aimed to help the company retain its profitability at the expense of human values. The place where the buck stops is often a distress area. Typically, laying off staff to reduce losses traumatizes executives who are forced to make the move.

Sacrifice of principle and values.   "Currents," a public affairs TV, series revealed the loss of softer traits and human values that result from executive practice. One guest, author Marilyn French contended that women risk unhappiness by competing on men's terms. Other speakers made the point that women are often criticized for being aggressive in an unladylike way or being ladylike and seeming unbusinesslike.

Frustration. The managing director of a large insurance organization reveals:

"Some women are still very naive as to the barriers" (that exist in the workplace). "I have certainly experienced frustrations in trying to win total professional acceptance in the upper echelons. At the end of the week I am often more exhausted from dealing with the absurd attitudes and perceptions of men than from the problems at hand."

Causes for upset are fairly common. A typical work situation contains many ingredients that, ranging from misunderstanding to a recalcitrant employee, can keep nerve-ends raw. However, for the seasoned manager, the usual antidote is a shrug, practical symptom treatment, and on to the next thing.

■ **Stress.** It's an executive affliction. But some women expect the rainbow flow of success to anneal the spirit. It seldom does. Claudia H. Duetsch, in the *New York Times,* describes the plight of a hotel manager who, as a result of "everything in the world being my responsibility" tries to offset the burden by overeating. Her bulimia forces her to force down junk food, regurgitate it, and eat more. Industrial psychologists speak of other consequences: "Women who experience the dark side of success compensate by excessive smoking, drug abuse and other forms of self-destructive behavior."

The discoveries of Hans Selye of the University of Montreal in analyzing and prescribing means of controlling stress (his work, *Stress and Distress,* contends that, "Stress is the spice of life," and is an excellent sourcebook) brought a much deeper understanding of the survival value of the phenomenon. A practical approach to lessening the negative consequences are summed up in three directive:

Change the situation. Examine the work situation for specific pressure points you can control or eliminate.

Change the people. Reshuffling assignments, putting better people at key operating points, can lessen your strain.

Defuse yourself. Everything from leaving your office for a breather, to trying for a better match of task and energy levels (see "Adjusting Your Schedule to Your Personal Daily Energy Cycle, page 4) can ease the strain.

2. Anticipate what you will be losing. In our present context, success means entry into the managerial echelons, or mounting to higher ones. The "new life" may require altered habits and associations. There may be an unexpected, and regrettable price to be paid:

"Breaking up the old gang."   It's not only wedding bells that can bring about this nostalgic shock. Your previous position had you close to colleagues, some of whom became friends to lunch with, to talk shop with, or to socialize with outside the work scene. Some of these may fall by the wayside, as new associates, new contacts, cut some of the ties that bound you together.

In addition to individual relationships affected, the groups of which you may have been a member—a "gourmet" club, people you could shop with at lunchtime—somehow slide out of reach.

"It's the restaurant I miss alot," says a new division head. "Kelly's, we used to love that place. It was as warm and comfortable as our own home. But now I feel strange there. My new office pals introduce me to a more elegant place, and it's nice, but that old feeling isn't there."

Promotion often means a new life.   You may or may not miss the old one, but like it or not, time moves it into the past.

3. Don't be surprised at a new you.   It would be surprising if everything around you changes and you didn't. You probably will. It's a consequence of growth. You go back to the house where you were brought up, and it seems half its size, the big backyard is now just a patch. The house hasn't changed, the yard hasn't changed, you have. A promotion may not be as vast a shift as one from childhood to adulthood, but it is often enough to change your perspective, your values, your interests.

"Different jobs make different people," says one V.P., Personnel. Her experience is that every rung of the advancement ladder creates new ways of thinking, feeling, and behavior.

The emergence of virtually a new person can be drastic or subtle. "Helen changed overnight," says a colleague, who has witnessed the transformation of a once carefree friend into a vice president with no time for socializing and the little goof-offs that make job life more relaxed and pleasant.

"Good old Alice," says her teammate. "She acts the same, and seems the same, but when I saw her coming in with eye makeup and a $100 silk scarf, I knew there's plenty going on below surface."

The changed behavior of a promotee is usually labeled "professional growth." The woman executive may like the change, or rue it. But when she sets her goals, consequences should be estimated realistically, so that success, when it comes, is not disillusioning and destructive but a constructive fate.

Fortunately, the "ailments" of success are usually curable. That's why there are few jobs in the higher echelons that go begging. Many a woman who has accepted advancement with some qualms, has been able to apply a benign version of the "minimax" approach: you *minimize* the negatives and *maximize* the positives. The paragraphs above highlight the potential negatives of success. Those that follow focus on the brighter side.

Special point: Don't be satisfied with "good enough" in seeking to maximize job satisfaction. Despite a tendency for the media to dwell on the professional burdens, many managerial women have found in full measure the fulfillment of their aspiration.

➲ THREE KEYS TO JOB ENJOYMENT

The recommendations below are equally suitable for men and women. They are included in this section because women are newer to the game, and are likely to find they fill a wider gap in experience or expectation.

Perhaps you see the goal of job enjoyment as icing on the cake, but if it seems like a rich dessert after a big meal, just remember, it's no-cal.

The more you enjoy your job the better you do it, the more you enjoy it. It's a benign cycle you will want to have working in your favor. Accordingly, consider these suggestions for increased pleasure:

1. Use your job for personal growth. "My job is one of the strongest maturing experiences I've ever had," says one West Coast executive. "It enlarged my vision of people, of relationships, and of myself."

A biologist, head of a pharmaceutical laboratory, says, "The executive job with its many contacts with people, its complex situations, is like a growth medium in which the executive is steeped. If she doesn't grow, there's something wrong."

2. Increase the challenge of your job. *Challenge.* The word has gone through the cycle from "in" word to cliché, but challenge adds excitement and stimulation to a job. How do you add challenge? Three ways:

- Be *frontier-minded;* seek the new, the leading edge of innovation in your business.
- Seek to perform the standard part of your job at *higher levels of excellence.*
- Set yourself a *special project,* something *not* required of you.

3. Make your job or career your personal monument. Develop what Bennett Cerf, well-known publisher and TV personality, called an "edifice complex." The desire to build something of value and permanence in your work can represent an ongoing and exciting target.

➲ WHAT TO DO ABOUT WHAT YOU WANT

To aspire or not to aspire, that may be the question. It's serious enough. It's a life matter and the individual must decide how she wants to live it. If she comes down on the career, or career too, side, some concluding thoughts:

Myra Strober of Stanford University, in a study of the changed patterns of women's entry into the workplace and its consequences says, "It's ironic. The problem of the 1970s was bringing women into the corporation. The problem of the 1980s is keeping them there." Perhaps.

The effort to "keep" women in corporations need not find women passive. It is desirable for employers to make the minor adjustments, such as adopting flextime, maternity leave, and child care practices that make it practical for women to work. But career women, for their part, must make the plans and take the actions that enhance their capabilities, not only for their own self-fulfillment but also to help build the management excellence of corporate America.

14. Fair Employment Practices

Starting in the early sixties, the Federal Government became directly involved in seeking to insure equality of treatment to all employees in business and organizational life in general. First efforts were directed toward those companies involved in government work. Contractors were required to adopt policies that would guarantee employment opportunities for members of minority groups.

Since those early beginnings, government control has continued to expand. The impact of the 1964 Civil Rights Act has been so broadened by the courts and subsequent legislative amendments that today the law is used to stamp out job discrimination in all areas: hiring, promotion, training opportunities, compensation practices, employee benefits, and firing.

Enforcement is growing constantly tougher: the cost of a misstep can be staggering. Penalties of $100,000 and $250,000 in back pay under the Equal Pay Act are not uncommon. And the Equal Employment Opportunity Commission (EEOC), the agency charged with enforcing the fair employment laws, has even required "front pay" in some cases; that is, employers can be obliged to pay out future earnings that may have been lost as a result of discrimination.

With the burgeoning "rights consciousness," not only of protected employee groups, but employees in general, there will be increasing corporate vulnerability to charges of discrimination in the years ahead. Executives must rid their firms of outmoded policies, and also eliminate the friction points that may cause a drain on productivity.

Continuing developments expand protection. Changes in the fair employment laws are made virtually every day. Just about every court interpretation involving the Federal antibias laws will have some kind of effect—extending them to additional employment practices, or attempting to set limits on just how far the law goes. For example, Congress has eliminated the age cap on the Age Discrimination in Employment Act (ADEA). When this law was first passed, an employee could be forced to retire at age sixty-five but not before. Later the law was amended to protect employees up to age seventy. Now, most employees have the right to work for as long as they want, or for as long as they can perform their jobs competently.

Continuing contribution to pensions.   In the employee benefits area, employers are now required to continue to contribute to and accrue employee pensions for as long as they are on the job. Previously, an employer could stop contributing when an employee reached age sixty-five. Age bias laws now also require companies to continue to carry older workers and their spouses on company-sponsored health plans—rather than shift that responsibility to Medicare when they reach age 65. The Retirement Equity Act addresses the problem of actuarial biases built into pension plans, not so much by employers as by insurers providing pension benefits, and extends pension protection to former spouses of employees.

SUMMARY OF ANTIDISCRIMINATION LAWS

Title VII of the Civil Rights Act of 1964

■ Prohibits job discrimination based on race, color, religion, sex, or national origin.

■ Covers the following:

. . . Employers engaged in an industry affecting interstate commerce who have at least 15 full-time employees in 20 or more weeks of the current calendar year (or who met the same test in the preceding year).

. . . Labor organizations that maintain a hiring hall or have 15 or more members.

. . . Employment agencies.

. . . State and local governments.

. . . Certain federal government units.

. . . Joint labor–management committees for apprenticeship and training.

. . . Educational institutions.

■ Exempts certain federal government units, Indian tribes, religious and government organizations, bona fide private membership clubs (other than labor organizations).

■ Enforced by the Equal Employment Opportunity Commission (EEOC).

Equal Pay Act
- Prohibits wage and benefit discrimination based on sex. The prohibition applies to both employers and unions.
- Covers all employers subject to provisions of the Fair Labor Standards Act. However, the exempt classes for Wage-Hour purposes (white-collar executive, administrative, professional employees) are not excluded from protection under the Equal Pay Act.
- Enforced by the EEOC.

Age Discrimination in Employment Act
- Prohibits job discrimination on the basis of age for all employees aged 40 and over.
- Covers the following:
. . . Employers in industries affecting interstate commerce who have at least 20 employees (including officers) in 20 or more weeks of the current calendar year (or who met the same test in the preceding year). Employees of U.S. companies who are working outside of the country are also protected by the Act.
. . . Labor organizations that maintain a hiring hall or have at least 20 members.
. . . Employment agencies.
. . . All federal, state, and local governments.
- Enforced by the EEOC.

The fair employment laws consist of a broad patchwork of state and federal antibias laws, as well as some common law theories. The major Federal laws include:

TITLE VII OF THE CIVIL RIGHTS ACT OF 1964.

This is the broadest of the antidiscrimination laws. It prohibits discrimination with respect to race, color, religion, sex, or nationality in the following situations:

- Hiring or firing;
- Setting compensation, terms, conditions, or privileges of employment;
- Dealing with, classifying, or otherwise limiting employees in any way that deprives an individual of employment opportunities or in some other way adversely affects his or her status as an employee;
- Printing or publishing or advertisements or notices that indicate a potentially discriminating preference, limitation or specification (NOTE: Keeping an eye

on the help wanted ads is one of the most obvious means that the Equal Employment Opportunity Commission has of monitoring discriminatory practices in the workplace directly);
■ Apprenticeship, training, or retraining programs.

Title VII covers "employers engaged in an industry affecting commerce"; that is, virtually every type of employer, who have at least fifteen employees on each working day for twenty or more weeks of the current calendar year (or who met the same test the previous year). In addition, it covers labor organizations that maintain a hiring hall or that have twenty-five or more members; and employment agencies.

Specifically exempted from Title VII are some government agencies, U.S. government-owned corporations, Indian tribes, religious and educational associations (to some extent), and bona fide private membership clubs (other than labor organizations).

Pregnancy Discrimination Act of 1978. This law amended Title VII specifically to include "pregnancy, childbirth and related medical conditions." In general, it requires that employers adjust their maternity leave, disability, and health insurance policies to assure that pregnancy-related disabilities are treated in the same way as any other disability with regard to insurance coverage and leave time.

Equal Pay Act. This law prohibits discrimination in wages and benefits on the basis of sex. Passed in 1963, it applies to employers and unions and all employees covered by the minimum wage provisions of the Fair Labor Standards Act. It has since been amended to apply as well to executives, administrators, professional employees, outside salespeople, and other exempt employees.

Age Discrimination in Employment Act. Passed in 1967, ADEA prohibits job discrimination based on age. Originally offering protection to employees and potential employees aged forty through sixty-five, the law has since been amended to protect all employees over age sixty-five. As with Title VII it applies to all employers with twenty or more employees (including officers) in twenty or more weeks in the current calendar year, or who met the test in the previous year.

Rehabilitation Act of 1973. This federal law applies only to companies that do business with the federal government, and requires them to have an affirmative action plan with regard to hiring *handicapped workers.* A number of states also have laws prohibiting discrimination against the physically and mentally handicapped.

Retirement Equity Act. This law was passed in 1984 to assure that women received equal treatment with men under annuity pension plans (i.e., that they get the same monthly payout from a pension plan as a man with the same seniority and salary) regardless of the accepted actuarial fact that women generally live longer than men. It also protects the pension rights of divorced or separated spouses of employees covered under pension and other retirement benefit plans.

➲ RACIAL DISCRIMINATION

Title VII clearly bans overt job discrimination on the basis of race; for example, paying minorities less for the same work, locking them into lower paying jobs, and the like. But many companies have encountered trouble in the courts with more subtle and frequently unintentional forms of discrimination.

No one at this point in time and experience needs to be told that segregated washrooms or Christmas parties would be discriminatory. But employers have also been tripped up when they thought they were following traditional business practices. For example, employment tests and skills requirements that screen out a greater percentage of blacks than whites have been found to be discriminatory where they can't be shown to be essential to performance on the job.

In particular, executives should be warned that announcing a nondiscrimination policy is not enough. EEOC and the courts are more than ever insisting that companies take positive action to assure that its equal employment policy is understood and adhered to at all levels of an organization. This does not necessarily mean affirmative action in the form of hiring or promotion quotas as it has generally been understood, but it does mean that employers must take steps to assure that executives, supervisors, managers, and rank-and-file employees don't discriminate, and to deal with discrimination immediately and effectively when it occurs.

The Supreme Court has been particularly hard on employers who have been lax in enforcing an antidiscrimination policy. In 1985, for instance, it heard a case involving a supervisor's sexual harassment of a female employee. When the company was sued for the supervisor's actions, it responded that not only did it not know about the harassment—the employee had not reported it at the time—but the supervisor had no hiring/firing power over the female worker.

When ignorance isn't bliss. Ignorance was no excuse, the Court said. Otherwise employers would have a reason to remain ignorant of what was going on in their workplaces. In addition, even if the supervisor had no official authority to hire and fire, "the mere appearance of a significant degree of influence in vital decisions gives supervisors the opportunity to coerce, intimidate, and harass employees," the Court said.

In practical terms, this suggests reviewing your company's antidiscrimination policy periodically with all managers and supervisors, investigating all discrimination claims immediately, and taking appropriate disciplinary action—up to and including discharge—when discrimination claims are found to have a basis in fact.

Employee screening. While racial discrimination has generally been eradicated, less visible forms could drag a company into court. For instance, with the steady erosion of the "employment-at-will" doctrine (or the "right to fire" any employee for any reason or for no reason as long as it isn't discriminatory), with the growing threat of drugs in the workplace, with the incredibly high cost of training workers for some positions, with the generally high cost of recruitment—employers are coming around to affirm the real need for effective employee screening. Employers are making use of polygraphs, drug tests, written "honesty" tests, aptitude tests, occupational skills tests, attitude tests, and personality profiles to guarantee to as great an extent as possible that the person they hire is the "right" one for the job. The problem is that the area of screening in general and testing in particular is rife with potential discrimination problems and controversy.

♦ THREE SCREENING HAZARDS FOR EMPLOYERS

Testing is just one method of selecting employees that has a potential for trouble. The chief problem is that many tests, particularly general aptitude tests, often screen out minorities in much higher proportions than they screen out "majority" prospects. This "adverse impact" is common and often unintentional but still may be viewed as discrimination.

Other types of employment standards that have been held to be discriminatory include requiring applicants to have a college degree. This tends to screen out minority applicants at a much higher rate. Even a high-school diploma requirement can be discriminatory in cases where an "adverse impact" can be made out.

Experience requirements may also be ruled discriminatory if the jobs from which that experience may be obtained have been traditionally dominated by white workers.

"Yellow sheet." Turning down an applicant on the basis of an arrest record can also be unlawful, according to the courts. In one such case, a policy of refusing to hire anyone who had been arrested "on a number of occasions" got an employer into trouble. A black applicant who had a record of arrests, but no convictions, sued when he was turned down as an applicant. The court ruled that even requesting this type of information on application forms or in job interviews was unlawful. Regardless of how fairly such a policy is administered, it tends to discriminate against minorities that may have a higher arrest rate than that of whites.

Test: "business necessity."   None of this means that tests or other employment screening techniques can't be used. "What Congress has forbidden," said the Supreme Court in one important case, "is giving testing or measuring procedures controlling force unless they are demonstrably a reasonable measure of job performance." The governing factor for all preemployment screening techniques should be "business necessity"—they must be related to the requirements of the job.

⮒ SENIORITY SYSTEMS SURVIVE FAIR EMPLOYMENT TEST

The traditional seniority system under a collective bargaining agreement is relatively sacrosanct under the Federal anti-discrimination laws. In a landmark decision in 1984 (Fire Fighters Local 1784 v. Stotts) the Court held in favor of senior white employees who had been laid off in place of minority employees with less seniority. The fire department had laid off the white employees under the provisions of a consent agreement with EEOC that required it to improve the racial balance of their workforce.

The Supreme Court, however, said that only employees who had been victims of past discriminatory practices should be entitled to this sort of preferential treatment, regardless of the terms of the consent agreement.

"Title VII protects bona fide seniority systems and it is inappropriate to deny an innocent employee the benefits of seniority in order to provide a remedy in a pattern or practice suit such as this," said the Court. It added that a seniority system is lawful as long as it does not attempt to provide different standards of "compensation, promotion, or employment conditions" according to race.

⮒ NATIONAL-ORIGIN DISCRIMINATION

National origin discrimination offers what may perhaps have even subtler pitfalls for the executive. The EEOC "Guidelines on Discrimination because of National Origin" were revised in 1980, for instance: "as a result of charges alleging denial of equal employment opportunity because an applicant's last name suggested association with a certain national origin group or because of an association with persons, schools, churches or other lawful organizations identified with a national origin group." In short, a woman might be denied a job because her married name was Hispanic, even if she was not.

Others claimed they were denied employment because of membership in churches, temples, or mosques that were readily associated with some ethnic group. As a result the EEOC has adopted a relatively broad definition of "national origin discrimination." It includes, but is not limited to: "the denial of equal employment opportunity because of an individual's, or his or her ancestor's place of origin, or because an individual has the physical, cultural or linguistic characterists of a national origin group."

In addition, the EEOC will examine with "particular concern" cases in which an individual has been denied employment opportunities for reasons such as:

- marriage to or association with persons of a national origin group;
- membership in or association with an organization identified with or seeking to promote the interests of national origin groups;
- attendance or participation in schools, churches, temples, or mosques, generally associated by persons of a particular ethnic group;
- because an individual's name or spouse's name is associated with a group of particular national origin.

➜ NATIONAL-ORIGIN TROUBLESPOTS

In general, executives should follow the "Uniform Guidelines on Employee Selection Procedures" as an aid to screening and selection. Particular hazards in terms of national origin bias that an executive should be aware of include:

Height and weight requirements.   According to the EEOC, these "tend to exclude individuals on the basis of national origin." As a result, employers are expected to evaluate these selection procedure for adverse impact, regardless of whether the total selection process has an adverse impact based on national origin.

Fluency-in-English requirements.   Denying a job or promotion because of a candidate's foreign accent or inability to communicate well in English is also unlawful, except where it can be demonstrated to be a "bona fide occupational qualification" or BFOQ. It would be reasonable to deny someone a position as an air traffic controller, for instance, because of poor-English-speaking ability. For other types of positions, however, the need for good English may not be as important as some employers may think.

Training or education requirements.   It's unlawful to deny employment opportunities because of an individual's foreign training or education or as a pretext for not hiring, or to require that an individual be foreign trained or educated.

➔ SPEAK-ENGLISH-ONLY RULES

It's unlikely that there would be good reason for a rule that requires employees to speak only English in the workplace at all times. The EEOC suggests that it is a denial of "essential national origin characteristics," and may create an atmosphere of "inferiority, isolation, and intimidation" that is likely to be discriminatory.

The Commission recognizes, however, that there might be a legitimate business reason for requiring only English at certain times—when communication or supervision are vital, for instance—but employees should be notified of the existence of any such rule, the reasons for it, and the consequences of violating it.

➔ ETHNIC HARASSMENT

Ethnic slurs and other verbal or physical conduct relating to an individual's national origin amounts to illegal harassment when:

- it has the purpose or result of creating a hostile or offensive work environment;
- it interferes with an individual's work performance;
- it adversely affects an individual's employment opportunities in any way.

➔ IMMIGRATION ACT COMPLICATIONS

Immigration laws enacted in 1986 make it unlawful for employers to hire illegal aliens (although a "grandfather" clause protects them against prosecution in regard to illegal aliens hired up to the time the Act became law in November 1986). Stiff penalties are incorporated into the law for employers who knowingly hire illegal aliens or who fail to require proof of citizenship or resident status or who fail to keep record of that proof for future reference. The law also warns employers that the law should not be used as a pretext for unlawful discrimination on the basis of national origin.

➔ RELIGIOUS DISCRIMINATION

Title VII offers the same protections against discrimination on the basis of religion as for race, sex, and national origin. And again, the EEOC defines what it means by "religion" rather broadly, including not only "theistic concepts," but also other ethical and moral beliefs that are held by an individual "with the strength of traditional religious views." This protection holds good whether or not those beliefs are part of a recognized religion.

➲ HOW MUCH ACCOMMODATION FOR EMPLOYEES' RELIGIOUS BELIEFS?

Regardless of how it has been defined, the issue involved with most religious discrimination suits brought over the years has been what adjustments an employer must make for employees' religious holidays observances and other practices.

EEOC guidelines say that an employer must make "reasonable accommodations" for the religious practices of employees and prospective employees. In fact, the employer has a "duty to accommodate" unless that accommodation would result in an undue hardship to the conduct of business.

Three points of conflict.   Religious practices and observances that most often come into conflict with business operations include:

Holiday observances.   When an employee cannot reconcile his or her work schedule with a religious holiday, the employer must examine all reasonable alternatives, including swapping, changing job assignments, flexible scheduling, etc.

Union membership.   An individual cannot be forced to become a member of a union if it is against his or her religious beliefs. Instead, the employee should be allowed to contribute a sum equal to union dues to an acceptable charitable organization.

Other religious practices.   Employers are also obliged to make reasonable accommodations for dietary requirements, dress, and grooming, and other practices.

➲ SEXUAL DISCRIMINATION

Though Title VII did prohibit discrimination on the basis of sex, its focus was really racial discrimination. In the years since 1964 legislative amendments such as the Pregnancy Discrimination Act, the Equal Pay Act, and numerous court interpretations have clarified some of the ambiguities that may have existed and provided working women with more specific protections.

While few employers need to be told that "male" and "female" job classifications or job application questions regarding child-bearing plans are unlawful, there are still some major areas of concern, both for employers and for female employees.

Employee benefits: a big sex discrimination trap.   It's unlawful under the Equal Pay Act for employers to offer medical plans, insurance coverage, pensions, disability benefits, vacation, or other benefits that discriminate in any way against female employees. This is true even if the cost of providing those benefits—such as with retirement or health benefits—is greater for women as a class than for men.

Pregnancy leave. Pregnancy of employees seems to have created a special problem for many employers, for some obvious and for not-so-obvious reasons. The Pregnancy Discrimination Act was intended to address some of those problems, and to provide guidelines on the rights of pregnant employees.

The law requires companies to treat a disability related to pregnancy and related conditions the same as other disabilities under any health, disability, insurance, or sick leave plan. Women cannot be denied a job or a promotion simply because she is pregnant—or had an abortion. The employee cannot be fired because of her condition, nor forced to take leave if she is physically capable of working. The courts have even held that the transfer of a pregnant employee to another position in some cases can be held discriminatory. In addition, women who take maternity leave must be reinstated under the same conditions as employees who return from leave after other disabilities.

Protection for fathers? The Equal Pay Act applies to men as well as to women. And while this would seem unlikely to create a problem, consider this: If a company offers "maternity" leave—paid or unpaid leave time over and above disability leave for the care of newborn or adopted children—it must offer the same benefit to male employees. While there have been relatively few cases in this area, the EEOC has said it would pursue claims against companies that offer infant care leave to female employees while denying it to male employees.

How long may a pregnant employee stay on the job? This question has gotten more than one employer into hot water. Pregnant employees will very often want to stay on the job for as long as possible. This is no problem for many types of jobs. Some jobs, however, may involve hazardous working conditions or a good deal of heavy physical activity. Many employers are understandably nervous about having a pregnant employee remain on the job. In most cases, however, as long as the employee is performing competently and wants to continue working, any attempt by an employer to force her to accept a transfer or to begin pregnancy leave opens the door to a discrimination suit.

While most employers are legitimately concerned for the pregnant employee's safety, they may be overly concerned. A recent study by the American Medical Association Council on Scientific Affairs suggests that a pregnant worker can probably do a lot more for longer into pregnancy than is often believed.

In most cases, the report says, "the pregnant worker should be able to continue productive work until the onset of labor." For work involving more strenuous activities, including prolonged standing, lifting, or climbing, an "alternative work assignment may be appropriate," the report says. In general, though, "the determination that a pregnant employee can or cannot work a particular job should be made on a case-by-case basis."

Compensation issues: equal pay and "comparable worth."   Equal pay for equal work is now one of the basic tenets of the workplace. It was not always so. At one time it was common for a woman to be paid less for performing the same job as a man. The Equal Pay Act and subsequent guidelines issued by the Department of Labor and later the EEOC set the standards for what was to be considered "equal work." Jobs should be compared on the basis of:

- equal skill—including such factors as experience, training, education, and ability.
- equal effort—"effort," according to the EEOC, refers to the physical or mental exertion necessary to perform the job.
- equal responsibility—this refers to the amount of accountability or "discretion" required in the performance of a job.
- similar working conditions—the mere fact that jobs are in different departments does not mean they are performed under different working conditions, the EEOC says. Significant differences would include hazardous surroundings that involve a greater potential of injury.

How to compare jobs.   To be equal, jobs need not be identical, but only "substantially equal." As one court put it, "insubstantial differences in the skill, effort and responsibility requirements of particular jobs should be ignored." In comparing jobs, the key questions, following the EEOC standards listed above, should be these:

- Do the jobs require equal skill, effort, and responsibility?
- Are they performed under similar working conditions?

The equal pay rules won't apply unless the jobs match on both of these tests. For example, two jobs may be performed under similar working conditions and require equal effort and responsibility, but if they demand different skills—or a different degree of skill—they won't be subject to the equal pay rules.

In determining whether jobs require equal skill, effort, and responsibility, it is important to remember two major points: It is necessary to look at jobs as a whole and over a full work cycle; and it is risky to rely too heavily on such criteria as job classifications, point value systems, and job titles, all of which may be misleading.

The "comparable worth" question. The notion of "comparable worth" takes the equal pay question a step further. It touches on the sticky question of the relative "value" of one job compared to another. In California, for instance, it was found that hospital pharmacists, a position dominated by men, were higher paid on the average than nurses, a position dominated by women, though the "value" of the respective positions to the hospital were judged to be about the same. Should the pay of hospital nurses on that basis be raised to equal that of pharmacists?

The question is by no means resolved. Thus far the issue of comparable worth has not gotten a very sympathetic hearing from the EEOC. According to that agency: "The mere predominance of individuals of one sex in a job classification is not sufficient to create an inference of sex discrimination in wage setting." Unless Congress is willing to rewrite the Equal Pay Act to address the issue, we're likely to see little change in that attitude.

Landmark Case in Affirmative Action

In March of 1987 the Supreme Court issued an unexpected and controversial affirmative-action ruling. In a 6-to-3 decision it upheld the promotion of Diana Joyce to a crew-dispatchers job in the Santa Clara County, California Transportation Agency. In competition for the job was Paul E. Johnson, who had scored slightly higher in interviews. But Joyce was chosen under the Agencies own voluntary affirmative action plan.

Johnson sued, charging discrimination under Title VII of the 1964 Civil Rights Act. The case reached the Supreme Court, which handed down its historic decision. The majority of the justices held that employers may give preference to women—and presumably other minorities—when the purpose is to erase a "manifest imbalance in traditionally segregated job categories." Since this situation often exists, the decision was taken as an important victory by women's and other minorities rights groups.

Traditionalists took the opposed view, claiming an unfair judgment. The dissent of Justice Antonin Scalia led the protest. He saw the decision as a reinforcement of "racism and sexism," to the detriment of the fairness doctrine.

To some, the Court's decision seemed belated justice for minorities who had been victimized by discrimination through the centuries. Critics were less willing to temporize. They branded it as blatant reverse discrimination that would cause more trouble than it would resolve.

One observer accused the court of error in which the ends didn't justify the means, asserting that the principle of nondiscrimination was being stood on its head, and that the future of Title VII was much in question.

A possible turn of the controversy was pointed out by Drew S. Days 3rd, of Yale Law School. According to the Yale professor, *Johnson v. Transportation Agency* suggests that affirmative action is not so much about selecting less qualified people, but taking a broader look at what is meant by qualifications.

The basic shock of the Joyce-Johnson case lies in its disturbance of what was thought to be a predictable evolution of affirmative action. The prospects seem to favor changes in judgments and practices as influenced by shifts in social values and political power.

Sexual harassment in the workplace.   Perhaps the leading fair-employment issue of recent years is that of sexual harassment. In a major ruling affecting fair employment practices (Meritor Savings Bank, FSB v. Vinson), the Supreme Court said that it was the employer's responsibility to provide a workplace free not only from active discrimination, but also from sexual harassment.

The Vinson decision did not set a specific standard for liability in sexual harassment, but did issue a series of findings that might serve as guidelines:

- Sexual harassment is a form of sexual discrimination in violation of Title VII of the Civil Rights Act.
- Victims need not suffer tangible economic damage; that is, loss or denial of a job, dismissal, to pursue a claim, but can also claim discrimination for "pervasive" sexual advances or harassment.
- Acquiescence to sexual advances must be put into the context of whether or not they were "welcome."
- How a victim dresses or behaves in the workplace—such as wearing provocative clothing or using inviting language—can play a part in determining whether sexual advances are "welcome" or not.

In most cases the employer will bear direct responsibility and liability for harassment stemming from a "hostile work environment"—one that fosters sexual intimidation, innuendo, abusive physical or verbal advances, and other evidence of harassment. In addition, the Meritor case determined that victims of sexual harassment can seek redress not only when he or she (men can be victims of sexual harassment as well as women) is threatened with "tangible economic damage," such as the loss or denial of a job or promotion, but also when the general work environment subjects the employee to a supervisor's or co-workers' "pervasive" sexual advances.

(Also see "Sexual Harassment and the Woman Manager," page 277.)

Six Major Problems of Sexual Harassment

What type of behavior constitutes sexual harassment? Here are some of the things the courts have held to constitute sexual harassment:

1. Sexual advances have to be "unwelcome" to be held unlawful, but even an employee who acquiesces to "unwelcome" advances can charge harassment.

2. Sexual harassment may involve not only conditions of employment such as evaluation, promotion, and continued employment, but also more general "aspects of career development," including training and travel opportunities, according to one federal court.

3. Employers are liable if sexual advances are made with their "active or constructive knowledge" and they do not act promptly to take remedial action. In other words, the employer can be held responsible for harassment when it *knows* of it or *should have known* of it, and did not act immediately to put and end to it.

4. Reverse discrimination is also a liability threat. Some courts have ruled, for instance, that an employee who has been passed over for a promotion or other advancement because another employee has acquiesced to a supervisor's sexual advances is also entitled to sue under Title VII.

5. Verbal or physical conduct can amount to harassment. Unwelcome touching, lewd or vulgar inquiries or comments, and other behavior have all invited harassment claims that have won a favorable hearing by the courts. As a result, more than one company has adopted a "no touching" policy for all supervisory employees.

6. Intolerable working conditions that compel an individual to quit rather than continue to work can amount to "constructive discharge" on the part of an employer.

How to avoid liability for sexual harassment.   A review of court cases and EEOC guidelines on sexual harassment suggest that there are a number of actions that companies can take to minimize the chance that they will become the target of a harassment claim. They include:

1. *Adopt a written antiharassment/discrimination policy.* Supervisors particularly should be apprised of your company's opposition to harassment of any kind.
2. *Notify supervisory employees directly.* In addition to written reminders, supervisory employees should also be cautioned directly, at management meetings or through periodic memos, that the company is opposed to discrimination and harassment.
3. *Stress the importance of documentation.* Written performance re-

cords, and records of warnings, discipline, absences, tardiness, and other job performance indicators, are an employer's best defense against charges of discrimination and harassment.

4. *Set up a formal procedure for handling complaints.* If a supervisor is sexually harassing an employee, the employee can't complain to that supervisor about the harassment. There should be some avenue by which the employee can go around any particular supervisor or manager to register a complaint.

5. *Investigate any charge of sexual harassment immediately.* To make this a matter of record, consider taking down notes of what is said, when, where, to whom, etc.

6. *Take immediate remedial action where appropriate.* If investigation pinpoints a guilty party, at a minimum a reprimand, verbal or written, may be in order.

➡ AGE DISCRIMINATION IN EMPLOYMENT

The Age Discrimination in Employment Act as amended protects all employees aged forty and over from discrimination because of age in the following situations:

- Hiring or firing;
- Setting compensation, terms, conditions, or privileges of employment;
- Segregating, classifying, or otherwise limiting employees in any way that deprives an individual of employment opportunities or in some way adversely affects his or her status as an employee.
- Printing or publishing advertisements or notices that indicate a preference, limitation, specification, or discrimination.

How the age bias law works.   More age discrimination claims are filed with the EEOC than any other type of claim, so employers need to be especially careful about their efforts to comply with the ADEA.

Employees aged forty and above (with no upper limit) are protected from hiring and firing practices that set arbitrary age restrictions (whether spoken or unspoken), discriminatory benefit plans, and promotion or layoff policies that favor younger workers. The law doesn't mean that older workers must be favored, but that they must be afforded the same opportunities and benefits as younger workers.

Question and Answer: Avoiding age bias in the workplace.   Here are some questions asked by employers about their obligations under the ADEA:

Q.   Does the elimination of mandatory retirement mean that an older employee can stay on the job for as long as he or she likes?

A. It means that older workers can no longer be forced to retire at an arbitrarily proscribed age—whether sixty-five, seventy, or ninety. The hiring, firing, or promotion of older workers must be based on the same performance standards, skills requirements, and additional factors other than age that are applied to younger workers.

An older worker can be terminated if he or she fails to perform to established standards, but those standards must be applied in the same way to all employees. In fact, employers may hestiate to "go easy" on older workers who are no longer facing a mandatory retirement age.

Q. How might an employee benefits plan be discriminatory?

A. The courts have held benefit plans to be discriminatory when because of the higher cost of coverage to older workers, employers have attempted to provide reduced benefits or required older workers to pay higher premiums for their coverage.

Two new benefits.   In addition, recent legislation has added two new benefit requirements:

- Employers may no longer discontinue pension plan contributions and accruals when an employee reaches age sixty-five. Employers must allow older workers to continue to participate in and benefit from these plans for as long as they are employed.
- Employers must continue to cover older workers—and older spouses of active workers—under company-sponsored health benefit plans until retirement. Employers cannot reduce coverage when an employee or spouse becomes eligible for Medicare coverage.

The law does permit some differences in coverage—in disability coverage or life insurance, for instance—if those reductions can be justified by "actuarially significant cost considerations."

Q. Can employees ever give up their right to age bias protection?

A. Though the EEOC has not yet given the green light to ADEA waivers, a U.S. appeals court has ruled that under certain circumstances an individual can waive his or her right to ADEA protection. For example, in return for a substantially more generous severance or retirement package, an employee might give up the right to make age discrimination claims with regard to employment or termination and agree to be eased into retirement. The court added, however, that such agreements must be entered into "freely and openly" and there be no evidence of threat or coercion.

Q. Can a company reduce its workforce by offering early retirement incentives to eligible employees?

A. For the most part, EEOC and the courts have not objected to early retirement incentives that seek to encourage workers to take voluntary retirement with enhanced pensions, part-time jobs, improved health benefits, and other incentives. Companies have gotten themselves into trouble, however, when such incentives are offered too selectively, when the early retirement "window" is too narrow to allow a clearly thought out election, and when there is the subtle (or not so subtle) threat that the alternative will be layoffs or other reprisals.

Q.   What about layoffs? Must an employer always lay off younger workers first?

A.   No, older workers don't have any special advantages during layoffs. But older, higher-paid employees are traditionally the first targets when staff reductions are in order. The courts have been very hard on companies where layoffs have had a substantially greater impact on older workers.

Q.   Are there any instances when an employee may still be forced to retire at a certain age?

A.   Companies may still rely on the "executive exemption" to ADEA to force key "policy-making" executives to retire at age 65. But again, the courts have been very narrow in their interpretations of a "high policy-making executive." High pay, for instance, is not the only criterion. The key is whether the executive's duties and responsibilities involve decision making or direct influence on company policy.

→ EMPLOYER LIABILITY FOR UNFAIR EMPLOYMENT PRACTICES

The question of liability for discriminatory practices is thorny, and one that should keep executives wary about what goes on in the workplace. Employers can be held responsible for discriminatory acts by supervisors, co-workers, and even outsiders—customers, clients, and others.

Being uninformed is no excuse. The employer is expected to ensure that the work environment is discrimination and harassment free for all protected workers. In one case the Supreme Court said, "employees have a right to work in an environment that is free from discrimination, intimidation, ridicule, and insult"—whether or not a promotion, raise, or other conditions of employment are threatened.

EEOC guidelines emphasize that employers can be held liable "regardless of whether the specific acts were authorized or even forbidden by the employer and regardless of whether the employer knew or should have known of their occurance."

Words alone don't do it. Even the existence of a formal antidiscrimination plan will not always exempt an employer from liability. In the case mentioned above, for instance, the Supreme Court ruled that the company's antidiscrimination policy "did not address sexual harassment in particular," and further, that its grievance procedure was ineffective "because it required an employee to complain first to a direct supervisor" who might have been the source of the discrimination.

Companies with formal antidiscrimination policies have been faulted because they failed to remind supervisors and other employees through periodic memos and other announcements of their antibias stand.

⊃ THREE LIABILITY TRAPS

Employers can be held responsible for discrimination shown by:

Managers and supervisors.   According to the EEOC, managers and supervisory employees are "agents of the employer" and their employer can thus be held responsible for their actions under the antidiscrimination laws.

Co-workers.   Companies are required to maintain a workplace free from discriminatory intimidation and harassment and can be held liable for actions of co-workers if they fail to take action to eliminate discriminatory conditions.

Outsiders.   Clients, customers, and others may also create discrimination or harassment problems for an employer. For instance, receptionists, truck drivers, salespeople, waitresses, and other employees can be targets of racial or sexual slurs or harassment. Employers can be held responsible when they fail to take the appropriate corrective actions to the "extent of their control and responsibility."

Warning to executives and supervisors.   In some recent cases, management and supervisory employees have been held personally accountable for discriminatory acts, even when the company could show that it was unaware of the discrimination and took an active stand against it. In other cases supervisors have been sued for discrimination-related damages in the state courts under common law theories. A recent Supreme Court decision opens up the possibility that there might be room for personal liability under Title VII of the Civil Rights Act as well. That is, in cases where the employer cannot reasonably be held to be responsible for discrimination, an individual supervisor could very well be.

⊃ BFOQ: THE SINGLE EXCEPTION

Title VII and the ADEA allow a single exception to the rules on discrimination in hiring. That is, when an employer can show that race, sex, religion, national origin, or age is a bona fide occupational qualification (BFOQ) and "reasonably necessary to the normal operation of that particular business or enterprise."

Blacks or women, for instance, might be excluded from certain acting or modeling jobs where it can be shown that only a white actor or male actor would be acceptable for a particular assignment. Education or skills requirements for certain positions—such as nuclear engineers or astrophysicists—would also be defensible in spite of the fact that they are likely to screen out minorities at a greater rate than white applicants. In general, though, it is extremely difficult for employers to demonstrate a BFOQ related to race.

The courts have stated repeatedly that if an company wants to establish sex or race or religion as a *bona fide occupational qualification* it would have to prove that there was reasonable cause to believe that "all or substantially all" of the members of a protected class would be unable to perform the job safely or effectively.

Age is more often accepted as a BFOQ, but still, employers must be ready to document their reasons for excluding individuals from any position on that basis. In 1975, for example, Greyhound Bus Lines was able to show that specific age limits in hiring new drivers were necessary for safety reasons.

More recently, however, the courts have been less willing to accept across-the-board limits on age in employment, and have required companies to show why hiring decisions can't be made on an individual basis using factors other than age.

➲ BOOBY TRAPS IN APPLICATION BLANKS AND INTERVIEWS

Preemployment inquiries regarding an applicant's race, color, religion, or natural origin can cause trouble. Such inquiries will weigh against a company in court, particularly when found in combination with other evidence of discrimination. Special care should also be taken so that those who interview job applicants don't inadvertently stray into areas of inquiry that are touchy. Here's a summary of questions that have been held to be unlawful by the New York Commission Against Discrimination:

- Original name of an applicant whose name had been legally changed.
- Birthplace of applicant, applicant's parents, spouse or other relatives.
- Requirement that applicant submit birth certificate, naturalization, or baptismal record.
- Inquiry into an applicant's religious denomination, religious affiliations, church, parish, pastor, or religious holidays observed.
- Requirement that an applicant affix a photograph to his or her employment form after interview, but before hiring, or at his or her option.
- Inquiry into whether an applicant's parents or spouse are naturalized or native-born citizens; the date when any of the above acquired citizenship.
- Questions about marital status, number of children, or child-bearing plans.
- Questions about child-care arrangements.
- Inquiry into language commonly used by applicant.

- Inquiry into how applicant acquired the ability to read, write, or speak a foreign language.
- Requirement that an applicant list all clubs, societies, and lodges to which he or she belongs.
- Inquiry into an applicant's general military experience.

However, the EEOC has said that an employer may inquire about an applicant's military service. It has also stated that a woman may be asked her maiden name, provided the information isn't used to discriminate.

➲ IF YOU AS AN EMPLOYEE ARE DISCRIMINATED AGAINST

Employees at all levels of an organization can be potential victims of discrimination, and discrimination doesn't have to be obvious or even intentional to be illegal. Not only entry level employees may be victims of discrimination. As women and minorities move up in any organization they are likely to face potential new sources of discrimination at every management and executive level. In other words, you too could be a victim of race or sex discrimination. It's important to know that if you are, you're not powerless, there are a number of steps you may take:

1. Contact the Equal Employment and Opportunity Commission for information on the types of discrimination and how to file a claim. They can provide you with information that will help you put together a case, and file a formal charge.

2. Report any perceived instance of discrimination, intimidation, or harassment to your supervisor or personnel department. Your first move to combat discrimination in the workplace should always be internal. Even the Equal Employment Opportunity Commission (EEOC) will seek a voluntary internal settlement to discrimination charges before it will take a case to the courts.

3. Make use of any available grievance procedure. If there is a formal grievance settlement procedure set up in conjunction with a union contract, chances are most courts won't even hear the complaint until it's exhausted this process.

4. File charges with the EEOC. Once you've exhausted any internal grievance procedure—and you're still unsatisfied—contact a local office of the EEOC. You'll have to spell out the details of your case in a letter or through oral testimony.

5. From here on it's largely up to EEOC. The agency will contact your employer and conduct an investigation. It's first move will be to attempt to negotiate some sort of settlement or compromise between you and your employer. If this is unsuccessful, the agency can either pursue the case on your behalf, or allow you to pursue the case through the courts on your own—with the help of an attorney.

6. Fear of filing. Understandably, you may have some hesitation about filing a claim with the EEOC or your employer. If so, remember that it's also illegal for an employer to retaliate against you for opposing an illegal employment practice, filing a claim with EEOC, or testifying, participating, or otherwise assisting in an investigation, proceeding, or hearing. But legal protection may be difficult to actuate. One test: How have employees involved in activity along any of these lines fared?

⊃ IF YOU'RE THREATENED WITH A SUIT

The best defense against an employment discrimination suit is to take active preventive measures to reduce the likelihood that such a suit will ever occur. This means implementing and enforcing an antidiscrimination policy in the workplace, publicizing and promoting that policy on a periodic basis through employee meetings, newsletters, posters, and other communications, and taking appropriate disciplinary measures when that policy is violated.

In general, the courts have also been more sympathetic to the employer's side of the story in discrimination claims when some kind of formal grievance procedure is in place as a way of mediating employee claims of discrimination internally. Of course, such procedures would have to be administered fairly and objectively.

If a claim does come up, you should investigate the charges immediately and attempt to mediate the claim internally, if possible. Get detailed statements from everyone involved as soon after the incident as possible, including witnesses. (If a case does end up in court, it could be several years before it is resolved, and you don't want your side supported entirely by recollection over so great a period of time. It also guards against subsequent "elaboration" of bias claims.)

If you receive notice of an investigation of discrimination charges from your local EEOC office it is best to participate as fully as possible. Stonewalling won't help. It is EEOC policy to work on the assumption that resistance to an investigation or unwillingness to cooperate indicates that a claim is valid.

EEOC will also attempt to negotiate a settlement between your company and the employee or applicant who has claimed discrimination, so there is still room for compromise, even at this point.

Once a discrimination claim reaches the courts, however, its course and conduct is largely in the hands of the attorneys. It can't hurt to repeat, however, that your case can stand or fall on evidence of a strong and effective antidiscrimination policy in use before the date of the claim being heard. That is, the most effective steps you can take to defend against a discrimination charge tomorrow is to implement an antidiscrimination policy today.

⮑ THE FUTURE OF FAIR EMPLOYMENT PRACTICE

The U.S. fair employment laws are in a continuing process of refinement and change. In fact, as the power and protection of organized labor fluctuates as an influence in the U.S. labor markets, state and federal governments increasingly will have to fill in to assure a minimum standard of worker rights and protections. We've already moved a great distance in that direction. In the future we can expect additional developments in a number of significant areas:

Equal pay.   "Comparable worth", while at present dormant, will once again become a major fair employment issue. There are a number of cases involving comparable worth—or equal pay for similar, though not identical, work—moving their way through the courts. There is also likely to be some effort at legislating a federal "comparable worth" standard.

Disability discrimination.   The federal laws dealing with discrimination against the handicapped currently apply only to federal contractors. The future will see more and more states offering employment protection for the disabled. One major area to watch is discrimination against victims of AIDS. A number of state legislatures are considering some form of antidiscrimination measure, and considering the widespread concern contact with AIDS victims—in the schools, in the workplace, in the health care setting—some form of federal standard is a strong possibility.

Job security.   The erosion of the employer's "right to fire" or to "terminate at will" is well documented. Before too long we could see the recognition of all employment relationships as "contractual," with the understanding that an employee can be fired only for "just cause." In addition, we are likely to see some form of federal plant-closing legislation within the next few years. One such bill considered by Congress would have required companies to provide advance notice of impending plant closings and layoffs, and to provide job-hunting and training assistance to affected workers.

The future of affirmative action.   A number of court cases have thrown some doubt upon the continued usefulness of affirmative action plans as a way of correcting employment discrimination. Even the Supreme Court has decided against such plans in some cases—such as when they conflict with established seniority systems. In particular the courts have been hard on affirmative action plans that adhere to rigid, inflexible quotas. For the future, while the courts, and EEOC will continue to press for affirmative action policies that actively seek, hire, and promote qualified minority applicants and employees, there will be much less emphasis on strict numerical quotas as a way of measuring the success of such policies.

2

REVIEWS AND
APPRAISALS

"How am I doing?"

Serious-minded executives can't help but ask this question. It's the key to their progress and achievement.

The reviews and appraisals that you find in this section give you a chance to assess your capability in key professional areas. In some cases, the self-ratings give you numerical evaluations. As an approximation of how well you are doing, your scores can be helpful in rule-of-thumb assessments. Further, in pinpointing weak and strong areas, you can derive the benefits of remedial moves that can further strengthen your professional capabilities.

You will find the assessment tools offered under three headings: I. People; II. Procedures; III. Personal Concerns.

I. People

The individuals and groups you deal with represent a resource for doing your job. The assessment tools that follow can help you spot strong points as well as those for further development.

➲ **SPOTTING COMMUNICATIONS WEAKSPOTS**

A key function of every executive is to receive and give information. How well are you doing? The questions below can turn up some useful answers:

311

1. In communications with your subordinates, do you often get:
   a. inaccurate information?
   b. more than you need?
   c. less?
2. Are you receiving only *routine* material, suggesting a hardening of communications arteries?
3. Do your subordinates complain that they get information late?
4. Do your people often have to check for:
   a. additional information (for example, to supplement a report)?
   b. clarification of a communication you've sent them?
5. From your superior do you usually get:
   a. all the information you need?
   b. information as soon as you need it?
   c. more information than you actually use?
   d. ambiguous, garbled, or unclear information?
6. In communications to your superior:
   a. do your replies to his or her reports or memos tend to be late?
   b. do phone calls take up more time than warranted?
   c. are you making the best use of written reports, phone calls, and face-to-face discussion?
7. In your communications with fellow executives:
   a. are you handicapped by any persistent gaps in information?
   b. are you sending any reports that no longer fill a purpose?
   c. are you receiving any reports that need revision?
   d. do you know of any change in method of communications that would improve results (e.g., switching from memos to conferences)?
8. Are your outside contacts (with customers, suppliers, and so on):
   a. snowing you under?
   b. frequent enough to provide satisfactory results?
   c. close enough to permit personal relationships?

No answers expose points that might benefit from attention. Three or more negatives suggest a need for a broad reassessment that may turn up such oversights as insufficient contacts, or uneven distribution of your communications time that means some people or echelons are being neglected.

➲ HOW WELL DO YOU RELATE TO YOUR SUBORDINATES?

Here's a chance to get some insight on how good you are at working with people. The questions are simple, but practical:

	Yes	No
1. Is your staff aware of your genuine interest in them as individuals?	( )	( )
2. Do you know both first and last names of all those in your group?	( )	( )
3. Have you shown sufficient interest in them (without being nosy) so that you know—		
a. names and ages of their children	( )	( )
b. where their children go to school or work	( )	( )
c. something about their home life and problems	( )	( )
d. their outside activities, talents, and hobbies	( )	( )
e. their health	( )	( )
f. their personal aspirations	( )	( )
4. Have you developed the right amount of friendliness without overfamiliarity?	( )	( )
5. Do you go out of your way to be personally helpful on things that don't relate to the job?	( )	( )
6. Are you willing to go all out for your people if the facts warrant it, even though it means some inconvenience for you?	( )	( )
7. Do you try to establish mutual interests with each subordinate—		
a. stressing a sincere interest in career objectives	( )	( )
b. showing an unaffected interest in personal interests, hopes, and so on	( )	( )
8. Do you try to keep the communication lines open and used, so that the times you seek out contacts with subordinates are not something special and ominous?	( )	( )
9. In the interviews that you have with subordinates, do you try to create a relaxed, unhurried air that helps each person feel at ease and emphasizes your receptivity?	( )	( )

Scoring: Give yourself 10 points for each question answered yes. Then rate yourself on the following scale:

90–100   You're good with your people, and they can be a fountainhead of strength and support to you.

70–80   You're pretty good. Try just a bit harder.

Below 70   You're not deriving all the benefits possible. Reread the quiz questions which you didn't answer yes. Each one suggests an area in which you have an opportunity to strengthen your rapport with people.

⮑ ARE YOU LISTENING?

From interviewing to handling complaints, success in many executive activites depends on *how well you listen*. The other person's opinions, information, suggestions, can pay off in a big way if you're "receiving" properly. But these same ideas don't have a chance if they fall on deaf ears. Here's a quick quiz that shows where you stand on this important skill.

1. Do you choke off an employee's conversation to—
   . . . ask digressive questions? □ Yes □ No
   . . . correct what he or she says? □ Yes □ No
   . . . tell *your* views: □ Yes □ No
2. Do you brush aside a subordinate's arguments because you're right? □ Yes □ No
3. Do you frequently have to backtrack because you misunderstood the information or instructions you received? □ Yes □ No
4. Are you quick to label a conversation or a speaker dull or boring? □ Yes □ No
5. Do you tend to squirm or fidget while others are speaking? □ Yes □ No
6. Do you "always know what they're going to say before they say it?" □ Yes □ No
7. Do you fail to listen for "feelings" or emotional content, as well as for sense? □ Yes □ No
8. Do you neglect to ask for a repeat or a restatement, when you haven't heard, or are not clear on meaning? □ Yes □ No
9. Do you think it's all right to only half listen to a conversation because you're already forming your answer to what's being said? □ Yes □ No
10. Do you prefer talking to listening? □ Yes □ No

Scoring: Give yourself 10 for each question answered No. 100–80 is good; 70–50 is poor. Anyone with a score below 50 is generally out of touch with people.

⮑ RATE YOUR LEADERSHIP

Of all management skills, leadership is most highly valued—and most difficult to define. Of course, a good leader may be easy enough to identify:

"His people will do anything he asks of them."
"She knows how to make her group pull together."

But even when we watch good leaders in action, we find it difficult to pinpoint exactly *what* they do and *how* they do it. Nevertheless, while there's a lot about leadership we don't know, some insightful checkpoints can provide a rule of thumb measure of this crucial skill. Try the quiz that follows, sticking reasonably close to your own experience.

	True	False
1. I do a good job of getting my people to cooperate in achieving goals	———	———
2. My people don't hestiate to bring their really tough work problems to me	———	———
3. When the heat's on, I can get my people to go full steam without any gripes from them	———	———
4. When I'm not around to supervise personally, my subordinates go on working pretty much as usual	———	———
5. I have a good record of helping individuals improve their job performance	———	———
6. I have never had a justified complaint about showing favoritism	———	———
7. I can usually get people to accept changes, even if they have to make a big adjustment	———	———
8. In case of an argument or controversy involving other departments, I back up my people when I know they are right	———	———
9. I have relatively little trouble in getting my people to level with me	———	———
10. I use encouragement often	———	———
11. My subordinates seem to take criticism from me and respond constructively	———	———
12. I find it easy to get volunteers	———	———
13. I make a special effort to be fair in assigning tasks, equitably	———	———
14. My people feel I'm readily available for assistance, as they need it	———	———
15. I am proud of my staff and don't hestiate to show it	———	———

Scoring: Give yourself 10 points for each item marked true, then rate yourself on the scale below.

130 to 150—You're an oustanding leader, a combination of Solomon and Caesar.

100 to 120—You're good, with only a slight case of Achilles' heel.

Under 100—You're not sure of your leadership ability, and this results in job headaches.

If you're dissatisfied with your score, go back over all the questions. Each one highlights a major opportunity for leadership performance. Questions you answered incorrectly are prime areas for improvement.

➲ **PERFORMANCE REVIEW OF YOUR SUBORDINATE MANAGERS**

Executives with department heads, supervisors, foremen, and other lower-echelon managers reporting to them, may want a checklist to assess how they're doing in a given time period—quarterly, semiannually, and so on. Here are the items that form the basis of such a performance review, and can pinpoint areas requiring consultation with you.

	Excellent	Satisfactory	Requires Att'n
1. Holding cost line	☐	☐	☐
2. Cooperation from work group	☐	☐	☐
3. Suggestions and ideas from work group	☐	☐	☐
4. Ability to handle rush or emergency orders	☐	☐	☐
5. Keeping up with work	☐	☐	☐
6. Flexibility of work group	☐	☐	☐
7. Improving employee skills (Training, job rotation, etc.)	☐	☐	☐
8. Relations with line departments	☐	☐	☐
9. Relations with staff and service departments	☐	☐	☐
10. Staying on top of personal workload	☐	☐	☐
11. Equipment maintenance and performance	☐	☐	☐
12. Self-improvement, updating of management skills	☐	☐	☐
13. Contacts with you—			
a. frequency	☐	☐	☐
b. quality	☐	☐	☐
14. Professional growth	☐	☐	☐
15. Drive for excellence	☐	☐	☐
16. Other (add your own)	☐	☐	☐
17. Other	☐	☐	☐
18. Other	☐	☐	☐

II. Procedures

Procedures are the means by which you "automate" regular activities. For example, the procedures you use for handling anything from production control to servicing customers are methodized so that you don't have to improvise a new plan every day. The items that follow touch on some key procedures in order to open them up for evaluation and possible rethinking.

➲ PROBLEM-SOLVING QUIZ

Unsolved problems are stones in the road of progress. The executive is confronted by an unending parade of problems day in, day out. Are you able to keep the stones out of the road? As an indication:

1. Do you go looking for problems in order to account for:
   a. plans that haven't jelled?
   b. unanticipated developments?
   c. unexpected behavior on the part of your people?
2. Do you agree that a problem clearly understood generally holds the clue to its solution?
3. When you're faced by a problem, do you automatically:
   a. start digging out the relevant facts?
   b. mentally line up the people who can help solve the problem?
   c. try to approach the situation on a logical, systematic basis?
4. Do you motivate the problem-solving activities of your subordinates by communicating to them the excitement and challenge of facing up to a tough problem?
5. Do you give your unconscious a chance to work on your problems by generating mental input—focusing on the circumstances and facts of the difficulty, thinking about the problem, and not trying to think through to a solution, leaving that to your unconscious mind?
6. As a starter for creative problem solving, do you examine and challenge the assumptions you may have about both the circumstances of the problem, as well as the possible solutions?

Executives with the best problem-solving records are not geniuses, but usually those who know how to mobilize their resources. Question 3b above, getting help from others, is often productive. You refine the move when you first, pick the right people, and second, avoid those who confuse matters, or who have a distorted sense of the practical. And knowing how to get to sources of information and how to use them is another important strength.

➜ ORDER-GIVING REVIEW

How good is your command of the order-giving process? Check—

1. Before giving orders, do you—
   a. clarify the end results you're after?
   b. prethink the moves required to meet objectives?
   c. decide on the right people to do the job?
   d. help make needed resources available to them?
2. In giving orders or instructions, do you—
   a. suit the type of order to the individual: direct and detailed orders for the beginner, "result-wanted" order for the veteran, etc.?
   b. indicate, wherever necessary, the additional information (data, reference material) they'll need to finish the job?
   c. try to put into your instructions the challenge that will create the strongest motivation for the individual?
   d. provide written instructions, and other "support" material, as needed?
3. In setting goals for subordinates' activities, do you:
   a. let them join in a discussion of the relevance and importance of goals?
   b. permit those with initiative enough leeway to exercise it?
   c. give those who lack self-confidence the opportunity to check back with you as often as will be helpful?
4. To aim at better teamwork, do you:
   a. give your group the opportunity, where possible, to share in planning operations?
   b. keep group goals clearly in view at all times?

➜ YOUR DECISION-MAKING PRACTICES

Your decision-making success depends on how well you can evaluate or compare alternative solutions to your problems, despite time pressure and insufficient data.

1. Do you avoid leaving yourself left high and dry, because of failure to decide on a course of action *in time?*
2. Similarly, do you avoid making decisions *before* you have to, and later receive information that would have changed your actions?
3. In developing alternative courses of action to problems, do you make use of the experience and knowledge of:
   a. your superior?
   b. colleagues?

    c. professional sources of know-how?

    d. your subordinates?

4. In evaluating the advantages and disadvantages of alternatives do you:

    a. list the pros and cons of each possibility in writing (at least for critical decisions)?

    b. check the opinions of experts or people with relevant experience?

    c. try to quantify as many factors as possible, to make comparisons easier and more meaningful? (see "Quantification, p. 100.)

5. In your final selection of a course of action, do you consider the possibility of combining the favorable aspects of two or more alterantives?

6. In analyzing decisions that misfired, was the reason:

    a. misunderstanding the objectives you were trying to achieve?'

    b. miscalculating the difficulties of the situation?

    c. overestimating the abilities of your subordinates?

    d. underestimating their abilities?

    e. failing to keep up with new developments affecting your decision?

    f. inadequate planning of the implementation.

⮌ PREINTERVIEW CHECKLIST

Before you begin the meeting—it may be with a new supplier or consultant—check these points:

1. Do you know as much as possible about the person in the context of the interview? For example:

    name and title

    nature of his or her responsibility or function

    name of company and what it does

    his or her superior

    business or work experience

    special interests

    accomplishments

2. Will the place selected be suitable?

3. Are there others who should be informed of the interview?

4. Are there others who should be present during the talk?

5. Are you prepared to discuss the subject?

6. Is the information or data you may want to use at hand?

7. Have you taken steps to minimize interruptions?

8. Do you have a list—mental or written—of the points you want to cover?

9. Do you know your objective?
10. Do you know the objective of your interviewee? What does he or she want to gain from the meeting?
11. Should you decide in advance to what extent you want to help satisfy the other's objectives?
12. Are there others who should be informed of the outcome of the interview?
13. Any follow-up steps to be taken—memos sent off, ideas to be followed, etc.?
14. Should a record of the interview be made?
15. If the interview is one of a series, should you note the ideas you've gained that should be reflected in subsequent talks?

↩ HOW EFFECTIVE IS YOUR INTERVIEW TECHNIQUE?

	Yes	No
1. Do your interviews generally run about as long as you feel they should?	☐	☐
2. Do you concentrate on helping the interviewee relax?	☐	☐
3. Do you check your notes during the meeting to make sure you cover the points and subpoints of your objective?	☐	☐
4. If unavoidable interruptions occur, do you try to minimize the annoyance for the interviewee—provide a book or magazine to glance at or, still better, material pertinent to your meeting?	☐	☐
5. Do you consider the advisability of terminating an interview short of its goal, if an unanticipated problem arises—unusual nervousness, or emotional upset of the other person, for example?	☐	☐
6. Do you strive for a positive and usually a satisfying ending to your interview—a pleasant word of thanks, or assurance of an action desired by the interviewee, if that's in the cards?	☐	☐
7. For repetitive interviews, would a checklist of points to cover be helpful for the sake of uniformity?	☐	☐
8. Are you aware of "stress interview" techniques—that is, pressuring the interviewee—to *avoid* them, as being unfair and unproductive?	☐	☐

Yes is the preferred answer, except for 7, where either answer is okay. *No* answers suggest points requiring remedy.

⊃ CHECK YOUR PLANNING PROCEDURES

The ability to study cause and effect, to see short-range difficulties in the light of long-range goals, is a key to overall executive accomplishment. Major effects fail or succeed depending on the concept and detail of your plans.

1. Do you review objectives periodically, so that your planning can be updated?
2. Do you take advantage of group brainpower by permitting subordinates to participate in planning procedures?
3. Would you benefit by formalizing your planning procedures, that is, allocating specific time periods to planning activities?
4. Do you use the basic "tools" of planning—calendar, pencil, paper, charts, graphs, pertinent records of past performance, and so on?
5. Is your planning flexible enough to meet changing conditions— higher standards, shorter deadlines, and so on?
6. Are your planning methods organized well enough for you to be able to explain them to someone else?
7. Do you try to develop the skills of your subordinates as an aid to achieving your most ambitious plans?
8. Do you devote "training time" to helping your subordinates plan their activities?
9. Are you planning the activity of any subordinates who should be on their own?
10. Are any of your subordinates performing planning functions that you should be doing—or vice versa?
11. Do you ask your superior for enough information to make your planning sufficiently long range?
12. Do you consult your superior for suggestions on your planning activities—covering everything from objectives to resources to methods and evaluation of results?

⊃ ARE YOU GOOD AT FOLLOW-UP?

Everybody's always telling everybody else to follow up. But what nobody tells anybody is exactly *how* you do it. The questions below can help you check yourself on some of the ABC's of the process.

Yes No

1. You give two subordinates assignments. One man is an old-timer, the other has been on the job only six months. Would you, in all cases, check back on the new man rather than on the old-timer?   ☐   ☐

	Yes	No
2. Do money considerations play a part in follow-up practices?	□	□
3. Does the fact that a particular job has been done again and again make follow-up unnecessary?	□	□
4. Is resentment at having you "breathing down their necks" a necessary consequence of follow-up?	□	□
5. Is it possible to toss the "follow-up ball" to the subordinate doing the assignment?	□	□
6. Can you delegate the follow-up responsibility?	□	□
7. Let's look up the ladder for a moment. Is there anything you can do to ease the follow-up burden of your superior?	□	□

Answers:

1. *No.* For example, if the old-timer was on a job with which he was unfamiliar, and the new employee was on his regular assignment, chances are it would be wiser to check the old employee.
2. *Yes.* Where sizable sums figure in the outcome of work being done, it's mandatory for you to keep a closer check.
3. *No.* Sag or boredom may set in. In addition to the possible dollar penalties of something going wrong, any critical operation—one involving risk to the employee, for example—demands your continued attention.
4. *No.* The manner you use in your follow-up can go a long way toward offsetting employee sensitivity.
5. *Yes.* Executives frequently use the device of having subordinates check back with them to report on developments or results.
6. *Yes.* In many routine jobs it's definitely in the cards for you to have an assistant or an experienced employee do the checking for you.
7. *Yes.* Provide the information needed—in the form of a progress report, for example—as soon as it's available.

Scoring: Give yourself 10 points for each correct answer.
70: You're perfect.
40 to 60: You're good.
0 to 30: Rereading the questions and answers can improve both your score and grasp of the follow-up process.

III. Personal Concerns

The executive's own skills and professional capabilities are often the key to job effectiveness. And for most executives, it's in the personal area and its potential that opportunities for career growth are to be found.

⮕ SKILLS RATING CHART

There are almost as many different sets of executive skills as there are management experts. The group used below represents twenty-one job-oriented areas of executive activity. Taken together in this quick quiz form, they give you a chance to rate your executive performance. You'll find an interpretation of your score following the items. To answer, ask yourself, "How do I rate my past performance in the given area?"

	Low	Medium	High
1. *Using the expert*—getting information, opinions, ideas from well-informed people inside or outside your company.	☐	☐	☐
2. *Building reputation*—making yourself known; developing a favorable name for yourself in the company.	☐	☐	☐
3. *Activating*—getting your people to understand and follow your instructions.	☐	☐	☐
4. *Imparting information*—making yourself understood by subordinates or superiors.	☐	☐	☐
5. *Judging people*—gauging individuals so as to be able to establish good relations and increase job satisfaction.	☐	☐	☐
6. *Working with subordinates*—establishing cordial and effective relationships with those who work for you.	☐	☐	☐
7. *Interviewing*—getting results from talking with people face-to-face.	☐	☐	☐
8. *Listening*—learning from the words of others how and what they think and feel.	☐	☐	☐
9. *Getting cooperation*—motivating people to join you in accomplishing departmental goals.	☐	☐	☐
10. *Maintaining good relations with your superior*—being both friendly and businesslike in your dealings up the line.	☐	☐	☐
11. *Using working time effectively*—being able to get sixty minutes of work out of every hour.	☐	☐	☐
12. *Decision making*—arriving at a logical conclusion and implementing it.	☐	☐	☐
13. *Planning*—developing a course of action to accomplish a definite objective.	☐	☐	☐

	Low	Medium	High
14. *Controlling paperwork*—maintaining the flow of interoffice communications, reports, and the like, to and from your desk.	☐	☐	☐
15. *Getting information*—uncovering the facts you need to advance your work.	☐	☐	☐
16. *Delegation*—making subordinates responsible for some of your activities, while retaining control.	☐	☐	☐
17. *Problem-solving*—licking the tough situations that interfere with efficiency.	☐	☐	☐
18. *Pacing your energy expenditures*—conserving yourself so as to be able to complete the day without undue fatigue.	☐	☐	☐
19. *Concentration*—being able to stick with a given task.	☐	☐	☐
20. *Memory*—remembering events, incidents, ideas, plans, or promises.	☐	☐	☐
21. *Self-scheduling*—accomplishing the objectives of your job by efficient allotment of your time.	☐	☐	☐

Selecting skills to improve.   Some executives feel that after making an overall assessment of their abilities, the next step is to concentrate on the weak spots.

This may be best. But note suggestions concerning your ratings in each of the three columns:

■ *Skills rated "high."*   The items marked "high" may be the ones in which you have the strongest natural proficiency. There's a tendency to pass over these. "Why bother doing anything about them?" the reasoning goes. There are some good reasons:

Locating fertile ground.   Since these "highs" are likely to represent natural strong points, you may find that with only slight effort they can be made outstanding.

Parlaying your strong points.   The parts of your job in which you've already been doing well may prove to be the best areas to work in. You're likely to be at an advantage, and you put yourself in a position to extend past successes.

Say you have a knack for "getting information" (#15 on the list). By concentrating on this item, you may win special assignments from your superior, involving trouble shooting or analytical inquiries, for example.

■ *Skills rated "medium."*   These may be your real danger areas.
In some cases the tip-off to trouble lies in the thought, "Let well enough alone."

Look over each item you've rated in the "medium" column. Supply actual working situations involving these skills. For example, if you've rated "imparting information" (#4 on the list) in this column, visualize the handicaps you've run into as a result. Ask yourself this question:

Do your instructions fail to get across, causing an assistant to fail to correctly carry out an assignment? An affirmative reply can set you on the road to new insight and remedy.

■ *Skills rated "low."*   These may be the toughest items to work on. Chances are that they are the areas in which you have least natural proficiency or experience.

Face that fact frankly. Improvement in these areas may require an uphill battle. You may have to go all out for a comparatively moderate gain. Yet, if the skill involved is a key to an objective you've set for yourself, it may be well worth the effort involved.

In general, selecting the skills to improve should be guided by these additional considerations:

Which do you *use* most?

Which play the *most important role* in the operation of your department?

And finally, this key question that takes your personal objectives into account:

Which are the *most important in helping you advance* toward your specific goal?

➲ **TENSION QUIZ**

Here's an amazing fact: many executives, including those laboring under greatest tension, don't know it. You may have to check to see how badly tension gets you down. The questions below can help you find out an unsuspected truth about yourself.

1. Your superior has asked you to see him. As you sit outside his office, what would be in your mind?
   a. "I wonder what's wrong."
   b. "I hope the boss has good news for me."
   c. Your mind turns to other matters completely unrelated to the coming sessions.
2. An employee asks for permission to see your superior, because she wants to complain about your handling of a situation. You're sure in

your own mind that you are beyond blame. Which move would you be most likely to make?

a. Tell the employee flatly that she is not to go to the boss.

b. Try to persuade her that it would be better if you and she settle the question between yourselves.

c. Say, "I always want you to feel free to see the boss at any time. Go right ahead."

3. You've suggested a new service policy to your boss. He likes the idea and suggests that you explain it to the board of directors. You're now sitting in a conference room with a dozen big shots. You feel:

a. As though you'd like to sink into the floor.

b. Completely calm.

c. Somewhat jittery, but exhilarated at the challenge you're facing.

4. You're sitting home reading. It's eleven P.M. Unexpectedly, the phone rings. Which reaction would be most likely for you?

a. "I wonder who's calling at this hour?"

b. "Oh, oh. Here comes trouble!"

c. "Probably a wrong number."

5. In the course of discussing a problem, you suggest a solution. A fellow executive takes violent exception to the idea, attacks it as "stupid." Your reaction:

a. You drop your wraps and come out fighting for your idea.

b. You're so upset that it takes a few seconds for you to recover.

c. You laugh and say: "Now that you've told us what's wrong with the idea, Bill, let's see if we can't incorporate the good points into our solution."

6. You've recently chosen a new assistant. She turns in an outstanding performance. Your reaction:

a. You're very pleased.

b. You go out of your way to tell your boss about your assistant's accomplishments.

c. You think maybe she's been more successful than you really want her to be, and is beginning to show you up in your own executive performance.

7. You and two other executives are being considered for promotion. The phone rings and it's the call to give you the decision. As you answer:

a. You feel pretty good because you're reasonably sure you got the job.

b. Your hand is shaking and you almost drop the receiver.

c. You're reasonably calm, because you know even if you missed out this time, eventually you'll make the grade.

8. You have to make a key decision that will affect the operation of your department for the entire year. Now, as in other decision-making situations, you are:
   a. Nervous and worried.
   b. So intent on digging into the facts and figures that you're not particularly aware you're doing anything special.
   c. In a Napoleonic mood, in which you feel yourself to be master of the situation.

Scoring.   Unlike most other self-tests, a "normal" score in this test is not one where all your answers indicate an absence of anxiety or tension. You'll find this fact reflected in the scoring directions below.   Answers that indicate you are predisposed toward tension: 1a, 2a, 3a, 4b, 5b, 6c, 7b, 8a.

For each question answered as above, deduct 10 points from a total of 80. Then rate yourself.

40 or less: You're too anxious.

50 to 70: You're anxious, but about average.

80: You're too perfect. Chances are you didn't answer the questions frankly, or you approach crises with an unnatural calm.

➔ CHECK YOUR DICTATION PRACTICES

A review of your dictating procedure may help you spot habits or practices that should be changed to boost efficiency. The list below touches some of the high spots:

1. Are your dictation periods timed so that they fall in the best possible spot in your daily routine? (For example, does your timing allow ample leeway for transcription before the last mail?)   yes   no
2. Do you make every effort to prevent unnecessary interruptions while you're dictating?   yes   no
3. Do you have at your fingertips all the information you require for the dictation you plan to give?   yes   no
4. Do you clearly state your instructions for each piece of dictated material—whether it's a memo, a letter, a report, or other type of communication?   yes   no
5. Do you clearly state your priorities—which items are to be rushed, which can be left for last?   yes   no
6. Do you ask for a rough draft when you anticipate changes in your copy?   yes   no

7. Do you spell out unusually difficult words, proper names, and technical phrases, and enunciate clearly all critical figures?   yes   no
8. If you use a stenographer, do you regulate your dictation speed to the steno's shorthand rate?   yes   no
9. When appropriate, do you give your stenographer an opportunity to ask questions on points that may not be clear?   yes   no
10. Do you indicate minor corrections in such a way that letters and reports need not be done over?   yes   no

Although you may have answered all the questions, keep in mind the possibility that some of your replies should be considered subject to review by your stenographer or transcriber. *Yes* is clearly desirable in each case.

⟳ YOU'RE A GOOD CONFEREE: TRUE OR FALSE?

	True	False
1. The conferee who does not have the problem being discussed can be a valuable contributor.	___	___
2. People sitting next to you influence you more than do those across the table.	___	___
3. A conferee who hears all that's said knows what is happening in a discussion group.	___	___
4. Conferences can be a promotion-gaining vehicle for a conferee.	___	___
5. Skilled conference leaders make good conferees.	___	___
6. The conferees who disagree with your view may be more help than one who agrees.	___	___
7. It is all right to tell a joke during a conference.	___	___
8. It's a good idea to "study up" on a subject before a discussion.	___	___
9. If you see that everyone in the group but you is heading in a direction you believe is wrong, you should keep quiet for the sake of peace and unanimity.	___	___
10. Any conferee can make or break a conference by being either aggressively negative or aggressively positive.	___	___

Scoring. To see how good you are as a conferee, give yourself 10 points for each question correctly answered. You may disagree with some of the "right" answers given. If you disagree violently, stick by your own answer and give yourself full credit. But generally, you'll find the answers given to be acceptable.

1. True. He or she may have the advantage of objectivity, can see the problem without emotional obstructions.
2. False. Tests show that the greatest interaction is between conferees sitting directly opposite one another.
3. False. Often, occurrences beneath the surface affect a conference more than visible factors do.
4. True. Many firms use conferences as a means of detecting superior and promotable people.
5. False. While their knowledge of problem handling, etc., equips them to help the leader eliminate disruptions, they sometimes cannot overcome the impulse to step in and start leading the discussion.
6. True. He or she obliges you to think harder and deeper in order to support your position.
7. True. A funny story is a big help, if it's relevant, illustrative, or eases tension.
8. True. You're better equipped to participate.
9. False. If you beleive your contrary view is valid, you do a disservice if you don't speak up, even though it may mean that, in a way, you pit yourself against the group.
10. True. One person can liven it up if it's dull, sour the whole group, raise spirits if defeatism is setting in, etc.

Rate yourself on the following scale:

80–100 . . . . outstanding
50 to 70 . . . . just about O.K.
Below 50 . . . . poor; suggest you reread questions answered incorrectly as a start in strengthening weak-points.

➲ YOU'RE A GOOD CONFERENCE LEADER: TRUE OR FALSE?

The dozen items below can test your conference leadership knowledge and skill. Indicate whether you believe each statement to be true or false. Then check your score according to the directions that follow.

	True	False
1. You may do nothing between your introduction and summary except ask questions, and still do a good job of leading a conference.	_____	_____

	True	False
2. Differences of opinion generally hamstring a conference.	___	___
3. When you "know the answer," you should save time by telling the conferees, rather, than use the slower method of leading them to think their way to the answer.	___	___
4. Leaders should state their views to encourage the conferees to state theirs.	___	___
5. When a conferee is "wrong" or advances an unpopular opinion and is attacked by the group, you have a responsibility to defend the person.	___	___
6. A side discussion can be stopped without chastising the participants.	___	___
7. Vote taking is the only approved device for settling disagreements.	___	___
8. Even long-winded conferees should be given full opportunity to say their piece.	___	___
9. "Atmosphere" changes in a conference can be detected before they erupt.	___	___
10. The best number of conferees is twenty-five.	___	___
11. An articulate expert is a constant help to a conference leader.	___	___
12. The leader is a dead duck if the conference gets out of control.	___	___

Scoring: To see how good you are as a conference leader, score your answers by giving yourself 10 points for each questions correctly answered. It may be that you may disagree with some of the "right" answers given below. If you disagree violently, stick by your own answers and give yourself full credit. Generally you will find the answers as given to be acceptable:

1. True. Socrates did it all the time, and look what a reputation for wisdom he gained! And the modern leader finds it an effective method.
2. False. They're an important asset. If everyone agrees, no one will go out smarter than when he came in.
3. False. The answer they think out acquires real meaning and acceptability.
4. False. There will always be a number of insecure individuals who will refrain from ever doing anything that even remotely smacks of bucking the boss or leader.

5. True. Actually the conferee is doing the group a favor—making it think.

6. True. For example, if you can assume they're talking about the conference subject, state that everyone would like to hear the idea they're discussing.

7. False. If there's that much lack of agreement, more discussion is needed.

8. False. The uncontrolled rambler is a prime conference killer. You must help someone in this category get to the point briefly.

9. True. Learning to recognize "feeling words," negative interactions, and subsurface meanings equips you to predict and counteract them.

10. False. Experience recommends six to twelve as optimum in most cases.

11. False. Sometimes the expert is best rendered inarticulate, so others can think and contribute.

12. False. The fact that a conference occasionally does wrench loose from its mooring is proof of its spontaneity. And it's seldom a problem to restore peace and direction.

> Rate yourself on the following scale:
> 100 to 120 . . . . outstanding
> 70 to 90 . . . . good
> 40 to 60 . . . . poor
> Below 40 . . . . reread questions answered incorrectly as a start in strengthening weak points.

⋑ HOW'S YOUR FAILSMANSHIP?

The worst has happened. You've fallen on your face and you have that "bottom-has-dropped-out-of-everything" feeling. But before laying out the price of a one-way ticket to Shangri-la, see if supplying the answers to some simple questions doesn't help, and without giving up the comforts of home:

1. Just what has been lost as a result of your failure? Write out this answer. Be specific. Mention amounts, time losses, delays in schedule, and so on.

2. Did you include "self-confidence" in your list above? If not, it's probably a serious omission. Add it.

3. Do you agree that as a result of your failure, you're wiser than you were before?

4. Write out what you've gained, point by point, from your failure?

5. If you find that you can't list anything in No. 4, just consider the

items submitted by an executive who failed in an all-out attempt to sell his boss on a program designed to expand the facilities in his department:

a. learned a lot about the dollar worth of present physical equipment
b. learned what was available in the market today
c. from boss's objection, got a better understanding of top management's views on cash investment
d. improved his ability to present a project in written form
e. realized for the first time that the boss has absolutely no imagination
f. from boss's questions, realized the need to supply and dramatize facts to support his contentions
g. put himself on record as being interested in building the area of his responsibility

6. Compare your answers to No. 1 and No. 4. Doesn't No. 4 constitute a more important factor in your future than No. 1?
7. Can you minimize or eliminate the items of loss you've noted in aswering No. 1?
8. Can you apply the items, noted in your answer to No. 4, in any future activity?
9. Don't you agree that the extent to which failure persists as an influence on your behavior is largely within your control?

If you can answer yes to No. 9, your Failsmanship is already of a high order.

➔ HOW FLEXIBLE ARE YOU?

Answer the questions below as accurately as possible. Even if you're able to spot the "right answers," try to indicate what you would actually do in the situation described. You'll find scoring directions at the end of the quiz.

1. You're in a room with three or four other executives. They're all wearing gray flannel suits; yours is brown tweed. Your reaction, if you noticed their garb at all, would be:
   a. To smile to yourself at their conformity.
   b. To suggest jokingly that at your next meeting they appear "out of uniform."
   c. To feel uncomfortable at being incorrectly dressed.
   d. To make a mental note to wear your gray flannel next time you are going to be in similar company.
2. Your office is to be moved to a different floor because of some

structural changes being made in the building. Your feeling is likely to be:

   a. Regret that you'll be leaving a place to which you've become accustomed.

   b. "Fine! New surroundings will be a welcome change."

   c. Interest in seeing that the new setup will be at least as good as the old.

3. You're in a conference called to decide whether or not the company should expand into a new field. Your probably course, all other things being equal, would be:

   a. To argue for the move.

   b. To argue against the move.

   c. To argue for the move, on condition that a careful study indicates good chances for success.

4. Your boss calls you into his office. "Jane," he says, "I've been wanting to talk to you about your job, but I don't know just how or where to begin. Now I want you to ask me for a raise. I think that will trigger the things I have to say." Your move is to say:

   a. "Boss, I'd like to have a boost of five thousand dollars a year, retroactive to the first of the year."

   b. "I couldn't. Let's wait until you can get going under your own steam."

   c. "Boss, our relationship must be getting awfully weak if you can't come right out and tell me what you want to say."

   d. You're tongue-tied.

5. Your boss calls you into her office. "Henry," she says, "let's go through our usual routine of discussing last week's problems. I'm not sure we're getting much benefit from this procedure, but I feel it's better than not doing anything at all." Your reply is:

   a. "Sure, just as you wish," and then you launch into the kind of monologue that has featured the previous sessions.

   b. "Since we're not getting satisfactory results, why not change our approach? How about . . . ," and you suggest a couple of alternative methods that you think might yield more information.

   c. "If you feel it's a waste of time, why do it at all?"

6. A customer is on the phone, telling you he must have delivery on an order by the end of the week. You tell him you can't make the stuff up to the standard of quality he wants and still ship within the time limit he has set. He insists; you insist. Finally:

   a. You tell him, "I'm sorry, Mr. White, but you're being unreasonable. No matter how much we'd like to, we just can't satisfy your request." And that's your final word.

    b. You ask him whether he could use material of the lower quality that would result from a speeded-up process.

    c. You say, "There is a possibility that we could get the work out on time, but it would mean running on a three-shift basis, and we're only set up for two. Would you be willing to pay the extra cost involved in our arranging a three-shift schedule?"

7. You've just got a new secretary. She's a good, capable worker who insists on dusting your desk every morning. The trouble is, she has her own ideas of how your desk equipment should be arranged: she puts your in-out box at the right instead of the left, puts your phone at the back of the desk, although you generally keep it toward the front, and so on. Would you:

    a. Let her have her way.

    b. Make it very clear that you have your personal preferences in the matter of desktop arrangement, and order her to place the items the way you've always kept them.

    c. Ask her why she feels her arrangement is better than the one you've been using.

8. You've made it a practice to have lunch with one of your colleagues every Tuesday. He calls you in the morning to say he can't make it. Which would be your likeliest move:

    a. Phone another friend or acquaintance and try to set up another lunch date.

    b. Feel quite disconcerted, go to lunch alone, and find yourself at loose ends for the entire hour.

    c. Go to lunch alone and enjoy the unaccustomed pleasure of an hour's solitude.

9. You get out of bed one morning and see it's a little late; you dress, gulp breakfast, and dash off to the station. To your surprise you notice the platform is practically empty; then you realize it's Sunday morning. Would you:

    a. Try to sneak back into bed without waking your spouse, so that you could keep the incident a dark secret.

    b. Feel the incident proves you're too deep in a rut, and cast about for some way of easing up.

    c. Decide to go into town anyway, to clean up a couple of overdue matters at the office.

Scoring.   First, realize that any one question by itself isn't too significant. Many of us can be flexible in some areas—matters of dress, personal working habits, for example—and inflexible in others, such as time schedules, and off-the-cuff reactions to abrupt changes.

However, a very high score in the quiz is probably a favorable indication of your flexibility in general; a very low one is apt to be unfavorable. Rate yourself as follows:

Start by giving yourself a perfect score, 90 points. Then, *subtract 10 points* for these "wrong answers": 1c or d; 2a; 3b; 4b or d; 5a; 6a; 7b; 8b; 9a.

Here's the rating scale:

70 to 90: You're as adaptable as a good boxer.

40 to 60: You tend to freeze a bit at the edges; ease up.

Below 40: A bit of rut-busting might do you a world of good.

➔ WHEN WILL YOU BE READY TO RETIRE?*

This questionnaire helps guide you, in due time, to consider when to retire. To shape your decision, you read the statements and check off the one that comes closest to describing your situation.

Each statement has a number or rating assigned to it. This helps weight your answers so as to give each its relative important in relation to other items concerning the same subject, and also as compared to other relevant factors.

For instance, *finances* is clearly a major factor in your decision. If you can't afford to retire early, then you may have to forget it, no matter how favorable other factors might be. Accordingly, the items relating to finances are weighted heavily. There are other crucial factors in addition to finances that must be considered if your retirement is to be a happy and productive experiences. Even if you are able financially to retire early, you may have to think seriously about whether it is wise and practical to do so.

Of course, with the passing of time your situation in relation to the factors listed may change. You can then take the quiz over again and the new score you get may suggest a different decision.

Go through each of the factors below and check off the one statement in each group that most closely approximates your situation. Make your responses accurate and honest. The usefulness of your score depends heavily on how carefully you do this. After the last factor, you'll find directions and an interpretation of your total score.

Finances

−50   ☐   I don't have enough reserves on hand to make it now.

5   ☐   I have just enough to scrape by, but I'm not sure about inflation.

* Adapted from *Over 50,* by Auren Uris, Chilton Book Company, 1979.

10 ☐ I can make it if I live "cheaply" and cut back on extras.

15 ☐ I'm okay for the foreseeable future at my present level of living.

25 ☐ I will do fine in almost any event.

50 ☐ Money is no consideration.

Health

− 5 ☐ My work keeps me zipping along, gives me exercise, and forces me to watch my diet and personal habits.

5 ☐ I feel that my work favors my health in that it keeps me busy and on a regular schedule.

15 ☐ My work generally leaves me dragged out at the end of the day. If it weren't for weekends, I'd be in a bad way.

50 ☐ My work is a terrible strain. It drains my energies, keeps me on edge, and doesn't let me sleep nights.

Relationships

− 5 ☐ If I retire now, I suspect my personal relationships will suffer badly; for example, I expect my wife and I will get on each other's nerves, I will lose some of my job friends, and so on.

0 ☐ I'm not sure if I have enough, and good enough, friends to make for a satisfactory social life if I stop work now.

10 ☐ I've never depended very much on people I met on the job for socializing, and I have a well-rounded group of friends and relatives who always have and will continue to make for a full social life.

25 ☐ The minute I stop working I'll be able to improve and devote more time to practically all of my relationships.

Emotional outlook

−10 ☐ I'm emotionally unprepared to stop work. If I retire now, I won't be able to make the many adjustments that are necessary.

5 ☐ I don't believe retirement is going to be much of a threat for me. I'm pretty flexible.

15 ☐ I find the prospect of retirement kind of exciting, an attractive adventure.

30 ☐ I can hardly wait for retirement. There are so many things I want to do.

Housing

− 5 ☐ If I stop working now, I'll have to give up my present living arrangements for something much less desirable.

5 ☐ My retirement won't affect my housing arrangements much one way or the other.

15 ☐ I expect benefits from my retirement: I'll be able to do a lot of work around the house that I've been putting off for years, which will mean not only enjoyable activity but also an increase in the value of the place.

20 ☐ If I retire now, I'll be able to move to another site in another part of the country (or whatever) that will give my whole life a lift.

Work

−15 ☐ I would miss it terribly. There is so much more I want to achieve before I quit.

0 ☐ Work? I can take it or leave it.

15 ☐ I'm proud of my work record. However, I feel my job achievement is behind me.

25 ☐ The day I leave the job will be one of the happiest of my life.

Activities

−10 ☐ I know I'll never find anything else to do that I will enjoy as much as I do my job.

5 ☐ I enjoy my life on the job as much as anything I might do on the outside.

10 ☐ I like the idea of getting into new things.

20 ☐ There are any number of things I've been eager to do and, when I leave my job, I'll finally have enough time to get to them.

Evaluating your score. In a moment, you'll be able to total your score and see what the implications are for you. But first, a word about the weighting. It's an attempt to make the score realistic. For example, consider the money factor; as was mentioned earlier, many other things might favor retirement, but if your financial situation is unsatisfactory, early retirement might be a catastrophe. That's why the money factor gets the highest value and why, if you put a check by the first of the statements suggesting that you are financially unprepared to stop work, other items would have to be very, very strong to compensate.

The same thinking explains the weighting of the health item. If your health is going to suffer if you continue in your job, it becomes a strong reason for retirement. And so on.

Now, go back over all your checkmarks (it's assumed you've made a choice for each factor) and total up your score.

Total Score: _____ .

If your score is over *100*, chances are you are both practically and mentally ready to consider early retirement. But don't act on the results of this questionnaire alone. Double-check such a move by an approach from a different perspective. Using the facts that you have in effect pinned down by using this tool, you can now discuss the move with interested parties—spouse, family or possibly a counsellor provided by your employer.

If your score is between *80* and *100,* the decision is up in the air. There seem to be advantages and disadvantages to the move that pretty well balance each other. Continue to explore the situation further. You can start by reconsidering the answers you checked off above. Make sure that they represent what you *really* think and feel. If no significant changes are made, then you may want to explore some of the key factors. In one case it may be your health; or perhaps your own financial picture isn't altogether clear. You may want to reexamine your net worth or any of the other factors that you feel may deserve clarification.

If you scored below *80,* indications are you are definitely not ready for retirement at this time. If this decision seems reasonable to you, you may want to let matters rest as they are for the moment. However, if you're really interested in retiring early, you may want to take steps that can improve the retirement possibilities for you. I've already emphasized the importance of the financial factor, but if, for instance, the matter of housing is particularly important, you may want to consider the actions that can change the picture so that your situation in this respect will be satisfactory.

Finally, keep in mind that the situation with respect to one or more of the factors may change. You may want to come back and recheck these factors. Where your situation has changed significantly, you will come up with a new score that may suggest the time is ripe to retire.

3

KEY

MANAGEMENT CONCEPTS

With the work of Frederick Winslow Taylor, the management of the business corporation developed a scientific orientation. Taylor's approach, called "Scientific Management," brought the idea of system and method to the working world.

Since Taylor's day, the science of management has moved ahead on the basis of concepts and innovative thinking contributed by industrial psychologists, management experts, and others dedicated to the world of the corporation.

Their ideas provide a treasury to strengthen the foundations and extend the professional thinking of contemporary managers.

The collection seems to divide naturally into two categories, the theoretical and practical. However, the division is not altogether satisfactory because management ideas are of value essentially for their eventual application. Labeling ideas as "theory" seems to minimize them vis-à-vis the "practical" ones. However, separating the two groups does make for a better coherence of presentation. For example, to follow McGregor's "Theory X, Theory Y" by the "Carelessness Diagnosis" would be mixing watermelons and grapes. Accordingly, "Food for Thought," is used for ideas that require further development for practical application, and "Ideas for Action" covers those that are closer to the application stage.

A. Food for Thought

The concepts that follow represent the best thinking of teachers and philosophers, most from academia, worthy disciples and successors to Frederick Winslow Taylor, the father of scientific management.

➲ HAWTHORNE EXPERIMENTS*

Any survey of management ideas must include the studies called the Hawthorne Experiments, an investigation started in the late 1920s and continuing for almost two decades. It proved to be a seminal effort that fundamentally transformed our thinking about productivity and the worker's role in it. Discussion as to findings and conclusions persists to this day and will doubtless continue into the future.

An appreciation of the impact of Hawthorne is best begun with an understanding of previous attitudes toward the worker. Typically, factory employees were called "hands." Some men were huskier and could undertake heavier work, and some were hungrier or more ambitious and might work harder. Mental capacity and individuality didn't count. Tom, Dick, and Harry, Tess, Dinah, and Harriet were just different names for the same thing. Hawthorne changed all that.

The Western Electric Company plant in Hawthorne, Illinois was known for its enlightened management. Employees had the latest pension plans, sickness and accident benefits, and recreation programs, but production wasn't up to expectations. Somebody thought lighting might have something to do with it.

Eventually Western Electric executives and management experts from Harvard University joined forces. They decided to study the effects of lighting on performance.

Two groups of operators were selected, Group One using the "normal" amount of light, and Group Two getting more light. Output from Group Two increased, which was expected. Unexpectedly, so did the production from Group One.

Then Group Two was given less light. Their output went up, and so did that of Group One. Two workers were put in a dark room, working by sense of touch, completely in the dark. Despite the handicap, increased output was maintained.

Next the researchers studied a group of six female assembly workers, checking their production under the following different conditions:

- An hourly wage rate was changed to piecework. Output rose.
- The women were given two five-minute rest periods. Output increased.
- Two ten-minute rest periods were given. Output continued to go up.
- The morning rest period was lengthened to fifteen minutes and the workers were served hot snacks. Production continued upward.

* "Hawthorne Experiments," along with "The Carelessness Diagnosis" and "Crisis Management" are adapted from *101 of the Greatest Ideas In Management*, by Auren Uris, John Wiley & Sons, 1986.

- The women were let off half an hour early. Output soared. They were let off a full hour earlier, and output stayed at the same high level.
- The women were put back to working that extra hour. Output shot up again, and remained at that high level even when weekly hours were cut from forty-eight to forty.

As a last test the original conditions were restored: The women went back to time work with no rest periods, no hot snacks, and a forty-eight-hour week. Output hit an all-time high.

The scientists thought they had gone back to the original working conditions but apparently they were mistaken. Something was now present that hadn't been there before. There was a change in the people themselves.

The researchers concluded that they had uncovered a psychological factor that influenced productivity. Exactly what that factor was and how it operated wasn't clear, and to this day there is disagreement. Some speculations follow:

- The women felt differently about themselves and about their work. Just separating them and using them in an experiment had made them feel important. They were more than small cogs in a large machine.
- Their work had taken on meaning, more than just turning out units. They had become a team whose help the company needed.
- As a result of recognition and special feelings about their roles and the purpose of their work, they had become motivated to exert effort toward producing more and better.

Awareness of the psychological factor and its effect on job performance suggested another experiment to the researchers. Twenty-one thousand Western Electric workers were interviewed and asked how they felt about their jobs and the company, what complaints they had, if any, and so on.

But the interviewing process itself turned up unexpected findings. Interviewers found the workers tended to stray from the questions asked and talked about other things such as their feelings, aspirations, and personal problems. After a while the interviewees were permitted to discuss whatever they wanted to.

Eventually the researchers concluded that there was a therapeutic benefit from the conversations. Mental stress seemed to ease after people expressed their feelings about their bosses, working conditions, and company management. And minimizing the distraction caused by upset made possible a return to normal performance. This finding opened up a new prospect: having managers or in some cases company-sponsored professionals talk with employees about problems that undercut their mental well-being and ability to perform.

Challenging insights emerged from the studies of the Western Electric—

Harvard investigators. Perhaps the most important result was the awareness of the worker's individuality, and potential for improved performance by policies and practices that would effect employee motivation.

This line of thought stimulated a new wave of management interest that came to be known as the "human relations" approach to managing people.

The Hawthorne findings relate to a number of key management areas:

■ **Personnel policy.** Reexamination of personnel policies may be in order to see whether restrictive rules or overcontrol has held people back as well as kept them in line.

■ **Manager training and indoctrination.** Could your managers be made more aware of the potential gains that can come from encouraging participation in problem solving and idea production? The question is simplistic as asked, but is intended to raise possibilities that, when followed up, can reap substantial improvements in relationships between employee and employer, to their mutual benefit.

■ **Departmental performance.** Companies may benefit by starting their managers on a study of the degree to which the positive and creative abilities of their employees are being used. This is a big job, but the efforts and hazards can be minor compared to benefits gained. If appropriate, the project might be kicked off with a review of the Hawthorne studies and their results.

The human relations school of management, created by Hawthorne, became a favorite subject of management writing in the years that followed it. Here is a helpful bibliography:

Management and the Worker, 1939, and *Counseling in an Organization,* by F. J. Roethliserger and W. J. Dickson, Harvard University Press, 1966; *Human Problems of an Industrial Civilization,* 1933, and *Social Problems of an Industrial Civilization,* 1933, by Elton Mayo, Harvard Business School; *Hawthorne Revisited,* by Henry Landsberger, Cornell University Press, 1965.

⮑ LIFECYCLE OF AN IDEA

Like old soldiers, ideas never die, and although they may fade away, they seldom vanish completely. This author's book, *Mastery of Management,* described the latency, growth, and downturn of interest in ideas that grasp management's imagination, flourish in seminars and practice, and then retire to a place as mysterious as the legendary graveyard of the elephants.

Here is a version of a chart developed to represent the fate of that long-lived management favorite, brainstorming.

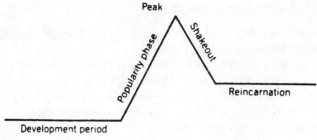

Lifecycle of an idea

Note the four phases:

Development period.   The time required for the idea to be fine-tuned and gain a degree of public interest and acceptance.

Popularity phase.   The months or years of its use by its adherents.

Shakeout.   Decimation of the user group.

Reincarnation.   Reemergence of interest and use.

Understanding the phases of interest can keep managers au courant on the changing array of subjects that claim the professional practitioner's attention. This knowledge can also help probe for the practical value of an idea, and divorce it from its popular appeal. The two don't always go hand in hand.

Brainstorming is a good example of a concept that won great favor, was practiced widely—in some organizations you couldn't open a meeting-room door without catching brainstormers in flagrante delicto—and then virtually disappeared from the management scene. And yet, the technique is still in use in companies where managers are aware of its unique benefits.

Using the concept.   You can put the life cycle concept to work in two ways; first your own use. For example, one executive gets considerable professional pleasure, and he says profit, by digging into a repositories of management wisdom, such as texts, magazines, and old training programs. He disinters some vein of thought of practice and develops updated applications. "I find perfectly good ideas neglected, usually because they lack widespread acceptance. It is no secret that management is taken up with fads just as is the general public, and every other profession."

Second, lower-echelon managers and managers in training can be made more hardheaded in their thinking. Their responsiveness to fads can be put into perspective, while stimulating them to search for new ideas, analyzing and evaluating old neglected ones.

➲ MASLOW'S HIERARCHY OF NEEDS

Industrial psychologist, A. H. Maslow, has made a major contribution to motivational theory on the work scene.

Maslow developed the "basic needs" concept that helped executives understand some puzzling factors about employee motivation. For example, money was supposed to be the great incentive. Yet, strangely, when people were asked what was most important to them in their jobs, money often took third or fourth place. Factors like "challenging work," "chance for advancement," and even, in some cases, "a good boss," ranked higher.

Dr. Maslow suggested a theory that explains the seeming contradiction. He suggested that there is a hierarchy of needs that exists for the human being. We give precedence to the first of these needs until it is satisfied. When the first need is satisfied, the second becomes dominant, and so on through the sequence. Here's Maslow's list:

Physiological needs.   Hunger, shelter, sexual gratification.

Safety needs.   These represent our needs for protection against danger and threat, either from the environment or from people.

Social needs.   After the physiological and safety needs are fairly well satisfied, the needs for love, affection, and "belongingness" tend to emerge.

Esteem needs.   These have to do with the wish that most of us have for self-respect and the good opinion of others.

Self-fulfillment.   Last on the list, but perhaps of most significance for future managers is the need for "self-actualization." This concerns the individual's feeling about the value and satisfaction of his or her work.

Failure to understand this need often lies behind the manager's complaint: "We've given our people everything: good pay, pleasant working conditions, all the physical comforts possible on the job—and yet they're dissatisfied." Dr. Maslow's concept explains the reason.   It's precisely because employees have had the four basic needs sufficiently satisfied that the fifth—the need for self-fulfillment—emerges. It will cause discontent unless and until the manager finds ways of satisfying it.

➲ HERZBERG'S MOTIVATOR/HYGIENE FACTOR CONCEPT

Dr. Frederick Herzberg, chairman of the Psychology Department at Western Reserve University, developed the concept that many management experts feel clarifies what makes an employee satisfied or dissatisfied in his job.

Herzberg developed the idea that two sets of conditions affect a person at work. He calls one set *motivators,* the other, *hygiene factors.* The first group is positive, with the power to satisfy an employee. The second group, hygiene factors, is negative, can dissatisfy or demotivate. Of the former, the five most important, according to Herzberg, are achievement, recognition, the work itself, responsibility,and advancement. Of the latter, the five most important are company policy and administration, supervision, salary, interpersonal relations, and working conditions.

The distinction between them says Herzberg, is that the first set of factors (the motivators) "describe man's relationship to what he does; his job content, achievement on a task, recognition for task achievement, the nature of the task, responsibility for a task, and professional advancement or growth in task capability."

The dissatisfiers (or hygiene factors) describe an employee's "relationship to the context or environment in which he does his job." They "serve primarily to prevent job dissatisfaction while having little effect on positive job attitudes."

This is a most important distinction. Dr. Herzberg's study shows that "the factors involved in producing job satisfaction are separate and distinct from the factors that lead to job dissatisfaction." The lack of satisfiers does not lead to dissatisfaction; the presence of hygiene factors does not lead to satisfaction, but to no dissatisfaction.

In other words, the presence of good company policies and administration, good supervision, good salaries, good interpersonal relations, and good working conditions will not motivate people over the long haul. What does motivate people is the challenge and pleasure they get out of the work itself, the sense of achievement they get from doing the work, recognition for a job well done, a feeling of responsibility, and the desire for advancement.

THEORY X, THEORY Y

Toward the end of the 1950s, management experts began to focus on the climate of work as a motivational factor. Behind this interest was an awareness that neither cash, nor stock incentive, nor punishment are effective as motivators in the long run. Professor Douglas McGregor of the Massachusetts Institute of Technology superseded these "pushing" types of motivators by the concept of a climate of concern that helps the individual develop his own internal reasons for wanting to excel.

Professor McGregor first explained his Theory X and Theory Y concepts at talks at MIT, and then expanded his ideas in a book, *The Human Side of Enterprise.*

McGregor's now-classic work suggests that two different approaches, or philosophies of management, are possible in business. Each is based on a set of assumptions about people. One can see the differences in approach—and at the same time test one's own assumptions about people—by looking at McGregor's descriptions:

Theory X Assumptions about People	Theory Y Assumptions about People
1. Human beings are inherently lazy and will shun work if they can.	1. For most people, the expenditure of physical and mental effort in work is as natural as for play or rest.
2. People must be directed, controlled, and motivated by fear of punishment or deprivation to impel them to work as the company requires.	2. People will exercise self-control in the services of objectives which they accept.
3. The average human being prefers to be directed, wishes to avoid responsibility, has relatively little ambition, and wants security above all.	3. Under proper conditions, the average human being learns not only to accept responsibility, but also to seek it.
	4. The capacity for exercising imagination, ingenuity, and creativity exists generally among people.

Which set of assumptions is true? Neither one, in a clear-cut objective way. But in general, managers tend to evaluate people either by the Theory X or Theory Y assumptions. And whichever position a manager takes, there are direct consequences in the way he handles his people. For example, consider the implications of McGregor's first assumption:

"Tom Smith is inherently lazy and will shun work if he can" (Theory X). If Tom Smith's boss believes he has an allergy to work, Tom Smith will be managed by a considerable amount of direct and close supervision. Rigid work schedules must be set for him. His progress and level of performance must be checked continually. These methods belong to the Theory X arsenal of management techniques.

Compare this with the second assumption:

"Tom Smith is energetic, enjoys his work, and prides himself in doing it well" (Theory Y). If Tom Smith's boss sees Tom as this type of person, he will spend considerably less time on direct supervision. Tom will be given objectives of assignments, and left to work out the ways of achieving them. He will also be trusted to turn out a satisfactory amount and quality of work, without overly frequent checking. These methods represent the Theory Y approach.

McGregor's ideas caused a furor in management circles. Many people, including management practitioners and consultants, contest McGregor's view that Theory Y is best for managing people.

One of the more articulate opponents of Theory Y, management consultant Dr. Robert N. McMurry in *Business Management,* pointed out a psychological basis for the superiority of Theory X:

"There appears to be little awareness that . . . the so-called victims (employees managed by Theory X) might relish their bondage. Why? For the simple reason that the rigid structure in which they find themselves is not fettering, but reassuring. It is even conceivable that rank and file employees deliberately seek regimented jobs because these positions are more comfortable and less demanding than jobs requiring initiative, creativity, and decision making."

In general, critics of Theory Y describe it as being impractical, unrealistic, and out of place in today's world of business. Moreover, the anti-McGregors argue, Theory X, whatever its shortcomings, works. Actually, objective observers now believe that these opposed views are more the result of misunderstanding and failure to agree on basic terms than of the irreconcilability of the two approaches.

Psychologists-and management experts are still discussing the pros and cons of McGregor's Theory X–Theory Y concepts. Yet Theory Y has not achieved the impact expected by some. True, many managers now give a responsible employee considerable latitude in his work, but more often than not, they've never heard of McGregor. What has failed to develop is any degree of broad testing of Theory Y that might lend eventual support to either side of the argument.

In other words, practicality and personal preference rather than theory—either X or Y—rules. Managers and executives develop their personal leadership styles that often are a mixture of both X and Y assumptions about people. We have not yet developed a concept of climate building that is sufficiently surefire as to result in general acceptance and use.

SKINNER'S BEHAVIOR MODIFICATION

Motivation theorists McGregor, Maslow, Herzberg, and most others stress the *why* of performance: for example, McGregor's Theory X Theory Y assumes that workers' feelings and attitudes determine effort. On the other hand, psychologist B.F. Skinner stresses *what* is done, behavior, as the key. Improved performance, says Skinner, can result from modifying behavior rather than trying to manipulate the psyche.

Skinner's major tool of behavioral change is *reinforcement,* positive and negative. *Positive* reinforcement acts as reward, *negative* as punishment.

His ideas are based on extensive experiments. He changed the behavior of rats and pigeons by *operant conditioning;* that is, evoking a desired action by training the subject to expect a reward for doing it. A pigeon is trained to peck at a dot by giving it a grain pellet after each peck. A worker, then, could be motivated to perform a task by knowing it would be positively reinforced, that is, rewarded. "Reinforce the behavior you want repeated," became a catch phrase.

Skinner's innovations further extend the field of motivation and provide you with additional ideas for consideration and workscene application. The experience of one company was widely studied:

Case in point.   Emery Air Freight launched a program in its shipping department. Workers were encouraged to set a production goal, which usually was higher than the goal the manager would have set, of the number of pallets they would stack with packages preparatory to shipping. Fulfilling or surpassing the goal won commendation and eventually, material rewards. Subpar performance was not mentioned. Productivity improved significantly.

Even Skinner's detractors admit the scientific discipline and success of his experiments. He was able to train pigeons past the dot-pecking to elaborate dance movements. A key disagreement concerned Skinner's claim that people could be trained as laboratory animals had been. But the attempts to apply behavior modififcation suffered from the same problems as other theories:

■ The procedures represented the addition of elements that were seen as artificial. Praise, for example, an effective stimulant, eventually wore out its effectiveness when used repeatedly as positive reinforcement.

■ It was necessary to continue positive reinforcement to prevent "extinction," the gradual dimunition of the conditioned response.

■ It was difficult for some supervisors and trainers to witness unsatisfactory work, such as errors and sloppy performance, without making a negative comment.

Attempts to use both positive and negative reinforcement overlooked the dictum that negative reinforcement cannot elicit desired behavior, it can only discourage unacceptable behavior.

Are we "too human?" The basic question as to whether success in conditioning animals could be duplicated with human beings is still unanswered. The human race, its behavior still reminiscent of its origins, may be viewed merely as intelligent animals. But the human brain and psyche's sensitivities, imagination, potential for spirituality, ability to create, aspire, and even its laxities and self-indulgence, represent forces weaning it away from purely mechanistic behavior.

For managers, Skinner's ideas contribute some practical elements, for example, his view of punishment and reward (the old carrot-and-stick idea in modern dress.) The Emery Air Freight example suggests the possibility of successful application. But attempts to duplicate it have not been satisfactory. This suggests that unidentified variables are at work.

At any rate, Skinner's ideas have a broad and provocative appeal. If motivation interests you, Skinner's ideas might make worthy fare. Among his books is a best-selling novel, *Walden II,* that dramtizes his theories. His major works, in order of fame, are *Beyond Freedom and Dignity,* 1971; *Schedules of Reinforcement,* 1957; *Analysis of Behavior,* 1961; and *About Behaviorism,* 1974. The novel, *Walden II,* was first published in 1948, with many editions to follow. Also of interest is a book about Skinnerian psychology, *Behavior Management: The New Science of Managing People at Work,* by Lawrence M. Miller, 1978. (Also, check "Motivation" in the Index.)

⮕ SENSITIVITY TRAINING

Sensitivity training developed in the management field out of a felt need. A growing segment of management came to believe that an executive's effectiveness depends largely on his or her interpersonal relationships. The problem of effective leadership then becomes one of the executive relating more effectivley to subordinates, colleagues, and so on. It is to this problem that sensitivity training addresses itself.

The popularity of ST peaked in the '70s and fostered wide interest in group confrontation and self-analysis. And it spawned movements that became mainstream preoccupations in and out of business. Its promise and percentage of successes—small but vocal—keep it alive in management awareness.

Sensitivity training got its start about 1946, as a result of work done by psychologist Kurt Lewin of M.I.T. In that year, Lewin and others conducted a workshop at the State Teachers' College in New Britain, Connecticut.

The workshop was divided into several groups, each with its own research observer. In the course of the workshop, Lewin became aware of two things. People who had been part of the same group experience had differing perceptions of what actually had occurred. And discussion of "my perception of reality" produced some startling interactions. One example, as recorded by the research observer:

> At 10:00 a.m. Mr. X attacked the group leader and then X and Mr. Y got involved in a heated exchange. Some other members were drawn into taking sides. Other members seemed frightened and tried to make peace. But they were ignored by the combatants. At 10:10 a.m., the leader came in to redirect

attention back to the problem, which had been forgotten in the exchange. Mr. X and Mr. Y continued to contradict each other in the discussion that followed.

Immediately Mr. X denied and Mr. Y defended the correctness of their views. Other members reinforced or qualified the data furnished by the observers. In brief, participants began to join observers and training leaders in trying to analyze and interpret behavioral events . . . participants reported they were deriving important understandings of their own behavior and the behavior of the group.

Lewin and his training staff felt a powerful process of reeducation had been hit upon. Group members, if confronted with their own behavior and its effects, might achieve highly meaningful learning about themselves, about the responses of others to them, and about group behavior and group development in general.

What had been created in 1946 is known today, variously as laboratory training, sensitivity training, and the T-group (training group); and it promises methods of altering the behavior of groups and individuals, and increasing their operating effectiveness.

"Sensitivity training," says Chris Argyris of Yale, one of its proponents, "is one of the most effective tools we have for developing human relations skills."

These are some of the benefits claimed:

- It improves an executive's control over personal frictions among subordinates.
- It gives him or her the ability to work more understandingly—and constructively—with superior and colleagues.
- It enables the executive to get subordinates and colleagues to "level" with him or her, be more open in day-to-day dealings.

The T-Group Experience.   About 60 percent of the total time of a typical sensitivity training course is spent in T-group meetings. In each group there is a staff member, usually an industrial psychologist, who guides the group to some extent. It would be a mistake to call him or her a leader, because the leader does little or no leading. At the first session, the staff person usually explains that the group will study behavior, that there is no agenda, and that any learning that occurs will depend upon the group itself. With that, he or she stops talking.

Since each unit is composed of different individuals, no group will operate in exactly the same way. Often a period of silence occurs—embarrassed, even awkward. Eventually, someone may suggest a topic to discuss, or the members will introduce themselves, or a participant will take it upon him or herself to try to lead the group. Whatever happens, the actions and statements of individual members are fair game for exploration.

It usually isn't long before the talk is free-wheeling. One contributing factor is, of course, the desire of the participants to gain as much as possible from the training. Another is the relative anonymity of the setting—executives from many companies who've just met and who'll be together for only a brief period. As a result the comments become open and personal.

Individuals who have participated in sensitivity training dwell at length on the vividness and depth of the experience. As a matter of fact, a more or less constant refrain from T-group participants is, "It's impossible to describe. You have to experience it to really understand what it's like."

To some extent, this is true. The T-group, with its ten or twenty participants and a psychologist-leader or trainer, is a microcosm, a small world with rules different from those "outside." As indicated, the usual amenities like politeness and small talk are absent.

In place of ordinary social conversation and small talk, participants begin reacting to one another in deep and significant ways. Complete openness, for example, is aimed for. And after a preliminary period of caution, participants feel free to level with one another, *really* voice their true opinions. This freedom to express what one really thinks and feels is based on trust in the group. T-groupers know they will not be penalized for honesty. It's at this point the life of the T-Group can be highly personal, revealing, and instructive.

As one participant expressed it: "The few days I spent in a T-group gave me more information about my comembers than I had learned about people I had worked with for ten years." Because such close knowledge is gained, faults and virtues, strengths and weaknesses become apparent. An individual sometimes gets a more accurate, even disturbing, picture of himself or herself than ever before available.

During the final week, the T-group members try to relate what they've learned about themselves, about each other, and about group dynamics to their jobs back home. For many managers, the result is personal growth and improved on-the-job relationships.

To understand why the compressed experience of a sensitivity session may be more helpful than uninterrupted immersion in real life—to understand, in short, why *this* particular compressed experience is a better teacher than "real" experience—it is necessary to understand, first, how the simulation works.

Participants in a typical group meeting at Bethel, Maine, headquarters of the National Training Laboratory seminars, included a minister, personnel director, a research scientist, two managers, and a trainer of hospital nurses.

Here's one participant's description of his experience, his increased self-awareness:

> At first, I was my usual self: hostile, aggressive, angry. In the past I'd always said "I don't care what so-and-so thinks, I'll be myself." You can say this. but you can't say, "I don't care what *people* think." You do care when everybody starts telling you the same thing.
>
> That's what happened. Ten people told me they disliked me—they'd disliked me from the beginning. When several people tell you something like that you have to say to yourself, "Maybe they're right." It's *not* one man's opinion. You begin examining yourself. I did, and I decided that my hostile manner was a thing I wanted to change about myself.

Instant feedback is what this man got from the group—something he had never gotten before. In the "real" world people are seldom told about their less desirable traits. Even when they are, there's a tendency to reject the statement as that of an "enemy." But the T-group is seen as helpful. The simulation of the T-group encourage candor, and the revelations and insights that emerge produce a desire to change.

A T-group is also referred to as a *behavioral laboratory*. And what participants soon come to realize is that this phrase is *literally* accurate. They can experiment with behavior. They can say what they really think, unlike the rule in the "outside" world. For example:

Participant A (to B): There's something about you I don't like.

Participant B: Well, what is it?

Participant A: I'm not sure . . . something about your size . . . yes, that's it . . . You seem so big, powerful . . . I'm afraid we might get into a fight. . . .

With the skillful help of the leader, Participant A, for the first time, becomes aware that he reacts negatively to men, who, because of their size, burliness, or other physical aspect, suggest aggressiveness. With this insight, he is able to comprehend for the first time why he avoids (or works poorly with) men who seem to be threateningly aggressive.

Similarly, Participant B develops new insights. He learns how his appearance and behavior might affect other people, and realizes why some individuals seem to become defensive in dealing with him. He can't change his appearance, but his new awareness helps him tone down his approach to people.

Note the benefits that emerge from this brief T-group interplay:

Participant A becomes aware of an *attitude* of *his* that affects his relationship with other people.

Participant B becomes aware of how some people *react* to *him* because of his physical appearance.

These two results taken together constitutes the "sensitivity," the increased awareness of interpersonal relationships by the T-group members.

In the T-group world, an individual may have *several* personal revelations in a few hours. Accordingly, the compression of experience is substantial. Most of us may go through *years* of real-life experience without a single such revelation.

Two key facts.   Although this controversial training method has its adherents, problems hinder progress. Two facts emerge:

Sensitivity training works.   A typical two-week program of sensitivity training at Bethel, Maine, sponsored by the National Training Laboratory, boasted a completely filled out roster of 120 participants. At the end of the two weeks, a sampling of opinion among the participants drew reactions that ranged from extreme enthusiasm to opinions such as, "Quite interesting;" and "Fairly helpful." However, three disenchanted participants left after two days.

Applications are a problem.   Not only the participants, but the professionals who conduct T-group sessions stress the obstacles to applying the benefits on the job.

The lore of the building trades provides a simple parallel: "You can't add new to old," says the plumber, the carpenter, and the stonemason. Anyone who has made a plumbing installation knows the problems of adding new fittings, pipe joints and so on, to old lines which may have different diameter pipes, different threading, and so on.

Similarly, it's difficult to have managers, back from T-group training, apply immediately what's been learned. Old habits, traditions, values, and points of view cannot be readily meshed with new ways of relating and working with one another. When "they're all out of step but Jim," no matter how keen a cadence Jim is treading, Jim can't really hope to have people change to conform to his style. However, if these obstacles can be minimized, it seems likely that the T-group experience may become an accepted, useful preparation for the business world.

B. Ideas for Action

The paragraphs ahead relate to activities and problems that continue to stymie managers, and for which practical solutions are suggested.

⮑ THE PARETO PRINCIPLE

Vilfredo Pareto, a nineteenth century economist, analyzed the distribution of wealth in his time and discovered that most of it was in the hands of a few people (the vital few), while the vast majority (the trivial many) existed in poverty.

In his book *Managing for Results,* Peter Drucker suggests that many management problems lend themselves to this approach. Drucker points out, "In the marketplace, a handful of products in the line produce the bulk of sales volume; a few salesmen out of the total roster produce 2/3's of all new business."

The Pareto principle can be applied to any management problem that can be quantified or broken down into units of relative importance. For example, a company asked its key officers to list the obstacles to increased profitability. When the lists were tabulated, they showed a total of thirty-seven problems—too many to handle at once. The list was sent back to the company officials with the request that they rate the problems in order of importance. The second set of lists showed that five of the problems fell into the category of the *vital few*. The rest fell into the category of the *trivial many*. The above example demonstrates the four basic steps involved in applying the Pareto principle:

> *First,* make a written list of the factors, units, or components involved in the problem.
> *Second,* arrange these items in order of importance relative to the problem.
> *Third,* identify the vital few.
> *Fourth,* identify the trivial many.

Another illustration of the application of how the four steps above apply: the president of a clock-making company eliminated one-third of the regular models when he found they added up to only 4 percent of the company's volume. Within six months, the company was doing a larger, more profitable volume.

In another case, the company analyzed 2,753 orders. The top 13 percent accounted for 66 percent of the sales volume in dollars, while the bottom 69 percent of the orders brought in only 7.1 percent of sales. In this case, the vital few, while accounting for 66 percent of the results, involved only 13 percent of the sales costs. The trivial many, bringing in only 7.1 percent of the sales were responsible for 68 percent of the costs. As Drucker puts it, "Results in costs stand in various relationship to each other." In this case it is clear, cutting of sales costs, to be most effective, must come from the trivial many.

➔ THE "HALO EFFECT"

When one trait of a person or aspect of a situation influences your judgment of another trait or another aspect, you have the "halo effect" in action. It's a management problem in cases like these:

■ **Interviewing prospective employees.** An executive permits the pleasant appearance and oral skills of an applicant to blind him or her to the fact that the man has a murky work history.

And, of course, the "halo effect" can work in the opposite way: an unattractive appearance or manner may blind one to an applicant's assets.

■ **Making assignments.** A subordinate does an excellent job of investigating and reporting a space situation in the company. His boss promptly gives him another task: analyzing poor reactions to requests for suggestions from the staff. The subordinate gets nowhere. Eventually his boss realizes that he's fine when dealing with tangibles: space, inventory, and so on. He's a babe in the woods in human relations situations.

■ **Judging job performance.** "Ellen's turning in a terrific job," a sales manager tells the V.P. in charge of sales. "This is the third week she's among the top three producers."

"You're overlooking something," observes the V.P. "Her cancellation rate from customers is tops also."

It's important for the executive not only to understand how the "halo effect" works but also how to use it practically:

1. Keep the "halo effect" in mind when rating people. Remind yourself from time to time that a person who's industrious is not necessarily cooperative; that a person whose job knowledge is excellent doesn't necessarily apply him or herself. And, remember that the person who is eager to please is not necessarily the best one for a demanding assignment.

2. Judge employees on one trait at a time. This is an added safeguard. Let's say you're rating employees' cooperation and initiative. By rating everyone on *cooperation* first, you get around the danger of letting Smith's cooperation rating influence his mark for initiative. By the time you get back to Smith to rate his initiative, you've broken through the "blinding" of the "halo effect."

3. Avoid putting similar traits close together if you make up your own rating form. For example, it's a good idea to follow a work performance trait like *job skill* with a personality trait like *initiative*.

The "halo-effect" concept is a good reminder that our judgments are susceptible to illogical pressures. Awareness of the "halo effect" phenomenon can be a major protection against unbalanced judgment.

● THE ZEIGARNIK EFFECT

Executives have noticed the behavior in others and in themselves:

"As soon as I finish this memo, I'll be right over," your subordinate tells you.

You're annoyed. What could be so important about the memo that would warrant the subordinate holding you up? You say O.K. and take care of a few loose ends while waiting.

Note that both you and the subordinate are dominated by compulsive behavior, a desire to stick with one task before turning to another one. This phenomenon is called the *Zeigarnik Effect,* named after the psychologist who studied it most intensively.

The finding explains some mysteries of behavior that traditionally puzzled managers:

- Why we don't like to "change horses in midstream."
- Why some employees will work after hours—overtime pay aside—to wrap up a project in which they are involved.
- Why employees may balk at interrupting one task to start another, even though the second is of higher priority.

The Zeigarnik idea not only sheds light in a few murky corners of human behavior, but also can help you in two areas:

1. Understand your subordinates' need to complete a task, and therefore chafe at what they consider unnecessary interruptions.

2. Ease the resistance of your group when it is asked to shift priorities, and swing over from a current unfinished task to a more urgent one.

Using the Zeigarnik. You can offset the constrictions of the pursuit of closure by three simple steps:

1. Make interruptions acceptable.   It helps to get the message across early, particularly if changing priorities make abrupt reassignments common in your department. Inform new people at the start of their orientation that flexibility of schedules is a normal aspect of the department's work. One manager tells her beginners, "From time to time the Sales Office asks us to put through a rush order. This means stopping one job and starting another. We pride ourselves in being able to make those switches smoothly. . ."

The idea of priority is an important element in tuning your people in on the need to be flexible in their work schedules. Since you undoubtedly are influenced by organizational needs in setting up work assignments, it will help to give your group some sense of the department's order of importance: "Since we're really a service unit for the Sales Division, we try to meet their requests at all times. . ." you remind your people.

2. Tie job deadlines to the workday stops and starts.   One manager says that he tries to match task deadlines to natural stops in the business day—lunchtime, rest periods, end of the work day. There is a double benefit. When a job is finished at a regular workbreak, the next assignment can have an easier start-up. This is true for physical reasons—the employee is rested—and psychological ones—the Zeigarnk compulsion is absent, and he or she can turn full attention to the new assignment.

3. Explain the switch. Understanding th actual reasons for a change is usually sufficient for the employee to go along with it. A phrase, a sentence as to why tasks must be reshuffled can go far to weaken the Zeigarnik reaction. The manager says, "The Front Office is in a bind to have that file updated for an important meeting. . ."

Obviously, the Zeigarnik can work for you. It may be another department's requirement, a request from a customer, or a practical consideration: "We've got to get that delivery on the night plane," that reinforces the need for completion.

Needless to say, the Zeigarnik Effect is a factor in planning your own work schedules. Point Number 2 above promises as much help in smoothing out your own stops and starts as it does for other echelons up and down the line.

➜ CRISIS MANAGEMENT

Professor Gerald Meyers, a teacher of crisis management at Carnegie-Mellon University says, "Crises are becoming more visible, more severe and of greater general concern. The media, our volatile economy and rapidly changing world have evolved to a point where managers can no longer ignore business disasters nor downplay business vulnerabilities."

The focus of Meyer's concern involves dangers like fire, flood, serious equipment malfunction, accidents with and without physical injury, earth slides, earthquakes, and terrorism. To have them happen is bad enough, to be unprepared is unmanagerial. Crisis management takes on dangers by preparing the countermeasures against them. Crisis planning and crisis teams can protect your organization from costly and even life-threatening events. No organization and/or department is free from fire hazard, equipment malfunction, physical injury, or health crisis. Flood or terrorist attacks have varying degrees of possibility for individual firms. Management should review preparedness in relation to its situation. Crisis plans and crisis-control elements—trained people and adequate equipment—-must be ready as needed. An example illustrates a crisis situation.

Case Example.   Workers in a small furniture plant in a suburban area are suddenly assailed by noxious fumes. A huge tank truck has crashed off the road and into the yard. The tank splits open. A toxic mist starts to penetrate the factory.

An alert executive has seen the accident and activates the fire alarm system. He rushes through the corridors shouting, "Everybody out!" A foreman runs up. "Shall I shut down the machines?" An employee says, "There's a sick woman in the ladies' room." The fumes are getting thicker and people are gagging as they flee. "Did anyone call the fire department?" someone shouts. "Should I phone the hospital for an ambulance?" yells another.

The company is lucky. The fumes aren't toxic. The worst casualties suffer from tearing eyes and irritated throats. Fire trucks and two ambulances arrive and the few people who feel sick are treated on the spot. The truck driver is badly shaken up but not badly hurt. He says the chemical isn't poisonous and management decides to let skeleton crews return and close down for the day. The big hero is the sweeper who went into the ladies room and carried a fainting clerk out to the parking lot.

"We'd better get organized," says the vice president who sounded the alarm. "We might not be so lucky next time."

Abjuring luck in favor of preparedness means thinking through the situations and decisions needed to devise or select protective materials or measures. All necessary facilities and experience should be brought to bear, with full backing for the effort from top management.

Indoctrination and training of personnel is a major need. How ambitious or modest your security training is depends on the nature and dimension of your risks. In any event, the training programs should be organized and presented to personnel, as needed, commensurate with the practicalities of your situation. Experienced managers know that catastrophes come in two sizes; department-wide and company-wide. Typically, a single department must have the capability to respond to a fire or accident. If the crisis involves two or more departments, the organization must be prepared to add its capabilities.

The department head can't prepare for all contingencies, but he or she should prepare for appropriate ones; for example, a toy factory in Bluebell, North Dakota needn't worry about a terrorist attack. The manufacturer of light machine guns in the town might be a target, however.

An overall approach by industrial psychologist Harry Levinson supplies helpful perspective. He says, "Everyone in the organization should recognize the four steps in managing crises: Impact; Recoil-turmoil; Adjustment; Reconstruction." Some suggested steps follow:

1. Call in a security consultant. Top management should consider employing an expert, preferably one with experience in its industry, or locale. Two areas for exploration by the expert along with selected members of your staff:

a. *Vulnerabilities.* A thorough survey of your premises, inside and out, by the combined staff-and-expert group should pinpoint every hazard, from a badly lighted stairway to a storage building near a gentle stream that may overflow its banks in the wet season. A typical hazards list should include:

- *Fire.* Wires to equipment may short out, hot plate in coffee area, careless smokers
- *Water.* Break in ceiling pipes, or from sprinklers
- *Injury.* Sprains or broken bones from slipping or falls
- *Health crisis.* Heart attack, stroke, fainting, and so forth
- *Emotional crisis.* Rage, depression, fear
- *Communications needs.*

This is a good start for most departments. Add your own: _____

_____

_____

b. Prevention. The group should develop your protection—equipment, procedures, labeling, and warning signs. Where analysis and decisions must be made to devise or select protective materials or measures, all necessary facilities and experience should be brought to bear, with full backing for the effort from top management.

Indoctrination and training of personnel is a major need. How ambitious or modest your security training is depends on the nature and dimension of your risks. In any event, the training programs should be organized and presented to personnel, as needed, commensurate with the practicalities of your situation.

2. Top management must take over the responsibility for overall crisis planning and implementation. And the effectiveness of measures adopted will depend on how skillfully the information and motivation is passed through management levels. Since the taskforce members will include a large percentage of rank-and-file employees, it is advisable to have them participate in the development of plans at their own level.

3. Organizing for trouble. A crisis group consisting of the most capable and cool-headed employees should be appointed. The taskforce approach of cutting through regular organization lines to get the people you need is suitable.

4. Special equipment and the skills to use it. Taskforce members should get whatever training they need. In one company, the president, who had recovered from a heart problem, saw to it that at least two people in each department were trained to deal with heart attack victims. Organizations shouldn't require that motivation to take this useful step, however. Whether it is handling a fire extinguisher, or pushing the alarm bell, make sure that even simple knowledge is not assumed. Under the pressure of events people lose abilities that haven't been fully mastered.

5. Maintenance.   After your plans and preparations are in place, they shouldn't be permitted to deteriorate. Check equipment and have occasional drills to test the taskforce operation.

6. Take the time element into account.   Conditions may change, and so may personnel. Yesterday's suitable taskforce may be depleted by people leaving or being promoted to other departments. Update regularly, retrain, and improve methods.

◑ THE HIDDEN AGENDA

The "hidden agenda" is a phenomenon observed in conversation and meetings: Discussion is under way when suddenly the talk switches to an unrelated topic. This topic is usually broached by the speaker for personal reasons, and may concern matters not expected by others. Its injection may be preplanned or spontaneous, but either way it is a digression.

By its nature the hidden agenda is a two-edged sword. If the interruption is benign, even desirable, it becomes a useful communication technique and adds spontaneity to the proceedings. If it is undesirable or destructive it becomes a problem that requires remedy.

Your awareness of the hidden agenda may come into play when:

- You are a conference leader and find the discussion taking off on a course neither expected nor desirable.
- You are conversing with a subordinate and are confronted by the launching of a subject that may be premature, improper, or otherwise out of order.
- You may see an opportunity and justification for broaching your own hidden agenda in a conversation or meeting.

In first two cases above, if the shift of subject is constructive, you go along with it. And when you have an impulse to open a new line of conversation aimed at satisfying your own interest, your alertness to your situation gives you a chance to second-guess yourself before you proceed: "Do I really want to mention this subject now, to this person?" or people. "Will it interfere with an important or higher-priority matter?" etc.

An example further clarifies the hidden-agenda situation:

Executive Dave Smith is talking to a subordinate about a feud she is waging with another manager. There is a pause in the conversation and the other says, "Something's been bothering me. It is almost two years since my last raise . . ." Smith interrupts her. "Let's set a date and go into that next week," and resumes the discussion. He doesn't show the annoyance he feels, and wonders at the other's poor judgment. However, the same hidden agenda might prove desirable if Smith realizes he has been remiss:

"I'm glad you reminded me. We should discuss it. Let's get together Wednesday first thing."

Familiarity with the hidden agenda phenomenon can add another facet to your sophistication in communications. Here are some ways to reap the benefits:

1. Recognize it when it happens.   Don't assume that every digression is a case of a hidden agenda. It may represent a poor sense of logic, or doubt as to what is expected from the speaker, or that the point of the discussion has been lost. Don't confuse a hidden-agenda digression with a thought that has suddenly come to the speaker and is worth attention.

2. Ask why.   The reason behind the introduction of a hidden agenda subject may be important for you to know. For instance, as untimely as the subject of a salary increase may have been in the talk between Dave Smith and subordinate, it may reveal some interesting possibilities:

- The subordinate has been stewing because she has heard, correctly, that the supervisor with whom she has been feuding has recently gotten a salary increase. Even though Smith feels that the raise was deserved in one case and not in the other, he knows he will have to discuss the matter with the complaining subordinate.
- Is poor communications the reason? Hidden agendas flourish when contacts between the parties are unsatisfactory. Then individuals may feel forced to bring up subjects that otherwise aren't likely to arise. Dave Smith's contact with his subordinate may have other serious gaps which the latter is trying to fill.

3. Should you go along?   Hidden agenda items are not necessarily unacceptable or a waste of time. Make a quick decision as to whether the subject deserves first priority or second. If it is the latter, you may want to say, "Let's talk about that just as soon as we complete the business at hand."

4. How about your own hidden agenda?   One executive says, "I have two or three subjects on tap to inject into conversations. I find that the fact that they are unexpected gets them special attention." In considering the usefulness of this approach:

- First, ask yourself why it should be a hidden topic. Is it because it is unpopular or touchy? Then you may want to rethink the advisability of broaching it at all.
- Next, ask yourself, "Why not add it in advance to a prepared agenda?" One reason for not doing so is that the subject may not be welcome to the chairperson. In this case you must make the judgment as to whether you want to force the issue in this manner.
- Is there a bridge? A subject you might think of as a hidden item may become suitable to an ongoing conversation or discussion if you can relate it. For

example, "While we're talking about deadlines, I think it's relevant to talk about an information bottleneck that has slowed me up, and perhaps troubled others, and that is the service from our library. Can we take some action that will accelerate our requests for information?"

As has been made clear, hidden agendas are not necessarily bad. Where they flourish, however, the implication is that ordinary communications channels may be clogged or not open to needs, particularly concerning subjects that have an emotional component. Occurrence of hidden agendas in the area of your responsibility may deserve some analysis. Beyond that, you may care to pass along your observations to others in the organization when they occur.

➲ MANAGEMENT BY OBJECTIVES

Basically, Management by Objectives is a simple concept: it is job performance and achievement guided by results desired. There are two types of application.

Unit performance.   The method may be used to set guides and evaluate results for departments, divisions, or whole companies.

Individual performance.   The Management by Objectives idea may be applied to the work of individual executives, managers, and employees. It is in this latter application, as a tool for motivating and measuring individual performance, that Management by Objectives can help the executive develop and evaluate subordinates.

An early innovator in the field, General Mills of Minneapolis, started to apply the Management by Objectives concept in 1957:

People from front line management echelons upward set job objectives for themselves after their immediate superiors presented them with statements of their accountability. An "accountability" is a result that the company expects for the satisfactory performance of the job. Each job at General Mills has from three to ten accountabilities. Accordingly, each manager of the company is annually presented with a list of three to ten results that he or she must accomplish—whatever the means chosen to accomplish them.

A company spokesperson gives an example: "I'm responsible for insuring that our salary structure compares favorably with our competitors." A front-line manager might be held accountable for maintaining an effective work force.

After the front-line manager has drawn up his statement of accountabilities, he writes out certain specific objectives; for example, "To improve the performance of employee John Doe by January 1." The manager creates as many of these specific goals as he thinks necessary to satisfy every accountability the company has placed upon him.

When he finishes, he meets with his superior to discuss whether the accomplishment of these objectives will satisfy the accountabilities. If need be, he modifies his objectives: adds more or changes some.

The method can be summed up in three steps:
Superior and subordinate work out realistic performance objectives.
They agree on the means for achieving specified results.
At the end of the agreed-on period, actual results are compared to expected results.

The manager commits himself to specific, measurable action with specific time limits. In so doing, he obviously takes the risk that he may fail and *that his superiors will know he has failed.*

Observers of the management scene has noted these problems in connection with Management by Objective:

Heel-dragging participation. In one company that tried to pursue an MBO program, resistance showed up during the orientation workshops. Some recalcitrants were insecure managers, afraid to give up the comfortable old ways. Others were afraid to be under the spotlight of having to tell their superiors what results they would achieve. And there were others who had been on plateaus. They weren't happy about having to stretch themselves—which MBO forces on a manager.

The participation of some managers was only half-hearted. As one executive observed: "They would get a business call and have to leave. Or they would prolong the conversation about the need for objectives so as not to have to write any. We encountered many delaying tactics."

The setting of low standards. In discussions with her boss, the subordinate sometimes committed herself to objectives that involved no challenge, hoping thereby to overachieve.

One executive reports on these situations: "People would become embarrassed, found difficulty talking about their conceptions—or misconceptions—of the job. Or a superior and a subordinate would both get embarrassed because both had misunderstood the subordinate's job. Sometimes the subordinate and his or her boss would realize, simultaneously, that the boss had failed as a manager—because of failure to communicate what was expected of the subordinate."

The problem of quantification. The difficulty in quantifying objectives can be a big stumbling block. For example, an executive of the Internal Revenue Service New York office, commented: "We tried to implement MBO for our group supervisors. But we found it difficult to set an objective for morale and attitude, which are the two most important contributions of our people." There are other jobs for which morale, willingness, call it what you will, is important. This can be a soft spot in Management by Objectives.

Clearly, the value of MBO is largely comparative. But it has some advantages over past methods for goal-setting and performance measure. Until a better tool comes along, it will have adherents.

⊃ THE MANAGERIAL GRID

Dr. Robert R. Blake and Dr. Jane S. Mouton, professors at the University of Texas and associates in the management consulting firm of Scientific Methods, Inc., Austin, Texas, developed an approach based on an "organic theory of change." They reject a static, mechanic view of the organization, seeing it, rather, as a developing set of interdependent net works of people. Their main emphasis, therefore, is on improving work relationships.

Dr. Blake and his associates feel that the most effective type of management is that of an integrated team operation, both from the standpoint of production and of an organization's ability to adapt swiftly and appropriately to rapidly changing conditions.

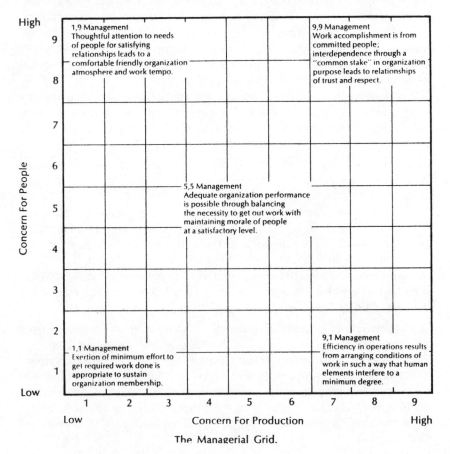

The Managerial Grid.

The "managerial grid" approach has two basic premises: (1) a manager or management can be measured according to two variables—a concern for people and a concern for production; (2) the best management is team management. If one accepts these premises, then the grid can be a useful tool in analyzing the manager's efforts as well as those of his subordinates.

On the grid, "concern for people" is measured vertically on a line divided into nine sections: "concern for production" is measured horizontally on a line similarly divided. The resulting grid has eighty-one "positions" which can be used to delineate various styles of leadership. Here are major styles discussed by the authors:

Task management.   Down in the lower right-hand corner of the grid one finds 9,1 management. It is characterized by strong emphasis on the task to be performed. People in themselves are of little consequence, except to the extent that they impede or further production. They are there to be used, somewhat like machines, and they should be replaced if they don't function effectively.

This type of leadership is strictly authoritarian. Subordinates are expected to carry out their orders unquestioningly and all conflict is suppressed. As a result, subordinates tend to lose initiative, their creative, approach to problems; and any increased skill and knowledge they develop is likely to remain untapped. One consequence of this type of leadership is the "gradual shift of many working and managerial persons in the direction of a 1,1 accommodation."

Country-club management.   Country-club management, located at 1,9 in the upper left-hand corner of the grid, is the very opposite of task management. Here the emphasis is all on people, the theory being that if they are kept contented and happy, high production will automatically follow. But whether production follows or not, the attitudes and feelings of people, "are valuable in their own right. They come first."

One possible consequence of this style of leadership is that production will suffer at the expense of harmonious human relations. But even here, conflicts are likely to be smoothed over and buried rather than resolved. And when this type of organization is called upon to increase efficiency, it is frequently unable to respond. As a result, it tends to succomb to competitive pressures.

Impoverished management.   Impoverished management, located in the lower-left-hand corner of the grid, couples low concern for production with low concern for people. This type of manager does just enough to get by. To all intents and purposes, he or she is "out of it," avoids involvement and concern because this, "can only lead to deeper frustration and discouragement."

An organization is seldom managed this way because, as Mouton and Blake point out, "a business operated under 1,1 concepts would be unable to survive very long." But an individual can sometimes persist for quite a long time as a 1,1 manager in a bureaucratic or country-club atmosphere. However, it's a situation of failure, not only for the individual, but for the company, since it involves the loss of a "potential productive contribution."

Dampened pendulum management.   In the middle of the grid at 5,5 is located the middle of the road, or dampened pendulum type of management. It avoids swinging to the extremes of 9,1 or 1,9. The 5,5 manager is aware of a conflict between people and production and tries to effect a happy compromise, to play it safe by not overemphasizing one or the other. Real problems are apt to be muted, and the climate is frequently paternalistic.

While 5,5 management is likely to be superior to any of the extremes mentioned so far, it too, has its limitations. According to the authors, "5,5 provides a poor basis for promoting innovation, creativity, discovery, and novelty. All of these are likely to be sacrificed by the adherence to tradition and 'majority' standards of conduct. Long term, then, the 5,5 or status quo, results in a gradual slipping behind as more flexible, progressive organizations take advantage of new opportunities or better management practices."

Team management.   The obvious goal of good management lies in the upper right-hand corner of the grid at 9,9. Here there is a high concern for both people and production. The result is a team approach to management where the "needs of people to think, to apply mental effort in productive work and to establish sound and mature relationships . . . with one another are utilized to accomplish organizational requirements."

Some of the gains attributed by the authors to a change toward 9,9 management are: (1) increased profitability; (2) improvement of intergroup relations; (3) more effective use of team action; (4) reduced frictions and increased understanding among individuals; and (5) increased individual effort and creativity and personal commitment to work.

In short, under team management, "the needs of individuals to be engaged in meaningful interdependent effort mesh with the organization requirements for excellent performance."

The managerial grid is a tool to help analyze one's managerial style, the styles of other managers, or the total management of a company. It's a way of structuring one's thinking about styles of management, and as such, both an analytical and constructive tool.

➲ SELECTIVE LEADERSHIP

Executives seeking practical guidance in leadership finds slim pickings in management literature. They will have no trouble in gathering numerous *general* statements: "A leader must be enthusiastic", "A leader must know how to motivate his people", "A leader must be able to empathize." And, as has been indicated in previous pages (see Index), the list of traits of the leader, or the situational factors that the leader must master to be effective, are readily come by. But theoretically sound and practically effective approaches are notable by their absence. Into this vacuum, the author, in the early 1950s, described in *How to Be a Successful Leader* (paperback edition titled *Techniques of Leadership,* McGraw-Hill, 1964) a systematic approach for leadership on the work scene. The concept, called "Selective Leadership," offers the executive an approach that has been used successfully in fields as varied as child rearing and the supervision of scientists working in a business setting.

Selective Leadership is a method that stems from experiments by psychologist Kurt Lewin at the University of Iowa. To explore the nature of leadership, Lewin set up two experimental groups:

1. One group was dominated by an "autocratic" leader, who determined policy; decided what was to be done and how it was to be done; assigned tasks and chose the work companions for each member; and was highly personal in his praise, criticism and general comments.

2. The second group was led by a "democratic" leader, who brought up matters of policy for group discussion; encouraged group members to participate in decisions; permitted individuals to choose their own work companions; and was highly "objective" in his comments.

Then came an unplanned and unexpected development: one of the individuals playing the role of "democratic" leader was found to be creating an atmosphere different from that of the other "democratic" leaders. He exercised virtually no control over the group. He permitted group members to shift for themselves to a large extent; and he had them tackle the problems that arose as best they could. The group's response to this technique differed from the reactions of other democratic groups. Lewin accordingly set up a third kind of group under this type of leadership, termed "laissez-faire."

Observers noted certain significant differences in atmosphere, behavior, feelings, and accomplishments among the three groups:

Autocratic. Group members were quarrelsome and aggressive. Some individuals became completely dependent upon the leader. When the leader was absent, activity tended to stop altogether. Work progressed at only a fair rate.

Democratic.   The individuals got along with one another on a friendly basis. Relations with the leader were freer, more spontaneous. The work progressed smoothly and continued even when the leader was absent.

Laissez-faire.   Work progressed haphazardly and at a slow rate. Although there was considerable activity, much of it was unproductive. Considerable time was lost in arguments and discussions between group members on a purely personal basis.

Although each method seems to have built-in strengths and weaknesses, as you will soon see, each method has its value.

Actually, the three methods developed in the University of Iowa investigations provide the framework of the Selective Leadership approach. Selective Leadership welds the three Lewin concepts into a unified and systematic method that has scored outstanding success in the management field.

Using the Selective Leadership approach, the manager *selects* whichever one of the three tools is most appropriate. For the sake of clarity, let's define the three tools as follows:

1. Autocratic leadership.   The leader mainly seeks obedience from his group. He or she determines policy and considers decision making a one-person operation—the leader of course, being the one person.

2. Democratic leadership.   The leader draws ideas and suggestions from the group by discussion and consultation. Group members are encouraged to take part in the setting of policy. The leader's job is largely that of moderator.

3. Free-rein leadership (Lewin's "laissez-faire" method).   The leader functions more or less as an information booth. He or she plays down the leader's role in the group's activity. He or she exercises a minimum of control.

These defintions provide the basis for a systematic approach to leading people. Autocratic, democratic, or free-rein methods may be considered as *three tools* of the management leader.

Contrary to common belief, the three approaches are *not* mutually exclusive. No one has to choose either the autocratic, democratic, or free-rein method. That would be like telling a golf player he or she must choose between using a driver or only a putter; in the course of a game both will be used.

Note Manager X in action:

- He *directs* (autocratic method) his secretary to make a report.
- He *consults* (democratic method) with his employees on the best way to push a special order through the shop.

■ He *suggests* (free-rein method) to his assistant that it would be a good idea to figure out ways in which special orders may be handled more smoothly in the future.

This type of leadership suggests that mastery lies in knowing *when* to use *which* method. In short, Selective Leadership is a logical adaptation of autocratic, democratic, and free-rein techniques to appropriate situations, seeking to put leadership on a rational basis.

(A description of Selective Leadership as a working procedure is included under the heading, "Selective Leadership: A Systematic Approach," page 172.)

➔ MANAGEMENT BY EXCEPTION

Lester R. Bittel, author of *Management by Exception,* published by Mc-Graw-Hill in 1964, describes the concept in these terms: management in its simplest form is a symptom of identification and communication. It tells the executive when his or her attention is needed in a particular activity or aspect of an activity, and conversely, when such attention is not required. The primary purpose is to simplify the management process; to permit the manager to find the problem that needs his or her attention, and avoid those which are routinely handled by subordinates.

Bittel views *Management by Exception* as having six key elements:

1. Measurement. Assign value—often numerical—to past and present performances. Without measurement of some sort, it would be impossible to identify an exception.

2. Projection. Analyze those measurements that are meaningful to business objectives and extend them into future expectations.

3. Selection. Pinpoint the criteria management will use to follow progress toward its objectives.

4. Observation. The phase of measurement that informs management of the current state of performance.

5. Comparison. Actual performance compared with expected performance identifies the exceptions that require attention and reports variances that exist.

6. Decision-making. What action must be taken to

■ bring the performance back into control, or
■ adjust expectations to reflect changing conditions, or
■ exploit opportunity.

⤴ PARTICIPATION IN GROUPS

Psychologists working in the field of group dynamics have long been aware that people behave differently in groups than they do as individuals. For example, studies conducted during World War II showed that housewives who participated in group discussions on the dietary value of citrus fruits tended to use citrus fruits to a greater degree than matched groups that were simply lectured at, on the same subject, by dieticians.

The implication for management was clear: if employees were given the chance to participate in decision making, they would accept the fiscal decision and be more wholehearted in working toward its implementation. Change, a continuing preoccupation of business, might then become more acceptable.

Yet here again the easy answer does not always apply. For example, Professor Arnold S. Tannenbaum of the University of Michigan describes an experiment in which a company divided its clerical staff into two groups, one to be managed participatively, the other in the usual way, with management making all decisions. In the participative group, the clerks discussed and decided things like rules for office conduct, size of work groups, length of coffee breaks, and so on. The other group was not allowed to participate in decisions.

The results? Although productivity in each group went up and the clerks in the participative group enjoyed their work more, productivity in the nonparticipative group rose most.

Professor Tannenbaum accounted for the results by suggesting that productivity went up in the participative group because of increased job satisfaction and in the other group because of the manager's increased control. Tannenbaum further suggested that output might have gone up more in the participative group, if the supervisor had realized that the purpose of participation was not to make personnel happy, but to improve their functioning inside the organizational context.

Academic findings and discussions aside, the practicing executive knows from experience that participation can help achieve a number of extremely desirable objectives:

■ **Communication.** By letting employees in on the "ground floor" of a problem or development, they're getting direct and early information, as compared to the garbling and confusion that may result from attempts at communication after the fact.

■ **Feedback.** The executive who gives his or her subordinates the opportunity to participate in discussions of problems, plan developments, and so on gains the benefits of the ideas and suggestions of subordinates as well as the modifications or extensions of his or her own ideas.

- **Training self-respect and dignity.**   Subordinates who have a chance to join you in discussions become exposed to your values, attitudes, and experiences in a most constructive situation. In addition, their response to being treated as "equal," as "being important enough to become important factors" in planning and other important activities will clearly have a desirable influence.

- **Motivation.**   Perhaps the greatest benefit of the opportunity for participation by your people is the sense of responsibility and willingness with which they undertake tasks that grow out of their participation.

⊃ **BOTTOM-LINE FALLACIES**

Bottom line is less a phrase than an invocation. The executive who says, "Let's look at the bottom line" is seen as tough-minded and result-oriented, willing to face up to the acid test of performance. And this high regard is probably deserved.

The bottom line, on a profit-and-loss sheet, the volume turned out by a production group, or final totals in an election, is often a definitive indicator. *But,* the most impressive bottom line may hide information at least as important as it reveals.

How the bottom line misleads.   An example yields important insights into those instances when the bottom line misleads:

Jed Tarleton is a hard-driving sales manager. His region usually wins the interregional annual contest, and although other groups are coming up, he is determined to finish on top again. And he does. His sales volume beats the next closest region by 4 percent, less of a margin than that of previous years, but enough to walk off with the prize.

One of the salespeople, who knows what has been going on, makes a list of the tactics Tarleton used to inflate the figures:

- Made some deals with under-the-table rebates.
- Got credit for poor-risk customers who subsequently defaulted.
- Offered best-possible terms usually restricted to special customers—cutting deeply into profitability—to those who demanded a last extra sweetener to sign a contract.
- Pressured salespeople to meet assigned quotas, no matter what.

Tarleton's short-range results were impressive, but his tactics will be ultimately injurious.

Checklist of hidden losses.   Most bottom lines are above reproach. But it helps to know some of the ways in which a total may hide important facts:

☐ A major consequence may be the hidden costs to get results.
☐ Individuals may have been pushed to the point of breakdown.
☐ Ethical principles may be sacrificed.
☐ Relationships may have been exploited, to their subsequent detriment.
☐ Future prospects may have been milked for a quick payoff, lessening ultimate benefit.
☐ Where ruthless competitive effort has produced winning results—as between divisions—future teamwork is likely to be impaired.
☐ Other: _____

A desirable end may be achieved by means that eventually prove too costly. Philosophers have said so for centuries.

➲ COGNITIVE DISSONANCE

Managers have been puzzled by behavior for which there seems to be no ready explanation. For example:

Manager Kevin Kidder has to fire Joe Harley, his subordinate and friend of many years. Kidder's boss has told him, "I know how you feel about Joe, but he hasn't been performing and it's costing too much to carry him."

Kidder goes through the unhappy business of telling Joe Harley the bad news as painlessly as possible, but he is upset for days afterwards. Then his thinking takes a turn. He tells himself, "The job was getting to be too much for Joe. Besides, he was using me, dropping in at all hours to discuss his problems, pressuring me to give favorable reports on his subpar performance." Somehow, by tearing Joe down, Kidder makes him seem a less worthy friend. He begins to feel better about firing him.

Psychologists say that Kidder's mental gyrations illustrate *Cognitive Dissonance* (CD). *The Dictionary of Psychology* defines the term as "an uncomfortable psychological state in which the individual experiences two incompatible beliefs or cognitions." In Kidder's case, the conflict is between loyalty to a friend and the need to act on the dollars-and-cents imperatives of the business world. His behavior is aimed at mitigating his sense of guilt.

Managers, both in their own behavior and that of others on the work scene, can find in CD an explanation for:

■ **Rationalizing a failure.** "I didn't want the promotion, anyway" and the rationalizer adds justification ranging from too much responsibility to insufficient pay. The dissonance is between the desire for advancement and the pain of not getting it.

■ **Explaining away a blow to one's self-esteem.** "Sure Paul's proposal won out over mine. He's got an in with the boss. Besides, my approach was too advanced for those knuckleheads." The conflict here is between vindication of one's feelings of superiority that would come with winning the competition and the bitterness of a putdown.

■ **Sacrificing principle to expediency.**   "I hated to disappoint Al, his company has been a dependable supplier, but I couldn't refuse the Big Boss's request to give the order to his nephew." The incompatible feelings are, loyalty to a trustworthy business contact, and submission to pressure from an authority.

Managers have found the CD concept helpful in understanding behavior, sometimes unexpected and strange, that shows up when people are in mental conflict. There are two areas of action in which CD applies:

1. With others, colleagues, subordinates, and possibly your boss.   Be aware of the cognitive dissonance possibility when you observe someone caught in a conflict of feelings.

- Let them sound off to you, and unload their feelings.
- If possible, tactfully supply the mitigations that help the person live with the situation. Your aim is to lessen the guilt or ease the upset. One executive tells a subordinate: "As J.F.K. said, it's not always a fair world, and this is your share of the unfair part. You may have to learn how to live with it, for now.

2. With yourself.

- Try to pinpoint the incompatible beliefs.
- Don't bottle up the conflict. Release it, if you can, by talking to a confidante—a spouse, colleague, or boss.
- Think through the factors that could put the dissonance in acceptable balance.
- Face up to the realities of the situation, distinguish between what you want to do, can do, and must do. If you are not satisfied with the results of your analysis, see whether there is some action that will get you out from under. This could include a discussion with your boss, a professional counselor or in serious cases, to pull out of the situation; for example, some people in Kevin Kidder's place have considered quitting.

The thing to remember about CD is its purpose: to minimize the stress of inner conflict.

⊃ **PERSONAL OBSOLESCENCE**

The Industrial Revolution made us aware of obsolescence. Today, craftspeople whose know-how is no longer needed, are joined by brain workers as victims. Scientists, engineers, medical practitioners, and business executives are vulnerable. Training that once lasted a lifetime now becomes outdated in a few years. In high-tech professions, frequent refresher courses are required. In some cases updating must be continuous.

Nature of the beast.   Executives can use the obsolescence threat as a reminder to remain current. More than just new machines and methods are involved. For example, two things can happen: (1) Cultural shifts may damage an entire industry—note the fate of the cinema as television burgeoned; and (2) young people newly trained, tend to replace older people because of their updated skills and willingness to work for lower wages.

Particularly vulnerable may be those in middle management. One instance: computer-industry employment data shows that while the lower and top echelons retain their employability, middle-range executives whose experience is heavy in yesterday's equipment and thinking did not fare as well.

Four telltale signs.   Career obsolescence appears in many ways and places. The manager's considerations should be made in the context of his or her own situation. Some guidelines:

Changes in your business.   In some cases developments are rapid, in others, less so. The rate of progress and obsolescence should be judged on an industry-by-industry basis.

Age rollback.   When the pace of change is rapid, a generation gap may be created. The experience of older people becomes irrelevant and younger competitors may be better qualified to perform.

Alienation.   This factor can be a major handicap. It is a result rather than an aspect of obsolescence, and intensifies the older person's discomfort at being among "strangers."

Skill and salary competition.   The older person can be at a disadvantage vis-à-vis a younger competitor. First, the latter benefits from updated training. Second, a younger person may take a job for less pay. Third, some companies favor younger employees to project a contemporary image and to assure future human resources.

For the dollar-shrewd employer, there may be other benefits. As one businessperson points out, "Terminating an older, not-yet-vested employee may make it unnecessary to pay a pension. And if vested, it cuts down on the pension amount that will have to be paid for their length of service."

Your antiobsolescence program.   For executives who feel they are at some risk, an obsolescence-minimizing program is advisable:

Ask yourself, "What do I want for the rest of my career?" It's a basic question for any contemplation of future plans, not easy to answer, but worth probing.

Check your organization's obsolescence-creating pattern. Consider both the company situation and your own profession or area of responsibility to determine whether the threat for you is real and imminent, mild and distant, or nonexistent.

Keep ahead of the game. There are a number of options:

Reeducation
Retraining
Courses, books, seminars, and so on
Shifting to a related, but for you more advantageous field
Being a consultant in your area of expertise
Starting your own business

Decide on your policy. Think through your situation and come up with a plan of action that can start a period of new growth and help improve your position for the present and future. (See "Winning the Fight Against Obsolescence," page 224.)

4

MANAGEMENT
TOOL KIT

"Man is a tool-using animal . . . without tools he is nothing, with tools he is all," said Thomas Carlyle.

Increasingly, the executive is getting to be a tool-using professional. As a matter of fact, the proliferation of tools available to executives today reinforces the professionalism of their calling.

In the pages that follow, you will find a sample group of practical tools executives use to improve communications, expedite planning, help develop training needs, and so on. Each of these tools can help you cope with specific mangement problems. Taken together, they represent an executive tool kit that may serve to sharpen your tool awareness and serve as a guide for the development of tools of your own devising.

➲ **COMMUNICATIONS CHANNEL CHOOSER**

Method	Advantages	Disadvantages
Phone	Speed. Permits give and take of questions. Doesn't call you away form your desk.	Words and figures might be misunderstood or garbled. Usually no record of conversation.
In Person	Visual. You can "show" and "explain." In many cases permits better meeting of the minds, closer rapport.	You may have to leave your office, lose time. The time may be inconvenient to either of you. Requires spontaneous thinking.
Informal Note or Memo	Brief. It can be "for the record"—in his files and a copy in your own.	You don't get an immediate reply. Your memo is at the mercy of a routine delivery and the bulk of his mail.
Formal Report	Complete. Permits time for organization of material. Can be reported to others.	Sometimes requires considerable time. May make for slow writing at one end, slow reading at the other.

➔ **COMMUNICATIONS ANALYZER**

Sending

Name of Communi-cation	To Whom Sent?	About What?	Method (Phone, written, face to face)?	Frequency (How often sent)?	Apply all questions to each item in the first column.
					Yes No
					1. Is the communi-cation really needed (that is, used) by the person receiving it? ☐ ☐
					2. If it is a request for information, are you sending it to the best source? ☐ ☐
					3. Does the com-munication ask for information already on hand in another form? (For example, payroll records may serve as an attendance record.) ☐ ☐
					4. Are you commu-nicating too frequently about the same things? (A monthly report substituted for a weekly one may cut the job by 75 percent.) ☐ ☐
					5. Are your com-munications frequent enough? ☐ ☐
					6. Are you using the best method of communicating for this material? (See the Channel Chooser Chart.) ☐ ☐

➲ COMMUNICATIONS ANALYZER

Receiving

Name of Communi- cation	From Whom?	About What?	Method (Phone, written, face to face)?	Frequency (How often received)?	Apply all questions to each item in the first column.
					Yes No
					1. Do you really need this com- munication (That is, do you use the information it contains)? □ □
					2. Does it get to you on time (when it's sched- uled to). □ □
					3. In time? (Geting to you "on time" may still not be in time to do any good.) □ □
					4. Does it contain all the informa- tion you need? □ □
					5. Do you need all the information it contains? (If not, you can take a load off the other fellow.) □ □
					6. Does everyone who needs some or all of the in- formation receive it? □ □
					7. Should you be passing along some of the information it contains? □ □
					8. Are you getting this communica- tion in the best possible form for your needs? (For instance, you can't file a phone call for record- keeping.) □ □

➲ PERT

The U.S. Navy calls this management tool "PERT," which stands for Program Evaluation and Review Technique. The Navy used the approach to expedite its gigantic Polaris missile program. It can also be used to overhaul an office or plan a factory project.

PERT works like the cook's approach to preparing a multi-course meal. He or she uses several burners and the oven simultaneously, starts the things that take longer first, and ends up at dinner time ready to serve.

Here's how to apply PERT to a task:

1. List everything that has to be done.   To take a simple example: Let's say you plan to transfer cartons of stored material from one room to another. These are the things you would have to do:

get a hand truck;
get two employees to do the moving;
make sure new area can take the load;
move cartons to the new locations;
sort and label the cartons;
check amount of material to be moved;
get okay by supervisor;
stack cartons, using the new system.

2. Put the jobs in sequence.   Go over your list of job steps and put them in the sequence in which they must be done.

In the list above, for example, the first step would be to make sure that the material you want to store will fit into the new area.

3. Estimate time for each step.   Express the time in minutes, hours, days, or as you will, and indicate time alongside each step on the sequence of operations you've listed. Now your list looks like this:

A. Check amount of material (.8 hours)
B. Check capacity of new areas (.4 hours)
C. Get truck (.2 hours)
D. Get employees (.1 hours)
E. Move material (5 hours)
F. Sort and label (2 hours)
G. Okay by supervisor (.5 hours)
H. Stack (3 hours)

4. Make an arrow diagram.   The PERT chart or "network" is a key step, shows how the various parts of the job interrelate. To draw the chart:

Use an arrow to indicate each step in the operation. The lengths of the arrows don't matter. But the *direction* of the arrow shows you how the step relates to the rest of the job.

Construct the diagram by asking three questions of each element in the sequence:

- *What immediately precedes this element?*
- *What immediately follows it?*
- *What other elements can be done at the same time?*

Here's how a PERT chart for the carton-moving operation might look:

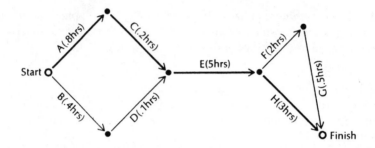

Note some of the things the chart tells you at a glance. First, Step E, the actual moving, can't take place until after Steps A-D are completed.

Second, it shows the general scope of the operation. Third, it helps you determine *the critical path.*

The critical path is the total of the longest consecutive jobs. In our chart, the critical path is shown by the heavy line. Knowing the critical path, you're now in a position to do several things:

Estimate the total time for the job.   In our example, it would be nine hours.

Spot bottlenecks.   Every operation on the critical path is, theoretically, a bottleneck. Operations *not* on the critical path (these are called *slack paths*) may generally be done at the same time as those on the critical path.

Since they take less time, it is the critical path that limits your schedule.

Expedite the schedule.   You have two alternatives, if you want to shorten your completion time: (1) have steps on the slack paths performed as much as possible at the same time as those on the critical path; (2) shorten critical path operations by making them crash activities, i.e., putting more people or equipment on the job, devising a more efficient method, and so on.

Used wisely, PERT can also help you keep costs down. You could, for example, devise two alternative charts, representing two different ways of getting a job done. Comparing person-hours, possible overtime, and other cost elements, and stacking completion time of one method against the other, you can come up with figures that tell you whether a "normal" production or a souped-up schedule is more desirable from a dollar and delivery standpoint.

◆ EMPLOYEE SKILLS AND ASSIGNMENT CHART

When you're under time pressure, it can be difficult to make work assignments efficiently. You may forget that Freda, who is temporarily out of your sight, might be best man for a given assignment, and you put Harry on it instead. Results may be unsatisfactory.

A simple chart can take some of the hit-or-miss quality out of job assignments. Here's a sample:

Names of Employees	Operation 1	Operation 2	Operation 3	Operation 4
Brown, C.	A	B	B	A
Coughlin, L.	C	A	A	—
Green, P.	B	A	B	B
Kinkead, R.	A	—	—	C

Legend: A—Fully competent
B—O.K. with slight assistance
C—Can do the job only with close supervision

You make the chart work by these steps:

■ **Step 1.**   List each employee on your staff down the left-hand column.

■ **Step 2.**   List each task or operation in your area, one task to a column, as in the chart.

■ **Step 3.**   Using the symbols "A," "B," or "C," give each employee a rating for each departmental task, if that employee is at *all* able to do the task. Meaning of the symbols:

A. Fully competent.
B. Knows the operation but needs a few pointers.
C. Can do the job, but only with supervision or with the assistance of a co-worker.

The rating symbol should be entered in the space *opposite* the employee's name and *below* each job. If he or she can't handle the job at all, leave the space blank.

When the chart is fully filled out, you may want to decide that you'll use "C" people only in pinches—when the work just has to be done and there's no one else to do it. You may also want to establish restrictions on the use of "B" people. Generally, assign "A" people, unless there's a reason for not so doing—lack of availability or higher-priority assignments.

The chart can have a secondary use: pinpointing training needs. If you don't have enough "A" people for a given task, it might be a good idea to undertake to upgrade the skills of "C" and "B" individuals.

➜ PLANNING GUIDE

This form is illustrative only. In the average case, a plan for a project of any size would require many pages.

1. Project Name:

_____

2. Purpose:

_____

3. Personnel:

_____

_____

4. Facilities:

_____

_____

5. Methods:

_____

_____

_____

6. Estimated Costs:

_____

_____

7. Schedule—Preparation:

_____

_____

8. Assignments:

_____

_____

9. Controls:

_____

_____

10. Evaluation of Results:

_____

_____

➲ SIX CHECKPOINTS FOR YOUR PLANNING

Here's a brief checklist to use before, during, and after planning. It can pinpoint a weakness, eliminate a kink that might wreck an effective program.

1. Should you subdivide?   You may benefit by dividing a large-scale program. Each subplan is parcelled out to a competent subordinate. The advantages: (a) no one person is snowed under by a load of details; (b) you benefit from the ingenuity of others and your people will cooperate more fully because they've had a voice in planning.

2. Do you need an alternative plan?   There are cases in which you must not fail. It's certainly a good idea to backstop yourself: locate a source for additional equipment; line up or train extra people who can lend a hand, just in case.

3. How far can you pretest?   Engineers have shown the way:

Rough planning.   Before you get lost in details, block out the program in its basic form. Suppose you are trying to develop a better method of indoctrinating new employees. It may be enough to simply work out four or five basic areas to be covered such as: (a) introductions to other employees; (b) helping newcomers get acquainted with physical layout, wash rooms, etc; (c) reviewing department functions; (d) reviewing company history; (e) explaining where they fit in the scheme of things.

Dry run.   Where feasible, a run-through of your plan helps you check methods, procedures, reactions.

Models.   Want to see your troubles before they get to you? No matter how well you can visualize, it pays to use:

a. _Scale models._ Let's say you're planning a new floor layout. You can spot flaws by laying out the room dimensions and using cardboard cutouts to represent equipment, workstations, and employees. Insufficient space in the aisles, awkward relationship of equipment, etc., will be revealed.

b. _Working models._ By having a carpenter make up a version of a projected auxiliary warehouse, an executive could check for feasibility.

Component tests.   When your car is serviced, it's under the microscope piecemeal: motor, tires, control mechanisms. Similarly, if your plan were to involve a series of report forms, you could scrutinize each one to see how well it furthers overall objectives.

4. Should you bring in your assistant?   The quickest way for a subordinate to develop a broader view of departmental problems is for you to delegate part of the planning. Do you have anyone you want to develop in this fashion?

5. Should you "step-plan"?   The situation may not allow you to lay out a complete course of action. Your efforts may involve two or more phases. You may have to stop after each part has been completed to appraise results before you can map the next step. Know the reassessment points in advance.

6. Does your plan need booster-shots?   Programs once started tend to run out of gas. If your plan covers an extended period of time, keep in mind the possible need to remotivate your people.

➲ EMPLOYEE SKILLS DEVELOPER

List the names of staff members whose skills you would like to improve. Under the section titled "Present Skills," list the various skills used in your departmental operations. Under the next section, titled "Extra Skills To Develop," list the skills you anticipate will be needed in the near future. Then, fill out the chart, using the following suggested code:

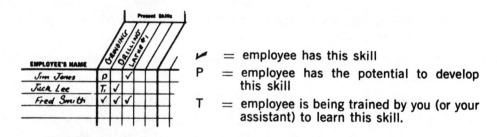

To indicate the state of the employee's training, you may want to use a simple rating from 1 to 5, with 1 equaling the beginning of training, 5 equaling the final stage. Thus you might put a T_3 next to an employee who is midway in training.

EMPLOYEE'S NAME	Present Skills			Extra Skills To Develop			Remarks	

Plans for Training. Many executives consider training to be a continuing process. Even so, changes in overall company plans or changes in departmental operations may dictate "emergency" training programs. In either case, the questions below can suggest worthwhile points for action.

1. Are the right people doing the training in your department?

   Notes: _____

   _____

2. Are you making use of the help available in your company: your boss? your colleagues? your highly skilled subordinates? Personnel?

   Notes: _____

   _____

3. Are you giving encouragement to those of your staff who feel their jobs are dead-end—showing them how they can train to get to the next step?

   Notes: _____

   _____

4. Are you emphasizing refresher training?

   Notes: _____

   _____

5. Are you using assignment rotation as a means of expanding employee skills?

   Notes: _____

   _____

6. Do you have people working at jobs requiring fewer or lesser skills than they have? If so, can he be transferred to higher-level work?

Notes: _____

_____

➲ THE FLOOR-PLAN CHART

When filled in, this chart will show the layout of all or part of your office or department, and will help you consider possible changes. It will also picture where the work originates and the steps followed to completion, and it will spotlight sources of trouble—badly located aisles, storage areas, and so on.

Wherever you have a problem that's rooted in poor layout, such as improper placement of equipment, a floor-plan chart can help. Here's how to proceed.

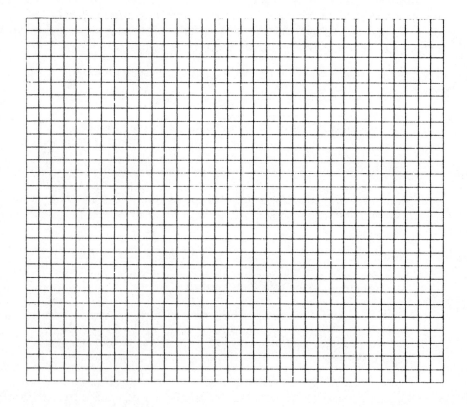

1. The Floor Plan. Draw a floor plan of your department. It doesn't matter how rough the drawing, but keep it in proportion, if possible. Use a ruler to draw the straight lines—walls, and so on. If you know the dimensions in feet, draw the area to scale. Once the general dimensions are worked out, draw in all the major equipment—desks, files, and so on.

2. Sequence of Operations. On another sheet, list the steps the work goes through.

Here's a list drawn up by the head of a production department producing spiral tubing:

a. Receive factory order.
b. Order material from stockroom.
c. Store material on shelf until needed.
d. Move material to spiral machine.
e. Fabricate tubing on spiral machine.
f. Store tube lengths.
g. Move tube lengths to slitting machine.
h. Slit tubes to size.
i. Spotcheck tubes for length and O.D.
j. Move tubes to assembly table.
k. Assemble cap on one end of tube.
l. Final-inspect tubes.
m. Pack and send to Shipping.

When you've written out the steps, show the flow of the work, as in the drawing below.

3. Making an improvement. The Floor-Plan Flow Chart can pay off substantially. In the situation illustrated (see Figure 1), the production head saw that the work was moving too long a distance, so he redid his drawing, and the actual arrangement, to look like Figure 2.

Note the improvement: by changing the location of the storage shelves, the distance between operations was cut considerably.

Of course, it's unwise to carry out such changes without consulting your subordinates, who may resent being left in the dark. To overcome any kickback later, give them the chance to work with you on improving the weak spots revealed by the chart. It's particularly advisable because the changes you're liable to make are the kind that affect them personally. Logical or not, the attachments people develop for "their" work sites are pretty strong. A one-sided decision to move a chair, a table, a machine, may cause more upset than the improvement is worth. Explanation and discussion can avoid this trouble.

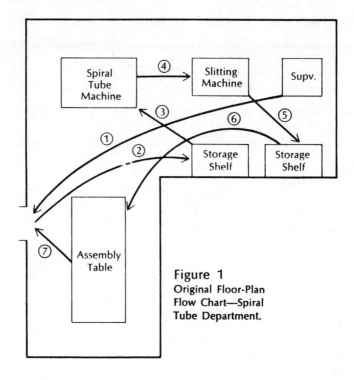

Figure 1
Original Floor-Plan
Flow Chart—Spiral
Tube Department.

➲ **ATTENDANCE ANALYZER**

Insert the appropriate information. An explanation for calculating an absentee rate (note the formula along the bottom of Chart 1) will be found in detail after the form. You may want to duplicate this form and use one copy at the end of each month.

Directions for calculating absentee rate.   If absence is a serious problem for you, consider duplicating the form and keeping accurate records, month to month. Executives find that record-keeping is often, of itself, a helpful remedy for diminishing absenteeism.

The chart provided is self-explanatory, though a note should be added about the column marked "Result of Discussion." It is based on the notion that it is a good practice to have returning employees see their superior before starting back to work. This interview will not only tell you the reason for the absence, but impress employees with your concern.

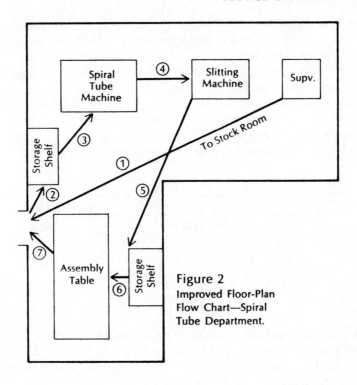

Figure 2
Improved Floor-Plan
Flow Chart—Spiral
Tube Department.

Name of Subordinate	Days Absent for Month of_____	Excused? Reason	Unexcused	Result of Discussion / Action to be Taken	Follow-Up, Remarks

$$\text{ABSENTEE RATE} = \frac{\text{Man-Days Lost: _____}}{\text{Man-Days Scheduled: _____}} \times 100 = \quad \%$$

Chart 1

394   MANAGEMENT TOOL KIT

The Absentee Rate is found by (1) taking employee-days lost in your department; (2) dividing them by employee-days scheduled; and (3) multiplying that figure by 100.

Here is how one manager performed this calculation. She had twenty employees in the department, each scheduled to work eight hours a day, twenty-four days a month. At the end of one month, recently, she found that seven employees hadn't been absent at all, but that five had been out one day each; four two days each; three three days each; and one man, twenty days. She roughed out the following chart:

No. of Employees	Days Absent	Man-days Lost
7	0	0
5	1	5
4	2	8
3	3	9
1	20	20
		Total 42

Next, she figured out the number of employee-days that were scheduled for this month: she multiplied the number of people in the department (20) by the number of work days in the month (24), to get 480. Filling in the formula, this manager's final calculation was:

$$\frac{42}{480} \times 100 = 8.75\%$$

An 8.75 percent absentee rate is very high (the national average is 4 percent). If your rate rises above 4 percent for any month, consider this recommendation: Concentrate on employees with the highest number of absences, whether excused or unexcused. Studies show that these same people will be repeaters unless checked.

➲ IDEA STIMULATOR: GETTING IDEAS FROM YOUR SUBORDINATES

Here is a form executives have used to facilitate the flow of ideas from their subordinates. The example below shows how the form looks when filled out:

Subject:	Plan to change locker room location.
Problem:	Present location is inconvenient.
	Time lost by workers between work area and lockers totals about 12 minutes per day per worker. (Include additional points as required.)
Proposal:	Move lockers to B storage room; using present locker room for storage.
Advantages:	Lockers would be next door to work area. (Include additional points as required.)
Disadvantages:	Change would occupy two men for three days. (Include additional points as required.)
Recommendation:	Locker location should be changed because it will save time and will be a morale builder worth the expense involved.

Ed Loman,
Supervisor

➲ EXECUTIVE TOOL RACK

Executives who have been able to figure out new applications for old standbys, such as charts and graphs, have successfully dekinked knotty tasks that previously slowed them down.

The executive who looks for help in the form of tools tends to develop a concept of efficiency, of "the better way" that is reflected in overall performance.

Tool catalog.   Below you'll find a list of devices widely found in executive offices. There isn't an executive alive who uses all or even most of them. But your use of a single one may prove to be the answer to an unsolved problem of efficiency that may have been bothering you for a long time. As you go down the list, keep in mind your own operations and the possible assistance you may gain by an application or adaptation of each item.

Charts and graphs.   All types and sizes of these are for organization control, production control, quality control, keeping track of orders received, processed, and shipped; overtime, and stock needed.

Phone adaptations.   You can have conference phones that sit on the desk and require no handling; double phones for three-way talks; phone side-switches to tell the switchboard whether the executive is in, away or, available by auto-call; timers to limit long-distance calls.

Blackboards and easel charts.   You can use these behind the desks, as well as in conference rooms, for problem-solving, illustration, etc.

Slides rules, adding, or calculating machines.   These make for easy computation in planning. "I run up a column of figures a dozen times a day," is a fairly typical statement from a top-level executive to explain the presence of equipment you wouldn't expect him to have.

Typewriters.   Some executives even prefer hunting and pecking to longhand. If you type by touch, you're ahead of the game.

Work tables.   You can get them large, medium, or small to use as a second desk, a clear work area, for quick huddles, blueprint examination, and so on.

Cameras.   Movie, candid, and still types can be used for getting visual evidence of a damaged shipment, supplies recieved in poor condition, safety malpractices, and many other occasions.

Clocks.   Include an alarm clock, to remind you when it's time to set out for an important meeting or date, Wrist models are becoming popular.

Projectors.   Slide or movie projectors are becoming more common in executive offices. As an adjunct to conferences, or as a briefing or training device, their rich possibilities are largely unexplored.

Dictating machines or recorders.   The use of a dictating machine for letters, and so on, is standard. But executives have found that putting a conference "on tape," for example, provides a verbatim record that at times is highly desirable.

➋ NEWEST AND MOST VERSATILE. . .

Of course, the wonder machine, whose application is limited by only three factors:

Your needs, the activities dictated by your job;
Hardware, the capabilities of your equipment;
Software suited to requirements, from word processing to special programs tailored to particular tasks—record keeping, analysis, decision making, problem solving—you may require.

Ongoing opportunity: try to keep up with hardware and software developments. New entries may ease a bottleneck for you or your department.

The possibilities for each tool itemized above are seldom limited. Your ingenuity in seeking out new uses may make a measurable improvement in your personal effectiveness, or that of your subordinates.

➔ WEEKLY SCHEDULING FORM

Many executives view their day as being divided into four parts, as indicated in the form below. In scheduling your week, you may use color coding to denote: important meetings or appointments, occasions for which some preparation is necessary, regular meetings such as conferences, or periodic discussions with staff or other executives. (This form may be photocopied and/or enlarged.)

	Monday	Tuesday	Wednesday	Thursday	Friday
Morning					
Pre-Lunch					
Post-Lunch					
Late afternoon					

➔ PERSONAL AND WORK RECORD OF YOUR STAFF

It's helpful to have at hand information about your subordinates, from the day they came with the company to auxiliary skills. The Roster Record is a convenient form for keeping such data. One caution: if you enter confidential notations, such as salary, or your evaluation of capabilities, the Record should be secured in a locked drawer or file. This form may be reproduced or photocopied.

ROSTER RECORD

Name, etc.	Date Data	Education and Previous Experience	Work Record (Attendance, health, promotions, raises)
☐ Mr. ☐ Ms. Home address: _____ _____ _____ Telephone: _____	Came with company _____ Joined your staff _____ Transferred _____ Separated _____ Birthday _____		

ROSTER RECORD

Name, etc.	Date Data	Education and Previous Experience	Work Record (Attendance, health, promotions, raises)
☐ Mr. ☐ Ms. _____ Home address: _____ _____ _____ Telephone: _____	Came with company _____ Joined your staff _____ Transferred _____ Separated _____ Birthday _____		

ROSTER RECORD

Name, etc.	Date Data	Education and Previous Experience	Work Record (Attendance, health, promotions, raises)
☐ Mr. ☐ Ms. Home address: Telephone:	Came with company ——— Joined your staff ——— Transferred ——— Separated ——— Birthday ———		

ROSTER RECORD

Name, etc.	Date Data	Education and Previous Experience	Work Record (Attendance, health, promotions, raises)
☐ Mr. ☐ Ms. Home address: ——— —————— —————— Telephone: ———	Came with company ——— Joined your staff ——— Transferred ——— Separated ——— Birthday ———		

ROSTER RECORD

Name, etc.	Date Data	Education and Previous Experience	Work Record (Attendance, health, promotions, raises)
☐ Mr. ☐ Ms. _____ _____ Home address: _____ _____ Telephone: _____ _____	Came with company _____ Joined your staff _____ Transferred _____ Separated _____ Birthday _____		

ROSTER RECORD

Name, etc.	Date Data	Education and Previous Experience	Work Record (Attendance, health, promotions, raises)
☐ Mr. ☐ Ms. Home address: _____ _____ _____ Telephone: _____	Came with company _____ Joined your staff _____ Transferred _____ Separated _____ Birthday _____		

403

➲ SELECTIVE DIRECTORY

Use the form below for recording addresses and so on of customers, colleagues, key employees, special contacts—a streamlined directory to keep at your fingertips.

Name	Address	Telephone Number	Remarks, Reminders

Name	Address	Telephone Number	Remarks, Reminders

INDEX

and leadership, 173
loss of, 126
maintaining, 112, 129–130
Constructivist, 71
Consultations, 18, 96
Cooperation, 175, 180–181
Copy, improving, 236
Correspondence load, 22–23. See also Mail
Cost-consciousness, 161
Cost-improvement program, 160–163
Costs
cutting, 183
estimating, 115
Counselors, guidance, 190
Country-club management, 367
Creativity, 10, 19, 80
creating climate for, 144–146
five steps to personal, 254–255
and leadership, 175
and problem-solving, 93–94
stimulating, 146–147
Credit, for decisions, 85
Crisis, 164
management, 359–362
Critical path, 384
Criticism, 184–185
of act, not person, 185
and dependent employee, 212
right time and place, 185
use of humor, 185
Crowd, flexible size, 51
Crying, 216, 217

Dampened pendulum management, 368
Daring to be different, 176–177
Days, Drew S., 3rd, 300
Deadlines, 11, 98, 102
Decision
avoiding arbitrary, 178
decisionless, 89
delegating, 79, 85–86
emergency, 108
and leadership trouble, 181
in meetings, 52
out-of-sequence, 87
scope and limitations of, 83
sour, 87–89
Decision making, 52, 76–91, 283, 371
ABC's of, 77–79
definition, 76

employee participation in, 372–73
fine-tuning intuitive, 80–81
follow-up, 79
historical model, 76–77
implementation, 83–86
and indecisive boss, 25–26
and meeting size, 58–59
minimizing uncertainty, 82
motivating, 85–86
noncognitive procedures, 79–80
practices, 318–19
psychological hurdles to, 81
self-rating, 89–91
six traps to, 86–87
by a team, 82–83
test run, 82
Dedication, 258
Defeatist thinking, 240
Delegate
authority of, 136–37
failure of, 130
getting cooperation for, 136–37
helping, 130–31
preparing, 136
selection of, 128
Delegation, 124–41
and achievement, 129
area of, 125
vs. assignment, 139
avoiding dependency, 132
benefits and consequences, 131
boomeranging, 137
checklist, 137–38
and communication, 19
and control, 129–30, 135–36
of decisions, 79
definition, 138
during absence, 134
in emergencies, 134
five basic situations, 133
occasions, 134–35
over-, 125
overcoming disadvantages, 126–27
of problems to subordinates, 102–3
progress chart, 132
psychology of, 125–26
reasons for, 124–25
of routine tasks, 14
scope of, 137
six steps to successful, 128–29